SOCIAL
MEASUREMENT

SAGE CLASSICS

———•◆•———

*T*he goal of the **Sage Classics Series** is to help bring new generations of social scientists and their students into a deeper, richer understanding of the roots of social science thinking by making important scholars' classic works available for today's readers. The Series will focus on those social science works that have the most relevance for impacting contemporary thought, issues, and policy—including increasing our understanding of the techniques, methods, and theories that have shaped the evolution of the social sciences to date.

The works chosen for the Series are cornerstones upon which modern social science has been built. Each volume includes an introduction by a preeminent leader in the discipline, and provides an historical context for the work while bringing it into today's world as it relates to issues of modern life and behavior. Moving into the future, opportunities for application of the findings are identified and references for further reading are provided.

It is our hope at Sage that the reissuance of these classics will preserve their place in history as having shaped the field of social science. And it is our wish that the Series, in its reader-friendly format, will be accessible to all in order to stimulate ongoing public interest in the social sciences as well as research and analysis by tomorrow's leaders.

Books in This Series:

1. SOCIAL EXPERIMENTATION *by Donald T. Campbell* • *M. Jean Russo*

2. UNOBTRUSIVE MEASURES (Rev. Ed.) *by Eugene J. Webb* • *Donald T. Campbell*
     Richard D. Schwartz • *Lee Sechrest*

3. SOCIAL MEASUREMENT *by Donald T. Campbell* • *M. Jean Russo*

Sage Classics 3

SOCIAL MEASUREMENT

Donald T. Campbell
M. Jean Russo

Sage Publications
International Educational and Professional Publisher
Thousand Oaks ■ London ■ New Delhi

For information:

Sage Publications, Inc.
2455 Teller Road
Thousand Oaks, California 91320
E-mail: order@sagepub.com

Sage Publications Ltd.
6 Bonhill Street
London EC2A 4PU
United Kingdom

Sage Publications India Pvt. Ltd.
M-32 Market
Greater Kailash I
New Delhi 110 048 India

Printed in the United States of America

Library of Congress Cataloging-in-Publication Data

Library of Congress Cataloging-in-Publication Data

Campbell, Donald Thomas, 1916-
    Social measurement / By Donald T. Campbell and M. Jean Russo.
        p.   cm. — (Sage classics series; v. 3)
Includes bibliographical references and index.
    ISBN 0-7619-0406-9 (cloth: alk. paper)
    ISBN 0-7619-0407-7 (pbk.: alk. paper)
    1. Social sciences—Methodology.   2. Social sciences—Statistical methods.   I. Russo, M. Jean.   II. Title   III. Series.
    H61.C2374   2000
    300'.7'2—dc21   00-012123

01   02   03   10   9   8   7   6   5   4   3   2   1

Acquiring Editor: C. Deborah Laughton
Editorial Assistant: Eileen Carr
Production Editor: Diana E. Axelsen
Editorial Assistant: Victoria Cheng
Typesetter/Designer: Janelle LeMaster
Indexer: Jeanne Busemeyer
Cover Designer: Michelle Lee

CONTENTS

————•◆•————

To *Donald P. Russo,*
my husband, my support in every way,
and
Roy C. Herrenkohl,
my mentor, esteemed colleague, and valued friend

———•◆•———

PREFACE

———— •◆• ————

*I*n the summer of 1995, Donald T. Campbell asked if I might be willing to work with him in editing two volumes of his works. Sara Miller McCune of Sage Publications, recognizing the significance and breadth of his achievements, encouraged Campbell to prepare his "intellectual legacy" for future generations of students. This anthology was to be different from previous collections in that it was to be aimed at the student. Campbell's own words in his formal proposal to Sage explained it this way: "This will not be a 'collected works' where loyalty to the original publication is required, but rather a user-friendly presentation of the essential content. Techniques for achieving this will include introductory overviews for each section and for each article, editor's explanatory insertions within the texts where needed, and the like."

As a student of Don Campbell's, I had been assigned many of these articles. I remember being struck by the enormous amount of information they contained, and sometimes I missed crucial themes by placing too much emphasis on minor details. There were certain areas that I found beyond my ken, but I was one of the fortunate ones who was able to sit across the table from Campbell in his classes (with his freely offered coffee and cookies between us) to discuss those subjects that I found puzzling. He referred to his students as his "co-teachers," and he encouraged us to ask questions, emphasizing that there was not a question he considered too simple-minded. My co-teachers and I took full advantage of this admonition, which led to some lively and informative discussions. It is hoped that this book, with its introductions and chapter overviews, will provide guidance to students who will not have this marvelous opportunity to discuss their questions with this world-renowned scholar and beloved teacher.

I was also well aware of Campbell's reputation, not only in psychology and research methodology, but across disciplines, such as sociology, evaluation studies, philosophy of science, and sociology of science. I was honored that he chose me for this editing task, and I jumped at the opportunity to work "at the feet of the master" on so many of the important contributions that made up his illustrious career. He chose the topics he wished to cover, the articles he wished to present, and the order in which they would appear. I had just begun my work of editing when my dream of working at his side was cut short through his death from complications of surgery in May 1996. In the years that followed, my goal was to produce two volumes that would serve as a tribute to this scholar and his great contributions to the field.

These volumes contain articles authored or coauthored by Campbell. They have been abridged, and slight changes may have been made in vocabulary or sentence structure to enhance the readability. When appropriate, editorial notes have been added, which are enclosed in brackets. The reference for the original work from which the chapter was excerpted can be found in a box at the bottom of the first page of the chapter. All of the work in these chapters should be credited to the authors of these original articles.

The first of the two volumes, *Social Experimentation,* was published by Sage in 1999. That volume stressed the importance of hard-headed evaluation of social programs. Campbell pondered whether a society rooted in the scientific principles of experimentation and evaluation was attainable or even desirable. He discussed methodological considerations, such as internal and external validity, and enumerated the threats to validity that had accumulated over the years through the mutually monitoring community of scientists. He provided the philosophical underpinnings that formed the basis for his belief in a validity-seeking theory of science, and addressed the arguments of those who emphasized the social construction of scientific beliefs and denied that reality played a role in scientific knowledge. He then offered practical advice to those evaluating social programs by outlining some of the research designs that he believed were most effective in rendering implausible many rival hypotheses.

This volume, as suggested by its title, deals with issues of social measurement. As the social sciences evolved from a philosophical orientation to a more scientific system, measurement assumed greater importance. It is a building block of science, and Campbell demonstrated an interest in measurement issues from the very earliest days of his career. In an article not included in this volume, "Social Attitudes and Other Acquired Behavioral Dispositions," Campbell (1963) recognized that social attitudes refer to acquired behavioral dispositions. Social psychologists of the time were divided in their approach to measuring attitudes—behaviorists observing their subjects and quasi-phenomenologists interviewing them. In Campbell's mind, attitudes involved both an individual's "view of the world" and a "predisposition to respond," making both types of measurement important.

Moreover, after the demise of logical positivism with its emphasis on definitional operationalism, Campbell stressed multiple operationalism or triangulation. He recognized the theoretical complexity of measures and the persistent effect of systematic biases, such as method effects. He emphasized that only by applying multiple measures using diverse methods is the social scientist able to achieve more valid approximations to the unobserved attitudes and traits underlying human interactions.

The chapters in this volume were authored or coauthored by Campbell and include topics that cover the scope of what is known of measurement in the social sciences. Part I includes his well-known and oft-cited article with Donald Fiske on the multitrait-multimethod matrix. All of the chapters in this section deal with this practical technique for establishing trait validity for newly constructed measures, providing a brief historic background, its philosophical underpinnings, examples, and methodological considerations. Another area of measurement in which Campbell is influential is unobtrusive measures, also referred to as nonreactive measures. The first chapter of this second section deals with validity issues for all measurement, and a later chapter provides many examples of nonreactive measures in a review of the early literature. Campbell is less well known for his support for qualitative approaches; however, in the third section, he gives us his view of the link between the quantitative and qualitative approaches, stressing their complementary nature. His experiences with cross-cultural research put him in touch with the problems faced by the anthropologist doing fieldwork, and he identified and addressed some of the biases that can occur when studying diverse cultures. In Campbell's eyes, providing a valid assessment of social programs is paramount, but he was well aware of the barriers, such as cost, to procuring the appropriate information for both experimental participants and controls. In the fourth part of this volume, he advocates the use of administrative records as an alternative to collecting original data. As always, he offers cautions on how they, too, can be misleading. He also stresses the importance of using the opinions of participants in the evaluation of a program. These stakeholders' comments should be collected not only with respect to the effectiveness of the treatment they received, but also regarding their perceptions of the quality of the services. In the final section, Campbell offers suggestions for the protection of the most valuable tool at the hands of the social scientist, the research participant. He offers procedures and suggestions to protect the privacy of these individuals and to afford them the respect they deserve as co-owners of the research.

Donald T. Campbell's contributions to the field are manifold and important. However, in an essay regarding Campbell's influence in social measurement, his colleague Lee Sechrest (1998) remarks, "note needs to be taken of the astonishing lack of influence that [Campbell's] insightful work on measurement has had in the social sciences." Sechrest believes that if the field had taken Campbell's insights and suggestions seriously,

> We would recognize more universally that the variables that interest us are latent, not measured variables; we would routinely use multiple and diverse measures; we would have statistical evidence for the influence of method variance in measures; we would use measures creatively to estimate or eliminate bias; and we would have better and more differentiated measures in the hands of practitioners. (p. 405)

Our failure to do this is "an indictment of the field, not of Don Campbell."

The planning of this volume was, perhaps, Campbell's one last attempt to assert that influence, by offering, in an integrated and unified work, these important concepts to future generations of social scientists who will be spearheading new research.

ACKNOWLEDGMENTS

———•◆•———

I am deeply grateful to Donald T. Campbell for inviting me to explore in depth the many facets of his extraordinary and extensive body of work. The many hours pondering these chapters to acquire a deeper understanding and to produce user-friendly summaries were hours well spent. I am honored that he chose me for the important task of imparting his ideas to a new generation of social scientists.

My sincerest thanks to two of the co-authors of these chapters, Andrew C. Gordon and Edward J. O'Connell, who kindly reviewed my overview and edited version of their respective chapters and offered helpful suggestions. I owe a debt of gratitude to Roy C. Herrenkohl and Brenda P. Egolf, who not only provided a careful reading of the introductions, but also provided encouragement and support throughout the project.

The graphics in this volume were reproduced from the original articles with the help of the Media Production Department at Lehigh. I appreciate their cooperation, their expertise, and the quick turn-around with which they provided the work.

Thanks also to C. Deborah Laughton, the senior editor at Sage, for her guidance and patience throughout this process.

Finally, there are no words to express the depths of my gratitude to my husband, Donald P. Russo, for his support throughout this project. He provided helpful editorial tips, numerous trips to the computer repair shop, many words of encouragement, and a constancy and concern without which this project could not have been completed.

PART I

VALIDITY OF ATTITUDE AND PERSONALITY TESTS

———•◆•———

*I*n his early training, Campbell was influenced by Egon and Else Frenkel-Brunswik and Edward Tolman, all psychologists who adhered to logical positivism, a predominant philosophical viewpoint of the time. Logical positivists denied underlying causes and did not invite speculation on objects that could not be observed. Instead, they advocated operational definitionalism, which Campbell described as "positivism's worst gift to the social sciences." This held that a single score defined a theoretical construct, which implies that the construct was measured without error.

As logical positivism was on the wane, Campbell embraced a hypothetical realism or critical realism. This suggests that an external reality exists, yet Campbell refers to it as a hypothetical reality, since we cannot observe it directly, but can only probe it. This philosophy rejects definitionalism, but it does not reject the need to operationalize constructs. In fact, measurement assumes greater importance with the recognition that all measures are fallible and theoretically complex.

When measuring an unseen attitude or personality trait, then, how can the social scientist be sure that the measure actually reflects the trait? How can the

1

test constructor determine whether a newly created measure is valid? Over the years, the field has developed several methods for establishing validity. If experts in the field surmise that an instrument measures the trait, it has face validity, sometimes called content validity. If it is used to predict successful candidates in a program, and it correlates highly with a subsequent measure of success, the measure has predictive criterion validity. If the outcome is measured at the same time as the validated measure, rather than at some future point in time, concurrent criterion validity has been established. Finally, construct validity demonstrates that the measure is related to other measures as a well-established theory would predict. Either it correlates highly with another measure of the same trait (trait validity), or it is related to measures of other constructs as theory would predict (nomological validity).

Since each measure is composed of true score and some quantity of extraneous error, there is no infallible criterion against which to compare a new measure. When trying to characterize a theoretical construct, therefore, multiple indicators should be used. The common variance among diverse indicators likely represents components of the trait, while the unique variance may be due to the type of method used or other sources of error.

This section deals with construct validity, more specifically with trait validity. For many years, even before the demise of positivism, test constructors trying to establish construct validity did so through convergent validity. This was established when the trait correlated highly with an existing measure of the trait. In their 1959 article "Convergent and Discriminant Validation by the Multitrait-Multimethod Matrix," Campbell and Fiske suggested that not only should the new measure correlate with existing measures of the same trait, but also it should be able to discriminate from measures of other unrelated traits. With the multitrait-multimethod (MTMM) matrix, the social scientist could examine these types of validity simultaneously. Sadly, although this is one of the most cited articles in the social sciences, this technique is not used extensively, and when it is applied, few measures successfully satisfy the suggested criteria. Still, the MTMM matrix offers the social scientist a unique tool for assessing the validity of a measure, and failure to establish convergence or discrimination may lead to conceptual developments rather than to the abandonment of the measure.

Chapter 1 presents a general and historical introduction to the multitrait-multimethod matrix via Campbell's response to an attack on the concept of construct validity. While not directly addressing the philosophical issues raised by Harold Bechtoldt, Campbell stresses the importance of construct validity in the practical business of validating new measures. Chapter 2 contains the greater portion of Campbell and Fiske's well-known article on the MTMM matrix. The original article contains many illustrations from the literature, some of which have been omitted in this volume. Since the MTMM matrix pointed out repeated instances of method variance, Chapter 3 examines whether this variance is additive or multiplicative. With evidence that it may be multiplicative, Campbell and O'Connell then explore whether the correlation between two measures may actually be attenuated when using independent methods. In Chapter 4, published in 1992, Fiske and Campbell recognize that their article popularizing the MTMM matrix is one of the most cited articles in the literature, and they point out what they believe to be the reasons for its popularity. They outline, however, some of the problems associated with the technique and express disappointment that little work has been done to examine these issues further. In Chapter 5, in an article in honor of Donald Fiske, Campbell discusses the philosophical underpinnings of the MTMM matrix. The final chapter of this section, by Campbell, Siegman, and Rees, examines a specific method factor by applying the MTMM matrix. The authors demonstrate the bias introduced by direction of wording in the California F Scale and the Minnesota Multiphasic Personality Inventory.

———•◆•———

OVERVIEW OF CHAPTER 1

————·◆·————

As social scientists recognized that underlying constructs could be measured, albeit with fallible measures, much of the discussion focused on how to verify that the measures were, in fact, tapping what they were intended to measure. Face and content validity, predictive and concurrent validity, and construct validity were offered as validation tools for the practitioner.

This article was written in response to an article written by Harold Bechtoldt in 1959 in which he attacked the category of construct validity. Campbell emphasizes that the philosophical issues posed by Bechtoldt should not detract from the importance of construct validity in the practical business of validating new measures.

Construct validity can be broken down into trait validity and nomological validity. Trait validity is established if test results are significantly correlated with another measure of that same trait. Nomological validity is established if test results are significantly related to other constructs as predicted by a formal theoretical network. The remainder of this chapter focuses on trait validity, which is an important tool for test validation.

In order to establish trait validity, one must demonstrate convergence with other measures that purport to measure the same trait, as well as divergence from other measures of different traits. Many tests that demonstrated convergence have been invalidated because of their failure to discriminate. Thus, it is this aspect of trait validity, discriminant validity, that has been so effective in invalidating useless tests.

In order to establish trait validity, Campbell suggests that all new measures be subjected to several analyses. New measures should be correlated with IQ tests administered in similar settings; with measures of other traits in which there is a tendency to describe oneself favorably; with tests in which the same multiple response levels are used; and with other simple self-ratings. Interpersonal perceptual accuracy tests should be correlated with scores of self-descriptions and stereotype scores. In all these instances, the newly constructed test should correlate more highly with a criterion measure. The ability of the new test to correlate with and discriminate from other traits can be tested by using a multitrait-multimethod matrix, which is discussed in greater detail in Chapter 2.

Campbell then discusses several impressions about construct validity held by others with which he disagrees. At the time of this article, many psychologists believed that construct validity was a new concept; however, Campbell points out that it is as old as the concept of test validity. Construct validity should not be applied only to tests developed in the context of formal theory, but can and should be applied to all new tests. In this way, trait validity can be established to increase confidence in a new measure. Construct validity is different from reliability in that it seeks agreement between measures of the same trait by using different and independent measurement procedures, whereas reliability seeks agreement using the closest possible method. This type of validity does not abandon operationalism, but calls for independent operations for comparison. This is in contrast to the early presentation of operationalism in which a single operation exhaustively defined a theoretical concept.

When construct validity was first applied to structured personality tests, the results were disappointing. This led researchers to use, instead, projective tests that were not subjected to competitive prediction against the same independent measures used to validate structured personality tests. Although they eluded validation procedures initially, subsequent tests showed projective tests performed even more poorly than the structured tests. Campbell warns that researchers should not use the failure to establish construct validity as an excuse to apply different measures that have not been tested for validity.

The wide variety of ways to conduct construct validity allows the possibility that a test may appear validated merely by chance or that a researcher may report only those instances in which a test's validity was confirmed. The multitrait-multimethod matrix avoids these pseudo-validations by requiring the investigator to specify in advance the correlations that will provide validating evidence. This matrix is also a useful tool in preventing test constructors and buyers from reifying a trait. Campbell warns that score-reifying, in which the score represents a perfect measure of the intended trait, is also dangerous. Finally, there is the danger of assuming that a test that has demonstrated a strong relationship with a criterion measure will have the same relationship with substitute measures of that criterion. The researcher must always consider other sources of systematic variance that may be a part of complex measures.

ONE

TYPES OF VALIDITY

Construct, Trait, or Discriminant Validity

————•◆•————

he occasion for this paper is the publication by Harold Bech-toldt (1959) of an eloquent attack on the category of construct va-lidity. The philosophical problems upon which Bechtoldt takes issue with Cronbach and Meehl (1955) are far removed from the practical business of designing, validating, and selling tests and are problems upon which competent philosophers are in disagreement. They are issues for which philosophy offers no orthodoxy upon which practitioners can depend and issues that make little or no difference to the practicing scientist, as Hochberg (1959) has argued. In this situation, it would seem inappropriate if the eloquence of Bechtoldt's attack led to the removal of the category of construct validity from the next edition of *Technical Recommendations for Psychological Tests and Diagnostic Techniques* (American Psychological Association [APA], 1954).

Campbell, D. T. (1960). Recommendations for APA test standards regarding construct, trait, or discriminant validity. *American Psychologist, 15,* 546-553.

Instead, it is here argued that there should be a considerable strengthening of a set of precautionary requirements more easily classified under construct validity than under concurrent or predictive validity as presently described.

While not denying the presence of a serious philosophical disagreement nor its relevance to psychology, this chapter will emphasize the common ground implicit in psychology's tradition of test validation efforts. The philosophical disagreement will remain, but it need not produce a lack of consensus about desirable evidence of test validity. Bechtoldt's argument is indeed more against the role of construct validity in discussions of philosophy of science and psychological theory, rather than an objection to specific statements of desirable evidence of test validity contained under that rubric. He probably would not claim, for example, that the presentation of concurrent, predictive, and content validity in the *Technical Recommendations* is an exhaustive statement of the desirable evidence of test validity.

Test validity and test reliability are not concepts belonging to the philosophy of science. Instead they are concepts that have developed in the course of the mutual criticisms of test constructors and test users, concepts that relate to the implicit and explicit claims of test constructors and test salesmen. Had test designers from the beginning been careful merely to present copies of their tests and those of others and to report correlation coefficients between them for specified populations on specified dates under specified administrators and conditions of administration, then no validity problem, no validity requirements, would have ever been developed.

The actual situation has always been different. In the labels given tests, in statements of intent and descriptive material, many explicit and implicit claims are made. These claims amount to assertions of empirical laws between the test and other possible operations. Requirements for evidence as to reliability and validity are requirements that some of these laws be examined and confirmed. Our insistence on the importance of such evidence comes from our cumulative experience, in which test constructors and users have frequently been misled. Test constructors and users have generally been prone to reifying and hypostatizing, prone to assume that their tests were tapping dispositional syndromes with other symptoms than those utilized in the test. The requirements of validity demand that the implications of such hypostatizing be sampled and checked. Were the hypostatizing tendency to be effectively eradicated, such requirements would indeed become obsolete. If indeed the hypostatizations are unjustified, there is no better way of extinguishing them than attempting to verify them. Validation procedures are just this.

CONSTRUCT OR TRAIT VALIDITY IN THE HISTORY OF TEST VALIDATION EFFORTS

Validation efforts have thus naturally been related to the intents and claims of the tests in question. In some instances, as occasionally for personnel selection tests, there have been quantitative or dichotomous institutional discriminations that it was economically advantageous to be able to predict. Where tests were offered as predictors of these practical decisions, evidences of the accuracy of prediction were the relevant validity data. Such validity efforts are subsumed in the *Technical Recommendations* under the terms *predictive* and *concurrent* validity. The latter is usually but an inexpensive and presumptive substitute for the former, and together they might be called *practical* validity. Note the asymmetry of the validational correlation of this type: Because of the socially institutionalized and valued nature of the "criterion," it is taken as an immutable given, even when, as in college grades or factory production records, it might be known to have many imperfections or sources of invalidity in itself, if judged from a theoretical point of view. Beginning with James McKeen Cattell's efforts to predict college grades from reaction time measures, many psychological tests have been validated and invalidated by this process.

But not all psychological tests have been designed solely to predict performance against extant institutional decision situations. There are, in fact, relatively few settings that produce such criteria; and these are often so patently complex in the determinants of success as to be uninteresting to the scientist, who would rather measure purer, more single-factored traits for which society produces no correspondingly pure criteria. A good half of the validation efforts for personality tests since 1920 have been of this latter type and cannot be readily subsumed under practical validity. They fit best under construct validity as first described in the 1954 *Technical Recommendations,* even though construct validity was described there primarily as a possibility for the future. Subsequent presentations (Cronbach & Meehl, 1955; Jessor & Hammond, 1957) have tended to tie construct validity to tests developed and validated in the context of explicit theoretical structures or "nomological nets." Such developed theory was usually lacking and was not typically employed in these older validation efforts, even where, as for the numerous introversion-extroversion tests, a theoretical background may have been present.

It may be wise, therefore, to distinguish two types of construct validity. The first of these can appropriately be given the old-fashioned name *trait validity*. It is applicable at that level of development still typical of most test development efforts, in which "theory," if any, goes no farther than indicating a hypothetical syndrome, trait, or personality dimension. The second type could be called *nomological validity* and would represent the very important and novel emphasis of Cronbach and Meehl on the possibility of validating tests by using the scores from a test as interpretations of a certain term in a formal theoretical network and, through this, to generate predictions that would be validating if confirmed when interpreted as still other operations and scores. When the Taylor Manifest Anxiety Scale is validated against psychiatrists' ratings (Taylor, 1956, pp. 316-317), trait validation is being illustrated. Validated by generating the correct predictions of performance in learning situations, when test scores are interpreted as differences in D in the Hull-Spence learning theory (Taylor, 1956, pp. 307-310), nomological validation is shown. The desirability of going still farther in designing tests in detailed consideration of formal theory is an aspect of nomological validity advocated by Jessor and Hammond (1957).

Among commercially published tests, nomological validity evidence is apt to be rare for some time to come, and it is therefore to trait validity criteria that this chapter is primarily addressed. If one prefers to regard this as merely the old commonsense notion of validity, and not needing any new label such as construct validity, this is acceptable. But the *Technical Recommendations* presentation of concurrent and predictive validity is not adequate to cover it. A number of distinctions between trait validity and practical validity can be noted. In trait validity, no a priori defining criterion is available as a perfect measure or defining operation against which to check the fallible test. Instead, the validator seeks out some independent way of getting at "the same" trait. Thus he may obtain specially designed ratings for the purpose. This independent measure has no status as the criterion for the trait, nor is it given any higher status for validity than is the test. Both are regarded as fallible measures, often with known imperfections, such as halo effects for the ratings and response sets for the test. Validation, when it occurs, is symmetrical and equalitarian. The presumptive validity of both measures is increased by agreement. Starting from a test, the validating measure is selected or devised on the joint criteria of independence of method and relevance to the trait.

The Downey Will-Temperament Tests, the moral knowledge tests, the introversion-extroversion tests, the social intelligence tests, the empathy tests: all have been invalidated without recourse to correlating test scores with criterion variables. They have instead been invalidated by cumulative evidence of the trait-validity sort. Trait validity is thus an important part of our cumulative experience in finding some tests worthless. It deserves to be represented among the precautionary standards attempting to prevent the needless publication and sale of worthless tests in the future.

Common to trait validity and practical validity is evidence of convergence or agreement between highly independent measures. Peculiar to trait validity considerations is the requirement of discriminant validity (Campbell & Fiske, 1959), the requirement that a test not correlate too highly with measures from which it is supposed to differ. Instances of invalidation by high correlation were already available when Symonds summarized the literature in 1931. He cites, for example, the moral knowledge tests. The interests of the 1920s had led to the development of such tests by several persons. These moral knowledge tests, it turned out, individually correlated more highly with intelligence tests than they did with each other and on this ground were abandoned. The case of the social intelligence tests (Strang, 1930; Thorndike, 1936) is similar. Predictive or concurrent validity considerations would not have invalidated these tests, as they did indeed predict the practical criteria that a general intelligence test would predict, although perhaps not as well. An ubiquitous class of cases in which high correlations have been invalidating are those instances of strong trait-irrelevant methods factors. These include the halo effects in ratings (Guilford, 1954; Thorndike, 1920), response sets (Cronbach, 1946, 1950), and social desirability factors (Edwards, 1957) in questionnaires, and stereotypes in interpersonal perception (Cronbach, 1958; Gage, Leavitt, & Stone, 1956). Where feasible procedures are available to check on the strength of these trait-irrelevant methods factors in their contribution to reliable test variance, such procedures should certainly be tried before offering the test for general use.

SUGGESTED ADDITIONS TO THE
RECOMMENDED EVIDENCES OF VALIDITY

Upon the basis of psychology's experience, the following additions to the *Technical Recommendations* in the category of construct validity are suggested:

1. Correlation With Intelligence Tests. A new test, no matter what its content, should be correlated with an intelligence test of as similar format as possible (e.g., a group intelligence test for a group personality test, etc.). If correlations are reported with independent trait-appropriate or criterion measures, it should be demonstrated that the new test correlates better with these measures than does the intelligence test.

This requirement is already somewhat recognized. Some test manuals for empathy and for personality traits report low correlations with intelligence as evidence favorable to validity. One major challenge to the validity of the F scale, for example, is its high correlation with intelligence and the fact that its correlations with ethnocentrism, social class, conformity, and leadership are correlations previously demonstrated for test intelligence (e.g., Christie, 1954).

2. Correlations With Social Desirability. A new test of the voluntary self-descriptive sort should be correlated with some measure of the very general response tendency of describing oneself in a favorable light no matter what the trait-specific content of the items. If correlations are reported with trait-appropriate or criterion measures, then it should be demonstrated that the new test predicts these measures better than does the general social desirability factor. In lieu of this, construction features designed to eliminate the social desirability factor should be specified, as in the forced choice pairing of items previously equated on social desirability. Edwards (1957) reviews the evidence necessitating this requirement.

3. Correlations With Measures of Acquiescence and Other Response Sets. Tests of the voluntary self-description type employing responses with multiple levels of endorsement (e.g., A-a-?-d-D, etc.) should report correlations with external measures of acquiescence response set and other likely response sets. For check lists, the correlation with general frequency of checking items independent of content should be reported. It should be demonstrated that the tests predict trait-appropriate or criterion measures better than do the response set scores. In lieu of this, it should be demonstrated that the test construction and scoring procedures are such as to prevent response sets from being confounded with trait-specific content in the total score, as through the use of items worded in opposite directions in equal numbers, and so on. Cronbach (1946, 1950) and others (e.g., Chapman & Bock, 1958) have illustrated the extent to which existing tests have produced scores predominately a function of such trait-irrelevant sources of variance. (This is not to rule out the deliberate utilization of response-set variance, where the intent to do so is made explicit.)

4. *Self-Description and Stereotype Keys for Interpersonal Perceptual Accuracy Tests.* Measures of empathy, interpersonal perception, social competence, and the like should compare the results of efforts to replicate the scores of particular social targets with the use of self-descriptions and stereotype scores as predictors; or such scores should be based upon competence in differentiating among social targets rather than upon the absolute discrepancy in predictions for a single social target. Gage et al. (1956) and Cronbach (1958) have described how misleading scores can be without such checks. Similarly, Q type correlations offered as validity data should be accompanied by control correlations based upon random matches, as in the manner of Corsini (1956) and Silverman (1959).

5. *Validity Correlations Higher Than Those for Self-Ratings.* Advocates of personality tests implicitly or explicitly claim that their scores are better measures (in some situations at least) than much quicker and more direct approaches such as simple self-ratings. While correlations with self-rating may in some circumstances be validating, it should also be demonstrated that the test scores predict independent trait-appropriate or criterion measures better than do self-ratings. The available evidence (as sampled, for example, by Campbell and Fiske, 1959) shows that this may only rarely be the case.

6. *Multitrait-Multimethod Matrix.* The demonstration of discriminant validity and the examination of the strength of method factors require a validational setting containing not only two or more methods of measuring a

given trait, but also the measurement of two or more traits. This requirement is implicit in several of the points above and has been present in the range of validational evidence used in our field from the beginning (e.g., Symonds, 1931). It is frequently convenient to examine such evidence through a multitrait-multimethod matrix. Particularly does this seem desirable where the test publisher offers a multiple-score test or a set of tests in a uniform battery. Achievement and ability tests need this fully as much as do personality tests. A detailed argument for this requirement is presented elsewhere (Campbell & Fiske, 1959).

DEMURRERS FROM
SOME CONNOTATIONS OF
CONSTRUCT VALIDITY

It is believed that the originators of the term *construct validity* would find in the above description of trait validity, including its discriminant aspects and the suggested additions, nothing incompatible with construct validity as they originally intended it. For this reason and for reasons of economy of conceptualization, it seems desirable to emphasize the essential identity. There may be, nonetheless, several points at which the connotations of the original presentation are at variance with the emphases of this chapter and of the orientation toward validity represented by the multitrait-multimethod matrix. These connotations may very well have been inadvertent aspects of the illustrations used in the presentation rather than intended. In other cases they may be connotations elicited only in the minds of a few readers. A primary source has been informal conversations with hardheaded psychologists who have failed to see the need for the concept or who have felt that they disagreed with it. These demurrers are deliberately overstated here for purposes of expository clarity. As will be seen from the discussions subsumed under them, there are included some complaints that the present writer feels are totally unjustified, as well as others upon which the presentation of construct validity may be in need of clarification.

   1. Construct validity is new. Through the use of hypothetical illustrations rather than classic instances, and through the references to formal theory, the connotation has been created that construct validity was offered as a new type of validation procedure. Actually it is as old as the concept of test validity itself, and it (or trait validity) is needed in any inventory of the useful procedures by which tests have been shown to be invalid in the past.

2. *Construct validity is only for tests developed in the context of formal theory.* While the illustrations of the *Technical Recommendations* presentation clearly contradict this, the term *construct,* the reference to nomological nets, and the accompanying argument from disputed positions within the philosophy of science have furthered this impression. The heterogeneity of validational approaches encompassable within construct validity is indeed so great that its subdivision into trait and nomological validation might well improve accuracy of communication at the practical level.

3. *Construct validity confuses reliability and validity.* While this criticism is perhaps accurately applied to some of the precursors to the concept of construct validity, and to some published claims of construct validity, details of the formal presentations belie this. Reliability is agreement between measures maximally similar in method. The best examples of concurrent, predictive, and construct validity all represent agreement between highly different and independent measurement procedures. This essential common component in all validity is spelled out in more detail by Campbell and Fiske (1959).

4. *Construct validity represents the abandonment of operationalism.* Like all of the pragmatist and positivist calls for observable evidence as opposed to untestable metaphysical speculation, construct validation is a kind of operationalism, as the term is generally used. Where verifying operations against which to check tests are not automatically available (as they are for predictive and concurrent validity), it calls for the generation of independent operations for this purpose. The only kind of operationalism with which it is in disagreement is the totally unpracticed kind referred to by Bridgman in his original presentation (1927), as when he said, "if we have more than one set of operations we have more than one concept, and strictly there should be a separate name to correspond to each different set of operations" (p. 10). We may call this "exhaustive-definitional-operationalism" if it is taken as alleging that for every theoretical construct there is one perfect defining operation and that

this operation exhaustively defines that theoretical construct. Bridgman probably no longer holds to this extreme view, if he ever did. No theoretical psychologist who attempts to relate theory with data employs this exhaustive-
definitional-operationalism.

The general spirit of operationalism as endorsed by such varied persons as
Margenau (1950, pp. 232-242; 1954), Feigl (1945), and Frank (1955) is certainly compatible with construct validity. Where the emphasis is upon test operations, distinguishing operations, operational verification, multiple operations (Frank, 1955), or convergent operations (Garner, 1954; Garner, Hake, &
Eriksen, 1956), the compatibility is particularly clear.

5. Construct validity makes possible pseudo-validation of invalid tests.
Many of us identified with structured measurement techniques and hard-
headed validational procedures are still smarting from having lost to projective
techniques in the late 1930s and early 1940s a battle that was never fought. As
we see it, the structured personality tests provided in the form of scores specific
predictions verifiable against other measures, such as ratings by psychologists
and peers, performance in experimental situations, and the like. The methodological commitments of the field made certain that these predictions be
checked, resulting in a disappointing collection of validity data, disappointing
not only because of numerous .00 correlations but also because .30s and .40s
looked like failure against expectations in the .80s and .90s. This record of
"failure" led to the wholesale supplanting of structured tests with projective
tests without any transition studies utilizing both types in competitive prediction against the same independent measures. On their part, the projective tests
were surrounded by an interpretive framework that evaded validation. The scientific evidence justifying the introduction of projectives was solely the evidence of the "failure" of the structured approaches and not in the least evidence
of the superior validity of the projectives. This seemed a very unfair victory.
Now, belatedly, projective tests are being checked in ways similar to those that
invalidated the structured tests, and the evidence for projectives looks even
worse. It would seem very undesirable if construct validity provided a rationalization for continued evasion of this evidence.

That construct validity could do so in some instances would be made possible by the joint application of several features. The presentation of construct
validity emphasized the wide variety of validational evidence, without pre-

scribing any particular type of evidence for all users. This makes possible a highly opportunistic selection of evidence and the editorial device of failing to mention the construct validity probes that were not confirmatory. When the multiplicity of possible evidences is combined with the small samples available in clinical studies, capitalizing on chance sampling variations from zero validity becomes a very real possibility. The multiplicity of extenuating circumstances known to the sensitive clinician in specific situations and for particular patients further dilutes the applicability of statistical tests. These possibilities should certainly be discouraged.

It is one of the valuable by-products of the rigid and "cookbook" character of the multitrait-multimethod matrix that it forces the investigator to specify in advance the correlations that will be validating if high, forces one to examine others that will be invalidating if high, and provides a setting for examining the comparative validity of techniques. Likewise, where a detailed and explicit nomological net is employed in the validational procedure, such evasion of invalidation seems unlikely. It is also unlikely where the test constructor commits in advance to the most appropriate independent data series for validational purposes and then attempts to predict this both with his new test and with simple self-ratings (or other rival devices).

When the evasion of invalidation is being considered, it seems well to note the evasion made possible by the combination of plausible a priori considerations, "face validity," and the kind of operationalism that says "intelligence is what the Stanford Binet (1916 edition) measures." Contrasted with this, the approach of construct validation forces the test designer into checking out the implicit and explicit claims by which he convinces others that his test is worth buying and using.

6. Construct validity encourages the reification of traits. Bechtoldt has ridiculed the proponents of construct validity on this score. Such ridicule is telling because we have all been taught to avoid naive reification, and we hate to appear unsophisticated. Were it not for such reasons of vanity, the simplest answer would be that test constructors and buyers are in fact prone to such reification. Such reification implies laws that can and should be sample-checked in the validation process. There is no better cure for such reification than entering the trait or the test in a multitrait-multimethod matrix. Even for the more successful tests, this is a humbling experience, generating modesty and caution.

Reifying tendencies are not limited to the trait-reifying construct validators, however. Still more pernicious is the score-reifying that has accompanied the popular use of intelligence, achievement, and vocational interest tests, for example. We are all occasionally appalled at the literal interpretations and assumptions of immutable three-digit perfection with which some users regard these test scores. Even test constructors are on occasion childishly naive in assuming their test scores to measure perfectly what they intended when they wrote the items. Often they use a pseudo-sophisticated operationalism to disguise this: What the test measures is the trait. Intent and achievement are slurred.

In such settings, one feels the need for a methodological perspective that emphasizes the imperfection inherent in scores: the variable effects of guessing, the biases in personality tests imposed by idiosyncracies in vocabulary, the impurities contributed by token compliance, the misreading of items, the clerical errors in answering, the response sets, the inevitable factorial complexity, and the like. A perspective that exhaustively defines constructs in terms of obtained test scores can only inconsistently or indirectly admit such imperfection. It is, however, an essential part of the critical-realist position that all measurement is, to some degree at least, imperfect; and this feature is one that strongly recommends it as describing the orientation of the scientist to scientific truth.

7. *Construct validity leads to a confusion of "significant correlation" with "identity."* There is in current psychological writing a frequent lapse into an implicit assumption of construct purity on the part of tests that have been found to be "valid" and an implicit assumption of complete intersubstitutibility on the part of different operations that have in one setting been found "significantly correlated." Too frequently there are inference sequences of this order: A correlates .50 with B. B correlates .50 with C, therefore A equals C —employed even when, with a little more work, the relation of A to C could be directly examined. Some users of the concept of construct validity have been guilty of this identification, but it is by no means limited to them, nor necessarily incurred as a result of their validity rationale. Some such thinking is involved whenever the implicit assumption is made that all of the correlates of a given test involve the same sources of systematic variance from within the inherently complex test. As a matter of fact, the emphasis upon the presence of

construct-irrelevant sources of variance in test scores should be a major deterrent to such lapses.

This paper has been improved through extended comments on a previous draft made by H. P. Bechtoldt, L. J. Cronbach, D. W. Fiske, K. R. Hammond, and J. Loevinger; and I [Campbell] wish to express gratitude for their generous help. This is not to imply that any of them would completely agree with the paper in its present form.

OVERVIEW OF CHAPTER 2

———•◆•———

While the validation procedures for measures of convergent and discriminant validity had been used for many years, Campbell and Fiske popularized a way to consider these two types of validity simultaneously. Convergent validity would suggest that a new measure of a trait has a high correlation with another measure of the same trait when independent methods are used to measure both. Discriminant validity would be established if the correlation were low between a new measure and an existing measure with which it was expected to differ. Each measure is a single trait-method unit; that is, it measures one trait using a specific method. A multitrait-multimethod (MTMM) matrix can be used when several traits are measured using several methods.

Using an example of three traits measured with three independent methods, Campbell and Fiske provide an illustration of such a matrix. The matrix includes reliability and validity diagonals; heterotrait-monomethod triangles, which include the correlations of different traits using the same method; and the heterotrait-heteromethod triangles, which contain the correlations of different traits using the different methods.

At the time this chapter was written it was a significant intellectual milestone because it alerted social scientists to the importance of considering method factors when correlating two measures of a trait to establish construct validity. Campbell's and Fiske's perspective for establishing convergent and discriminant validity depended on examining the pattern of correlations in the MTMM matrix. This signaled a major advance in the field. The criteria they used are outlined below in order to illustrate the intuitive process that led them to consider the influence of the method factor. It should be noted, however, that more recent work using latent variable models has shown that the criteria used by Campbell and Fiske can sometimes lead to erroneous conclusions (Reichard & Coleman, 1995). Reichard and Coleman believe that using model-specific criteria provides more information about convergent and discriminant validity than an examination of the matrix. Yet, even with this more advanced method, problems can arise if there is uncertainty about the model or the model does not adequately fit the data. Still, they believe that researchers should be aware of the limitations of Campbell's and Fiske's criteria.

Campbell and Fiske suggest four ways this matrix can be used to establish the validity of the measures. First, the validity diagonals should be reasonably high to establish convergent validity. Second, the validity value of a variable should be higher than the correlations of that variable with any other trait using other methods. Third, the variable should correlate higher with a measure of the same trait using a different method than with other traits employing the same method of measurement. Fourth, the same pattern of interrelationships should be apparent in all of the triangles, both heterotrait-monomethod and heterotrait-heteromethod.

Recognizing some of the shortcomings of these criteria, Campbell and Fiske point out that an absolute determination of validity can be made only when the traits and methods are totally independent. One can never be certain that this is the case, so the best that one can hope for is a measure of the relative validity. This relative validity is an estimate of the common variance specific to a trait over and above the shared variance due to the method.

Much of the literature on measurement contained only fragments of the multitrait-multimethod matrix, and these studies often failed to point out the strength of the method variance. When the full matrix was reported, the validity of the tests was not supported. The authors discuss a number of studies that failed to establish trait validity of all or parts of newly developed measures. A final example presents a measure that fared better through analysis of the multitrait-multimethod matrix. This study, by Kelly and Fiske, provided an assessment of clinical psychologists, and although none of the traits has a validity higher than all other values in the heteromethod block, a number of the traits do very well.

This discussion of construct validity is more concerned with confirmation of a test as a measure of a construct, rather than how the construct relates to other constructs predicted by theory. Campbell and Fiske believed that establishing the validity of the measure was a necessary step before examining relationships with other constructs. Since the literary conception of a construct can be quite different from the instrument that is supposed to measure it, the test constructor is asked to produce several different measures of the same construct using vastly different methods to measure it. Rather than supporting single operationalism, Campbell and Fiske advocate a multiple operationalism and methodological triangulation.

Each value in the multitrait-multimethod matrix must be considered in light of other factors. For example, the validity coefficients must be analyzed relative to the reliability coefficients. Also, the sample used for the analysis should not be limited with respect to one or more traits. Differential restrictions on different traits can lead to serious misinterpretations.

Campbell and Fiske believe that judgments about convergent and discriminant validity should consider the stage of development of the constructs, the hypothesized relationships, the level of refinement and the independence of the methods, and relevant characteristics of the sample. One of the greatest contributions of the matrix is to guide the test constructor in the next steps to constructing a better test. Validity coefficients of any stage can be evaluated based on improvements over the preceding stages.

To design a multitrait-multimethod matrix, it is necessary to try to select suitable, yet optimally different, methods to measure a trait, allowing the values in the heteromethod-heterotrait triangles to approach zero. When independent methods are ruled out by the nature of the trait, researchers should seek as much diversity in the classes of stimuli or the experimental context.

To establish convergent validity, a convergence of two traits measured with different methods is sufficient, providing the methods show little overlap in the heterotrait-heteromethod triangles. Discriminant validity has no such hard and fast rules; you can only demonstrate that a trait A has little convergence with B or C.

The monomethod correlation between two measures of a trait should be rather high, and the heteromethod correlations should all be positive. Failure to demonstrate convergence may lead the constructor to rule out one or both methods for measuring a trait, or perhaps recognize that the trait is not being measured at all. This can and should lead to further development of the test rather than abandonment.

TWO

MULTITRAIT-MULTIMETHOD VALIDITY MATRIX

———•◆•———

*J*n the cumulative experience with measures of individual differences over the past 50 years, tests have been accepted as valid or discarded as invalid by research experiences of many sorts. The criteria suggested in this chapter are all to be found in such cumulative evaluations and subsequent discussions of validity. These criteria are clarified and implemented when considered jointly in the context of a multitrait-multimethod matrix. Aspects of the validational process receiving particular emphasis are these:

1. Validation is typically convergent, *a confirmation by independent measurement procedures.* Independence of methods is a common denominator among the major types of validity, and it is this independence of methods that distinguishes validity from reliability.

Campbell, D. T., & Fiske, D. W. (1959). Convergent and discriminant validation by the multitrait-multimethod matrix. *Psychological Bulletin, 56,* 81-105.

2. *For the justification of novel trait measures,* for the validation of test interpretation, or for the establishment of construct validity, *discriminant* validation as well as convergent validation is required. Tests can be invalidated by too high correlations with other tests from which they were intended to differ.

3. *Each test or task employed for measurement purposes is a trait-method unit,* a union of a particular trait content with measurement procedures not specific to that content. The systematic variance among test scores can be due to responses to the measurement features as well as responses to the trait content.

4. *In order to examine discriminant validity,* and in order to estimate the relative contributions of trait and method variance, *more than one trait* as well as *more than one method* must be employed in the validation process. In many instances it will be convenient to achieve this through a multitrait-multimethod matrix. Such a matrix presents all of the intercorrelations resulting when each of several traits is measured by each of several methods.

To illustrate the suggested validational process, a synthetic example is presented in Table 2.1. This illustration involves three different traits, each measured by three methods, generating nine separate variables. It will be convenient to have labels for various regions of the matrix, and such have been provided in Table 2.1. The reliabilities will be spoken of in terms of three *reliability diagonals,* one for each method. (In Table 2.1, the reliabilities are presented within parentheses.) The reliabilities could also be designated as the monotrait-monomethod values. Adjacent to each reliability diagonal is the *heterotrait-monomethod* triangle (a solid triangle in Table 2.1). The reliability diagonal and the adjacent heterotrait-monomethod triangle make up a *monomethod block.* A *heteromethod block* is made up of a *validity* diagonal (*italicized*), which could also be designated as monotrait-heteromethod values, and the two *heterotrait-heteromethod* triangles (enclosed with dotted lines) lying on each side of it. Note that these two heterotrait-heteromethod triangles are not identical.

In terms of this diagram, four aspects bear upon the question of validity. In the first place, the entries in the validity diagonal should be significantly different from zero and sufficiently large to encourage further examination of validity. This requirement is evidence of convergent validity. Second, a validity diagonal value should be higher than the values lying in its column and row in the

Table 2.1 A Synthetic Multitrait-Multimethod Matrix

	Traits	Method 1			Method 2			Method 3		
		A_1	B_1	C_1	A_2	B_2	C_2	A_3	B_3	C_3
Method 1	A_1	(.89)								
	B_1	.51	(.89)							
	C_1	.38	.37	(.76)						
Method 2	A_2	.57	.22	.09	(.93)					
	B_2	.22	.57	.10	.68	(.94)				
	C_2	.11	.11	.46	.59	.58	(.84)			
Method 3	A_3	.56	.22	.11	.67	.42	.33	(.94)		
	B_3	.23	.58	.12	.43	.66	.34	.67	(.92)	
	C_3	.11	.11	.45	.34	.32	.58	.58	.60	(.85)

NOTE: The validity diagonals are the three sets of italicized values. The reliability diagonals are the three sets of values in parentheses. Each heterotrait-monomethod triangle is enclosed by a solid line. Each heterotrait-heteromethod triangle is enclosed by a broken line.

heterotrait-heteromethod triangles. That is, a validity value for a variable should be higher than the correlations obtained between that variable and any other variable having neither trait nor method in common. This requirement may seem so minimal and so obvious as not to need stating, yet an inspection of the literature shows that it is frequently not met, and may not be met even when the validity coefficients are of substantial size. In Table 2.1, all of the validity values meet this requirement. A third requirement is that a variable correlate higher with an independent effort to measure the same trait than with measures designed to get at different traits that happen to employ the same method. For a given variable this involves comparing its values in the validity diagonals with its values in the heterotrait-monomethod triangles. For variables A_1, B_1, and C_1, this requirement is met to some degree. For the other variables A_2, A_3, and so on, it is not met and this is probably typical of the usual case in individual differences research. A fourth desideratum is that the same pattern of trait interrelationship be shown in all of the heterotrait triangles of both the monomethod

and heteromethod blocks. The hypothetical data in Table 2.1 meet this requirement to a very marked degree, in spite of the different general levels of correlation involved in the several heterotrait triangles. The last three criteria provide
evidence for discriminant validity. [Note: Reichard and Coleman (1995) suggest that using model-specific criteria provides more reliable information
about convergent and discriminant validity than the criteria outlined above.]

Before examining the multitrait-multimethod matrices available in the literature some explication and justification of this complex of requirements
seems in order.

*Convergence of Independent Methods: The Distinction Between Reliabil-
ity and Validity.* Both reliability and validity concepts require that agreement
between measures be demonstrated. A common denominator that most validity concepts share in contrast to reliability is that this agreement represent the
convergence of independent approaches. The concept of independence is indicated by such phrases as "external variable," "criterion performance," "behavioral criterion" (American Psychological Association, 1954, pp. 13-15) used
in connection with concurrent and predictive validity. For construct validity it
has been stated thus: "Numerous successful predictions dealing with
phenotypically diverse 'criteria' give greater weight to the claim of construct
validity than do . . . predictions involving very similar behavior" (Cronbach &
Meehl, 1955, p. 295). The importance of independence recurs in most discussions of proof. For example, Ayer (1956), discussing a historian's belief about
a past event, says "if these sources are numerous and independent, and if they
agree with one another, he will be reasonably confident that their account of the
matter is correct" (p. 39). In discussing the manner in which abstract scientific
concepts are tied to operations, Feigl (1958) speaks of their being "fixed" by
"triangulation in logical space" (p. 401).

Independence is, of course, a matter of degree, and in this sense, reliability and validity can be seen as regions on a continuum (cf. Thurstone, 1937,
pp. 102-103). Reliability is the agreement between two efforts to measure the
same trait through maximally similar methods. Validity is represented in the
agreement between two attempts to measure the same trait through maximally
different methods. A split-half reliability is a little more like a validity coefficient than is an immediate test-retest reliability, for the items are not quite iden-

tical. A correlation between dissimilar subtests is probably a reliability measure, but is still closer to the region called validity.

Some evaluation of validity can take place even if the two methods are not entirely independent. In Table 2.1, for example, it is possible that Methods 1 and 2 are not entirely independent. If underlying Traits A and B are entirely independent, then the .10 minimum correlation in the heterotrait-heteromethod triangles may reflect method covariance. What if the overlap of method variance were higher? All correlations in the heteromethod block would then be elevated, including the validity diagonal. The heteromethod block involving Methods 2 and 3 in Table 2.1 illustrates this. The degree of elevation of the validity diagonal above the heterotrait-heteromethod triangles remains comparable and relative validity can still be evaluated. The interpretation of the validity diagonal in an absolute fashion requires the fortunate coincidence of both an independence of traits and an independence of methods, represented by zero values in the heterotrait-heteromethod triangles. But zero values could also occur through a combination of negative correlation between traits and positive correlation between methods or the reverse. In practice, perhaps all that can be hoped for is evidence for relative validity, that is, for common variance specific to a trait above and beyond shared method variance.

Discriminant Validation. While the usual reason for the judgment of invalidity is low correlations in the validity diagonal (e.g., the Downey Will-Temperament Test [Symonds, 1931, p. 337ff]), tests have also been invalidated because of too high correlations with other tests purporting to measure different things. The classic case of the social intelligence tests is a case in point (see below and also Strang, 1930; Thorndike, 1936). Such invalidation occurs when values in the heterotrait-heteromethod triangles are as high as those in the validity diagonal, or even where within a monomethod block, the heterotrait values are as high as the reliabilities. Loevinger, Gleser, and DuBois (1953) have emphasized this requirement in the development of maximally discriminating subtests.

When a dimension of personality is hypothesized, when a construct is proposed, the proponent invariably has in mind distinctions between the new dimension and other constructs already in use. One cannot define without implying distinctions, and the verification of these distinctions is an important part of the validational process. In discussions of construct validity, it has been expressed in such terms as "from this point of view, a low correlation with athletic ability may be just as important and encouraging as a high correlation with reading comprehension" (American Psychological Association [APA], 1954, p. 17).

The Test as a Trait Method Unit. In any given psychological measuring device, there are certain features or stimuli introduced specifically to represent the trait that it is intended to measure. There are other features that are characteristic of the method being employed, features that could also be present in efforts to measure other quite different traits. The test, or rating scale, or other device, almost inevitably elicits systematic variance in response due to both groups of features. To the extent that irrelevant method variance contributes to the scores obtained, these scores are invalid.

This source of invalidity was first noted in the "halo effects" found in ratings (Thorndike, 1920). Studies of individual differences among laboratory animals resulted in the recognition of "apparatus factors," usually more dominant than psychological process factors (Tryon, 1942). For paper-and-pencil tests, methods variance has been noted under such terms as "test-form factors" (Vernon, 1957, 1958) and "response sets" (Cronbach, 1946, 1950; Lorge, 1937). Cronbach has stated the point particularly clearly: "The assumption is generally made . . . that what the test measures is determined by the content of the items. Yet the final score . . . is a composite of effects resulting from the content of the item and effects resulting from the form of the item used" (Cronbach, 1946, p. 475). "Response sets always lower the logical validity of a test. . . . Response sets interfere with inferences from test data" (p. 484).

While E. L. Thorndike (1920) was willing to allege the presence of halo effects by comparing the high obtained correlations with commonsense notions of what they ought to be (e.g., it was unreasonable that a teacher's intelligence and voice quality should correlate .63), and while much of the evidence of response set variance is of the same order, the clear-cut demonstration of the presence of method variance requires both several traits and several methods. Otherwise, high correlations between tests might be explained as due either to basic trait similarity or to shared method variance. In the multitrait-multimethod matrix, the presence of method variance is indicated by the difference in level of correlation between the parallel values of the monomethod block and the heteromethod blocks, assuming comparable reliabilities among all tests. Thus the contribution of method variance in Test A_1 of Table 2.1 is indicated by the elevation of $r_{A_1B_1}$ above $r_{A_2B_2}$, that is, the difference between .51 and .22, and so on.

The distinction between trait and method is of course relative to the test constructor's intent. What is an unwanted response set for one tester may be a trait for another who wishes to measure acquiescence, willingness to take an extreme stand, or tendency to attribute socially desirable attributes to oneself (Cronbach, 1946, 1950; Edwards, 1957; Lorge, 1937).

SEVERAL EXAMPLES OF
MULTITRAIT-MULTIMETHOD
MATRICES IN THE LITERATURE

Multitrait-multimethod matrices are rare in the test and measurement literature. Most frequent are two types of fragment: two methods and one trait (single isolated values from the validity diagonal, perhaps accompanied by a reliability or two), and heterotrait-monomethod triangles. Either type of fragment is apt to disguise the inadequacy of our present measurement efforts, particularly in failing to call attention to the preponderant strength of methods variance. The evidence of test validity to be presented here is probably poorer than most psychologists would have expected. [Note: The original version of this chapter contains a number of studies for which multitrait-multimethod matrices were analyzed. Only a selection of these studies is presented below.]

One of the earliest matrices of this kind was provided by Kelley and Krey in 1934. Peer judgments by students provided one method, scores on a word-association test the other. Table 2.2 presents the data for the four most valid traits of the eight he employed. The picture is one of strong method factors, particularly among the peer ratings, and almost total invalidity. For only one of the eight measures, School Drive, is the value in the validity diagonal (.16!) higher than all of the heterotrait-heteromethod values. The absence of discriminant validity is further indicated by the tendency of the values in the monomethod triangles to approximate the reliabilities.

R. L. Thorndike's (1936) study of the validity of the George Washington Social Intelligence Test is the classic instance of invalidation by high correla-

Table 2.2 Personality Traits of School Children From Kelley's Study $(N = 311)$

		Peer Ratings				Association Test			
		A_1	B_1	C_1	D_1	$\cdot A_2$	B_2	C_2	D_2
Peer Ratings									
Courtesy	A_1	(.82)							
Honesty	B_1	.74	(.80)						
Poise	C_1	.63	.65	(.74)					
School Drive	D_1	.76	.78	.65	(.89)				
Association Test									
Courtesy	A_2	*.13*	.14	.10	.14	(.28)			
Honesty	B_2	.06	*.12*	.16	.08	.27	(.38)		
Poise	C_2	.01	.08	*.10*	.02	.19	.37	(.42)	
School Drive	D_2	.12	.15	.14	*.16*	.27	.32	.18	(.36)

tion between traits. It involved computing all of the intercorrelations among five subscales of the Social Intelligence Test and five subscales of the George Washington Mental Alertness Test. The model of the present chapter would demand that each of the traits, social intelligence and mental alertness, be measured by at least two methods. While this full symmetry was not intended in the study, it can be so interpreted without too much distortion. For both traits, there were subtests employing acquisition of knowledge during the testing period (i.e., learning or memory), tests involving comprehension of prose passages, and tests that involved a definitional activity. Table 2.3 shows 6 of Thorndike's 10 variables arranged as a multitrait-multimethod matrix. If the three subtests of the Social Intelligence Test are viewed as three methods of measuring social intelligence, then their intercorrelations (.30, .23, and .31) represent validities that are not only lower than their corresponding monomethod values, but also lower than the heterotrait-heteromethod correlations, providing a picture that totally fails to establish social intelligence as a separate dimension. The Mental Alertness validity diagonals (.38, .58, and .48) equal or exceed the monomethod values in two out of three cases, and exceed all heterotrait-heteromethod control values. These results illustrate the general conclusions reached by Thorndike in his factor analysis of the whole 10×10 matrix.

Table 2.3 Social Intelligence and Mental Alertness Subtest Intercorrelations From Thorndike's Data ($N = 750$)

		Memory		Comprehension		Vocabulary	
		A_1	B_2	A_2	B_2	A_3	B_3
Memory							
Social Intelligence (Memory for Names and Faces)	A_1	(_)					
Mental Alertness (Learning Ability)	B_1	.31	(_)				
Comprehension							
Social Intelligence (Sense of Humor)	A_2	*.30*	.31	(_)			
Mental Alertness (Comprehension)	B_2	.29	*.38*	.48	(_)		
Vocabulary							
Social Intelligence (Recognition of Mental State)	A_3	*.23*	.35	*.31*	.35	(_)	
Mental Alertness (Vocabulary)	B_3	.30	*.58*	.40	*.48*	.47	(_)

The data of Table 2.3 could be used to validate specific forms of cognitive functioning, as measured by the different "methods" represented by usual intelligence test content on the one hand and social content on the other. Table 2.4 rearranges the 15 values for this purpose. The monomethod values and the validity diagonals exchange places, while the heterotrait-heteromethod control coefficients are the same in both tables. As judged against these latter values, comprehension (.48) and vocabulary (.47), but not memory (.31), show some specific validity. This transmutability of the validation matrix argues for the comparisons within the heteromethod block as the most generally relevant validation data, and illustrates the potential interchangeability of trait and method components.

A conspicuously unsuccessful multitrait-multimethod matrix is provided by Campbell (1953, 1956) for rating of the leadership behavior of officers by themselves and by their subordinates. Only 1 of 11 variables (Recognition Behavior) met the requirement of providing a validity diagonal value higher than any of the heterotrait-heteromethod values, that validity being .29. For none of the variables were the validities higher than heterotrait-monomethod values.

Table 2.4 Memory, Comprehension, and Vocabulary Measured With
Social and Abstract Content

		Social Content			Abstract Content		
		A_1	B_1	C_1	A_2	B_2	C_2
Social Content							
Memory (Memory for Names and Faces)	A_1	(_)					
Comprehension (Sense of Humor)	B_1	.30	(_)				
Vocabulary (Recognition of Mental State)	C_1	.23	.31	(_)			
Abstract Content							
Memory (Learning Ability)	A_2	*.31*	.31	.35	(_)		
Comprehension	B_2	.29	*.48*	.35	.38	(_)	
Vocabulary	C_2	.30	.40	*.47*	.58	.48	(_)

In a paper by Borgatta (1955), 12 interaction process variables were measured by quantitative observation under two conditions, and by a projective
test. In this test, the stimuli were pictures of groups, for which the subject generated a series of verbal interchanges; these were then scored in Interaction
Process Analysis categories. For illustrative purposes, Table 2.5 presents the
five traits that had the highest mean communalities in the overall factor analysis. Between the two highly similar observational methods, validation is excellent: Trait variance runs higher than method variance; validity diagonals are in
general higher than heterotrait values of both the heteromethod and
monomethods blocks, most unexceptionably so for Gives Opinion and Gives
Orientation. The pattern of correlation among the traits is also in general confirmed.

Of greater interest because of the greater independence of methods are the
blocks involving the projective test. Here the validity picture is much poorer.
Gives Orientation comes off best, its projective test validity values of .35 and
.33 being bested by only three monomethod values and by no heterotrait-
heteromethod values within the projective blocks. All of the other validities are
exceeded by some heterotrait-heteromethod value.

Table 2.5 Interaction Process Variables in Observed Free Behavior, Observed Role-Playing, and a Projective Test ($N = 125$)

		Free Behavior					Role-Playing					Projective Test				
		A_1	B_1	C_1	D_1	E_1	A_2	B_2	C_2	D_2	E_2	A_3	B_3	C_3	D_3	E_3
Free Behavior																
Shows solidarity	A_1	(_)														
Gives suggestion	B_1	.25	(_)													
Gives opinion	C_1	.13	.24	(_)												
Gives orientation	D_1	-.14	.26	.52	(_)											
Shows disagreement	E_1	.34	.41	.27	.02	(_)										
Role Playing																
Shows solidarity	A_2	.43	.43	.08	.10	.29	(_)									
Gives suggestion	B_2	.16	.32	.00	.24	.07	.37	(_)								
Gives opinion	C_2	.15	.27	.60	.38	.12	.01	.10	(_)							
Gives orientation	D_2	-.12	.24	.44	.74	.08	.04	.18	.40	(_)						
Shows disagreement	E_2	.51	.36	.14	-.12	.50	.39	.27	.23	-.11	(_)					
Projective Test																
Shows solidarity	A_3	.20	.17	.16	.12	.08	.17	.12	.30	.17	.22	(_)				
Gives suggestion	B_3	.05	.21	.05	.08	.13	.10	.19	-.02	.06	.30	.32	(_)			
Gives opinion	C_3	.31	.30	.13	-.02	.26	.25	.19	.15	-.04	.53	.31	.63	(_)		
Gives orientation	D_3	-.01	.09	.30	.35	-.05	.03	.00	.19	.33	.00	.37	.29	.32	(_)	
Shows disagreement	E_3	.13	.18	.10	.14	.19	.22	.28	.02	.04	.23	.27	.51	.47	.30	(_)

The projective test specialist may object to the implicit expectations of a one-to-one correspondence between projected action and overt action. Such expectations should not be attributed to Borgatta, and are not necessary to the method here proposed. For the simple symmetrical model of this chapter, it has been assumed that the measures are labeled in correspondence with the correlations expected, that is, in correspondence with the traits that the tests are alleged to diagnose. Note that in Table 2.5, Gives Opinion is the best projective test predictor of both free behavior and role-playing Shows Disagreement. Were a proper theoretical rationale available, these values might be regarded as validities.

Carroll (1952) has provided data on the Guilford-Martin Inventory of Factors STDCR and related ratings that can be rearranged into the matrix of Table 2.6. (Variable R has been inverted to reduce the number of negative correlations.) Two of the methods, Self-Ratings and Inventory scores, can be seen as sharing method variance, and thus as having an inflated validity diagonal. The more independent heteromethod blocks involving Peer Ratings show some evidence of discriminant and convergent validity, with validity diagonals averaging .33 (Inventory × Peer Ratings) and .39 (Self-Ratings × Peer Ratings) against heterotrait-heteromethod control values averaging .14 and .16. While not intrinsically impressive, this picture is nonetheless better than most of the validity matrices here assembled. Note that the Self-Ratings show slightly higher validity diagonal elevations than do the Inventory scores, in spite of the much greater length and undoubtedly higher reliability of the latter. In addition, a method factor seems almost totally lacking for the Self-Ratings, while strongly present for the Inventory, so that the Self-Ratings come off much the best if true trait variance is expressed as a proportion of total reliable variance (as Vernon, 1958, suggests). The method factor in the STDCR Inventory is undoubtedly enhanced by scoring the same item in several scales, thus contributing correlated error variance, which could be reduced without loss of reliability by the simple expedient of adding more equivalent items and scoring each item in only one scale. It should be noted that Carroll makes explicit use of the comparison of the validity diagonal with the heterotrait-heteromethod values as a validity indicator.

Table 2.6 Guilford-Martin Factors STDCR and Related Ratings (*N* = 110)

	Inventory					Self-Ratings					Peer Ratings				
	S	T	D	C	–R	S	T	D	C	–R	S	T	D	C	–R
Inventory															
S	(.92)														
T	.27	(.89)													
D	.62	.57	(.91)												
C	.36	.47	.90	(.91)											
–R	.69	.32	.28	–.06	(.89)										
Self-Ratings															
S	.57	.11	.19	–.01	.53	(_)									
T	.28	.65	.42	.26	.37	.26	(_)								
D	.44	.25	.53	.45	.29	.31	.32	(_)							
C	.31	.20	.54	.52	.13	.11	.21	.47	(_)						
–R	.15	.30	.12	.04	.34	.10	.12	.04	.06	(_)					
Peer Ratings															
S	.37	.08	.10	–.01	.38	.42	.02	.08	.08	.31	(.81)				
T	.23	.32	.15	.04	.40	.20	.39	.40	.21	.31	.37	(.66)			
D	.31	.11	.27	.24	.25	.17	.09	.29	.27	.30	.49	.38	(.73)		
C	.08	.15	.20	.26	–.05	.01	.06	.14	.30	.07	.19	.16	.40	(.75)	
–R	.21	.20	–.03	–.16	.45	.28	.17	.08	.01	.56	.55	.56	.34	–.07	(.76)

RATINGS IN THE ASSESSMENT
STUDY OF CLINICAL PSYCHOLOGISTS

The illustrations of multitrait-multimethod matrices presented so far give a rather sorry picture of the validity of the measures of individual differences involved. The typical case shows an excessive amount of method variance, which usually exceeds the amount of trait variance. This picture is certainly not as a result of a deliberate effort to select shockingly bad examples: These were encountered without attempting an exhaustive coverage of the literature. The several unpublished studies of which we are aware show the same picture. If they seem more disappointing than the general run of validity data reported in the journals, this impression may very well be because the portrait of validity provided by isolated values plucked from the validity diagonal is deceptive, and uninterpretable in isolation from the total matrix. Yet it is clear that few of the classic examples of successful measurement of individual differences are involved, and that in many of the instances, the quality of the data might have been such as to magnify apparatus factors, and so on. A more nearly ideal set of personality data upon which to illustrate the method was therefore sought in the multiple application of a set of rating scales in the assessment study of clinical psychologists (Kelly & Fiske, 1951).

In that study, "Rating Scale A" contained 22 traits referring to "behavior which can be directly observed on the surface." In using this scale the raters were instructed to "disregard any inferences about underlying dynamics or causes" (Kelly & Fiske, 1951, p. 207). The subjects, first-year clinical psychology students, rated themselves and also their three teammates with whom they had participated in the various assessment procedures and with whom they had lived for 6 days. The median of the three teammates' ratings was used for the Teammate score. The subjects were also rated on these 22 traits by the assessment staff. Our analysis uses the Final Pooled ratings, which were agreed upon by three staff members after discussion and review of the enormous amount of data and the many other ratings on each subject. Unfortunately for our purposes, the staff members saw the ratings by Self and Teammates before making theirs, although presumably they were little influenced by these data because they had so much other evidence available to them (see Kelly & Fiske, 1951, especially p. 64). The Self and Teammate ratings represent entirely separate "methods" and can be given the major emphasis in evaluating the data to be presented.

In a previous analysis of these data (Fiske, 1949), each of the three heterotrait-monomethod triangles was computed and factored. To provide a multitrait-multimethod matrix, the 1952 heteromethod correlations have been computed especially for this report. [Note: There are some discrepancies between these values and those originally reported, since several cases were dropped from the subsequent analysis due to clerical errors.] The full 66×66 matrix with its 2,145 coefficients is obviously too large for presentation here, but will be used in analyses that follow. To provide an illustrative sample, Table 2.7 presents the interrelationships among five variables, selecting the one best representing each of the five recurrent factors discovered in Fiske's (1949) previous analysis of the monomethod matrices.

The picture presented in Table 2.7 is, we believe, typical of the best validity in personality trait ratings that psychology had to offer to this time. It is comforting to note that the picture is better than most of those previously examined. Note that the validities for Assertive exceed heterotrait values of both the monomethod and heteromethod triangles. Cheerful, Broad Interests, and Serious have validities exceeding the heterotrait-heteromethod values with two exceptions. Only for Unshakable Poise does the evidence of validity seem trivial. The elevation of the reliabilities above the heterotrait-monomethod triangles is further evidence for discriminant validity.

A comparison of Table 2.7 with the full matrix shows that the procedure of having but one variable to represent each factor has enhanced the appearance of validity although not necessarily in a misleading fashion. Where several variables are all highly loaded on the same factor their "true" level of intercorrelation is high. Under these conditions, sampling errors can depress validity diagonal values and enhance others to produce occasional exceptions to the validity picture both in the heterotrait-monomethod matrix and in the heteromethod-heterotrait triangles. In this instance, with an N of 124, the sampling error is appreciable, and may thus be expected to exaggerate the degree of invalidity.

Within the monomethod sections, errors of measurement will be correlated, raising the general level of values found, while within the heteromethods block, measurement errors are independent, and tend to lower the values both along the validity diagonal and in the heterotrait triangles. These effects, which may also be stated in terms of method factors or shared confounded irrelevancies, operate strongly in these data, as probably in all data involving ratings. In

Table 2.7 Ratings From Assessment Study of Clinical Psychologists ($N = 124$)

		Staff Ratings					Teammate Ratings					Self-Ratings				
		A_1	B_1	C_1	D_1	E_1	A_2	B_2	C_2	D_2	E_2	A_3	B_3	C_3	D_3	E_3
Staff Ratings																
Assertive	A_1	(.89)														
Cheerful	B_1	.37	(.85)													
Serious	C_1	-.24	-.14	(.81)												
Unshakable Poise	D_1	.25	.46	.08	(.84)											
Broad Interests	E_1	.35	.19	.09	.31	(.92)										
Teammate Ratings																
Assertive	A_2	.71	.35	-.18	.26	.41	(.82)									
Cheerful	B_2	.39	.53	-.15	.38	.29	.37	(.76)								
Serious	C_2	-.27	-.31	.43	-.06	.03	-.15	-.19	(.70)							
Unshakable Poise	D_2	.03	-.05	.03	.20	.07	.11	.23	.19	(.74)						
Broad Interests	E_2	.19	.05	.04	.29	.47	.33	.22	.19	.29	(.76)					
Self-Ratings																
Assertive	A_3	.48	.31	-.22	.19	.12	.46	.36	-.15	.12	.23	(_)				
Cheerful	B_3	.17	.42	-.10	.10	-.03	.09	.24	-.25	-.11	-.03	.23	(_)			
Serious	C_3	-.04	-.13	.22	-.13	-.05	-.04	-.11	.31	.06	.06	-.05	-.12	(_)		
Unshakable Poise	D_3	.13	.27	-.03	.22	-.04	.10	.15	.00	.14	-.03	.16	.26	.11	(_)	
Broad Interests	E_3	.37	.15	-.22	.09	.26	.27	.12	-.07	.05	.35	.21	.15	.17	.31	(_)

such cases, where several variables represent each factor, none of the variables consistently meets the criterion that validity values exceed the corresponding values in the monomethod triangles, when the full matrix is examined.

To summarize the validation picture with respect to comparisons of validity values with other heteromethod values in each block, Table 2.8 has been prepared. For each trait and for each of the three heteromethod blocks, it presents the value of the validity diagonal, the highest heterotrait value involving that trait, and the number out of the 42 such heterotrait values that exceed the validity diagonal in magnitude. (The number 42 comes from the grouping of the 21 other column values and the 21 other row values for the column and row intersecting at the given diagonal value.)

On the requirement that the validity diagonal exceed all others in its heteromethod block, none of the traits has a completely perfect record, although some come close. Assertive has only one trivial exception in the Teammate-Self block. Talkative has almost as good a record, as does Imaginative. Serious has but two inconsequential exceptions and Interest in Women three. These traits stand out as highly valid in both self-description and reputation. Note that the actual validity coefficients of these four traits range from but .22 to .82, or, if we concentrate on the Teammate-Self block as most certainly representing independent methods, from but .31 to .46. While these are the best traits, it seems that most of the traits have far above chance validity. All those having 10 or fewer exceptions have a degree of validity significant at the .001 level as crudely estimated by a one-tailed sign test. [Note: The procedure for this test estimation is explained in a note in the original version of this article.] All but 1 of the variables meet this level for the Staff-Teammate block, all but 4 for the Staff-Self block, all but 5 for the most independent block, Teammate-Self. The exceptions to significant validity are not parallel from column to column, however, and only 13 of 22 variables have .001 significant validity in all three blocks. These are indicated by an asterisk in Table 2.8.

This highly significant general level of validity must not obscure the meaningful problem created by the occasional exceptions, even for the best variables. The excellent traits of Assertive and Talkative provide a case in point. In terms of Fiske's original analysis, both have high loadings on the recurrent factor Confident Self-expression (represented by Assertive in Table 2.7). Talkative also had high loadings on the recurrent factor of Social Adapt-

Table 2.8 Validities of Traits in the Assessment Study of Clinical Psychologists as Judged by the Heteromethod Comparisons

	Staff-Teammate			Staff-Self			Teammate-Self		
	Val.	Highest Het.	No. Higher	Val.	Highest Het.	No. Higher	Val.	Highest Het.	No. Higher
1. Obstructiveness*	.30	.34	2	.16	.27	9	.19	.24	1
2. Unpredictable	.34	.26	0	.18	.24	3	.05	.19	29
3. Assertive*	.71	.65	0	.48	.45	0	.46	.48	1
4. Cheerful*	.53	.60	2	.42	.40	0	.24	.38	5
5. Serious*	.43	.35	0	.22	.27	2	.31	.24	0
6. Cool, Aloof	.49	.48	0	.20	.46	10	.02	.34	36
7. Unshakable Poise	.20	.40	16	.22	.27	4	.14	.19	10
8. Broad Interests*	.47	.46	0	.26	.37	6	.35	.32	0
9. Trustful	.26	.34	5	.08	.25	19	.11	.17	9
10. Self-Centered	.30	.34	2	.17	.27	6	-.07	.19	36
11. Talkative*	.82	.65	0	.47	.45	0	.43	.48	1
12. Adventurous	.45	.60	6	.28	.30	2	.16	.36	14
13. Socially Awkward	.45	.37	0	.06	.21	28	.04	.16	30
14. Adaptable*	.44	.40	0	.18	.23	10	.17	.29	8
15. Self-sufficient*	.32	.33	1	.13	.18	5	.18	.15	0
16. Worrying, Anxious*	.41	.37	0	.23	.33	5	.15	.16	1
17. Conscientious	.26	.33	4	.11	.32	19	.21	.23	2
18. Imaginative*	.43	.46	1	.32	.31	0	.36	.32	0
19. Interest in Women*	.42	.43	2	.55	.38	0	.37	.40	1
20. Secretive, Reserved*	.40	.58	5	.38	.40	2	.32	.35	3
21. Independent Minded	.39	.42	2	.08	.25	19	.21	.30	3
22. Emotional Expression*	.62	.63	1	.31	.46	5	.19	.34	10

NOTES: Val. = value in validity diagonal; Highest Het. = highest heterotrait value; No. Higher = number of heterotrait values exceeding the validity diagonal.
* Trait names that have validities in all three heteromethod blocks are significantly greater than the heterotrait-heteromethod values at the .001 level.

44

both high correlations between them and significant discrimination as well. Even at the commonsense level, most psychologists would expect fellow psychologists to discriminate validly between assertiveness (nonsubmissiveness) and talkativeness. Yet in the Teammate-Self block, Assertive rated by self correlates .48 with Talkative by teammates, higher than either of their validities in this block, .43 and .46.

In terms of the average values of the validities and the frequency of exceptions, there is a distinct trend for the Staff-Teammate block to show the greatest agreement. This can be attributed to several factors. Both represent ratings from the external point of view. Both are averaged over three judges, minimizing individual biases and undoubtedly increasing reliabilities. Moreover, the Teammate ratings were available to the Staff in making their ratings. Another effect contributing to the less adequate convergence and discrimination of self-ratings was a response set toward the favorable pole that greatly reduced the range of these measures (Fiske, 1949, p. 342). Inspection of the details of the instances of invalidity summarized in Table 2.8 shows that in most instances the effect is attributable to the high specificity and low communality for the self-rating trait. In these instances, the column and row intersecting at the low validity diagonal are asymmetrical as far as general level of correlation is concerned, a fact covered over by the condensation provided in Table 2.8.

The personality psychologist is initially predisposed to reinterpret self-ratings, to treat them as symptoms rather than to interpret them literally. Thus, we were alert to instances in which the self-ratings were not literally interpretable, yet nonetheless had a diagnostic significance when properly "translated." By and large, the instances of invalidity of self-descriptions found in this assessment study are not of this type, but rather are to be explained in terms of an absence of communality for one of the variables involved. In general, where these self-descriptions are interpretable at all, they are as literally interpretable as are teammate descriptions. Such a finding may, of course, reflect a substantial degree of insight on the part of these subjects.

The general success in discriminant validation coupled with the parallel factor patterns found in Fiske's earlier analysis of the three intramethod matrices seemed to justify an inspection of the factor pattern validity in this instance. One possible procedure would be to do a single analysis of the whole 66 × 66 matrix. Other approaches focused upon separate factoring of heteromethods blocks, matrix by matrix, could also be suggested. Not only would such methods be extremely tedious, but in addition they would leave undetermined the precise comparison of factor-pattern similarity. Correlating factor loadings over the population of variables was employed for this purpose by Fiske (1949), but while this provided for the identification of recurrent factors, no single overall index of factor pattern similarity was generated. Since our immediate interest was in confirming a pattern of interrelationships, rather than in describing it, an efficient shortcut was available: namely to test the similarity of the sets of heterotrait values by correlation coefficients in which each entry represented the size values of the given heterotrait coefficients in two different matrices. For the full matrix, such correlations would be based upon the N of the $22 \times 21/2$ or 231 specific heterotrait combinations. Correlations were computed between the Teammate and Self monomethods matrices, selected as maximally independent. (The values to follow were computed from the original correlation matrix and are somewhat higher than that which would be obtained from a reflected matrix.) The similarity between the two monomethods matrices was .84, corroborating the factor-pattern similarity between these matrices described more fully by Fiske in his parallel factor analyses of them. To carry this mode of analysis into the heteromethod block, this block was treated as though divided into two by the validity diagonal, the above-diagonal values and the below-diagonal representing the maximally independent validation of the heterotrait correlation pattern. These two correlated .63, a value that, while lower, shows an impressive degree of confirmation. There remains the question as to whether this pattern upon which the two heteromethod-heterotrait triangles agree is the same one found in common between the two monomethod triangles. The intra-Teammate matrix correlated with the two heteromethod triangles .71 and .71. The intra-Self matrix correlated with the two .57 and .63. In general, then, there is evidence for validity of the intertrait relationship pattern.

DISCUSSION

Relation to Construct Validity. While the validational criteria presented are explicit or implicit in the discussions of construct validity (APA, 1954; Cronbach & Meehl, 1955), this chapter is primarily concerned with the adequacy of tests as measures of a construct rather than with the adequacy of a construct as determined by the confirmation of theoretically predicted associations with measures of other constructs. We believe that before one can test the relationships between a specific trait and other traits, one must have some confidence in one's measures of that trait. Such confidence can be supported by evidence of convergent and discriminant validation. Stated in different words, any conceptual formulation of trait will usually include implicitly the proposition that this trait is a response tendency that can be observed under more than one experimental condition and that this trait can be meaningfully differentiated from other traits. The testing of these two propositions must be prior to the testing of other propositions to prevent the acceptance of erroneous conclusions. For example, a conceptual framework might postulate a large correlation between Traits A and B and no correlation between Traits A and C. If the experimenter then measures A and B by one method (e.g., questionnaire) and C by another method (such as the measurement of overt behavior in a situation test), his findings may be consistent with his hypotheses solely as a function of method variance common to his measures of A and B but not to C.

The requirements of this chapter are intended to be as appropriate to the relatively atheoretical efforts typical of the tests and measurements field as to more theoretical efforts. This emphasis on validational criteria appropriate to our present atheoretical level of test construction is not at all incompatible with a recognition of the desirability of increasing the extent to which all aspects of a test and the testing situation are determined by explicit theoretical considerations, as Jessor and Hammond have advocated (Jessor & Hammond, 1957).

Relation to Operationalism. Underwood (1957, p. 54), in his effective presentation of the operationalist point of view, shows a realistic awareness of the amorphous type of theory with which most psychologists work. He contrasts a psychologist's "literary" conception with the latter's operational definition as represented by his test or other measuring instrument. He recognizes the importance of the literary definition in communicating and generating science. He cautions that the operational definition "may not at all measure the process he wishes to measure; it may measure something quite different" (p. 55). He does not, however, indicate how one would know when one was thus mistaken.

The requirements of the present chapter may be seen as an extension of the kind of operationalism Underwood has expressed. The test constructor is asked to generate from the literary conception or private construct not one operational embodiment, but two or more, each as different in research vehicle as possible. Furthermore, one is asked to make explicit the distinction between the new variable and other variables, distinctions that are almost certainly implied in his literary definition. In the very first validational efforts before the paper goes into print, the test constructor is asked to apply the several methods and several traits jointly. The literary definition, the conception, is now best represented in what the independent measures of the trait hold *distinctively* in common. The multitrait-multimethod matrix is, we believe, an important practical first step in avoiding "the danger . . . that the investigator will fall into the trap of thinking that because he went from an artistic or literary conception . . . to the construction of items for a scale to measure it, he has validated his artistic conception" (Underwood, 1957, p. 55). In contrast with the *single operationalism* now dominant in psychology, we are advocating a *multiple operationalism,* a *convergent operationalism* (Garner, 1954; Garner, Hake, & Eriksen, 1956), a *methodological triangulation* (Campbell, 1953, 1956), an *operational delineation* (Campbell, 1954), a *convergent validation.*

Underwood's presentation and that of this chapter as a whole imply moving from concept to operation, a sequence that is frequent in science, and perhaps typical. The same point can be made, however, in inspecting a transition from operation to construct. For any body of data taken from a single operation, there is a subinfinity of interpretations possible; a subinfinity of concepts, or combinations of concepts, that it could represent. Any single operation, as representative of concepts, is equivocal.

Our insistence on more than one method for measuring each concept departs from Bridgman's (1927) early position that "if we have more than one set of operations, we have more than one concept, and strictly there should be a separate name to correspond to each different set of operations" (p. 10). At the current stage of psychological progress, the crucial requirement is the demonstration of some convergence, not complete congruence, between two distinct sets of operations. With only one method, one has no way of distinguishing trait variance from unwanted method variance. When psychological measurement and conceptualization become better developed, it may well be appropriate to differentiate conceptually between Trait-Method Unit A_1 and Trait-Method Unit A_2 in which Trait A is measured by different methods. More likely, what we have called method variance will be specified theoretically in terms of a set of constructs. (This has in effect been illustrated in the discussion above in which it was noted that the response set variance might be viewed as trait variance, and in the rearrangement of the social intelligence matrices of Tables 2.3 and 2.4.) It will then be recognized that measurement procedures usually involve several theoretical constructs in joint application. Using obtained measurements to estimate values for a single construct under this condition still requires comparison of complex measures varying in their trait composition, in something like a multitrait-multimethod matrix. Mill's joint method of similarities and differences still epitomizes much about the effective experimental clarification of concepts.

The Evaluation of a Multitrait-Multimethod Matrix. The evaluation of the correlation matrix formed by intercorrelating several trait-method units must take into consideration the many factors that are known to affect the magnitude of correlations. A value in the validity diagonal must be assessed in the light of the reliabilities of the two measures involved: for example, a low reliability for Test A_2 might exaggerate the apparent method variance in Test A_1. Again, the whole approach assumes adequate sampling of individuals; the curtailment of the sample with respect to one or more traits will depress the reliability coefficients and intercorrelations involving these traits. While restrictions of range over all traits produce serious difficulties in the interpretation of a multitrait-multimethod matrix and should be avoided whenever possible, the presence of different degrees of restriction on different traits is the more serious hazard to meaningful interpretation.

Various statistical treatments for multitrait-multimethod matrices might be developed. We have considered rough tests for the elevation of a value in the validity diagonal above the comparison values in its row and column. Correlations between the columns for variables measuring the same trait, variance analyses, and factor analyses have been proposed to us. However, the development of such statistical methods is beyond the scope of this chapter. We believe that such summary statistics are neither necessary nor appropriate at this time. Psychologists today should be concerned not with evaluating tests as if the tests were fixed and definitive, but rather with developing better tests. We believe that a careful examination of a multitrait-multimethod matrix will indicate to the experimenter what his next steps should be; it will indicate which methods should be discarded or replaced, which concepts need sharper delineation, and which concepts are poorly measured because of excessive or confounding method variance. Validity judgments based on such a matrix must take into account the stage of development of the constructs, the postulated relationships among them, the level of technical refinement of the methods, the relative independence of the methods, and any pertinent characteristics of the sample of subjects. We are proposing that the validational process be viewed as an aspect of an ongoing program for improving measuring procedures and that the "validity coefficients" obtained at any one stage in the process be interpreted in terms of gains over preceding stages and as indicators of where further effort is needed.

The Design of a Multitrait-Multimethod Matrix. The several methods and traits included in a validational matrix should be selected with care. The several methods used to measure each trait should be appropriate to the trait as conceptualized. Although this view will reduce the range of suitable methods, it will rarely restrict the measurement to one operational procedure.

Whenever possible, the several methods in one matrix should be completely independent of each other; there should be no prior reason for believing that they share method variance. This requirement is necessary to permit the values in the heteromethod-heterotrait triangles to approach zero. If the nature of the traits rules out such independence of methods, efforts should be made to obtain as much diversity as possible in terms of data sources and classification processes. Thus, the classes of stimuli *or* the background situations, the experimental contexts, should be different. Again, the persons providing the observations should have different roles *or* the procedures for scoring should be varied.

Plans for a validational matrix should take into account the difference between the interpretations regarding convergence and discrimination. It is sufficient to demonstrate convergence between two clearly distinct methods that show little overlap in the heterotrait-heteromethod triangles. While agreement among several methods is desirable, convergence between two is a satisfactory minimal requirement. Discriminative validation is not so easily achieved. Just as it is impossible to prove the null hypothesis, or that some object does not exist, so one can never establish that a trait, as measured, is differentiated from all other traits. One can only show that this measure of Trait A has little overlap with those measures of B and C, and no dependable generalization beyond B and C can be made. For example, social poise could probably be readily discriminated from aesthetic interests, but it should also be differentiated from leadership.

Insofar as the traits are related and are expected to correlate with each other, the monomethod correlations will be substantial and heteromethod correlations between traits will also be positive. For ease of interpretation, it may be best to include in the matrix at least two traits, and preferably two sets of traits, that are postulated to be independent of each other.

In closing, a word of caution is needed. Many multitrait-multimethod matrices will show no convergent validation; no relationship may be found between two methods of measuring a trait. In this common situation the experimenter should examine the evidence in favor of several alternative propositions: (a) Neither method is adequate for measuring the trait; (b) One of the two methods does not really measure the trait. (When the evidence indicates that a method does not measure the postulated trait it may prove to measure some other trait. High correlations in the heterotrait-heteromethod triangles may provide hints to such possibilities.) (c) The trait is not a functional unity, the response tendencies involved being specific to the nontrait attributes of each test. The failure to demonstrate convergence may lead to conceptual developments rather than to the abandonment of a test.

SUMMARY

This chapter advocates a validational process utilizing a matrix of intercorrelations among tests representing at least two traits, each measured by at least two methods. Measures of the same trait should correlate higher with each other than they do with measures of different traits involving separate methods. Ideally, these validity values should also be higher than the correlations among different traits measured by the same method.

Illustrations from the literature show that these desirable conditions as a set are rarely met. Method or apparatus factors make very large contributions to psychological measurements.

The notions of convergence between independent measures of the same trait and discrimination between measures of different traits are compared with previously published formulations such as construct validity and convergent operationalism. Problems in the application of this validational process are considered.

Some of the data analyses reported in this paper were supported by funds from the Graduate School of Northwestern University and by the Department of Psychology of the University of Chicago. We [Campbell and Fiske] are also indebted to numerous colleagues for their thoughtful criticisms and encouragement of an earlier draft of this paper, especially Benjamin S. Bloom, R. Darrell Bock, Desmond S. Cartwright, Loren J. Chapman, Lee J. Cronbach, Carl P. Duncan, Lyle V. Jones, Joe Kamiya, Wilbur L. Layton, Jane Loevinger, Paul E. Meehl, Marshall H. Segall, Thornton B. Roby, Robert C. Tryon, Michael Wertheimer, and Robert F. Winch.

OVERVIEW OF CHAPTER 3

———•◆•———

In a review of multitrait-multimethod matrices, Fiske points out that many measures of personality do not exhibit a great deal of validity. Even when convergent and discriminant validity have been established, validity coefficients are not very high. Triangulation was thought to be the answer; in the personality domain, however, it has not been as useful as first believed. Clarity through triangulation is of two types: objective clarity and subjective, or perceived, clarity. Triangulation, through the multitrait-multimethod matrix, reduces subjective, perceived clarity in measuring personality traits. Even when triangulation occurs to some extent, we do not always get an improved picture.

One must consider that there may not be an objective reality to measure, and that humans may behave differently in each social role or setting. While Fiske's review of studies with poor convergent and discriminant validity may suggest this, there are enough instances where these types of validity are demonstrated. Therefore, methodology must be considered. The purpose of this chapter is to encourage methodologists to search for better methods that will improve the clarity of personality measurement.

The authors of this chapter, Campbell and O'Connell, in an earlier publication noted that the higher the correlation between two traits, the greater that relationship increased when the same method was shared.

Also, when two traits were independent, even using the same method did not increase the correlation. This seemed inconsistent with what was known of method factors, so the authors set out to determine why this was so. Allen Yates (1980), in revising the conceptualization of factor analysis, suggested that sharing the same method increases the correlations of two measures above the true relationship. Campbell and O'Connell wished to examine the reverse of this conceptualization, suggesting that using different methods might actually lessen, or attenuate, the true relationship.

Using a hypothetical multitrait-multimethod matrix, the authors demonstrate how correlations can be derived from trait factor loadings and method factor loadings. When the correlations in the heterotrait-monomethod triangle are compared to those in the heterotrait-heteromethod triangle, the patterns are similar, even though those in the monomethod triangle are higher. When the correlation values in the heteromethod triangle are plotted against those in the monomethod triangle, the regression line appears to be 45 degrees. Campbell and O'Connell hypothesize that if the traits and method factors varied more than those shown in their hypothetical example, the parallelism would continue, but the scatter would be larger. If one assumes that the trait loading is independent of the method loading, the slope would be approximately 45 degrees.

As illustrated earlier, the variance in a correlation is made up of the trait variance and the method variance. One would assume that as the correlation between two traits increases, the method-factor loadings would decrease, since it would be contributing less to the total variance. It was believed that, in this instance, the net slope would be less than 45 degrees, less than 1.00. When the multitrait-multimethod matrix was expanded, these expectations were not borne out. The net slope was actually greater than 1.00. This suggests that traits with a high correlation have an even higher correlation when the same method is used.

The authors then ask the question of whether the correlations using the same method might be truer descriptions of the underlying relationships between the variables. The attenuation of the true relationship due to different methods may be the same type of process that occurs in constant attenuation of correlations over time, known as the autoregressive model. This model suggests that synchronous measures have higher correlations that erode at a constant rate over time. Campbell and O'Connor posit that the lower correlations in the heteromethod block may be due to attenuation similar to the attenuation noted over time. The remainder of the chapter attempts, first, to see if the autoregressive model fits for the multimethod erosion model and, then, to try to understand why this is so.

To begin, they present eight validity studies' correlations of the monomethod and heteromethod triangles and the slopes that occur when the correlations are plotted. When Kelly and Fiske plotted the correlations and the regression lines for the two methods (Self and Staff), the mean intercept at .13 on the vertical axis supported the additive method factor model; that is, the method variance would be estimated to be .13. A different result was apparent, however, when the correlations between the Edwards Personal Preference Schedule and the Taylor Manifest Anxiety Scale were plotted. The zero-zero intercept for this plot supports the autoregressive model. When this procedure was done for all 22 methods in the eight validity studies, the following conclusions can be drawn.

With the narrow pinch of all the plotted regression lines close to the zero-zero intercept, the multiplicative method appears to be supported, that is, the higher the correlation between two measures of a trait, the greater the effect of the method factor. In certain cases, where the vertical intercept is above zero on the vertical axis, the additive method is also present, indicating that there is, indeed, a method factor operating, which affects all correlations. For a number of methods with substantial slopes that pass through zero, the possibility of an attenuation model rather than a multiplicative model is explored.

A first example involves ink blot tests taken in two forms. In one form, the individual records his or her own responses in a group setting; the other form is administered individually. The set of blots used for each method is different; thus, it evoked somewhat different responses for a specific trait, lowering the correlations. If the tests were infinitely long, the correlations would be higher. For these rather limited tests, therefore, a correction for test length would be in order (in the attenuation mode). These same correlations would be higher within a single method (e.g., group administration only), since the diluting effect of method would not be present. This phenomenon represents the erosion attenuation model. However, the correlation of the sampling error within a given form (method) switches to the augmentation model. Correlated error within a given method will increase the correlation, and this increase would not be present when the correlations involved two forms or methods.

The authors then go on to discuss specific examples of studies that might be characterized as erosion attenuation models or multiplicative augmentation models. They admit to biases in favor of the augmentation model, where correlated error and rater theories exaggerate the correlation between already highly correlated traits.

This chapter is an important one, because Campbell's and O'Connell's insights about the two broad classes of models, additive and multiplicative, may have been the inspiration for later researchers who specified and tested such models using structural equation modeling techniques.

THREE

DOES THE METHOD
OF MEASUREMENT
ADD IRRELEVANCIES
OR DOES IT DILUTE?

———•◦•———

*F*iske's review of the validity of personality measurement as seen through the multitrait-multimethod matrix correctly presents a very disappointing picture. We measure stable aspects of personality very poorly—if indeed there are any—but we do not recognize how poorly we measure them unless we compare different methods. Even when we find some evidence of both convergent and discriminant validity, the validity correlations are low and only slightly higher than the heterotrait-heteromethod values. Even when we have good evidence of both convergent and discriminant validity, we do not know how to combine these multiple

Campbell, D. T., & O'Connell, E. (1982). Methods as diluting trait relationships rather than adding irrelevant systematic variance. In D. Brinberg & L. Kidder (Eds.), *New directions for methodology of social and behavioral science: Forms of validity in research* (Vol. 12, pp. 93-111). San Francisco: Jossey-Bass.

images into a single personality description, either for a single person or as a portrait of the true trait relationships for the conceptual domain.

Triangulation and binocular convergence were initially encouraging metaphors (Campbell, 1959a, 1961a, 1966; Campbell & Fiske, 1959), but in the personality domain we have not received the benefits that triangulation provides in binocular vision or in land surveys. In both of these instances, triangulation results in both increased clarity and additional information about the depth dimension. The clarity provided is of two types, objectively valid clarification and subjective or perceived clarity. Visual triangulations usually provide both, except in extremely atypical situations, such as the stereoscope, in which perceived clarity is not always accompanied by objective clarification. Illusions of the latter sort, however, have to be contrived by a psychologist who knows the laws of vision. Haphazard degrading of visual information does not produce them. The rare occurrence in visual space perception of illusory clarity and illusory depth is not relevant to the disappointing results of triangulation in the study of personality. Methodological triangulation in the personality domain—using multiple methods with multiple traits—has greatly reduced subjectively perceived clarity. Moreover, even when the resulting matrix gives hints of triangulation on an objective reality, it does not pare away the irrelevant components and present us with an improved net picture.

One answer is, of course, that perhaps there are no such objects to be perceived—that no matter what ideal method we might use, no clarifying triangulation could result. The disappointment may be valid. Individuals can differ reliably in very specific settings, but the setting-person interactions are so strong that no trans-setting personality traits exist. (This was Robert Tryon's view after much work on individual differences in rats and humans. In his teaching Campbell about apparatus factors in rat research, Tryon is the grandfather of the multitrait-multimethod matrix.) Such a finding would correspond to the sociologist's dogma that behavior is to be predicted from social role and social setting, not from permanent traits that individual persons impose on all situations. Learning theory can lead to similar conclusions. If, for example, we were to have five rats concurrently learn five discriminable mazes to asymptotic accuracy, we would certainly be better able to predict the right-or-left turn at a given instant by knowing not which rat it is but which unit in which maze, if we cannot know both. Even if we were dealing with rats that have only half-learned the maze and that confuse it with another or if we are dealing with humans whose mazes, roles, and settings we only partially know, perhaps nothing like personality traits would emerge. These may be the correct conclusions from the experience that Fiske reviews. However, the degree to which we sometimes discover convergent and discriminant validity for generalized personality traits—even if the validity coefficients are only between .30 and .50—leads us to suggest that this negative discovery may not be the whole story and that we should also consider putting the methodology on trial.

In this spirit, this chapter is intended to encourage a new generation of methodologists, perhaps with new techniques of spectral analysis borrowed from radio and space flight astronomy, to reexamine our problem of obtaining clearer images from noisy, static-ridden, and biased channels and to look for other means by which triangulation in the personality measurement domain can lead to greater clarity.

This chapter proposes no definitive new answers, only some tentative suggestions aimed at provoking readers to reexamination of basic methodological assumptions.

THE EMPIRICAL PUZZLE

In an obscurely published and never cited (viz: Social Science Citation Index) paper, Campbell and O'Connell (1967) presented evidence of several kinds showing that methods factors interact in a specific multiplicative way with trait factors: The higher the basic relationship between two traits, the more that relationship is increased when the same method is shared. In contrast, if two traits are basically independent, their correlation is still essentially zero even when they are measured by the same method. We regarded this discovery as incompatible with the original conceptual bases of methods factors and factor analysis. We called upon the psychometric tradition to meet this challenge. We spent several frustrating years on computer simulations of the problem, but we published nothing more. While our paper met with no published response, Allen Yates (1980) addressed the issue by revising the conceptualization of simple structure in factor analysis. Yates's approach more closely resembles the kind of possible solution that we had in mind in our earlier explorations than it does what we propose here. This is because it retains the notion that *sharing the same method increases the correlations between two measures above the true*

Table 3.1 A Traditional Model Multitrait-Multimethod Matrix

		3.1A—Factor Loadings				
		Trait Factors			Method Factors	
	Measures	t	u	r	m	n
Method 1	A_1	.50	.41	.31	.50	
	B_1		.70		.51	
	C_1			.80	.52	
Method 2	A_2	.51	.40	.30		.42
	B_2		.71			.41
	C_2			.81		.40

		3.1B—Correlation Matrix					
		A_1	B_1	C_1	A_2	B_2	C_2
	A_1	(.76)					
	B_1	.54	(.75)				
	C_1	.51	.27	(.91)			
	A_2	.51	.28	.24	(.69)		
	B_2	.29	.50	.00	.46	(.67)	
	C_2	.25	.00	.65	.41	.16	(.82)

relationship. The conceptual reversal that we will argue here is that *using different methods actually dilutes or attenuates the true relationship,* so that it appears to be less than it should be. To present this insight, we need to backtrack. In Table 3.1, we present an example of the traditional factor analytic model that underlies both the original multitrait-multimethod matrix (Campbell & Fiske, 1959) and our 1967 paper (Campbell & O'Connell, 1967). The trait factors t, u, v, w, x, and so on are presumed to explain the nonindependence of the traits when method is not involved, that is, when correlations share no method, as in the heterotrait-heteromethod triangles. There are several method factors—m, n, o, p, q, and so forth. For now, and for most of our earlier imagery, each single method, M_1, M_2, . . . involves only a single methods factor; thus, methods are totally independent. (In Table 3.1A, zero loadings are left blank.)

In the multitrait-multimethod matrix illustrated in Table 3.1B, the reliability coefficients are placed in parentheses. These are the sum of the squares of the factor loadings for each measure, including, of course, the method factors. [For example, in Table 3.1, $r_{A_1A_1} = (.50)^2 + (.41)^2 + (.31)^2 + (.50)^2 = .76$.] The other values are correlation coefficients between two separate measures; they are derived from the factor loadings as the sum of products of the loadings of the two variables on each factor. [For example, $r_{A_1A_2} = (.50)(.51) + (.41)(.40) + (.31)(.30) + (.50)(0) + (0)(.42) = .51$.] The validity values are italicized. The pattern of intertrait relationships is displayed in four triads of correlations, one within each method, and two that are independent of shared methods. In the jargon of Campbell and Fiske (1959), these four intertrait patterns are the two heterotrait-monomethod triangles and the two heterotrait-heteromethod triangles lying above and below the validity diagonal. Note that the two heterotrait-heteromethod triangles are not identical. The two correlations of A with B ($A_1B_2 = .29$ and $A_2B_1 = .28$) share no array of scores in common. The parallel values in Table 3.1A have been made trivially different so as to highlight this point.

While the matrix of Table 3.1B is not too different from the best examples of Campbell and Fiske (1959) and of the subsequent literature, the reader may well be appalled at the simplification laid bare by the chosen factor loadings. The trait factors are set almost identical for each method, and the methods loadings are set almost identical for the different traits. The manifest methods share no underlying method factors. Methods and traits are conceptualized as belonging to entirely separate and independent realms.

This conceptualization leads to the empirical puzzle examined in this chapter. At the risk of confusion, however, some parenthetical comments are in order. Campbell and Fiske (1959) regarded a matrix as not completely interpretable or decomposable if the lowest heterotrait-heteromethod correlations did not reach zero. This required both that one method was completely independent of a second method and that one trait was completely independent of a second trait. While they used mainly this very simple conceptualization, they also considered more complex possibilities. For example, they illustrated that traits and methods could reverse roles, turning a multitrait-multimethod matrix inside out. Degrees of similarity among methods (shared methods factors) were recognized and discussed, as in the gradations between ideal extremes of pure reliability, where both methods and traits were completely shared, and validity, where methods were entirely independent, and only traits were shared. However, the likelihood of a method that mixed both trait and method factors was not considered. There are the beginnings of such discussion in the context of response sets and the F scale of authoritarian personality (Campbell, Siegman, & Rees, 1967; Chapman & Campbell, 1957b), and such complexity may seem needed where the two heterotrait-heteromethod triangles show asymmetry. However, many other possible and likely complexities remain totally unexplored, and they are worth considering before the radical solution offered here is accepted.

A PRIORI EXPECTATIONS

Look at two parallel heterotrait triangles in Table 3.1B: the monomethod triangle for Method 1 (with values of .54, .51, and .27) and the heteromethod triangle below the validity diagonal (with values of .29, .25, and .00). Both triangles show a very similar pattern of intertrait relationships. Traits A and B are the most closely related, and B and C, the least. The monomethod values are all higher, about .26 correlation points higher—the additive contribution in the monomethod values of their shared method factor. Figure 3.1A crudely plots this relationship for the three paired values. The three dots represent BC (.00 and .27), AC (.25 and .51), and AB (.29 and .54). Four such plots can be derived from each multitrait-multimethod matrix by pairing values from each of the heteromethod triangles with parallel values from each of the monomethod triangles.

It is apparent from Table 3.1A that, if we expanded this model to include more traits and thus many more heterotrait values, the scatter of points would lie parallel to the 45 degree line, which represents identical values and zero method-factor contribution. It is our anticipation that, were methods factors and trait factors randomly varied to a larger degree than in the overly idealized Table 3.1, this parallelism would continue, but with a larger scatter. This assumption needs more exploration, but it seems implicit in the combination of the additive model shared by all factor analytic methods with the assumption that the method loading is independent of the trait loading. We employed, then as now, visually judged scatter plots in our argument, and we computed a net slope rather than the regression line of monomethod values on heteromethod values, since we wanted an index of slope that was independent of degree of scatter. If the regression were used, greater variability of trait loadings and method loadings across measures would increase the scatter and produce a flatter regression line, less than 45 degrees, less than a slope of 1.00.

In constructing a hypothetical example like Table 3.1 that starts from arbitrarily selected factor loadings, one is apt to be embarrassed by generating correlation coefficients larger than 1.00. This points to a major implausibility of the model. It would be much more realistic to start with a table of unstandardized components of variance and then to introduce a standardizing process. The overall result would cause those variables with the larger trait variance to have smaller method-factor loadings, since the contribution of methods to the total variance would be decreased. In general (although not in our arbitrary example of Table 3.1), variables with higher trait loadings produce higher intertrait correlations, and as a result their correlations are less enhanced when their measures share the same method. In general, intertrait correlations that were truly zero in the heteromethod triangle would increase more if method were shared than basically high intertrait relations would. If one were to consider a net slope measure that was independent of scatter, the expected slope on this basis would also be less than 45 degrees, less than 1.00.

OUTCOMES

The expectations raised by these a priori considerations (the first for slopes of 1.00 paralleling the identity diagonal, the second for slopes less than 1.00) are refuted by what we found. Slopes larger than 1.00 were the rule. Figure 3.1B shows data on staff and teammate ratings from the study by Kelly and Fiske (1951) as reanalyzed by Campbell and Fiske (1959). Figure 3.1B, like Figure 3.1A, is a scatter plot of intertrait correlation coefficients, expanded from three traits and three intertrait coefficients to include the 231 intertrait correlations among the 22 traits used in the study. Note, first, that the pattern of intertrait correlations is quite similar in the heteromethod triangle, where no shared method is involved, and in the monomethod triangle, where all traits are measured by the same raters. In fact, the correlation r_t is .80. Note, too, that there is evidence of a method factor, in that the monomethod values average higher than the heteromethod values. Note the visual impression of slope: The intertrait correlations that are most augmented by being measured by the same

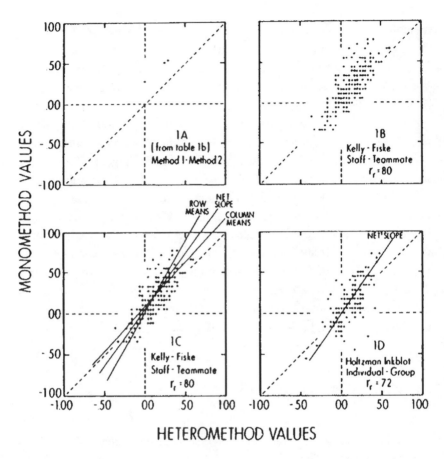

Figure 3.1. Scatter Plots for Similarity of Monomethod and Heteromethod Estimates of Intertrait Correlations

NOTE: In each case, the monomethod values are for the first method listed (see text for explanation).

raters are the larger ones. A basically zero intertrait relationship is zero, whether it is measured by the same rater or by different raters.

Figure 3.1C repeats the scatter plot of Figure 3.1B, but with the two standard regression lines and a net slope superimposed in order to introduce the scatterfree or net slope index that we will be using subsequently. Note, in judging the fit between the scatter points and the fitted lines, that the scatter plot program could put only one point in a cell, no matter how many cases fell there. The visual impression that results is sometimes misleading. In preparing the scatter plots, some variables were reflected; that is, they were reversed in sign to maximize the number of positive correlations. Where there were three methods, this was done separately for each pair. Only the two sets of monomethod values were used in making decisions on reflection. In Figure 3.1C, the line labeled Column Means is one of the two ordinary regression lines, to wit the best-fitting line predicting monomethod values from heteromethod values. For an eyeball fitting of such a line, imagine a best-fitting line that goes through the mean values for each column and gives heavier weight to the columns with more cases. The line labeled Row Means is the other standard regression line. The net slope is an intermediate slope, the line on which the two ordinary regression lines would converge if there were no scatter, that is, if the r_r were +1.00. (This turns out to be the ratio of the two standard deviations plotted through the two means.) It is this net slope line that we will be using in what follows. Note that, in this case, the net slope passes close to the zero-zero axis.

Other Data. Figure 3.1D is included as the only case from our earlier paper (Campbell & O'Connell, 1967) that did not involve ratings. The data came from the experiment by Holtzman, Mosely, Reinehr, and Abbott (1963), where 100 persons took the Holtzman Inkblot Test in both individual and group form. The responses were scored on 18 variables. We find the same pattern again; in this case, the net slope intersects the zero-zero origin almost exactly. In our paper of 1967, there were 17 matrices from eight separate studies, and four scatter plots were examined for each. In these 68 instances, the slopes were of this multiplicative sort, larger than 1.00, 63 times according to the net slope index.

In 1967, we presented the puzzle, explored a variety of considerations, and did extensive precautionary analyses, such as examining the effect for each trait separately and recomputing one matrix on Ns of 25, 50, 100, and 200, in order to assure ourselves that it was a real puzzle. We noted that transforming our graphs by plotting r^2 or z' in place of r only exaggerated our puzzle and did not remove it. We wondered whether the basic model of factor analysis should be challenged not only for multitrait-multimethod matrices but for all uses, since we noted the abnormality of cumulative-additive relationships in explanatory theoretical mathematical models, as opposed to nonexplanatory predictive equations in the successful sciences, and we wondered whether factor analysis should be reformulated on a multiplicative basis. However, we did not suggest an adequate solution to our puzzle.

THE AUTOREGRESSIVE MODEL

Because colleagues were also doing shotgun searches for causal relations in cross-lagged panel correlations, we had several multitrait-multitime matrices available. The most dramatic of these is shown in Figure 3.2E. As seen from our present perspective, this slope and its zero-zero intercept are exactly what would be expected from the most appropriate mathematical model available. In longitudinal or panel studies of intelligence, achievement, attitudes, and peer ratings involving several waves of measurement, it is regularly found that correlations are lower for longer time lapses than for intermediate lapses. This has come to be called the *simplex* pattern of correlations. This general pattern is compatible with an autoregressive model developed initially for long time series on a single individual or object. Usually, a first-order Markov process provides a good fit. In the simplest model, where one-occasion reliabilities in the main diagonal of the correlation matrix would be 1.00, a formula of this form is appropriate:

$$X_t = pX_{t-1} + x_t$$

where X is a score at time t or $t - 1$, x_t is a new random component added in at time t and thereafter absorbed as part of X, and p is a coefficient, less than 1.00, that can be interpreted as the correlation coefficient between X_1 and X_{t-1} under stationary conditions.

It is usually inappropriate for the one-occasion reliabilities to be 1.00, so the preceding formula can be modified by interpreting the X as a latent score and generating the observed score X_t* by this formula:

$$X_t* = X_t + e_t$$

where e_t is a time-specific error that is not absorbed into the base for the next time period's $X*$ or X. That is, the autoregressive process is for the latent X rather than the observed X_t*. In either case, correlations decrease over more time periods by a constant proportion p. Thus, if the synchronous $r_{x_i x_i} = .90$ and if $p = .80$, then

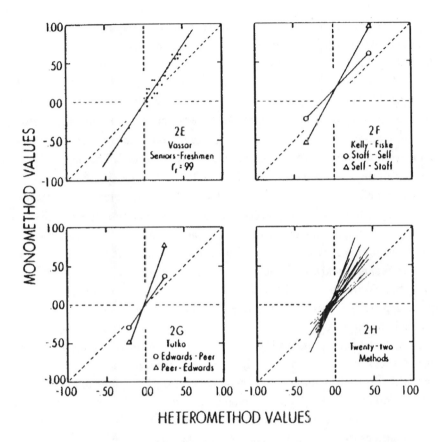

Figure 3.2. Net Slopes for Similarity of Monomethod and Heteromethod Estimates of Intertrait Correlations

NOTE: In each case, the monomethod values are for the first method listed (for 3.2F, substitute *time* for *method*; see text for explanation).

$$r_{x_t x_{t-1}} = .72, \; r_{x_t x_{t-2}} = .576, \; r_{x_t x_{t-3}} = .4608$$

and so on, each correlation being .8 as large as the correlation for the next shorter time gap.

To extend this model to cross-trait, cross-time correlations, we need to assume that the latent factors explaining the intertrait correlations are autoregressive. The groundwork for an autoregressive mathematical model and analysis procedures for multitrait-multitime or multioccasion matrices exist (Jöreskog, 1969, 1970; Jöreskog & Sörbom, 1979; Werts, Linn, & Jöreskog, 1977). These are both conceptually and empirically appropriate to the data of Figure 3.2E. They generate the expectation that a high synchronous correlation between two attitudes will be more attenuated or eroded over time than a low synchronous correlation. A synchronous correlation of zero can erode no further, and it remains zero when computed across a time lapse. The elegant intersection of the zero-zero origin of Figure 3.2E affirms the appropriateness of such a model. (The r_r of .99 also implies that all the latent factors have the same p.) For multitime matrices, one could conceive of an augmentive additive or multiplicative spurious time-specific correlated error shared by all the measures taken on a specific occasion. But, for a data outcome such as from the Vassar freshman and senior retesting, a reductive imagery focused on the synchronous correlations, as truer than the time-spanning correlations, seems more appropriate than an augmentive imagery. Genuine changes in character and belief over the 3-year period will undermine a high correlation more than they will a low one. Misidentification of responses from different persons on the two occasions as responses from the same person (this is perhaps unlikely in the Vassar study, but it is hard to avoid completely in a public opinion panel study) will disrupt a high correlation but not a zero correlation, and so forth.

Can this subtractive, erosion, dilution model be transferred from multitime matrices to multimethod matrices? As we noted in passing in 1967, the concept of attenuation of correlations as a result of the unreliability of measures has a multiplicative character, since high correlations are more attenuated by unreliability than low ones. The correction-for-attenuation algebra seems closer to the autoregressive model than to the additive model of factor analysis. Can we imagine attenuation as the result of invalidity as well as of unreliability? Can we conceive the values in the monomethod triangle as truer descriptions of the intertrait relationships, and the heteromethod triangles as an eroded, attenuated, corrupted version? (In the past, we must note, we have thought of the heteromethod values as purer, because they lacked the irrelevant augmentation produced by a method factor.)

Two types of considerations are relevant. The first is the fit of the data to the model, which we shall examine first. Even if we choose an augmentive methods-factor conceptualization in the end, the Jöreskog mathematical model could still be used to capture its multiplicative nature. However, the gestalt switch attempted here also requires the conceptualization of processes that make an attenuation or erosion model appropriate to multimethod matrices. We will attempt this on a case-by-case basis in the final section.

THE FIT OF THE AUTOREGRESSIVE MODEL

To examine the data fit with the autoregressive model, we performed a supplementary analysis of detailed tabular material presented in 1967 (Campbell & O'Connell, 1967). Here, as a result of the autoregressive model, we are now interested in the degree to which the net slope passes through the zero-zero intercept. Thus, the 1967 counterparts of Figures 3.1B, 3.1D, and 3.2E did not have the slopes drawn in, nor was the proximity with which that line passed through the zero-zero intercept commented upon. We graphed the slope for eight validity studies, each involving two or three methods and one or two populations—a total of 22 methods. For these new graphs, only slopes, not scatters, are provided. Figure 3.2F is an example, showing the slopes for two methods (Staff and Self) examined by Kelly and Fiske (1951) when in the same matrix. (The lines are drawn for two σ's lengths above the means and for two below the means.) Self shows a slope of 1.02, with a constant elevation above the identity diagonal, and intercepts the vertical axis at .13, which corresponds to a mean elevation of .13, in perfect conformity with the additive method factor model. When paired with Teammates (not presented here), Self shows a similar picture, with a slope of only 1.14, and intercepts the vertical axis at .12, approximating a mean elevation of .13. Table 3.2 presents all these values, together with background information on the number of traits, the number of persons being measured, and the intertrait pattern similarity index between monomethod and heteromethod triangles (r_i). (In Table 3.2 and in Figures 3.2F, 3.2G, and 3.2H, we depart from the 1967 article and Figures 3.1B, 3.1C, and 3.1D by pooling the two heterotrait-heteromethod triangles, rather than relating each separately to each monomethod triangle, thus reducing the number of indices to be considered by half.) The elevation column summarizes the strength of the method factor under the additive model, that is, the difference between the average intertrait correlation in the monomethod and heteromethod blocks. The slope is the net slope.

Table 3.2 Method Strength, Net Slope, and Intercepts in Eight Validity Studies

	Background			Method Strength		Zero Intercepts	
	K	N	r_r	Elev.	Slope	Vert.	Hor.
Kelly-Fiske (1951)							
Staff/Teammates*	22	124	.75	.09	1.31	.05	−.04
Staff/*Teammates*	"	"	.82	.10	1.14	.08	−.07
Staff/Self	"	"	.54	.17	1.81	.12	−.07
Staff/*Self*	"	"	.48	.13	1.02	.13	−.13
Teammates/Self	"	"	.63	.17	1.77	.12	−.07
Teammates/*Self*	"	"	.46	.13	1.14	.12	−.11
Carroll (1952)							
Guilford-Martin/Peer	5	110	.57	.30	1.83	.18	−.10
Guilford-Martin/*Peer*	"	"	.80	.19	1.33	.14	−.11
Guilford-Martin/Self	"	"	.66	.17	1.68	−.01	.01
Guilford-Martin/*Self*	"	"	.54	−.07	.86	−.03	.04
Self/Peer	"	"	.14	.04	1.27	−.01	.00
Self/*Peer*	"	"	.64	.17	1.79	.05	−.03
Tutko							
Self/Peer	16	100	.68	.04	.91	.04	−.04
Self/*Peer*	"	"	.76	.08	2.06	.05	−.03
Self/Edwards	"	"	.45	.00	1.34	−.02	.01
Self/*Edwards*	"	"	.56	.02	1.30	.01	−.00
Peer/Edwards	"	"	.50	.16	2.68	.08	−.03
Peer/*Edwards*	"	"	.46	.01	1.42	−.01	.01
Meeland (Becker, 1960)							
Peer/Cattell AFHL	4	102	.62	.27	1.30	.17	−.13
Peer/*Cattell AFHL*	"	"	.50	−.05	1.15	−.10	.09
Wetzel (Peterson, 1965)							
Self/Parent	24	72	.54	.06	1.61	.01	−.01
Self/*Parent*	"	"	.43	.08	1.68	.03	−.02
Self/Peer	"	"	.56	.10	1.38	.09	−.07
Self/*Peer*	"	"	.60	.13	1.50	.12	−.08
Parent/Peer	"	"	.42	.14	1.65	.13	−.08
Parent/*Peer*	"	"	.55	.11	1.87	.09	−.05
Banta							
Fathers/Mothers	21	500	.68	.02	1.31	.00	−.00
Fathers/*Mothers*	"	"	.68	.04	1.30	.02	−.02
Projection Project							
Self/Peer (Fem)	27	204	.50	.21	2.29	.19	−.08
Self/*Peer* (Fem)	"	"	.55	.27	2.48	.24	−.10
Self/Peer (Male)	27	200	.60	.14	1.42	.13	−.09
Self/*Peer* (Male)	"	"	.68	.30	2.52	.23	−.09
Holtzman et al. (1963)							
Individual/Group	18	100	.75	.02	1.45	−.02	.01
Individual/*Group*	"	"	.76	.06	1.40	.02	−.02

NOTE: * Italics indicate the method to which the row values apply.

Also in the Kelly-Fiske data, one estimate for Teammate as a method (when paired with Staff) approaches the additive model, with a slope of 1.14, but the other estimate of Teammate (when paired with Self) has a slope of 1.77. In Table 3.2, there are only two other cases of slopes near 1.00 or below, and these occur in instances where the elevation measure indicates no method variance (Tutko Self, when paired with Peer, and Meeland Catell AFHL).

Figure 3.2G shows the Edwards Personal Preference Schedule (PPS), plus Taylor Manifest Anxiety as a 16th variable, and Peer ratings on the same variables from Tutko's unpublished study. (At Northwestern University around 1962, Thomas A. Tutko collected data from fraternities and other residential groups. In addition to taking the Edwards Schedule and the Taylor scale, subjects rated themselves and coresidents on scales intended to tap the 16 test dimensions.) Here, the Edwards conforms to the autoregressive model by going through the zero-zero origin. In Table 3.2, the last two columns present the net slope's zero intercepts on the vertical axis and on the horizontal axis in an effort to convey numerically the net slope's proximity to the zero-zero origin. For the Edwards of Figure 3.2G, these values are −.01 and .01; for the Vassar seniors and freshmen of Figure 3.2E, they are −.02 and .02. The other five multitrait-multitime matrices in our 1967 paper give intercept values generally close to zero, although some are as large as .03 and −.03, and this might be taken as a tentative upper limit for a purely autoregressive model.

Figure 3.2H plots net slopes for the 22 separate methods of Table 3.2. (Where there are three methods, Table 3.2 presents two slopes for each method. To reduce the redundancy that results, only the first that occurs has been plotted, although, as we have noted for the Teammates of Kelly and Fiske, the two are sometimes quite different.) If we take Figure 3.2H as an overall summary, we can draw a number of tentative conclusions. The multiplicative nature of method factors is preponderant. The narrowest pinch of the sheaf of slopes is nearer the zero-zero origin than to anything else, but it is also generally biased away from it in the upper left direction. The same fact is shown numerically in the column for vertical intercept in Table 3.2, where most of these values are positive, with only a third of them being equal to or less than the .03 maximum found in the multitime matrices, the median being .09. The horizontal intercepts are predominantly negative, that is, to the left of the origin, the median being −.05.

There is a slight bias in the same upper left direction for the multitime matrices, since nine tenths of the vertical intercepts are positive (median .02). It is possible that such bias is an artifact of the predominantly positive values ensured by our reflection of variables to that end and that it is made larger for the validity matrices by their lower r_r. However, it seems more likely that, for the validity matrices with large vertical intercepts, an additive method component is combined with a multiplicative process.

It is worth remarking, however, that a number of methods have substantial slopes that pass through the origin. To recapitulate, these include the Holtzman Ink Blot study, both individual and group methods, both the Edwards PPS and the Self ratings of Tutko's study, and the Banta study of 500 youths rated by both father and mother on 21 variables (in 1967 [Campbell & O'Connell, 1967], we called this the Banta study, because we obtained the data from Thomas J. Banta during his postdoctoral period at Northwestern University in 1959-1960. The data came from Leonard Eron's Rip Van Winkle Foundation study.). For these few studies, an attempt to conceptualize processes that would be more like attenuation than multiplicative augmentation seems worthwhile. (It is also conceivable that an augmentation model could employ the mathematics of the autoregressive or correction-for-attenuation form to improve on factor analysis for validity matrix summarization.)

ATTENUATION VERSUS MULTIPLICATIVE AUGMENTATION

Let us examine some specific examples and see what we can do to add realistic content to the attempted reconceptualization. We confess in advance that we are such long-standing participants in the old augmentation paradigm of halo effects, response sets, correlated error, and shared method-specific content-irrelevant variance that we may not give the new paradigm a fair shake.

Let us start with the study by Holtzman and others (1963). Individuals took both form A and form B, one in group administration (no examiner inquiry, recording their own responses on record forms, etc.), the other in the individual administration typical of the Rorschach test. Each form had a different set of blots, and although the sets were selected for equivalent average drawing power, each blot set stimulated somewhat different responses. Heterogeneity in small stimuli samples attenuates relationships that would be stronger if each form was infinitely long. A correction for test length is in order, in the attenuation mode. For relationships between variables within one form, the specific ink blots are, of course, the same, and the diluting effects of short test length are reduced. This is how an erosion attenuation model could be read. But, note how easily this gestalt slips back into the augmentation mode. The sampling of both blots and responses involves chance sampling errors. Within a given form, correlation of two traits involves correlation of sampling error. When each trait is measured by a separate form, this correlated error is absent, and the correlations are, therefore, lower. To fit these data, the correlated error must augment high basic correlations, not zero correlations. If a given response to a given aspect of a blot is validly scored for both of two dimensions, then those two dimensions have some intrinsic correlation. Chancy, stochastic aspects in the emission of such a response will exaggerate such intrinsic correlation when it is correlated within the same administration of the same form. Nothing that we have come up with here would be unique to a validity study, in contrast to a multitrait two-administration reliability matrix. Holtzman and others (1963) offered such matrices for both group-group and individual-individual, but we did not analyze them in our paper of 1967.

In three of the studies, multiple structured-item self-description personality questionnaires are compared with peer ratings, self-ratings, or both. In Carroll's (1952) study of five factor scores from the Guilford-Martin inventory, some single-item responses were scored for more than one factor. This was done where the factors were intrinsically correlated, and the multiple scoring introduces correlated error that would amplify the correlations. Where two trait-scoring keys shared no items, no correlated error would be added, and the base correlation would be apt to be zero. (Carroll's study has only five traits, and hence it has only 10 intertrait correlations on which to base r_r, net slope, etc.; as a consequence, the results are quite unstable.)

The practice of using one item response on more than one trait's scoring key is lacking in the Edwards PPS study. In both of its pairings in Tutko's study, the Edwards fits the autoregressive model well, and our handiest correlated-error multiplicative enhancement model is not obviously appropriate. Can we come up with an attenuation erosion, subtractive model? We will try: The sentence, nine-response level rating scales employed were devised in an attempt to epitomize the variable tapped by the questionnaire. This attempt was inevitably imperfect, and the imperfection attenuated high intertrait correlations more than it did low ones. The imperfect translation hypothesis is supported by one detail from our 1967 paper. When all the methods use the same rating scales (e.g., Staff, Teammates, and Self in the study by Kelly & Fiske, 1951), the r_r between the two monomethods tends to be as high as or higher than the r_r between one monomethod and the heteromethod triangle; for the Edwards study, this is not so. While Peer and Self monomethods produce an r of .72, they correlate with the Edwards monomethod only .18 and .19, very weakly indeed. That the monohet r_r s in the Edwards are as high as .45 to .56 is remarkable indeed. For the Edwards PPS, the erosion, reductive model seems more plausible than the augmentive, correlated-error, add-on-of-irrelevant-methods variance model.

Seven of the eight studies involve personality ratings with a single rating scale per trait. For six studies, two or three of the other, separate methods employed for analysis involve separate classes of raters who use identical rating scales to describe the same persons. It is on these six studies that we will focus our final speculations. Let us first address an extreme that is not exemplified by any of the studies that we examine here: Two raters each rate 100 persons on 12 personality scales. The ratings are made independently, and they are based on independent samples of each person's behavior. The two raters do not share a common community of gossip about the personalities of those whom they rate. They do, however, agree on meanings for the personality trait terms. Each behavior sample can provide valid information on more than one personality trait. The small number and difference of the behavior samples attenuate the correlations across raters. Greatly increasing the number of samples that each rater has for comparable social settings will reduce this attenuation, even if the specific samples continue to have no overlap. Increasing the sample size will make their samples more nearly equivalent to having the same sample, thus, making the heterorater intertrait correlations more like the monorater correlations. For short and distinct behavior samples, the monorater correlations are more like those hypothetical asymptotic large-sample correlations. The heterorater correlations are attenuated versions of them, more attenuated for the high monorater values.

This is the best that we can do for a reductive, erosion model. It may have a certain amount of validity as part of the explanation for the higher correlations in the monomethod blocks. However, even in this idealized scenario, the case for an augmentation model may seem stronger. The small behavior samples have chance unrepresentativeness or sampling error. This is correlated error for trait ratings by the same rater, and it is probably more enhancing for high intertrait relations than for low ones. Large-sample asymptotic values will be different from small-sample values, and the correlations would probably be lower, if behavior sampling were the only problem involved.

Exemplified by higher correlations when third variables are correlated with teacher-rated intelligence than with measured intelligence, halo effects in ratings were the first methods factor to be noted in the psychometric tradition—around 1920 or earlier. It is possible that halo effects were represented in our multitrait-multimethod matrix thinking as additive factors, but if they were, it was thoughtlessly done. From the very beginning, the halo effect involved rater theories of intertrait relationships, in which holding the theory created or at least augmented the correlations among ratings. Some theories may have been totally fictional, such as the belief that popular pupils make fewer errors in calisthenic drills, as in the Zillig (1928) study featured in Klineberg's (1940) influential social psychology text. Such popularly accepted false theories, and their specific attributions to individuals, will account for heterorater agreements under at least two conditions: if both raters share in a gossip community about the ratees (this is ruled out in the preceding scenario), or if one of the traits (such as physical beauty or talkativeness) is reliably noted by independent raters. In either condition, a rater's chance unevenness in diagnostic judgments, coupled with the theory that carries the related trait along, will produce higher monorater than heterorater correlations, thereby generating the multiplicative halo effect pattern. Shweder and D'Andrade (1980), Nisbett and Ross (1980), and Ross and Lepper (1980) review the extensive modern rediscovery and elaboration of such findings. Even where the theorized intertrait relationships have some grain of truth, they are exaggerated when they are noted at all. These exaggerated beliefs about relationships dominate the monorater correlations. It is probably the higher real correlations that are the most apt to be noted and exaggerated, thus providing the multiplicative form of the halo-effect correlation enhancement for even our simple insulated-rater ideal model. This will be the case even if the subjective personality theories or meanings given to the trait terms are identical. Idiosyncrasies in these regards will further increase the contrast between monorater and heterorater estimates of intertrait correlation. (Perhaps these idiosyncrasy effects should be regarded as attenuating the heterorater correlations.)

None of our personality-rating studies conforms to this simple scenario, where each of two independent raters (the two methods) rates all the ratees. For Carroll, Tutko, Meeland, and our Projection Project, the Peer ratings were collected from coresidents in student housing, who rated each other in clusters ranging from 5 to 20 or so. (On the Wetzel study, a unique peer, usually a roommate, was obtained for each ratee.) The average rating (excluding self-ratings) that each ratee received was used as the Peer rating. The Ns of 100 to 204 have been made up of a number of such clusters, both raters and ratees differing from cluster to cluster. Shared personality trait theories as a source of error augment intertrait correlations under this condition, while idiosyncratic ones tend to get averaged out. Insofar as there are trends, the peer ratings tend to show the strongest methods factors by both elevation and net slope; they may also show more nonzero intercepts. The Teammates in the study by Kelly and Fiske (1951) also were collected in small clusters. Staff was constant across all ratees, although its members experienced the latter by teams and had access to teammate ratings before making their own.

In another rating model, each ratee is rated by a different rater. Banta's study of 500 youths rated by both father and mother is typical. This study is noteworthy for its conformity to the autoregressive model, since the slope passes right through the zero-zero origin. In general, by either elevation or slope, the method factors were low. The Self ratings in all studies are also of this nature, and in general they have lower methods factors than the Peer ratings of the same study. They conform unevenly to the multiplicative model, as illustrated by Figure 3.2F. Insofar as all raters share a common subjective theory of personality, this should enhance monomethod correlations. The case for the attenuation model is no better here than in the two-rater scenario.

OVERVIEW

This chapter has called attention to an overlooked puzzle posed by methods factors in the use of multitrait-multimethod matrices in the personality domain. The authors have presented an alternative interpretation, in which differences in method attenuate relationships that are more validly shown when method is held constant than in cross-method correlations. This interpretation has been contrasted with the concept that shared method augments intertrait correlations above their true values, which are more validly shown in their heteromethod form. For the attenuation model, the autoregressive statistics of time series analysis could be considered appropriate, and many of the data sets show superficial conformity to it. When conceptualizing specific processes, however, a multiplicative augmentation model seems most appropriate in most instances. In this model, correlated error and rater theories of personality exaggerate the correlation between the more highly correlated traits.

This chapter was supported in part by National Science Foundation Grant BNS 7925577. The authors [Campbell and O'Connell] have profited from suggestions made by David A. Kenny, Charles S. Reichardt, and Robert L. Linn.

OVERVIEW OF CHAPTER 4

———— •·• ————

Cumulative research experience provided criteria for accepting or discarding measures because of their validity. With the multitrait-multimethod (MTMM) matrix popularized by Campbell and Fiske, a new criterion was added. Not only were validity coefficients to be positive, but now these positive correlations were to be higher than the correlations of different traits measured by different methods. The how-to-do-it recipe for establishing construct validity and the assertion that a measure need not be treated as a perfect criterion was, perhaps, responsible for the high citation rates of the 1959 Campbell and Fiske article.

Examinations of multitrait-multimethod matrices reported in past research provided disappointing results. Often the validity coefficients did not satisfy the criteria for validity, and when they did, the coefficients were very low. Many of the matrices in the literature may have been published simply because it is so common to produce matrices that demonstrate poor validity. In this chapter, Fiske and Campbell ask the question: Is it possible to have a matrix that exhibits convergent and discriminant validity?

Studies that cite the Campbell and Fiske article fall into two groups: those that refer to the basic concepts in the article, and those that report a matrix and apply the eyeballing procedures that were suggested. Few researchers dealt with the unresolved problems associated with the

MTMM matrix. While some researchers explored methods for providing summary statistics and estimations for MTMM matrices, no single method was preferred by all researchers.

Two questions need to be addressed when examining an MTMM matrix. First, how can the methods be improved? Second, how can the concept be improved? Although work has been done on the general conceptualization problems, these matrices have not been used extensively to test the proposed measures of these constructs.

Since methods and traits may be highly related, perhaps the unit of study should be a "trait-method." In doing this, one must be careful not to fall into operationalism, in which a distinct operation is required for each combination. When an MTMM matrix is applied, however, and the results are unsatisfactory, the measure should not be discarded. Rather, this method of validation should be a part of a step-by-step process aimed at improving the measure for the next study.

Most of the time, MTMM matrices had been applied to measures of personality, attitude, or aptitude. Questions remain: Are these the easiest domains in which to apply MTMM, or are these areas simply more interesting to researchers? How do we define and describe a method? Does the method variance change based on the trait being measured? What gains can be expected when these questions are answered? In 1995, Campbell chose this article to appear in this volume. He felt that these questions still had not been addressed to his satisfaction, and he hoped to extend the challenge to the new generation of methodologists.

THE CURRENT STATUS
OF RESEARCH ON THE
MULTITRAIT-MULTIMETHOD
VALIDITY MATRIX

———————•◆•———————

*I*n the cumulative experience with measures of individual differences over the past 50 years, tests have been accepted as valid or
discarded as invalid by research experiences of many sorts. The
criteria suggested in this chapter are all to be found in such cumulative evaluations, as well as in the recent discussions of validity. These criteria are clarified
and implemented when considered jointly in the context of a multitrait-
multimethod (MTMM) matrix. [Note: See Chapter 2 in this volume.]

Although the notions of convergent and discriminant validation are rather
simple, they needed to be identified and labeled. Each of us had encountered, in

Fiske, D. W., & Campbell, D. T. (1992). Citations do not solve problems. *Psychological
Bulletin, 112,* 292-295. Copyright © 1992 by the American Psychological Association.
Adapted with permission.

his own research, instances in which several measures with the same label simply had too low intercorrelations and in which scores for different variables, when derived from the same instrument, had what seemed to be too high correlations, that is, they lacked discriminant validity. Many others had noticed these tendencies before us. Guilford (1954, p. 279) noted that halo effects were recognized in 1907 and named in 1920. We generalized to all variables when measured by any method. We added a new comparison base for validity scores: Not only should they be positive, they should also be larger than the "heterotrait-heteromethod" values, that is, the correlations between measures differing in both method and trait—values rarely if ever examined before modern computers churned them out as a by-product of a whole-matrix approach to getting the wanted values.

Although the method has never been incorporated into the American Psychological Association's official test standards, in spite of a pointed effort (Campbell, 1960b), it has become an orthodoxy. It combined obvious desiderata with an explicit how-to-do-it recipe, and it captured an important part of Cronbach and Meehl's then newly promulgated construct validity (Cronbach, 1989). The validational recipe did not require that any measure be treated as a perfect criterion, thus meeting the needs of the great majority of personality trait or attitude measurers. Perhaps these virtues are enough to explain the high citation rates.

In 1959, we presented all of the matrices we knew about, plus some newly computed ones. [Note: A selection of these studies was included in Chapter 2.] The results were very disappointing. Validity values (monotrait-heteromethod) were generally not as high as the heterotrait-monomethod values; reliable method-specific variance was ordinarily higher than reliable trait-specific variance. Worse than that, validity values significantly different from zero were often not as high as heterotrait-heteromethod correlations involving the same measure. And even when this low standard was met, the "successful" validity coefficients were typically .30 to .50, disappointingly low.

We have looked at only a fraction of the applications of the multitrait-multimethod (MTMM) method, in part because the matrices continued to be discouraging. We have elsewhere expressed our disappointment with published outcomes (Campbell & O'Connell, 1982; Fiske, 1982, the latter providing some suggestions for extensions).

A widely read and widely cited *Psychological Bulletin* article is one that researchers can use. Is our article being used as a crutch? Matrices published today continue to be about as unsatisfactory as those published more than 33 years ago. Editors and readers are accepting matrices showing limited convergence or discrimination, or both, perhaps because these are so typical, so common in the published literature. The only published ones that are fairly good are those using rather similar methods or quite disparate traits or other attributes or both. We have yet to see a really good matrix: one that is based on fairly similar concepts and plausibly independent methods and shows high convergent and discriminant validation by all standards. Is such a matrix possible?

What is surprising is that the citation rate continues to be high: over 100 a year in recent years. (The increase in annual rate is probably associated with the increase in the number of psychologists.) Keeping up with just that literature would be quite a task. We have looked at a few dozen of the citations in recent years (our sample being perhaps biased by our picking papers that were more readily available). Most of the citations fall into one of two groups, either a passing reference to the basic concepts or to the matrix or an application of the eyeballing procedures we suggested, sometimes alongside some sophisticated statistical analyses. (It has also been used in scale construction, e.g., Jackson, 1970; Jackson & Carlson, 1973). Regrettably, there have been very few examinations of the underlying and unresolved problems.

A substantial literature exploring formal summary statistics and component estimations for MTMM matrices has developed. With one early exception (Boruch & Wolins, 1970), the great majority have made use of Karl Jöreskog's confirmatory factor analysis (Jöreskog & Sörbom, 1979), with Browne's (1984) composite direct product coming in more recently. Many of our friends involved in these efforts are pessimistic. Wothke (1984) found difficulties in all of the many models he studied but came out in favor of scale-free variance component models. Kenny and Kashy (1992) say that after 30 years, "we still do not know exactly how to evaluate statistically these two [convergent and discriminant] validities" (p. 170). They recommend, nonetheless, their own "correlated uniqueness" model. Marsh (1988) states that no generally accepted solution has emerged. Jackson (1975), an early pioneer, is now optimistic about Browne's (1984) approach (Goffin, 1987; Goffin & Jackson, 1992), as is Bagozzi (Bagozzi, Yi, & Phillips, 1991).

The study of any obtained matrix seeks answers to two major problems: What can one do to improve the methods that were used, and what can one do to improve the concepts? Although much work has been done on general problems of conceptualization, little of it has used these matrices to test proposed delineations of constructs.

Our article reinforced the concern with method variance. It seems likely that psychologists can do more about that problem, which is largely "out there," than about the problem of conceptualization, which is all too much in psychologists, in their intuitions. One substantive research program has productively confronted the method problem, dividing it into the instrument and the agent providing the datum: Patterson's group has made considerable substantive progress in handling the method difficulties in their studies of children and families (cited in Bank, Dishion, Skinner, & Patterson, 1990).

Method and trait or content are highly interactive and interdependent. We may have to settle for the practice of studying "trait-method units" (as we called them in the original article) if we can do so without entering the blind alley of pure operationalism: having a distinct operation for each such combination. In the meantime, eyeballing an MTMM matrix in terms of the weak criteria proposed in the original article seems like a sound first step, especially when one has an extended research program and sees the particular matrix as only a step toward constructing an improved set of measuring procedures. Presumably, one is not going to stop with the particular matrix but is going on to further study of the variables by methods improved by carefully interpreting the results at hand. A given study is carried out to make the next study a better one.

Note that most of the examples in the original article were from the personality, attitude, or aptitude domains; it is in these individual-differences areas that the MTMM techniques continue to be most frequently used. Are researchers in those areas the ones that are most concerned with convergent and discriminant validation? Do researchers in other areas find it difficult to identify and apply alternative methods of measuring their dependent variables?

Cronbach (1989) has summarized the situation well:

> The Campbell-Fiske paper has been enormously popular because it offered a recipe for investigating CV [construct validity]. . . . Campbell and Fiske . . . produced a software package, the multitrait-multimethod . . . matrix, to help

beginners make a start toward CV. Unfortunately, users of their package rarely go beyond it, to match inquiry specifically to the construction under test. (p. 153)

So what are the unresolved questions? What do we mean by method? How can one identify and describe a method? Is a method modified when it is used for measuring a particular attribute or other trait (just as a trait seems to change with the method used to measure it)? Why have almost all the empirical studies using MTMM matrices involved personality, attitudes, and similar judgments? How much will psychology gain when these questions are well answered? There is much still to be done.

Our article had impact because it raised a problem: the links between psychological methods and psychological constructs. The problem is still with us 33 years and more than 2,000 citations later.

We [Fiske and Campbell] are indebted to Barbara Page Fiske, Louis Fogg, and Werner Wothke for their valuable comments on a draft of this article.

OVERVIEW OF CHAPTER 5

——————•◆•——————

As a part of a festschrift honoring Donald Fiske, Campbell presents his own perspective on philosophy of science, which he believes is compatible with the scientific practices of Fiske. Campbell and Fiske's 1959 article on the multitrait-multimethod (MTMM) matrix challenged logical positivism, which stressed definitional operationalism of theoretical terms. While definitional operationalism suggested that the score of a measure defined the construct and contained no error, Campbell and Fiske asserted that all measures were compositionally complex and included method variance as well as trait variance. They considered themselves postpositivists, but Fiske was not entirely comfortable with Campbell's fallibilist-realist assumptions about constructs—that they are real entities only imperfectly observed.

Early in his career, Fiske recognized that the criterion measures against which new measures were compared were, themselves, imperfectly valid and reliable. In his early work, he reported on methods factors, halo effects, and response sets, which demonstrates his distance from definitional operationalism. With the MTMM matrix, the zero correlation that was assumed between the heterotrait-heteromethod correlations was replaced by two criteria: the validity values should be higher than the heterotrait-heteromethod correlations; and the validity values should be higher than the heterotrait-monomethod correlations. While the MTMM matrix provides a quantitative way of making these comparisons, these criteria were employed by Fiske and others prior to 1959.

Campbell is quick to point out that the fallibilistic scientific realism that he espouses is different from logical positivism. Still, he admits that some social scientists tend to view these two in the same light, and in doing so, reject any superiority of scientific methods. There were two major reactions to the demise of logical positivism. Campbell and others still admired the achievements of science and believed that a revised theory of science could be applied to the social and psychological sciences. Others, including Fiske, either believed that science did not provide an effective approach to increasing validity, or believed that scientific methods would not be effective in the social sciences.

Campbell goes on to explain his beliefs regarding how we acquire knowledge. By recognizing that measures can be validated only with other fallible measures, Campbell and Fiske showed themselves to be postpositivists who practice nonfoundationalism. Foundationalism holds that there are certain pieces of infallible knowledge upon which all knowledge and truth are based. Campbell uses the word *hermeneutics* to describe the new consensus on the theory of science. Hermeneutics is a method for interpretation, which was used initially in the translation and decoding of ancient texts. While he rejects an ontologically nihilistic hermeneutics, which accepts all interpretations as equally plausible, Campbell does advocate a validity-seeking hermeneutics. While hermeneutics means "interpretative," logical positivism tried to eliminate all interpretation; facts were based on observables, and theories were to be dictated by the "facts." Hermeneutics did not treat texts as foundational, that is, limiting the interpretation of a text to that text without regard to the author, the circumstances, or time in which the author wrote. This would allow a scholar interpreting a text to suggest that an error had been made by the scribe, rather than assuming that a written text should be interpreted as if it were infallible.

Campbell then presents nine principles of hermeneutics, which he invites young scholars to consider in their search for a validity-seeking process for the social sciences. The first is the hermeneutic spiral in which we arrive at a better approximation of our theoretical constructs through an iterative process he labeled the part-whole iteration. The principle of charity suggests that we can make interpretations of the actions and words of others by assuming that the "actor" is "just like me."

The coherence strategy of belief revision suggests that we improve the validity by accepting the majority of our beliefs while revising only a small number; Campbell described this as the 99-to-1 trust-doubt ratio. Maximizing the interpretive horizon implies that interpretations are most valid when viewed in context. The "whole of science" should be the unit against which an individual belief must be compared. Another principle, described as contextualism, indexicality, and unconfounding rival interpretations through triangulation, suggests that, when an unknown word is used in several different contexts, a single interpretation may fit all the contexts, ruling out rival interpretations. This sort of triangulation is the principle behind the MTMM matrix and experimental design.

The following principles must be understood using the conceptualization of a spherical web of belief. At the core of this sphere are the laws of logic and fundamental beliefs of the world. At the periphery are the things we perceive and experience. The in-between connections are our beliefs about physical objects and our theories, which include concepts and invisible entities. The principle of privileging perception means that we should more readily revise our theories than our sensual perceptions, although revising these, too, may be reasonable at times. Privileging the core suggests that we be reluctant to revise the laws of logic and fundamental beliefs in order in the world, and instead, we question our specific theories. When making revisions to the web, adjacent and nearby links should be readjusted; this is called the principle of proximal readjustment in the web of belief. The final hermeneutic principle suggests that pattern similarity is a sign of validity. With the term *hermeneutics* and the discussion of the nine principles arising from the hermeneutic tradition, Campbell attempted to characterize the theory of science that provided the underpinnings for Fiske's and his work on attitude measurement.

FIVE

THE CONTEMPORARY PHILOSOPHY OF SCIENCE APPROPRIATE TO THE MULTITRAIT-MULTIMETHOD VALIDITY MATRIX

————•◆•————

*D*uring Donald Fiske's long career at the frontiers of psychological measurement, the paradigmatic dogma of logical positivism, with its definitional operationalism for theoretical terms, has come and gone. While always a participant in the exciting philosophy of science discussions as they affected psychology, Fiske has been consistently postpositivist in his research. I am thinking of the following: (a) 1947 wartime

Campbell, D. T. (1995). The postpositivist, nonfoundational, hermeneutic epistemology exemplified in the works of Donald W. Fiske. In P. E. Shrout & S. T Fiske (Eds.), *Personality, research, methods, and theory: A festschrift honoring Donald W. Fiske*. Hillsdale, NJ: Lawrence Erlbaum.

(World War II) research on the validation of naval aviation selection tests, in which low validity coefficients were explained as due, in part, to invalidity and unreliability in the criterion measures; (b) warnings about the biases due to individual differences in response fluency in Rorschach test scoring (Fiske & Baughman, 1953); (c) many studies of intraindividual variability between 1955 and 1974; and (d) subtle and creative preoccupation with invalidity in its many forms, which can be found in his individual articles and books: *Measuring the Concepts of Personality* (1971), *Strategies for Personality Research* (1978), and *Problems With Language Imprecision* (1981).

To characterize Fiske's measurement research as "postpositivist" alerts us to the fact that postpositivism need not mean giving up the traditional goals of scientific objectivity and quantification. Instead, logical positivism was a mistaken characterization of science. Giving up the definitional operationalism of scientific terms, or giving up taking observations and meter readings as "foundational," does not entail giving up science's more general goals. This needs stressing at the onset because, in his most explicit recent excursion into postpositivist (and, indeed, postmodern) philosophy of science (Fiske & Shweder, 1986), Fiske (1986) is happy to play the scientific extreme on the "social science commitment continuum" (Frankel, 1986).

Our coauthored "Convergent and Discriminant Validation by the Multitrait-Multimethod Matrix" (1959; see Chapter 2, this volume; see also Fiske & Campbell, 1992) was a part of that career—a small part, but the part I know best. In it we explicitly rejected the dogma of operational definitions of theoretical terms and thus challenged the overwhelmingly dominant logical positivist philosophy of science of that period. Since that time, a major conceptual revolution or paradigm change has occurred among philosophers of science, in which logical positivism has by now been almost totally rejected. Although no new consensus has emerged that is as strong, this chapter aspires to present a current perspective compatible with the scientific practice exemplified by Fiske's work, including the multitrait-multimethod (MTMM) matrix.

The operationalist-positivist consensus we challenged was as dominant in would-be scientific psychology as in philosophy of science. As Smith (1986) made clear, this was due as much to a convergence of independent developments as to the persuasive influence of the logical positivists. Even within the philosophy of physics, Bridgman's (1927) demand for operational definitions of theoretical constructs was an independent and anticipatory development. In addition to the confluences Smith documented, those in psychometrics had the decades-old custom of defining validity in terms of the correlation of a test with the criterion (be it college grades or insurance salesmen's sales volume). We psychometricians were also practitioners of Karl Pearson's partial- and multiple-correlation coefficients, with their implicit definitional operationism of the so-called independent variables, treated as if measured perfectly, with all of the imperfection in the relationship projected into the dependent variable. Associated with this was the likelihood of having read Pearson's (1892) *The Grammar of Science,* a positivist diatribe against speculating about unobserved variables.

However multiple were the sources, our colleagues of the 1940s and 1950s were all discussing the issues in terms of the logical-positivist philosophy of science (e.g., Bergmann & Spence, 1941; Cronbach & Meehl, 1955; Jessor & Hammond, 1957; Loevinger, 1957; MacCorquodale & Meehl, 1948). Fiske had been an undergraduate philosophy major at Harvard. I had acquired my reading habits in philosophy of science from Egon and Else Frenkel-Brunswik and Edward Tolman, all psychologists who embraced logical positivism. By 1959, Fiske and I were both trained in, and generally committed to, logical positivism and "operationalism." (Campbell and Fiske remained committed to operationalism in the form of operational explicitness. What they boldly rejected in 1959 was the definitional operationalism of theoretical terms.)

The MTMM matrix was not the first conspicuous rejection of logical positivism in psychology. A polarizing defense of operational definitions by Bechtoldt (1959) pointed out the complexities. Speaking for Gustav Bergmann (a young member of the Vienna Circle, by then at Iowa with appointments in both philosophy and psychology) and Kenneth Spence (psychologist), he attacked the concept of construct validity (Cronbach & Meehl, 1955) and all of us who aligned ourselves with it (e.g., Campbell & Fiske, 1959; Jessor & Hammond, 1957; Loevinger, 1957). Bechtoldt wanted test validity limited to criterion-defined variables, for which "predictive" and "concurrent" validity were the acceptable forms.

But Cronbach and Meehl had explicitly written from within the logical-positivist framework. They explicitly accepted the definitional operationalism of concurrent and predictive validity, and were adding construct validity to the acceptable types. Although they allowed unobserved theoretical entities to be involved in the theoretical linkage between observed variables, this required a formal, logical ("nomological") linkage. The empirical confirmation of such a predicted relationship supported (albeit did not prove) the whole linkage involved, including the posited existence of the unobserved variable. But the unobserved variable was not regarded as being "measured" by any of the "observed" variables. Moreover, construct validity was limited to settings in which formal theory (in a logical or mathematical form) had been employed, and was thus primarily a possibility for the future.

Fiske and I went farther than this in claiming that all measures were compositionally complex; all were, at best, "trait-method units," not pure trait measures, and thus could not be definitional of the intended trait because of contamination by "method variance." We regarded explorations of validity of the sort sometimes feasible through use of an MTMM matrix as preliminary to the use of measures in theory-confirming construct validation. However, we omitted mention of the fallibilist-realist assumptions about traits that I believe are implicitly involved in the concept of alternative methods of measurement of "the same" trait, and indeed Fiske was not fully comfortable with my "hypothetical realism" (Campbell, 1959a). It was such realism about not directly observables that was a major target of logical positivism. A rebuttal to Bechtoldt (Campbell, 1960b) more explicitly acknowledged my own critical-realist commitments. Although many postpositivist positions among philosophers of science involve a fallibilist realism of some sort, the application of the realist strategy to the personality test domain, via the MTMM matrix or otherwise, has been very frustrating, as Fiske (1982) and I (Campbell & O'Connell, 1982) have noted. This is a field of application that does little to encourage belief in "real but imperfectly observed" entities.

Although it is convenient for me to focus on the MTMM matrix, I want the reader to be clear that its important postpositivist features were already present in Fiske's work prior to that article. I have already noted that Fiske (1947) recognized that the criterion measures one employs are imperfectly reliable and imperfectly valid. In contrast, definitional operationalism defines one set of measures as perfect. By centering his agenda in personality measurement, Fiske no doubt reduced the tendency found in personnel selection test development to contrast "criterion measures" with "predictors." Ten years before the MTMM article, Fiske (1949) had already recognized the egalitarian, mutually validating nature of agreement among ratings by different sets of observers, without treating any one of the sets as the criterion. (The fact that he was still a graduate student when this was written may have helped him resist the temptation to treat ratings by "experienced Ph.D. clinicians" as the criterion, against which ratings by fellow trainees and self-ratings were to be validated.) In his work on Rorschach test scoring, Fiske (Fiske & Baughman, 1953) had already added to the literature on what we called "methods factors" in 1959 (and of which "halo effects" in ratings and questionnaire "response sets" were other prior exemplars).

The MTMM matrix seems to offer the possibility of quantitative comparison of the strength of the methods factors in different methods, and of the strength of trait factors in comparison with methods factors. But such seeming possibilities turn out to be hard to cash in on [see Chapter 4]. As we [Campbell and Fiske] (1959) pointed out, one has to find and assume a true zero correlation in the heterotrait-heteromethod triangles. One must also assume no specific trait- method interactions. One may have to assume the methods variances constant across methods, as Stanley (1961) did, each rater being treated as a different method. Finally, the MTMM matrix provides two substitutes for the implicit zero value that is usually used as the comparison base for validity coefficients:

1. Validity values should be higher than any of the heterotrait-heteromethod correlations (i.e., between measures sharing neither method nor trait) involving either of the measures (often met, but perhaps in no more than half of computed MTMM matrices).
2. Validity values should be higher than the heterotrait-monomethod correlations involving either of the two measures.

These are all nice gains where MTMM matrices are feasible, but they are only formalizations of criteria already employed, if less systematically, by Fiske and others prior to 1959. Thus, the epistemology and philosophy of science discussion to follow is not at all specific to the MTMM.

Fiske's commitment to multimethodism has at times reached ludicrous extremes. He and I have jointly authored two famous papers. Unfortunately for our citation counts, but perhaps fortunately for our promotions to tenure (scientific sobriety was required of assistant professors in those days), the second of these was anonymous, never submitted for publication, and famous only as a famous paragraph in a famous book:

In a report whose authors choose to remain anonymous (Anonymoi, 1953-1960), it was discovered that there is a strong association between the methodological disposition of psychologists and the length of their hair. The authors observed the hair length of psychologists attending professional meetings and coded the meetings by the probable appeal to those of different methodological inclinations. Thus, in one example, the length of hair was compared between those who attended an experimental set of papers and those who attended a series on ego-identity formation. The results are clear cut. The "tough-minded" psychologists have shorter-cut hair than the liberal-minded psychologists. Symptomatic interpretations—psycho-analytic inquiries as to what is cut about the clean-cut young men—are not the only possibilities. The causal ambiguity of the correlation was clarified when the "dehydration hypothesis" (that is, that lack of insulation caused the hard-headedness) was rejected by the "bald-head control," that is, examining the distribution of baldheaded persons (who by the dehydration hypothesis should be most hardheaded of all). (Webb, Campbell, Schwartz, & Sechrest, 1966, pp. 116-117; Webb, Campbell, Schwartz, Sechrest, & Grove, 1981, pp. 203-204)

Perhaps we were overcautious in our choice of anonymity, but now we can reveal our names. While ludicrous, this was a real study, with extremely high chi-squares.

LOGICAL POSITIVISM AND ITS COLLAPSE

Already in this chapter, fallibilist scientific realism has been contrasted with logical positivism in a way that conflicts with some current social scientists' tendency to lump realism and positivism together, using both as synonyms for scientism. They then identify the announced failure of logical positivism as discrediting all efforts at being scientific in the social sciences, or as discrediting all claims for the superiority of scientific beliefs and methods. The discussions of logical positivism in psychology in the 1940s and 1950s, and that in mainstream philosophy of science, were quite different. I cannot speak with authority on Auguste Comte and the sociological tradition of positivism, which may indeed support a link between positivism and materialism (and hence a materialistic realism). But our tradition, going back through the logical positivists (e.g., Ayer, 1959) to Mach and Hume, always took a systematically agnostic and skeptical view toward invisible and underlying causes and real objects, seeking instead to ground science purely in observations, and logically/mathematically predict future observations.

The rejection of logical positivism came from many independent sources, some being from within the movement, as in Nelson Goodman's paradoxes of induction (see Brown, 1979, for a postpositivism so based). Quine's rejection of "Two Dogmas of Empiricism" (1951) and "Epistemology Naturalized" (1969a) are also rejections by a sympathetic insider. Although Popper's (1959, 1963) widely influential writings are commonly regarded as still positivist, I join him in regarding his works as major contributions to the demise of logical positivism. Kuhn (1962) has been most influential. For me, Polanyi (1958), Hanson (1958), and Toulmin (1961) have been equally important. Suppe (1977) is widely respected as an entry into the postpositivist consensus, such as there is. Meehl (1986), the chief philosopher of science among us tests-and-measurements psychologists, announced the demise and provided wise advice on how to react on it. Meehl (1990, 1992) has also provided his own important (albeit obscurely published) version of what the new consensus should be.

Two major streams of reaction to the demise of positivism must be distinguished. Most philosophers of science, including all those cited in the previous paragraph (plus psychologists such as Cronbach, Meehl, Fiske, and myself), continue in admiration of the achievements of the physical and biological sciences, reject logical positivism's description of science's achievements, and seek a revised theory of science that might also be relevant to the social and psychological sciences. This is the thrust of the present chapter.

The other major stream regards this demise as either discrediting science's claims to be an especially effective approach to improving the validity of belief even in the physical sciences, or discrediting efforts to be scientific in the social sciences. Fiske and Shweder (1986) and Shadish and Fuller (1994) offered entry into these literatures.

NONFOUNDATIONALISM

Most postpositivist philosophies of science display this badge with pride. Anybody like Fiske, who is willing to validate personality measures using no criteria measures but only other measures of dubious validity, is practicing nonfoundationalism. Quine often cites Neurath's (1959) metaphor, which I paraphrase: In science we are like sailors on a raft at sea, who must replace one particularly rotten beam while depending on others almost as decayed and that we later will have to replace. Popper (1959) has a similar metaphor, again paraphrased: In science we are like those who build upon a bog. Our pile-driver never drives the piles we build upon down to bedrock; whenever we stop, we could have driven down further; our pile-driver itself sits upon such piles. Some modern analytic philosophers whom I admire, such as Alvin Goldman (e.g., 1985), still attempt to justify some beliefs by means of others not needing justification because they are based on "reliable" channels of belief acquisition. However, reliable justifications do not guarantee validity, and in this sense at least they are nonfoundational. Probably all modern epistemologists agree that we cannot confirm or justify any belief by direct comparison of a belief with the reality it purports to describe. Instead, validating or justifying involves comparing a belief with other beliefs, none of which has been proven to be true. Quine (1951) said that not only may observations be held up for revision, but also basic laws of logic. Cook and I (1986) have designated this point omnifallibilism.

HERMENEUTICS

We need an affirmative name and a focal conception for the alternative candidates for a new consensus on the theory of science. "Antipositivism" is too ambiguous and fails to connote why we are "anti," and what our substitute is like. Currently (e.g., 1991), I [Campbell] am trying out *hermeneutics,* referring to the older validity-seeking hermeneutics coming out of the translating and decoding of ancient texts (perhaps in unknown languages) exemplified by Schliermacher and Dilthey, who around 1900 first introduced a hermeneutic model for the human and social sciences. If applied to science, it may offer a better theory of knowledge than does logical positivism. In the avant-garde social science epistemology of today (sampled in Fiske & Shweder, 1986), there is an ontologically nihilistic hermeneutics that I reject. But of the modern hermeneuts, I [Campbell] classify Habermas (1971, 1983) as *validity seeking.*

Hermeneutic means interpretative. Logical positivism sought to eliminate all interpretation—all subjective discretion—from science. Facts were to be public meter readings that all saw alike, totally independent of theory and hence available to test theory. Theory choice was also to be nondiscretionary, impersonally dictated by "the facts" and by the formal logic that linked facts together in the theory under test. Both nondiscretionary aspects have proved to be untenable. Instead, the facts that produce anomalies for accepted theories are, at their firmest, only social consensuses on interpretation, socially negotiated among the active scientists in a given field (Campbell, 1993). Theory choice has a similar interpretative discretionary character, never logical proof.

The hermeneutics of translation, although focused on texts and manuscripts, never treated texts as foundational (even though some contemporary hermeneutic theories may do so). This is perhaps most clearly illustrated by the frequent achievement of scholarly consensus that a specific anomalous detail represented some early scribe's clerical error in copying a prior manuscript. To get a feel for this nonfoundational achievement, try to recollect the first time you identified a misprint in a foreign language text you were studying.

Prodded by the zealous philosophy students enrolled in my Knowledge Processes course at Northwestern in the 1960s and 1970s, and by young theorists of social science methodology in anthropology and sociology, I have been half-heartedly monitoring the literature on hermeneutics for many years. Once it became apparent that founders Dilthey and Schliermacher were proposing a validity-seeking process quite in contrast to the ontological nihilism of most of the young advocates in the social sciences, I began looking for listings of hermeneutic principles that social scientists might use, but have not yet found any such list. I am presenting here in skeleton form some principles I feel reasonably sure are there, as an effort to pass the torch to younger scholars. I am not even helping by providing citations to those sources I still remember skimming. (I make an exception for my deceased friend Arthur Child, 1965, because of the great likelihood it would be missed.) Crude as the list is, and overlapping as the principles be, I distinguish nine in what follows. All hermeneutic principles are heuristic, rather than methodological universals guaranteeing truth.

The Hermeneutic Spiral or Circle. The hermeneutic circle or spiral is the only principle that I have found repeatedly mentioned in self-consciously hermeneutic literature. I (1986) translated this as "part-whole iteration." A guess is made at the meaning of the whole (e.g., the text). This helps, but does not fully dominate the interpretation of a part (e.g., a word), an experienced plausibility at this level then changes the interpretation of the whole, and so on in re-cursive revisions. Such iterative reinterpretations can amount to bootstrap-ping, or to effectively using an interpretation as a scaffolding that is later rejected on the basis of the later achievement, which could not have been made without it. The development of intelligence tests illustrates this. The earliest efforts by James McKeen Cattell using reaction times were rejected because they did not agree at all with teachers' and peers' rankings. Binet and Simon se-lected more cognitive items that did agree to considerable extent with teachers' evaluations, and on which older children in general did somewhat better than younger ones. Yet soon these very tests were being used to discredit teacher and peer ratings because of the halo effects found in those ratings, and to distin-guish mental age from chronological age. In 1923, Boring (an anticipatory log-ical positivist and definitional operationalist) defined *intelligence* as what the 1916 Stanford-Binet measured. Fortunately the author of that test, Lewis Terman, paid no attention and set to work improving the test and removing known imperfections and anomalies—actions quite incomprehensible if the 1916 version defined the concept being measured.

For those in the field of tests and measurements, another example of the hermeneutic cycle is available in item analysis using total scores of the same test as a criterion, typical of personality and attitude test construction. One ar-tistically generates a large number of items that one thinks might exemplify the attitude or trait one seeks to measure. Tentatively trusting that the totality of these items is on the mark, one generates total scores on this first version, and correlates each item with that total (algebraically removing that item's correla-tion with the total; i.e., correlating each item with the sum of the other items). One then removes the items that correlate negatively, zero, or low positive with the total. One could then generate a new purified total and repeat the process. (Factor analysis and multidimensional scaling can also be hermeneutically in-terpreted.) This process must be theory driven. If one believes that there really are methods factors such as acquiescence response sets, one must generate items for each pole of the attitude or trait (e.g., writing serene items as well as anxious ones). Otherwise, this part-whole iteration will maximize reliability by confounding trait and response-set variance (Campbell, Siegman, & Rees, 1967). Both item selection based on total scores and precautions against re-sponse sets are contrary to definitional operationalism and are antifounda-tional.

The Principle of Charity. In interpreting an utterance, a text, or a human action, this principle exhorts us to assume, wherever possible, that the speaker (writer, actor) is a fellow human being with a rationality shared with the interpreter (Quine, 1960). If this other person comes from an exotically different culture, physical environment, or historical period, this "just like me" assumption requires fallible empathetic guessing as to what "I" would have been intending had I been reared in that strange culture. This is a modification that Davidson (1984) rejects. This is probably the second-most-cited hermeneutic principle. But only Hesse (1980) explicitly identified it with the hermeneutic tradition.

This is the only principle in my list that is specific to the social sciences. I would assert that the others can be applied to the physical sciences as well.

The Coherence Strategy of Belief Revision. Under this title, I try to make more specific the metaphors of Neurath's boat or raft, and Popper's pile driver, introduced under the Nonfoundationalism section previously. We have no choice but to improve the validity of our beliefs by trusting the great bulk of our beliefs and revising as few as possible to improve the overall coherence. There is a continental version, attributed to Hegel, in which coherence defines truth. In contrast, the Anglo-American tradition tentatively uses coherence as a symptom of truth, but retains correspondence between belief and referent as defining the meaning and goal of truth, even while recognizing that such a comparison is not available as a "truth test" for specific beliefs. Lehrer (1974, 1990) contrasted such a coherentist epistemology with a perceptual or factual foundationalism. Harmon (1985) and many others share such a position, as does Quine.

To the turn of the century philosopher G. E. Moore is attributed the modern rejection of the older epistemological strategy of holding all belief in abeyance until the possibility of knowledge was first proven, thus rejecting also the Cartesian strategy of total doubt. Moore suggested that the problem of knowledge be studied assuming one had lots of it. For me, this fails to answer the valid quibbles of the skeptics. But taken as Quine (1951) does, as the strategy of tentatively trusting the validity of the great bulk of one's beliefs (unproven though they be) while critically revising a few, it describes how we get by in everyday life, and in science. (I have sloganized this as "the 99 to 1 trust-doubt ratio" [Campbell, 1988].) This bulk of trusted beliefs, collectively, is the only foundation we have in choosing between beliefs. Although the constituent beliefs are all potentially fallible, collectively they do act like a foundation against which beliefs most incoherent with them are judged to be in error.

Maximizing the Interpretive Horizon. A single letter, syllable, or word in isolation is profoundly equivocal in interpretation. If the word is in a sentence, it is less so. If it is in a paragraph or a book, still better. The larger the context (the more extensive the contemporaneous texts in the same language and from the same culture), the more certain is the interpretation or translation, and the more convincing a diagnosis that there has been a clerical error in transcription.

From recent Bible translation comes an example of the value of expanding the interpretive horizon. There has been a dispute over the meaning of a Hebrew word that occurs only once in the Pentateuch. In the last 50 years or so, there have been discovered extensive cuneiform libraries of a pre-Hebraic Semitic language, Ugaritic, in which the corresponding word appears more frequently and in a sufficient variety of contexts to permit a working consensus on its interpretation. This interpretation has made possible a tentative consensus on the meaning of the disputed Hebrew sentence. The value of expanded context is again and again illustrated in the heroic decipherments of Cretan Linear B and Mayan.

Speaking for science, or more generally for the link between belief and the world, Quine (1951) has said:

> Russell's concept of definition in use was . . . an advance over the impossible term-by-term empiricism of Locke and Hume. The statement, rather than the term, came with Russell to be recognized as the unit accountable to an empiricist critique. But what I am now urging is that even in taking the statement as unit we have drawn our grid too finely. The unit of empirical significance is the whole of science. (p. 39)

"The whole of science" is but a metaphorical exaggeration of the important hermeneutic principle of greater validity from larger interpretative horizons. Unfortunately, under the slogan of *holism* it has been taken as postponing indefinitely the issue of truth, or selection between competing beliefs, and in support of a nihilistic attitude toward the issue of validity (Campbell, 1991).

Fiske's and my MTMM matrix is a formalized way to extend the interpretive context.

The *interpretive horizon* part of this principle is almost authentically hermeneutic. It comes from Rudolph Bultmann and Hans Georg Gadamer, who used that concept to emphasize a horizon-specific relativity to the truth of an interpretation. Without having done any scholarship to support it, I deconstruct their motives in doing this with a metahermeneutics of their hermeneutics. They came from a tradition of Protestant, Bible-citing preachers (even though they were opposed to Biblical literalism) who asserted the continual up-to-date relevance of the holy scriptures for the current moral and religious needs of their congregations. For this purpose, the ancient writings did require an ever-changing truth in response to the ever-changing moral and religious needs of their parishioners. (Bultmann introduced into the horizon of his day the concept of religiously and ethically valid myths.)

Contextualism, Indexicality, and Unconfounding Rival Interpretations Through Triangulation. We can be more specific on how an increased interpretive horizon, an increased number of relevant texts, reduces equivocality. The incidental phrase (previously in regard to Ugaritic) "sufficient variety of contexts" points the way, and to the triangulation exemplified in the MTMM matrix.

For a disputed translation of a given word, many parallel uses, repeating the same context of other words, are not very helpful because the rival interpretations all remain plausible in each such instance. Varied contexts offer the chance of choosing the one interpretation that would make sense in each. Such triangulation partakes of John Stuart Mill's "cannons of cause," "concomitant variation," and "similarities and differences," and is the essence of both the MTMM matrix and experimental design.

Privileging Perception. Fiske and I (Campbell & Paller, 1989) remain empiricists, albeit nonfoundationalist empiricists. So, too, does Quine in the inspiredly postpositivist last 15 paragraphs of his "Two Dogmas of Empiricism" (1951). He describes a spherical web of belief extending from a "sensory periphery" to a "core," with the in-between connections involving "posits of [perceivable] physical objects" and theory, including concepts of *forces* and *invisible entities*. Among the many links in this web of belief, we should be much less willing to revise the "sensory periphery" and the "posits of [perceivable] physical objects," compared with the intermediate theoretical links. This does not make the "sensory periphery" foundational, however. We may find that, in following his rule of making minimal revisions in the overall web of belief when change is necessary, we may, in Quine's phrase, "plead hallucination." Nonetheless, he recommends in general that we privilege "experience," being less willing to revise it than the more interior theoretical links. As a hermeneutic principle in its original translation context, it would involve a nonfoundational privileging of the manuscript.

Privileging the Core. In describing the web of belief, Quine (1951) also spoke of a core that contains the laws of logic and fundamental beliefs in order in the world (i.e., in the possibility of scientific knowledge, over and above any specific scientific theories). Although Quine dramatically stated that a theoretical statement that seems to conflict may be retained "by amending certain statements of the kind called logical laws. . . . Revision even of the logical law of the excluded middle has been proposed as a means of simplifying quantum mechanics; and what difference is there in principle between such a shift and the shift whereby Kepler superseded Ptolemy, or Einstein Newton, or Darwin Aristotle?" (p. 40). Nonetheless, overall in these paragraphs, I think it clear that Quine recommends we be more reluctant to change these core beliefs than the intermediate ones of specific theory.

Proximal Readjustment in the Web of Belief. The hermeneutic, interpretive, discretionary flavor of Quine's (1951) last 15 paragraphs includes an emphasis on the looseness of the web of belief and, concomitantly, a recognition that, for most of the theory-substituting revisions, only adjacent and nearby links in the web of belief need revision. Although I judge this to be inconsistent with his occasional use of the terms *logical* and *entail* for these links, I claim this emphasis on proximal readjustment as a more general hermeneutic principle of revision.

Pattern Matching. This is a recurrent hermeneutic tactic. Overall patterns may be validly perceived even if the specific signals (e.g., the radar pixels) are full of static. Fiske's (1949) early use of pattern similarity as a sign of validity, and our repetition of its use (in part on the same data) in 1959, exemplifies this interpretative principle. Elsewhere (Campbell, 1966), I have collected illustrations of this principle in Bertrand Russell and many others.

SUMMARY

As much as 12 years before, Fiske was already employing the concepts epitomized in our joint article on the MTMM matrix. Thus, his research has always been postpositivist, avoiding the operational definition of theoretical terms and foundationalism more generally.

In an effort to spell out what a postpositivist consensus on scientific method and Fiske's research strategy might be, I explore an extension of validity-seeking hermeneutics. Nine hermeneutic principles are tentatively offered. These turn out to be more indebted to Quine (and, in particular, the last 15 inspired metaphoric paragraphs of his "Two Dogmas of Empiricism") than to the hermeneutic literature per se.

OVERVIEW OF CHAPTER 6

———•◆•———

It is no longer assumed that an attitude scale or personality test is a pure measure of the dimension one wishes to measure. Many factors affect a test score, including psychological, sociological, and linguistic factors. While it is important to examine and study these factors, Campbell, Siegman, and Rees warn against the extremist attitude that all test scores are merely response sets. In an effort to avoid this attitude, some test constructors have become too complacent, advocating that new scales be constructed without attention to response sets. This chapter is intended to address this latter group of test constructors, particularly with regard to the problem of direction of wording. The intent was to show that there are direction-of-wording effects, and that they can be found in the California F Scale measure of authoritarian personality trends as well as in the Minnesota Multiphasic Personality Inventory (MMPI).

Campbell and his colleagues explored this problem by studying the correlations among scales designed to measure different topics, attitudes, or traits. For these scales, both positive and negative direction-of-wording versions were available, and these versions were assumed to measure the same attitude. The MMPI produced equivalent scales with a reversed scale, while reversed scales for the F scale failed to produce equivalence. By looking at the way in which the F scale relates to other scales that have been successfully reversed, direction-of-wording effects can be studied. Two such scales are the California E scale and the Taylor Manifest Anxiety Scale (MA), which have both a "pro" scale, signified by a "p," and a "con" scale, signified by a "c."

While the positive and negative versions of the F scale correlate only .53 when corrected for attenuation, the positive and negative versions of the E and MA scales correlate at .94 and .98, respectively, when corrected for attenuation. When the positive and negative versions of the E scale were correlated with the positive version of the F scale, they produced disparate correlations. The same phenomenon occurred when the MA scales were used. This suggests that there is a correlation between the content component of the F scale and the direction-of-wording factor. This would result in a higher correlation between the positive scales of F and E (since both the content component and the direction-of-wording effects of F correlate with those of the positive E), and a reduced correlation between the positive scale of F and the negative scale of E (since the content component correlates positively, but the direction-of-wording effect correlates negatively). The authors concluded that the best way to study the direction-of-wording effect is to examine the difference between the average of the correlations of like-direction-of-wording scales [F_p, E_p and F_c, E_c] and the average of the correlations of the cross- direction-of-wording scales [F_p,E_c and F_c,E_p].

One possible statistical explanation for direction-of-wording effects involves the average proportion of the population endorsing the item in the trait-scored direction, indicated by a P value. When the P values for the pro and con scales differ greatly, there will be a constraint on the correlation between the pro and con totals. This is not the case, however, for the F scale, which has essentially identical values for the pro and con scales.

When multiple attitude tests with pro and con items are used in a study, the intercorrelations demonstrating direction-of-wording effects are rarely reported. One exception is the first study discussed in this chapter in which the direction-of-wording effects for the F scale were reported by Chapman and Campbell.

Data from other studies are reexamined to determine direction-of-wording effects for the F scale. Three studies are discussed: one by Peabody, one by Wrightsman, and another by Chapman and Campbell. In all of these studies, the F scale for the authoritarian personality demonstrates distinct direction-of-wording effects in relation to other scales.

The authors then analyze the Minnesota Multiphasic Personality Inventory (MMPI) in the same way. The scales in the MMPI were first modified to eliminate items that appeared on more than one scale. The direction-of-wording effects in the modified scales were even greater than those found in the F scale (with the exception of the Peabody study). The authors point out, however, that the F scale was less vulnerable to the direction-of-wording effect since the reversed items preserved the content of the original items or were drawn from the same content pool. In the MMPI scales, the reversed items did not share equivalent content. But even this does not explain why correlations between measures of the same content but with different direction of wording were so much lower than those in which the content differed but the direction of wording was the same. This demonstrates that there is a systematic relationship represented by or confounded with direction-of-wording effects.

The authors suggest that, in addition to direction-of-wording effects, another systematic factor might be affecting these correlations, namely the pole of description. For example, sick and healthy are opposite poles of the continuum. The authors suggest that perhaps four items would fully describe a bipolar trait—"I am healthy," "I am not sick," "I am not healthy," and "I am sick." While the first two describe the same condition, they are opposite in direction of wording; the same is true of the last two statements. In examining the correlations among the pro and con scales of the MMPI, there is only one positive correlation between a pro scale and a con scale, and this involves two scales that contain the greatest number of items with the same pole focus, for example, both with "sick-pole" items.

Rorer (1965; Rorer & Goldberg, 1965) reworded the MMPI items to eliminate content differences among the pro and con scales. Correlations show that there still is a dependable direction-of-wording effect. It is felt, however, that test constructors can be equally successful by using commonsense reversals rather than the awkwardness that comes when reversals are made without changing content.

While the direction-of-wording effect has been uniformly present, the authors do not believe there is enough evidence to suggest that the relationships with other attitudes were totally due or even predominantly due to the response set.

BIASES IN ATTITUDE
AND PERSONALITY SCALES

———•◆•———

*J*f there was a time when as definitional operationists we could complacently assume that our attitude scale or personality test was a pure measure of our dimension of interest, that day is past. We now know on grounds of both theory and experience that the scores we get inevitably are complex products of numerous psychological, sociological, and linguistic factors, many of which are irrelevant for our purposes. Already we have in our literature specifications of a number of the systematic irrelevancies contributing to test scores. Undoubtedly we will accumulate more and improve the effectiveness with which we avoid or compensate for them. For example, future research will almost certainly deal in more detail with the effects of grammatical form, with subcultural differences in the threshold for the use of evaluative terms, and with vocabulary difficulty.

Campbell, D. T., Siegman, C. R., & Rees, M. B. (1967). Direction-of-wording effects in the relationships between scales. *Psychological Bulletin, 68,* 293-303. Copyright © 1992 by the American Psychological Association. Adapted with permission.

Within this tradition, it is of course possible to exaggerate the role of the irrelevancies, or even to take a reverse "purist" position that the scores measure nothing but response sets. Such excesses must also be corrected. Two such corrective efforts have, however, been so extreme and so persuasive as to run the very real risk of convincing a new generation of test constructors that the problems can be neglected, that, for example, new scales should be constructed without attention to response sets (Block, 1965; Rorer, 1965). It is in the service of correcting this overcorrection on the specific problem of direction of wording that the present chapter is directed.

The burden of the chapter will be to establish these points:

1. A dependable, albeit often small, direction-of-wording effect can be found in the interrelationship among scales.
2. This effect is particularly pronounced for the California F Scale measure of authoritarian personality trends (Adorno, Frenkel-Brunswik, Levinson, & Sanford, 1950; Chapman & Bock, 1958). Even if all reversed forms are disregarded as unsuccessful, the effect appears in the relationship of the original F scale with pro and con forms of successfully reversed scales.
3. The effect is also marked for the weaker scales of the Minnesota Multiphasic Personality Inventory.

The approach of this chapter will be to focus on the interrelationships among scales designed to measure different topics, attitudes, or traits. This line of attack has been almost completely neglected in the studies of the F scale. Instead, attention has been paid only to the relationships between original and reversed items presumed to be codiagnostic of that one attitude. When in such a study the correlation between an original set of items and a set of reversals is less than expected from the reliabilities, this may be due to the fact that different topics are being measured rather than due to response-set variance. On the other hand, in many item-reversal studies the correlation may be judged misleadingly high due to the use of both members of an item-reversal pair. Repeating the same illustrative specifics in a positive and negative form produces a higher correlation than typical of interitem relationships among independent items. These problems are, on the whole, avoided in the cross-trait correlations. In studies of the MMPI, the factor-analytic studies have, of course, used interrelationships among traits, but with the ambiguity of optional choices in rotation producing an equivocality exploited by the contestants.

Table 6.1 Direction-of-Wording in Correlations Among the F Scale of
Authoritarian Personality Trends, the Ethnocentrism Scale,
and the Manifest Anxiety Scale

Scale	F_p	F_c	E_p	E_c	MA_p	MA_c
F_p	(.71)	.53	.76	.56	.41	.27
F_c	.29	(.42)	.36	.58	.12	.10
E_p	.57	.21	(.80)	.94	.13	.06
E_c	.39	.31	.70	(.69)	.05	.10
MA_p	.32	.07	.11	.04	(.87)	.98
MA_c	.21	.06	.05	.08	.84	(.85)
Number of Items	30	30	19	19	50	50
Average item P	.18	.21	.28	.29	.08	.11

NOTES: P = average proportion of the population endorsing the item in the trait-scored direction
Correlations involving the same direction of wording are italicized.

STUDIES INVOLVING THE F SCALE
AND OTHER SOCIAL ATTITUDES

It is a paradox of Rorer's (1965) review that he exonerated the MMPI and the F
scale on opposite and contradictory grounds. He exonerated the MMPI because his item-reversal effort produced equivalent scales, and direction-of-wording effects were negligible. He exonerated the F scale because no
efforts to develop a reversed scale had succeeded in producing an equivalence.
While for the F scale this recurrent failure has been used persuasively by many
as evidence of a response-set problem, Rorer's rejection of the reversal efforts
can be tentatively accepted and a direction-of-wording effect can still be demonstrated by looking only at data involving the original F scale items in relation
to the scales that are "successfully" reversed. Tables 6.1, 6.2, 6.3, and 6.4 are
relevant to this issue.

Table 6.1 presents data on the correlation between the F scale measure of
authoritarian personality trends (Adorno et al., 1950), the California E Scale
measure of ethnocentric, primarily antiminority, attitudes (Adorno et al.,
1950), and the Taylor Manifest Anxiety (MA) scale (Taylor, 1953). These are

each represented by a "pro" form in which the items are worded in advocacy of the authoritarian (F_p), ethnocentric (E_p), and anxious (MA_p) pole, and a "con" form, worded in the nonauthoritarian (F_c), tolerant (E_c), and unanxious (MA_c) form. While most of the data to be presented in this chapter are new, in this case they have been presented before (Chapman & Campbell, 1959a, 1959b), although neglected in Rorer's (1965) review. The data are based upon the responses of 184 college students in an introductory psychology class (66 male, 118 female). Each F scale had 30 items, each E scale had 19, and each MA scale had 50. All items were presented in the true-false format typical of the MA scale. The reliabilities in the diagonal of Table 6.1 are based upon Kuder-Richardson Formula 20. Values above the diagonal are corrected for attenuation.

The data of Table 6.1 illustrate one of the more "successful" reversals of the F scale, since the correlation between F_p and F_c is at least positive. However, it is low, and when corrected for attenuation reaches but .53. On the other hand, the E scale and the MA scale seem almost completely free of acquiescence bias, since direction of wording made almost no difference and the correlations between positive and negative forms approached unity (.94 and .98) when corrected for attenuation. But while the two forms of each seem equivalent, they are far from identical in the correlations they produce with F_p, the original F scale. F_p correlates .57 with E_p, but only .39 with E_c (difference significant at $p < .0002$). The difference cannot be due solely to reliability differences, for it persists when corrected for attenuation (.76 vs. .56). Although MA is still more immune to direction-of-wording effects than is E, a parallel picture obtains here: F_p correlates .32 with MA_p versus .21 with MA_c (difference significant at $p < .01$); corrected for attenuation, the values become .41 and .27. Thus, direction of wording is highly relevant to the magnitude of the correlation with the F scale even when only the "successful" reversals are used, the weak F_c being omitted from consideration.

Note that this effect is significantly present, even though no constant additive direction-of-wording component uniformly affects all the relationships in the matrix. Note also that the correlation of E and MA shifts from .11 when both are positive to .04 or .05 when one or the other is negative. This is probably due to the fact that E and MA have small loadings on the direction-of-wording factor, as is also indicated by the magnitude of their high intrascale pro-con correlations, corrected for attenuation. F, on the other hand, has a high loading by both lines of evidence.

While the correlation difference between F_pE_p and F_pE_c undeniably indicates a direction-of-wording effect, it possibly exaggerates it in that it is highly plausible that the F content factor and the direction-of-wording factor are correlated (e.g., Chapman & Campbell, 1957b; Leavitt, Hax, & Roche, 1955). A correlation between the F content component and direction-of-wording variance in E would augment the F_pE_p correlation and reduce F_pE_c. This hypothesis also provides an explanation of why in some instances F_p is a better predictor of E_c (or the con forms of other ethnic prejudice measures) than is F_c (as in the uncorrected correlations of Table 6.1, in the American data of Table 6.2, and in Table 6.3). For this reason, perhaps the best index of the effect of direction of wording on the F-E relation is not the .18 correlation point difference between F_pE_p and F_pE_c, but is rather the difference between the averages of the two like-directioned values (F_pE_p and F_cE_c) and the two cross-directional ones (F_pE_c and E_cE_p), which is only .14 points, $[(.57 + .31)/2]$ $[(.21 + .39)/2]$. (This value is .17 if the z' transformation is used.) Corrected for attenuation, however, the two indicators are essentially the same. The $F_pE_p - F_pE_c$ difference is .20, while the mean like-directional versus mean cross-directional difference is .21 (z', .32).

Table 6.1 includes the "average item P" for each scale. This is the average proportion of the respondent population endorsing the item in the trait-scored direction. Thus on the average F_p item, 18% of the respondent population gave the authoritarian answer of agreeing with the item. On the average F_c item, 21% gave the authoritarian answer of disagreeing. These values are provided to make possible the examination of a possible statistical explanation of direction-of-wording effects. Lloyd Humphreys, in a personal communication in November 1966, pointed out that where the pro and con scales differ greatly in these P values, the resulting statistical constraint on interitem correlations involving pro and con item pairs produces a corresponding constraint on the correlation between pro and con totals. The literature on item-difficulty factors in dichotomously scored tests, particularly where product-moment or phi coefficients are used (Wherry & Gaylord, 1944), point to the same conclusion. The essentially identical values for the pro and con forms of each scale rule out such explanations in the case of Table 6.1.

While many multiple attitude studies have contained several scales, each with balanced subsets of pro and con items, it is rarely that the intercorrelations are reported as a function of direction of wording. Table 6.1, in fact, represents

Table 6.2 Direction-of-Wording Effects in Peabody's Study of Scales of Authoritarianism, Dogmatism, Anti-Semitism, and Conservatism

Scale	F_p	F_c	D_p	D_c	AS_p	AS_c	PEC_p	PEC_c
American Data ($N = 88$)								
F_p	(.69)	.33	.93	−.02	.59	.55	.02	.28
F_c	.18	(.42)	−.20	1.01^a	.22	.52	−.19	.24
D_p	.61	−.10	(.62)	.37	.46	.18	.07	−.17
D_c	−.01	.47	.21	(.51)	.15	.49	−.33	.07
AS_p	.46	.13	.34	.10	(.87)	.81	.03	−.03
AS_c	.39	.29	.12	.30	.65	(.74)	−.08	−.05
PEC_p	.01	−.09	−.04	−.17	.02	−.05	(.51)	1.12
PEC_c	−.18	.12	−.10	.04	−.02	−.03	.61	(.58)
Number of items	14	14	20	20	10	10	8	8
Average item P	.45	.25	.45	.24	.24	.19	.64	.54
British Data ($N = 75$)								
F_p	(.82)	.60	.84	.03	.68	.36	.09	−.05
F_c	.36	(.44)	.15	.92	.41	.60	−.08	.05
D_p	.63	.08	(.68)	.30	.60	.30	.16	−.14
D_c	.02	.49	.20	(.64)	.25	.51	−.11	−.01
AS_p	.54	.24	.44	.18	(.78)	.97	−.14	−.30
AS_c	.30	.37	.23	.38	.79	(.86)	−.16	−.10
PEC_p	.07	−.05	.12	−.08	−.11	−.13	(.79)	.94
PEC_c	−.04	.03	−.10	−.01	−.23	−.08	.74	(.78)
Number of items	14	14	20	20	10	10	8	8
Average item P	.50	.22	.50	.21	.35	.19	.52	.37

NOTES: Values above the diagonal have been corrected for attenuation.

a. In this table and in Table 6.5, a combination of high correlations and underestimated reliability values provides paradoxical corrected values over 1.00.

the only published data on this of which we are aware. Tables 6.2, 6.3, and 6.4 represent such data resurrected and/or recomputed from otherwise published studies. In Peabody's (1961) study, all subjects were administered pro and con

Table 6.3 Wrightsman's Correlations by Direction of Wording for Authoritarianism, Segregation, and Machiavellianism

	F_p	F_c	S_p	S_c	M_p	M_c
F_p	(.44)		.68	.39	.53	−.64
F_c	.10	(.04)				
S_p	.43	.17	(.92)	.96	.33	−.08
S_c	.24	.18	.84	(.83)	.41	.16
M_p	.22	−.18	.20	.24	(.39)	.80
M_c	−.33	−.11	−.06	.11	.38	(.59)
Number of Items	10	10	25	11	10	10
Average item M[a]	.15	−.47	−.27	−.46	−.70	−.88

NOTES: N = 207 women.
a. Possible range of −3.00 to 3.00.

versions of the F scale, Dogmatism (D) scale (Rokeach, 1956, 1960), and the Anti-Semitism (AS) and Politico-Economic Conservatism (PEC) scales (Adorno et al., 1950). While in the initial report he did not present the intertrait correlations, he kindly provided them for this report, as shown in Table 6.2. The reliabilities are split-half corrected. These data confirm the presence of direction-of-wording effects, differentially important for different contents. Looking first at the within-scale correlations corrected for attenuation, we find that F and D are reversed with the greatest difficulty (F_pF_c = .33 American, .60 British; D_pD_c = .37 American, .30 British) while AS and PEC show little effect.

Again if one looks only at the original F_p, its correlations are higher with "successfully" reversed scales such as AS and PEC as a function of the direction of wording of the latter. The pattern of F and AS for the British data is particularly striking. Dogmatism also shows a striking direction-of-wording effect in its relationship with AS, again even if only the original scale, D_p, is used. Pooling the British data and the American, and using both directions of wording, direction of wording makes a difference of .15 (z' .17) in the FAS correlation, or .21 (z', .28) when corrected for attenuation. For D and AS the value is .21 (z', .22), or .29 (z', .34) corrected for attenuation. For F and D it is .55 (z', .56) or .93 corrected for attenuation, both scales being highly susceptible. At the other extreme, for AS and PEC, both very successfully reversed, the value

Table 6.4 Intercorrelations Among Authoritarianism, Superior-Subordinate Orientation, Alienation, Identification With Discipline, and Noncooperativeness as a Function of Pro or Con Wording of Items

Scale	F_p	F_c	SS_p	SS_c	Al_p	Al_c	ID_p	ID_c	NC_p	NC_c
F_p	(.62)	−.06	.54	−.28	.46	−.18	.46	−.16	.36	−.36
F_c	−.03	(.41)	−.47	.20	−.33	.17	.01	.25	−.09	.39
SS_p	.29	−.21	(.47)	.53	.28	−.33	.75	−.10	−.29	−.54
SS_c	−.14	.08	.23	(.42)	−.35	.46	.12	.40	−.22	.11
Al_p	.28	−.20	.15	−.18	(.61)	.31	.21	−.51	−.24	−.57
Al_c	−.10	.08	−.16	.21	.17	(.48)	−.57	.04	−.35	.23
ID_p	.24	.00	.35	.05	.09	−.27	(.45)	.26	.15	−.15
ID_c	−.09	.12	−.05	.19	−.27	.02	.13	(.54)	.22	.63
NC_p	.20	−.04	−.14	−.10	−.13	−.16	.07	.11	(.48)	.64
NC_c	−.22	.20	−.29	.05	−.35	.11	−.08	.36	.35	(.61)
Number of Items	15	15	10	10	14	14	7	7	13	13
Average item M[a]	1.91	1.93	1.91	1.81	1.66	1.79	2.01	2.71	2.14	2.31

NOTES: Values above the diagonal have been corrected for attenuation.
a. Possible range of 0 to 4.00.

is but .06 (z', .06) or .08 (z', .08) corrected for attenuation. The other intersections are intermediate. While the average item Ps of pro and con forms are somewhat more discrepant than in Table 6.1, they still are so similar as to provide no explanation of the effects.

Wrightsman's (1965) study used pro and con subsets of items for F (10 items each form; Christie, Havel, & Seidenberg's 1958 reversals), Christie et al.'s (1958) Machiavellianism (M) scale (10 items each form), and Komorita's (1963) Segregationism (S) scale (S_p has 25 items, S_c has 11 items). He has provided the correlations shown in Table 6.3. (Because the split-half reliability for F_c is such an underestimate as to provide one corrected correlation of 1.46, deattenuated values involving this measure are not presented.) Again, F is poorly reversed, while S, representing ethnocentrism content, is very successfully measured by both pro and con items. The direction-of-wording effect on the F-S correlation is .10 (z', .11) points; on the F-M correlation, .31 (z', .32);

and on the M-S correlation, .07 (z', .07). If one looks only to the original F_p, rejecting F_c as unsuccessful, the correlation of F_p with S is shifted .19 points (.29 corrected for attenuation) by direction of wording. The correlation of F_p with M is shifted .55 points (1.17 corrected for attenuation).

Wrightsman's scores are based on six levels of endorsement; if the item is omitted, it is scored as a zero, making seven possible levels of scoring. Average item means are therefore reported instead of item Ps. Though this method of scoring removes most of the item-marginal restraints on interitem and interscale correlations, some degree of the problem still remains (Carroll, 1961). Considering that the means could potentially range from –3.00 to 3.00, the pro-con forms are judged similar enough in average item marginal to provide no statistical explanation for the direction-of-wording effects found.

A final study reworks data presented earlier by Chapman and Campbell (1957a). All five levels of endorsement (Agree Strongly, Agree, Undecided, Disagree, Disagree Strongly) have been used in the scoring, and the Coefficient Alpha version of the Kuder-Richardson reliability formula (Cronbach, 1951) has been computed. The following scales were used: F scale of authoritarian personality trends, F_p consisting of 15 of the original scale items (Adorno et al., 1950) and F_c consisting of 15 items worded in the nonauthoritarian direction, revised following item analysis of a previous effort; an SS scale of superior versus subordinate orientation, the items of which had gone through several prior studies with item analysis; an AI scale of alienation, developed from a number of scales used previously; an ID scale of identification with discipline, revised from prior use; and an NC scale reflecting noncooperative or nonsocial tendencies and preferences, used by Chapman and Campbell (1957a) for the first time. The direction of scoring and labeling for NC were reversed from the earlier report to maximize positive correlations. The resulting matrix based upon data from 144 male undergraduates enrolled in an introductory psychology course is reported in Table 6.4, with values above the diagonal corrected for attenuation by the reliabilities given in the diagonal.

In Table 6.4 none of the scales is very successfully reversed, judging by the pro-con correlations corrected for attenuation, which range from –.06 to .64—each of the previous studies had provided some corrected correlations in the .90s. Again, the F scale comes off very poorly. Again, the direction-of-wording effect can be shown using only F_p, disregarding the unsuccessful F_c, with an average effect of .39 (z', .38) points, or .70 (z', .64) points when corrected for attenuation. Since all of the scales are relatively susceptible to direction-of-wording effects, this value is higher than those in the previous studies. For both directions of wording, the F correlation with the other scales shows an average direction-of-wording effect of .31 (z', .31), or .59 (z', .55) corrected for attenuation. For the intertrait relations among the other four scales, the average effect is .26 (z', .26), or .51 (z', .52) corrected for attenuation. In this regard, the F scale seems little more susceptible than the average of the others, although all are dangerously so. Again, average item means are such as to produce minimal statistical restraints on the correlations.

Thus, in all studies available, the F scale (in original form alone if one prefers) has shown distinct direction-of-wording effects in its interrelations with other scales. In varying degrees, these other scales have likewise shown susceptibility to direction-of-wording effects.

TWO MMPI STUDIES

In the MMPI in its original form, all of the diagnostic scales had some items for which agreement was a symptom and some items for which disagreement was a symptom. Intercorrelations of these part scales analogous to those of the previous tables have shown a strong direction-of-wording factor (e.g., Jackson & Messick, 1962), but this interpretation has been challenged on a variety of grounds. One of these is that item overlap between scales predicts this same pattern of intercorrelations (Block, 1965). While the high frequency of shared items precludes removing the overlap simultaneously from all scales, it can be done for a partial set. Since it was established that some MMPI contents are relatively immune to direction-of-wording effects (e.g., the MA scale—see Table 6.1 and Chapman & Campbell, 1959a), four scales were chosen that seemed most likely to be susceptible to such effects. These were the four scales showing the lowest or most negative pro-con correlations in an unpublished matrix provided by L. G. Rorer and in the results of Jackson and Messick (1962). For these, *Hy, Pd, Ma,* and *Pa* overlap-free pro and con keys were prepared by eliminating items from the longer of the scales sharing them, resulting in the eight modified scales shown in Table 6.5, with numbers of items ranging from 11 to 34. [The items used in these modified scales can be found in the original version of this chapter.]

Table 6.5 Intercorrelations as a Function of Direction of Wording Among Four Susceptible MMPI Scales Scored Without Item Overlap

Scale	Hy_p	Hy_c	Pd_p	Pd_c	Pa_p	Pa_c	Ma_p	Ma_c
Hy_p	(.57)	.26	.69	.03	.75	−.36	.39	−.50
Hy_c	.13	(.44)	−.33	.87	−.14	.65	−.49	.15
Pd_p	.44	−.18	(.71)	−.19	1.01	−.73	.83	−.38
Pd_c	.01	.34	−.10	(.36)	.10	.62	−.55	.28
Pa_p	.42	−.07	.63	.05	(.54)	−.67	.79	−.42
Pa_c	−.19	.30	−.43	.26	−.35	(.49)	−.75	.53
Ma_p	.23	−.26	.55	−.26	.45	−.41	(.62)	−.27
Ma_c	−.23	.06	−.19	.10	−.19	.22	−.13	(.36)
Number of items	13	34	21	20	21	14	27	11
Number negatively worded	0	10	3	5	0	2	5	2
Average item P	.12	.41	.17	.42	.11	.48	.22	.50

NOTE: Data in this table were computed by Jack Block. $N = 205$ (95 males, 110 females).

Jack Block was kind enough to score and compute correlations for these eight scales on a population of 205 college students (95 men, 110 women) providing the results shown in Table 6.5. The reliabilities were computed by Kuder-Richardson Formula 20. For these weak scales, direction-of-wording effects remain dramatically strong even with item overlap removed. A few caveats in interpreting this result are in order.

Note first that removal of item overlap reduces the apparent direction-of-wording effect. For this same population, the average direction-of- wording correlation difference for the full keyed version of these four traits is .71 (z', .65). The value for Table 6.5 is .53 (z', .51), or 1.00 corrected for attenuation, large but distinctly less.

While the value of .53 is high compared with most of the F scale results (except the F and D relationship in Peabody's Table 6.2 data—.55, [z', .56], or .93 corrected for attenuation), the conditions of item wording are distinctly less favorable. In the F scale studies, two conditions exist: (a) Experimental reversals have been made for each item, preserving the specific illustrative content, and both the original and reversed member of each pair have been used, one in the pro form and one in the con. This is true of the studies represented by Tables 6.1 and 6.2, and provides the most favorable condition for minimizing apparent direction-of-wording effects. (b) Experimental item reversals have been employed, but only one member of any pair has been used. This is characteristic of the F scales of Tables 6.3 and 6.4. While this is less favorable, it still provides considerable assurance that the pro and con items have been drawn from the same content pool and differ mainly in direction of wording. In neither case was randomization used to decide which member of a pro-con pair would be used. Instead, item-correlational evidence and judgment were used to select successfully reversed items, a condition that probably minimized content differences even more than randomization.

In the original MMPI, of course, neither of these assurances of equivalent content are present, and there is good evidence, as Block indicates, of systematic differences in content between the positively and negatively keyed items of a given scale. This in itself, however, does not explain the negative pro-con correlations or why the correlations should be so strikingly positive and high within wording direction across content. Note in Table 6.5 that the highest within-content correlation, when corrected for attenuation, is .26 (the others are .19, .67, and .27). In contrast, 11 of the 12 different-trait but same-direction correlations exceed that .26, the average value being .63. Whatever the vagaries of item development in the MMPI, something highly systematic is present here, represented by or at least confounded with direction of wording.

One possible additional systematic factor can be suggested—the *pole* of description. For a clearly bipolar trait or attitude, four item types rather than two might be considered, for example, pro conservative, con liberal, con conservative, and pro liberal. While the complexity and subtlety of the MMPI items resist any smooth application of such a priori categories, the corresponding four types would be "I am sick," "I am not healthy," "I am not sick," and "I am healthy." Types 1 and 2 are pro in the sense of the tables in this chapter; Types 3 and 4 are con. However, it is Types 2 and 3 that are grammatically negative. To indicate crudely the relative prevalence of these four types, without getting into the detailed morass of MMPI item wordings (some items seem miskeyed by this typology), we have indicated the frequency of grammatical negatives in each of the eight scales of Table 6.5.

The pro items of all scales are, by this criterion, almost exclusively of the "I am sick" type, except for three Pd_p items and five Ma_p items of the "I am not

Table 6.6 Direction-of-Wording Effects in the Correlation Between Block's EC-5 and ER-0 Scales for the MMPI

	$EC\text{-}5_p$	$EC\text{-}5_c$	$ER\text{-}O_p$	$ER\text{-}O_c$
$EC\text{-}5_p$	(.54)	.86	−.03	.06
$EC\text{-}5_c$	.50	(.64)	−.22	.16
$ER\text{-}O_p$	−.02	−.16	(.84)	.77
$ER\text{-}O_c$	.04	.12	.65	(.85)
Number of Items	16	16	53	53
Average item P	.53	.57	.77	.81

healthy" class. The con items are, on the other hand, preponderantly of the "I am healthy" type. This focal-pole attribute provides a content-like common denominator among scales worded in the same direction. In this regard, it may be meaningful that the one con scale with a substantial number of sick-pole items is Hy_c (10 out of 34 items of the "I am not sick" variety), and that Hy is the only trait where the pro-con correlation is positive. Pole of focus and direction of wording are confounded in most studies but should certainly be segregated in future research. Pole of focus may turn out to be the same as what Jackson and Messick (1965) have called an "acceptance of characteristics as self-descriptive" factor.

Note that Table 6.5 shows a systematic difference between pro and con scales in item popularity. Were all correlations positive, these might help explain part of a direction-of-wording effect. They do not help explain the strong negative correlations, however.

Table 6.5 represents an effort to pick out the *most* susceptible of the MMPI scales. Table 6.6, prepared by Block from the same respondents, shows the direction-of-wording effect for his two main MMPI factors, Ego Resiliency Obvious (ER–O), and Ego Control Version 5 (EC–5). Here, direction of wording nets only .11 (z', .11) correlation points, or .15 (z', .15) when corrected.

The data of Rorer's (1965; Rorer & Goldberg, 1965) own study make possible the examination of direction-of-wording effects with the content differences in pro and con versions of each scale removed, and he has kindly computed Table 6.7. His original and reversed-form testings are here treated as though a single test. For each of the MMPI scales, a pro score has been generated combining the original pro items from the first testing plus the reversals of the originally con items from the second testing. The con scores are a combination of con items from the first testing plus reversals of the originally pro items from the second testing. The resulting pattern in Table 6.7 shows, overall, a small but generally consistent direction-of-wording effect. The average difference between same-direction and different-direction correlations is but .09 (z', .11). In 32 of the 36 intertrait intersections, the two same-direction values averaged higher than the two different-direction values ($p < .001$; exceptions involved Hs). For the four highly susceptible scales used in Table 6.5, Hy, Pd, Pa, and Ma, the average difference was .16 (z', .17) points with all of the six intersections showing much the same degree of effect, ranging from .135 to .185. In the 10 intersections among the other five variables, the average value was only .05 (z', .09), with a range of −.01 to .125. Thus with content closely controlled and looking only at the intertrait effects, not the intratrait ones, a small but generally dependable direction-of-wording effect appears, which is more marked for some traits than for others.

Rorer's rewordings were meticulously designed to eliminate possible content differences and to produce item marginals comparable to the originals. The great reduction in effects between Table 6.5 and Table 6.7 and the even item P values of Table 6.7 testify to his success in this regard. However, he produced no evidence that his emphasis on logical reversals at the expense of simplicity of wording was necessary. The equally successful experience using commonsense reversals with the Manifest Anxiety sample of the same item pool in Table 6.1 indicates that logical reversals are not required. The following sample of Rorer's wordings will illustrate the problem:

Original	Rorer's Reversal
I have a good appetite.	I do not have a good appetite (or it is about average).
My father was a good man.	My father was not a good man (or he was about average).
I seldom or never have dizzy spells.	It is not true that I seldom or never have dizzy spells.
I am not easily angered.	It is not true that I am not easily angered.
I daydream very little.	I daydream more than a very little.
It does not bother me particularly to see animals suffer.	It is not true that it does not bother me particularly to see animals suffer.

Table 6.7 Intercorrelations Among Pro and Con Scales in Rorer's MMPI Study

Scale	F_p	F_c	Hs_p	Hs_c	D_p	D_c	Hy_p	Hy_c	Pd_p	Pd_c	Pa_p	Pa_c	Pt_p	Pt_c	Sc_p	Sc_c	Ma_p	Ma_c
F_p																		
F_c	.65																	
Hs_p	.53	.41																
Hs_c	.53	.39	.80															
D_p	.48	.25	.57	.52														
D_c	.39	.28	.49	.54	.70													
Hy_p	.27	.01	.48	.41	.39	.22												
Hy_c	.07	.01	.26	.39	.18	.34	.63											
Pd_p	.60	.46	.41	.43	.37	.30	.35	.16										
Pd_c	.47	.49	.26	.27	.20	.36	.16	.26	.71									
Pa_p	.25	.10	.21	.21	.26	.11	.40	.19	.28	.04								
Pa_c	.20	.16	.11	.07	.15	.12	.28	.38	.16	.27	.52							
Pt_p	.57	.44	.60	.65	.66	.54	.14	-.02	.46	.29	.31	.06						
Pt_c	.57	.50	.56	.63	.54	.62	.06	.08	.45	.44	.17	.12	.88					
Sc_p	.70	.61	.60	.65	.57	.45	.20	.03	.62	.44	.34	.13	.84	.78				
Sc_c	.64	.70	.52	.59	.58	.51	.06	.08	.54	.58	.14	.20	.72	.83	.82			
Ma_p	.29	.41	.26	.29	.02	-.06	.02	-.11	.48	.32	.19	-.01	.39	.31	.50	.41		
Ma_c	.17	.40	.21	.22	-.16	.01	-.09	.10	.29	.40	-.08	.07	.17	.31	.30	.47	.63	
Number of Items	64	64	33	33	60	60	60	60	60	60	40	40	48	48	78	78	46	46
Average item P	.07	.08	.14	.10	.33	.32	.36	.36	.26	.27	.24	.26	.23	.24	.12	.16	.35	.37

NOTE: The pro scales pool those items originally scored positively and Rorer's reversals of those originally scored negatively; the con scales are a corresponding pool. $N = 221$ (96 men, 125 women).

The awkwardness is so great that it probably would not have been feasible, in terms of student rapport, to have presented the reversed form as the first administration. What is needed for practical control of direction-of-wording effects are items that can be inconspicuously mixed. In providing recommendations to future test constructors, it needs to be emphasized that there is no research evidence of the superiority of Rorer's reversals over such simpler wordings as "I have a poor appetite," "My father was not a good man," "I often have dizzy spells," "I am easily angered," "I daydream a lot," and "It really disturbs me to see animals suffer." While these simpler wordings would probably result in less item-by-item identity in P values, as long as the sets did not substantially differ there would be no disadvantage from this. Rorer seems to mistakenly demand much greater identity between pro-con item pairs than is required between two same-directional items belonging to a single scale.

MAGNITUDE OF EFFECTS

In the studies reported here the direction-of-wording effect has been uniformly present, but in greatly varying degree. Even in its strongest appearance, the evidence has not been such as to justify the characterization of a relationship as due totally or even predominately to response set. Take as an extreme example the FD relationship of Table 6.2, which in rounded and averaged form looks like this:

$$.50 \qquad .00$$
$$.00 \qquad .50$$

Such a picture would result if each of the four measures had a factor loading of .50 on the shared trait factor, and ±.50 on the direction-of-wording factor (.50 for the two pro forms, .50 for the two con forms), thus augmenting the codirectional correlations and canceling out the trait covariance on the heterodirectional ones.

For all of the relationships between F and ethnocentrism (anti-Semitism, segregationism), the trait covariance is much larger than the direction-of-wording effect. Only in Table 6.4 do we find intertrait relations in which shared method is approximately as large as shared trait variance.

The original study on which this chapter was based was supported in part by National Science Foundation Grant SS1309X. This chapter was based in part on an earlier research report supported by Project C998, Contract 320 001 with the United States Office of Education. The authors [Campbell, Siegman, and Rees] are indebted to Jack Block and Leonard G. Rorer for new computations made especially for this report, and to Dean Peabody, Lawrence S. Wrightsman, and Loren J. Chapman for providing computations not previously published.

~ PART II ~

INDIRECT MEASURES

———•◆•———

ampbell defines indirect measures as "structured, quantitative, disguised measures of social attitudes." Indirect measures can be carried out in a variety of ways. One example would be a pen-and-paper test that is disguised as a test of knowledge, but actually measures an individual's attitude. Another example, used to estimate the public's interest in a specific topic, would be a count of the number of times the particular subject was broached in a public place, such as a bus or waiting room. Another rather unusual indirect measure involves gauging the popularity of museum exhibits by measuring the relative amount of wear on the floor tiles in front of the exhibits.

Campbell's interest in these types of measures stems from early in his academic career. In 1950, he reviewed the literature in a paper titled "The Indirect Assessment of Social Attitudes." While at the University of Chicago in the early 1950s, he participated in studies that examined attitudes toward blacks. To study this issue, he and his colleagues developed an indirect measure of attitude based on nonrandomness of seating patterns in university classrooms.

In the 1960s, inspired by Campbell's earlier work, Eugene Webb, Richard Schwartz, and Lee Sechrest joined with Campbell to publish a volume on indirect measures. *Unobstrusive Measures: Nonreactive Measures in the Social*

Sciences was first published in 1966. According to Sechrest's description in *The American Journal of Evaluation,* the work received a great deal of attention in many fields, but it did not inspire many studies that utilized the principles laid out in the book. A 1981 revision of the book, which dropped the term "unobtrusive measures" from the title, did not fare as well and went out of print several years ago.

In 1970, after a request to reprint his earlier review of the literature, Campbell along with Louise Kidder updated that review, beginning the article with a reassessment of indirect measures. They maintained that unobtrusive measures can be ingenious and innovative, and illustrate psychological laws to a greater degree than do direct measures. Also, since the biases associated with indirect measures are so different from the biases of direct measures, they are a useful tool for triangulation. At the same time, unobtrusive measures may constitute an invasion of privacy; they expose the research subjects to possible exploitation; and they tend to perform poorly in comparisons with direct attitude measures.

Once again, Campbell presents the following chapters in the hope that budding social scientists might accept the challenge of exploring new indirect measures or employing current ones along with the more commonly used direct measures. Only with an accumulation of such studies can the effectiveness of indirect measures be established and their weaknesses exposed. Chapter 7 is a chapter that appeared in the revised volume on unobtrusive measures. Campbell, along with Webb, Schwartz, Sechrest, and Grove, discusses 15 validity issues affecting all measures. They are divided into three groups: error stemming from those being studied, error that comes from the investigator, and error associated with sampling imperfections. The next chapter, Chapter 8, contains excerpts of the revised literature review written with Louise Kidder. All the instruments discussed in this review are indirect measures, but they are further divided on whether they are voluntary versus objective or free-response versus structured. In Chapter 9, Campbell, Kruskal, and Wallace present the findings of their study on seating arrangements as a measure of attitude toward blacks. The chapter contains an enlightening discussion of the issues that were considered during the conception of this measure.

————•◆•————

OVERVIEW OF CHAPTER 7

———— •◆• ————

This chapter, written by Webb, Campbell, Schwartz, Sechrest, and Grove, deals with unobtrusive measures, their usefulness, and some of the methodological issues associated with them. Measurement always involves comparison. Three approaches help social scientists to achieve interpretable comparisons. They are experimental design, index numbers, and plausible rival hypotheses. Experimental design involves randomization, and although the authors feel this is the most successful approach, they feel it is underused. Index numbers control sources of irrelevant variance by transforming raw data and using weighted aggregates. By using indexes, such as percentages, per capitas, or annual rates, meaningful comparisons can be made across time and space. Indexes have their pitfalls, as shown in the example of the erroneous report of the rising percentage of illegitimate black births in 1976. While the authors call for greater use of index numbers to improve interpretability, they caution that one must pay special attention when analyzing them. Two indexes may appear to be correlated simply because they share common elements or because they are both changing systematically over time when, in fact, there is no relationship between the two. In time-series analyses, detrending may be necessary, although this effort, too, can lead to invalid interpretations. Still, the authors endorse the continued use of indexes, although they should not be used indiscriminately.

The final approach to comparison is plausible rival hypotheses. This approach asks the researcher to consider plausible interpretations that might be responsible for noted differences other than the treatment of interest. The mutually monitoring community of scientists offer other possible rival explanations. These rival explanations are only threats, and do not negate the belief that the results are due to the variable of interest unless the threats become as plausible as the laws we seek to demonstrate. These rival interpretations can be ruled out by using experimental methods or indexes, by checking the commonly relevant threats to validity, or by doing additional analyses. Yet even with a thorough examination of these issues, the authors recognize that a theory can never be proven, but merely probed.

A list of 15 validity issues affecting all measures is preceded by a discussion of the distinction between internal and external validity. Internal validity asks whether or not a difference exists and whether that difference is due to the treatment. External validity asks whether the difference can be generalized to other populations, occasions, and measures. The 15 frequent threats to valid interpretation are divided into three groups: error that may be traced to those being studied; error that comes from the investigator; and error associated with sampling imperfections.

The first four threats can be traced to those being studied. The first threat involves reactive measurement effects that can occur when the respondent is aware that he or she is participating in research. Wishing to make a good impression, the respondent gives responses that are suggested by the measuring instrument. This threat can be lessened by using archival records instead of gathering new data, by ensuring anonymity or confidentiality, or by masking the purpose of the measure. The best way to establish the plausibility of the reactivity threat is to do validating studies in which behaviors observed under nonreactive conditions are compared with behaviors after reactive conditions are introduced. The second threat is role selection, in which the respondent makes a decision as to the "role" he or she will assume when responding. The extent to which this role selection affects the results may depend upon many factors. Among these are the educational level of the respondent, or the individual's familiarity with the subject matter or testing methods of the study. Measurement as change agent, the third threat involves instances where the measurement itself produces a change in the activity being measured. This may be permanent attitude changes resulting from the measure, or may occur through practice on a pretest that, in turn, improves posttest scores. The final threat in this category consists of response sets. This involves direction-of-wording effects, which is discussed in greater detail in Chapter 6 of this volume. Other possible biases involve the preference for strong statements over moderate ones, or selecting right-hand or left-hand responses, for example. These four types of error, which can be traced to those being studied, can be avoided by using research measures that do not require the cooperation of the respondent. At the very least, researchers should try to estimate the degree of bias introduced by error from the respondent.

Threats five through nine involve error introduced by the investigator. Interviewer effects have been noted when different interviewers were used. The race, age, religion, or social class of the interviewer may produce systematic differences. Further, the interviewer may influence the individual's responses by the tone of voice or the wording or order of the questions. These types of influences are difficult to avoid, and perhaps the best way is to circumvent them altogether. Changes in the research instrument is another threat to valid interpretation. The research instrument can be the interviewer. For example, interviewers may change over time by becoming more skilled in their recording or interpreting of responses. They may become more fatigued or bored with the subject matter, which can, in turn, add error into those responses. This source of error is not limited to interviewers; changes in record-keeping can also produce spurious effects. The next threat, varieties of sampling error, involves the selection of respondents. The researcher should keep in mind that there are other alternatives to selecting respondents, for example, to sample time or space or to examine aggregates, such as agencies or precincts. For the next threat, population restrictions, the researcher must consider how the included universe differs from those who are not included. For example, an age group may be overrepresented because of its availability; respondents may be restricted because of requirements for a certain reading level; or volunteers may be different from the population being studied. These restrictions may produce bias, since the groups are not representative of the populations to which the results are being generalized. The eighth threat involves population stability over time. If samples are taken in different seasons or on different days of the week, there is a potential for bias. Randomly selecting times for measurement or using a narrower universe with a more stable population can reduce time sampling problems. The final threat in which error is introduced through the investigator is population stability over areas. If the researcher is studying drastically different areas, comparisons may produce invalid results. A thorough examination of background data may be necessary to establish the representativeness of the groups.

The authors recognized that these threats to validity may be discouraging to many researchers, since every method appears to have weaknesses and biases. Used together, however, convergence of findings can strengthen support for a particular theory.

Another group of threats are those involving access to content. The method chosen often depends on its ability to probe the content of the research area of interest. There are restrictions on the content that can be examined by each class of research methods.

The first in this group of threats involves restriction on content. If diverse methods are used, the content that can be probed by each type of method must be considered. Observational methods can be used only when the differentiating factor can be observed, for example, race versus religion. Stability of content over time is the next threat that must be considered. Because the results produced by an observational method can be affected by events or cycles, it may be best to sample different time periods when collecting the data. Next is a similar threat involving stability of content over areas. If two areas are being compared, one must try to determine if they are comparable with regard to the content being studied.

The final group of threats can be serious or nonexistent, depending on the method that is used. The first, dross rate, refers to the irrelevant information that is gathered during the course of an interview. The level of dross rate is less when the interview is structured, whereas an unobtrusive sampling of conversations to gauge attitudes toward a certain subject may yield a high dross rate. Access to descriptive cues should be considered when evaluating which methods should be used to study a population. Gathering descriptive clues about a population can be done most easily through survey methods. It is possible, however, to gather certain background data without causing reactive effects by sampling of times of the day or days of the week. A final consideration in evaluating methods is the ability to replicate. Data provided through interviews and surveys allow replication, whereas archival records or physical evidence provides a fixed amount of data.

A score on any measure can be explained in many ways. One of the ways it can be explained is that it is a valid measure of that which it is intended to measure. However, the awareness of possible rival explanations should induce the researcher to gather the information in such a way as to rule out these rivals or gather supplementary information that can rule them out.

All people perform the same processes that scientists do; they have a hypothesis, test it out by experimenting, and then change their ideas based on their interpretation of the test. Ordinary people generally do not use the surveys or questionnaires used by scientists. Rather, they use self-reports and unobtrusive measures. Scientists differ from ordinary people by being more systematic and by collecting more data. Scientists can be more confident in their research results if they apply multiple measures of the same phenomenon for comparison. Using a variety of methods—for example, both survey data and unobtrusive measures—is the best way to avoid the threats mentioned above and to increase our confidence in the validity of the results.

SEVEN

FIFTEEN VALIDITY ISSUES AFFECTING ALL MEASURES

———•◆•———

*I*n this chapter we deal with methods of measurement appropriate to a wide range of social science studies. We assume that the goal of the social scientist is always to achieve interpretable comparisons, and that the goal of methodology is to rule out those plausible rival hypotheses that make comparisons ambiguous and tentative.

Often it seems that absolute measurement is involved, and that a social instance is being described in its splendid isolation, not for comparative purposes. But a closer look shows that absolute, isolated measurement is meaningless. In all useful measurement, an implicit comparison exists when an explicit one is not visible. "Absolute" measurement is a convenient fiction and usually is nothing more than a shorthand summary in settings where plausible rival hypotheses are either unimportant or so few, specific, and well known as to be taken into account habitually. Thus, when we report a length "absolutely"

Webb, E. J., Campbell, D. T., Schwartz, R. D., Sechrest, L. B., & Grove, J. B. (1981). *Nonreactive measures in the social sciences*. Boston: Houghton Mifflin.

in meters or feet, we immediately imply comparisons with numerous familiar objects of known length, as well as comparisons with a standard preserved in some Paris or Washington sanctuary.

If measurement is regarded always as a comparison, there are three classes of approaches that have come to be used in achieving interpretable comparisons: experimental design, index numbers, and plausible rival hypotheses. The most satisfactory of the three is experimental design. Through deliberate randomization, the *ceteris* of the pious *ceteris paribus* prayer can be made *paribus*. [*Ceteris paribus* is Latin for "other things being equal."] This may require randomization of respondents, occasions, or stimulus objects. In any event, the randomization strips of plausibility many of the otherwise available explanations of the difference in question. It is a sad truth that randomized experimental design is possible for only a portion of the settings in which social scientists make measurements and seek interpretable comparisons. The number of opportunities for its use may not be staggering, but, where possible, experimental design should by all means be exploited. Many more opportunities exist than are used.

Index Numbers

The second approach to comparison, a quite different and historically isolated tradition, is that of *index numbers*. Here, sources of variance known to be irrelevant are controlled by transformations of raw data and weighted aggregates. The goal of this social science tradition is to provide measures for meaningful comparisons across wide spans of time and social space. Real wages, intelligence quotients, and net reproductive rates are examples, but an effort in this direction is made even when a percentage, a per capita, or an annual rate is computed. The current interest in a variety of "social indicators" involves many types of index numbers. To be meaningful, most social indicators must be transformed into some sort of an index number.

Index numbers cannot be used uncritically because the imperfect knowledge of the laws invoked in any such measurement situation precludes computing any effective all-purpose measures. Furthermore, the use of complex compensated indexes in the assurance that they measure what they are devised for has in many instances proved quite misleading. A notable example is found in the definitional confusion surrounding the labor force concept (Jaffe & Stewart, 1951; Moore, 1953). Often a relationship established between an overall index and external variables is found due to only one component of the index. An instance of a flagrant and harmful index number that had been widely disseminated and cited was the proportion of black infants being born out of wedlock. In 1978 the government's National Center for Health Statistics reported that in 1976 for the first time more than 50% of all black births involved unmarried mothers. However, a subsequent analysis, not so widely publicized, indicated that a large proportion of what appeared to be an increase in illegitimacy is accounted for by the fact that married black women are having fewer children with the result that the numerator of the index, the absolute number of illegitimate children, was growing, but the denominator was shrinking. The absolute rate of illegitimacy per 1,000 black women had been shrinking for 6 straight years by 1976. Thus, illegitimacy among blacks is falling, not rising (Drummond, 1978).

Despite these limitations, index numbers, which once loomed large in sociology and economics, deserve more current attention and should be integrated into modern social science methodology (Morgenstern, 1963).

The tradition is relevant in two ways for the problems discussed in this chapter. Many of the sources of data suggested here, particularly secondary records, require a transformation of the raw data if they are to be interpretable in any but truly experimental situations. Such transformations should be performed with the wisdom accumulated within the older tradition, as well as with a regard for the precautionary literature just cited. Properly done, such transformations often improve interpretability even if they fall far short of some ideal (cf. Bernstein, 1935).

A second value of the literature on index numbers lies in an examination of the types of irrelevant variation that the index computation sought to exclude. The construction of index numbers is usually a response to criticisms of less sophisticated indexes. They thus embody a summary of the often unrecorded criticisms of prior measures. In the criticisms and the corrections are clues to implicit or explicit plausible rival interpretations of differences, the viable threats to valid interpretation.

Take so simple a measure as an index of unemployment or of retail sales. The gross number of the unemployed or the gross total dollar level of sales is useless if one wants to make comparisons within a single year. Some of the objections to the gross figures are reflected in the seasonal corrections applied to time-series data. If we look at only the last quarter of the year, we can see that the effect of weather must be considered. A "gain" over the same quarter last year may reflect the unusual lowness of last year rather than a true gain for this year. Systematically, winter depresses the number of employed construction workers, for example, and increases the unemployment level. Less systematically, spells of bad weather keep people in their homes and reduce the amount of retail shopping. Both periodic and aperiodic elements of the weather should be considered if one wants a more stable and interpretable measure of unemployment or sales. So, too, our custom of giving gifts at Christmas spurs December sales, as does the coinciding custom of Christmas bonuses to employees. All of these are accounted for, crudely, by a correction applied to the gross levels for either December or the final quarter of the year.

Some of these sources of invalidity are too specific to a single setting to be generalized usefully; others are too obvious to be catalogued. But some contribute to a general enumeration of recurrent threats to valid interpretation in social science measures.

The technical problems of index number construction are heroic. "The index number should give consistent results for different base periods and also with its counterpart price or quantity index. No reasonably simple formula satisfies both of these consistency requirements" (Ekelblad, 1962, p. 726). The consistency problem is usually met by substituting a geometric mean for an arithmetic one, but then other problems arise. With complex indexes of many components, there is the issue of getting an index that will yield consistent scores across all the different levels and times of the components.

In his important work on economic cycles, Hansen (1921) wrote, "Here is a heterogeneous group of statistical series all of which are related in a causal way, somehow or another, to the cycle of prosperity and depression" (p. 21). The search for a metric to relate these different components consistently, to be able to reverse factors without chaos, makes index construction a difficult task. A case in point is provided by the work of Brenner (e.g., 1973, 1975), attempting to develop index numbers for both economic conditions and such social ills as mental disorder and crime. Although Brenner believes that his work demonstrates a relationship between economic cycles and the rates of mental disorder and crime, the problems inherent in attempting to correct for all the extraneous factors have brought Brenner's work under intense criticism (e.g., Eyer, 1976). But the potential payoff from construction of indexes is great. For good introductory statements of issues in the use of index numbers see Yule and Kendall (1950), Zeisel (1957), and Ekelblad (1962). More detailed treatments can be found in Mitchell (1921), Fisher (1923), Mills (1927), Mudgett (1951), and Morgenstern (1963).

Ruist (1978), Hoover (1978), and McCarthy (1978) have surveyed a much larger literature for the *International Encyclopedia of Statistics*. However, so far as we are aware, there is as yet no adequate review of the booby traps that lie in wait when one goes beyond looking at a single index for its "direct" informational value and uses series of readings from "the same" index over time or across social units, correlating these with other indexes, or inferring the impact of specific historical events, and so on. No one has done for index numbers what Cronbach (1958) did so well for spurious effects in social perception accuracy scores.

An index number is formed by some combination of other numbers, often by dividing one number by another. Hence, an index number will reflect the values of all the numbers that go to make it up. An index of disposable income per family and an index of savings might be related because both would reflect total income and necessary expenses. To take an obvious case, but one not invariably avoided, indexes of the percentage of pupils who are white and the percentage who are black in schools will be highly related to each other unless there are sizable numbers of pupils of other ethno-racial designations. The relationship will, of course, be negative. In fact, if index numbers were constructed randomly by pairs, with the restriction that each pair had to have one common element, the two sets of numbers would be likely to be substantially correlated. For example, if Index A = a/c and Index B = b/c, then A and B might be correlated just because they share the variability in c. Typical situations in which such index series might be constructed would be to represent characteristics of different nations, cities, or census tracts, and so forth, or situations in which characteristics of some units of interest, perhaps nations, perhaps families, are correlated over time. As an example of the first kind of study, an investigator might be interested in the relationship between size of police force and number of burglaries across a number of cities. Each item of interest would be likely to be indexed by size of population: police officers per 1,000 population, and burglaries per 1,000 population. The two indexes would thus share city population as a denominator and might have a built-in correlation. We note, however, that Long (1980) has shown that the correlations between index numbers sharing common elements are complexly determined and may take nearly any value. Spurious, artifactual correlations may even stem from measurement error alone when one number, including error, is shared across two indexes. We concur with Long's injunction that any ratio used as an index should make theoretical sense as a ratio. For example, auto accidents per registered vehicle makes sense; auto accidents per number of telephones does not. Ratios that are not rational are probably especially likely to cause problems.

The second type of study would be exemplified by the work of Brenner (1973, 1975), who attempts to show that such forms of personal and social pathologies as mental disorder and crime change over time with economic cycles. The problem that may tend to produce spurious correlations is that, even though two indexes do not share any common elements in terms of the numbers that go to make them up, both may be changing systematically over time. For example, during a period extending from 1882 to 1930, cotton prices were gradually increasing and the number of lynchings in the United States was gradually decreasing (Hovland & Sears, 1940), permitting the erroneous conclusion that lynchings stemmed from the frustrations of low cotton prices. A problem exists with many economic indicators from the very beginning because they often need to be expressed in "constant dollars." Presumably it is the income to be obtained from cotton sales relative to the costs of things that have to be bought that is the important factor in any frustration from prices. Even if prices were expressed in constant dollars but were increasing or decreasing steadily over time, it would be hazardous to assume any causal link between those prices and a similarly changing series. Many things change regularly over time. It has even been demonstrated, as an instance, that suicides have increased regularly with the increasing number of telephones! Probably in the period from 1882 to 1930, the number of deaths attributable to falling off horses decreased, but scarcely in any way attributable to rising cotton prices. The fact that the link between cotton prices and lynchings seems more sensible does not make it truer.

Any time-series analysis must begin with "detrending" of the data, an analytic step that involves determining for each observation the degree to which it deviates from any overall trends. In their analysis of cotton prices and lynchings, for example, Hovland and Sears (1940) ran straight lines through the data for cotton prices and lynchings, plotted separately and determined whether each data point fell above or below the line (which had been drawn to a least squares fit). It was these "detrended" data that they then analyzed, and for which they found the negative relationship between cotton prices and lynchings. The process of detrending is, however, often not so simple, and Mintz (1946) showed that the use of straight lines did not deal at all well with the trends in either cotton prices or lynchings, and when he used more appropriate procedures, the negative correlations largely disappeared.

There can also be perturbations in time series that result from specific features of data systems. Some months have more weekends than others, and those months will have more crimes. Numerator data tend to be collected and corrected over shorter time periods than denominator data. Crimes, for example, are usually counted and reported by months, but population data are not likely to be corrected more than yearly, if that often. Thus, if there is an abrupt increase in estimated city population every January, the drop in crime rate between December and January will be greater than would be expected on the basis of true seasonality. The reporting of 1980 census data will result in corrections in many indexes, probably mostly in the denominators, with the result that there may be a good many discontinuities in many common indexes between 1980 and 1981. To some extent these problems may be avoided by the use of a "moving average" that expresses each data point as a departure from a longer period of which it is the center. If data are reported monthly, the moving average might be calculated for successive 12-month periods. Various other corrections are possible. Since the amplitude of fluctuations is often proportional to absolute level (e.g., burglary rates will be more variable during seasons when burglary rates are high), logarithmic transformation prior to seasonal correction is usually preferable with raw data consisting of frequency counts. Even so, seasonal corrections probably very often undercorrect and produce subtle forms of correlated error. At the very least in a time-series analysis, the analysis should be run separately for each element in the index.

Erroneous inferences due to part-whole correlation may emerge if the correlation between an index and its correction base becomes of interest and is calculated. A common instance is an index of gain accompanied by an interest in whether people at different original levels gain differentially. Since a gain may be defined as $C = $ Post-measure $-$ Premeasure, a big spurious negative correlation between gain and original level is inevitable, leading to the erroneous conclusion that, the worse off people were originally, the more they will have improved. An analogous positive correlation arises when an element is correlated with a total of which it is a part; for example, the correlation between students' grade point averages in their majors will be correlated with their overall grade point averages in part because the former is part of the latter. If the elements have some degree of independent variability, the spuriousness will diminish with an increasing number of elements. Thus, the briefer the course of study in the major and the longer the course of study outside the major, the lower the built-in correlation.

These warnings should not be taken as discouraging the use of index numbers altogether, but as a caution against their unthinking and indiscriminant use and interpretation. They have a long and generally honorable history and probably as long a future, perhaps one whose prospects can be improved.

Plausible Rival Hypotheses

The third general approach to comparison may be called that of plausible rival hypotheses. It is the most general and least formal of the three and is applicable to the other two. Given a comparison that a social scientist wishes to interpret, this approach asks what other plausible interpretations are allowed by the research setting and the measurement processes. The more of these, and the more plausible each is, the less validly interpretable is the comparison. Platt (1964) and Hafner and Presswood (1965) have discussed this approach with a focus in the physical sciences.

A social scientist may reduce the number of plausible rival hypotheses in many ways. Experimental methods and adequate indexes serve as useful devices for eliminating some rival interpretations. A checklist of commonly relevant threats to validity may point to other ways of limiting the number of viable alternative hypotheses. For some major threats, it is often possible to provide supplementary analyses or to assemble additional data that can rule out a source of possible invalidity.

Backstopping the individual scientist is the critical reaction of fellow scientists. Where plausible rival hypotheses are missed, colleagues can be expected to propose alternative interpretations. The culture of science seeks to systematize the production of rival plausible hypotheses and to extend them to every generalization proposed. While this may be implicit in some fields, scientific epistemology requires that the original and competing hypotheses be explicitly and generally stated.

Such a commitment could lead to rampant uncertainty unless some criterion of plausibility were adopted before the rival hypothesis was taken as a serious alternative. Accordingly, each rival hypothesis is a threat only if we can give it the status of a law approximately as credible as the law we seek to demonstrate. If it falls much short of that credibility, it is not then "plausible" and can be ignored. Even in a "true" experimental comparison, an infinite number of potential laws could predict this outcome, but do not let this logical state of affairs prevent us from interpreting the results. Instead, practical uncertainty comes only from those unexcluded hypotheses to which we, in the current state of our science, are willing to give the status of established laws: These are the plausible rival hypotheses. While the north-south orientation of planaria may have something to do with conditioning, no interview studies report on the directional orientation of interviewer and interviewee. And they should not.

For those plausible rival hypotheses we give the status of laws, the conditions under which they would explain our obtained result also imply specific outcomes for other sets of data. Tests in other settings that attempt to verify these laws may enable us to rule them out. In a similar fashion, the theory we seek to test has many implications other than that involved in the specific comparison, and the exploration of these is likewise demanded. The more numerous and complex the manifestations of the law, the fewer singular plausible rival hypotheses are available, and the more parsimony favors the law under study.

Our longing is for data that prove and certify theory, but such is not to be our lot. Some comfort may come from the observation that this is not an existential predicament unique to social science. The replacement of Newtonian theory by relativity and quantum mechanics shows us that even the best of physical science experimentation probes theory rather than proves it. Modern philosophies of science as presented by Popper (1935, 1959, 1963), Quine (1953), Hanson (1958), Kuhn (1962), and Campbell (1966, 1969a, 1974a) make this point clear.

Before listing some of the most common sources of invalidity, it will be helpful to alert the reader to our occasional use of a distinction between internal and external validity. For our present purposes, focused on measurement and comparison in a broad range of contexts, internal validity asks whether or not a difference exists at all in any given comparison. It asks whether or not an apparent difference can be explained away as some measurement artifact. External validity deals with the problem of generalization: To what other populations, occasions, and measures may the observed finding be generalized. We find the distinction useful, but we are aware that at deeper levels and from other perspectives the boundary of the distinction shifts or disappears. In consideration of experimental design, for example, internal validity has been described as hinging on whether or not in a given instance the experimental treatment has made a difference (Campbell & Stanley, 1966). Thus a genuine difference attributable to a change-agent other than the experimental treatment is a challenge to the internal validity of an experiment. Here, as in our first edition, such a problem is a matter of the external validity of a measurement. For experimental validity, Cook and Campbell (1979) have reviewed the criticisms of the external-internal validity distinction and present an expanded typology.

SOURCES OF INVALIDITY OF MEASURES

In this section, we review frequent threats to the valid interpretation of a difference—common plausible rival hypotheses. They are broadly divided into three groups: error that may be traced to those being studied, error that comes from the investigator, and error associated with sampling imperfections. This section is the only one in which we draw illustrations mainly from the most popular methods of current social science. For that reason, particular attention is paid to those weaknesses that create the need for multiple and alternate methods.

In addition, some other criteria such as the efficiency of the research instrument are mentioned. These are independent of validity but important for the practical research decisions that must be made.

Reactive Measurement Effect:
Error From the Respondent

The most understated risk to valid interpretation is the error produced by the respondent. Even when he or she is well intentioned and cooperative, the research subject's knowledge that he is participating in a scholarly search may confound the investigator's data. Four classes of this error are discussed here:

awareness of being tested, role selection, measurement as a change agent, and response sets.

1. The Guinea Pig Effect—Awareness of Being Tested. Selltiz and her associates make the observation:

> The measurement process used in the experiment may itself affect the outcome. If people feel that they are guinea pigs being experimented with, or if they feel that they are being "tested" and must make a good impression, or if the method of data collection suggests responses or stimulates an interest the subject did not previously feel, the measuring process may distort the experimental results. (Selltiz, Jahoda, Deutsch, & Cook, 1959, p. 97)

Guinea pig effects have been called "reactive effect of measurement" and "reactive arrangement" bias (Campbell, 1957; Campbell & Stanley, 1966). It is important to note early that the awareness of testing need not, by itself, contaminate responses. It is a question of probabilities, but the probability of bias is high in any study in which a respondent is aware of his or her subject status.

Although the methods to be reviewed here do not involve "respondents," comparable reactive effects on the population may often occur. Consider, for example, a potentially nonreactive instrument such as the movie camera. If it is conspicuously placed, its lack of ability to talk to the subjects doesn't help us much. The visible presence of the camera undoubtedly changes behavior and does so differentially, depending upon the labeling involved. The response is likely to vary if the camera has printed on its side "Los Angeles Police Department" or "NBC" or "Foundation Project on Crowd Behavior." Similarly, an Englishman's presence at a wedding in Africa exerts a much more reactive effect on the proceedings than it would on the Sussex Downs.

A specific illustration may be of value. In the summer of 1952, some graduate students in the social sciences at the University of Chicago were employed to observe the numbers of blacks and whites in stores, restaurants, bars, theaters, and so forth on a south side Chicago street intersecting the black-white boundary (East 63rd). This, presumably, should have been a nonreactive process, particularly at the predominantly white end of the street. No questions were asked, no persons stopped. Yet, in spite of this hopefully inconspicuous activity, two merchants were agitated and persistent enough to place calls to the university, which somehow got through to the investigators; how many others tried and failed cannot be known. The two calls were from a store operator and the manager of a currency exchange, both of whom wanted assurance that this was some university nosiness and not a professional casing for subsequent robbery (Campbell & Mack, 1965). An intrusion conspicuous enough to arouse such an energetic reaction may also have been conspicuous enough to change behavior; for observations other than simple enumerations the bias would have been great. But even with the simple act of nose-counting, there is the risk that the area would be differentially avoided. The research mistake was in providing observers with clipboards and log sheets, but their appearance might have been still more sinister had they operated counters with hands jammed in pockets.

We argue strongly for the use of archival records. Thinking, perhaps, of musty files of bound annual reports of some prior century, one might regard such a method as totally immune to reactive effects. However, were one to make use of precinct police blotters, going around to copy off data once each month, the quality and nature of the records would almost certainly change. In actual fact, archives are kept indifferently, as a low-priority task, by understaffed bureaucracies. Conscientiousness is often low because of the lack of utilization of the records. The presence of a user can revitalize the process—as well as create anxieties over potentially damaging data (Campbell, 1967a). When records are seen as sources of vulnerability, they may be altered systematically. Accounts thought likely to enter into tax audits are an obvious case (Schwartz, 1961), but administrative records (Blau, 1955) and criminal statistics (Kadish, 1964) are equally amenable to this source of distortion. The selective and wholesale rifling of records by ousted political administrations sets an example of potential reactive effects, self-consciousness, and dissembling on the part of archivists.

These reactive effects may threaten both internal and external validity, depending upon the conditions. If it seems plausible that the reactivity was equal in both measures of a comparison, then the threat is to external validity or generalizability, not to internal validity. If the reactive effect is plausibly differential, then it may generate a pseudo difference. Thus, in a study (Campbell & McCormack, 1957) showing a reduction in authoritarian attitudes over the course of one year's military training, the initial testing was done in conjunction with an official testing program, while the subsequent testing was clearly under external university research auspices. As French (1955) pointed out in another connection, this difference provides a plausible reactive threat jeopardizing the conclusion that any reduction has taken place even for this one group, quite apart from the external validity problems of explanation and generalization. In many interview and questionnaire studies, increased or decreased rapport and increased awareness of the researcher's goals or decreased fear provide plausible alternative explanations of the apparent change recorded.

The common device of guaranteeing anonymity demonstrates concern for the reactive bias, but this concern may lead to validity threats. For example, some test constructors have collected normative data under conditions of anonymity, while the test is likely to be used with the respondent's name signed. Making a response public, or guaranteeing to preserve privacy, will influence the nature of the response. This has been seen for persuasive communications, in the validity of reports of brands purchased, and for the level of antisocial responses. There is a clear link between awareness of being tested and the biases associated with a tendency to answer with socially desirable responses.

There are several fairly common ways in which investigators attempt to reduce the reactivity of their measures, of which the promise of anonymity is one. Investigators may assure subjects that the information they give is for important scientific purposes and that they should, therefore, be truthful. Even when data are not collected under the promise of anonymity, almost always the promise of confidentiality is made. Questionnaires on a single topic often contain "filler" items that are not to be scored but that are thought to reduce somewhat the awareness of the subject of the true purpose of the questionnaire. Unobtrusive measures are but among a fairly extensive variety of measurement procedures addressed to the same problem, ample testimony to the widespread recognition that there is a problem.

The considerations outlined above suggest that reactivity may be selectively troublesome within trials or tests of the experiment. Training trials may accommodate the subject to the task, but a practice effect may exist that either enhances or inhibits the reactive bias. Early responses may be contaminated, later ones not, or vice versa (Underwood, 1957).

Ultimately, the determination of reactive effect depends on validating studies—few examples of which are currently available. Behavior observed under nonreactive conditions must be compared with corresponding behavior in which various potentially reactive conditions are introduced. Where no difference in direction of relationship occurs, the reactivity factor can be discounted.

One procedure for which a good bit of information is currently being developed is the randomized response technique (Boruch & Cecil, 1979) by means of which a randomizing device seen only by the respondent keeps the interviewer from knowing which particular question is being answered by the respondent but that permits a statistical estimation of true responses for groups. An example of the type of finding emerging is that if female college students are queried about their participation in various sexual activities, the estimate of the frequency of such activities is higher from the randomized response technique than from direct questionnaire data (Fidler & Kleinknecht, 1977).

In the absence of systematic data, we have little basis for determining what is and what is not reactive. Existing techniques consist of asking subjects in a posttest interview whether they were affected by the test, were aware of the deception in the experiment, and so forth. While these may sometimes demonstrate a method to be reactive, they may fail to detect many instances in which reactivity is a serious contaminant. Subjects who consciously try to deceive during an experiment may do so afterward for the same reasons. And those who are unaware of the effects on them at the time of the research may hardly be counted on for valid reports afterwards.

The types of measures surveyed in this monograph have a double importance in overcoming reactivity. In the absence of validation for verbal measures, nonreactive techniques of the kind surveyed here provide ways of avoiding the serious problems faced by more conventional techniques. Given the limiting properties of these "other measures," however, their greatest utility may be in their capacity to provide validation for the more conventional measures.

2. *Role Selection.* Another way in which the respondent's awareness of the research process produces differential reaction involves not so much inaccuracy, defense, or dishonesty, but rather a specialized selection from among the many "true" selves or "proper" behaviors available in any respondent.

By singling out an individual to be tested (assuming that being tested is not a normal condition), the experimenter forces upon the subject a role-defining decision—What kind of a person should I be as I answer these questions or do these tasks? In many of the "natural" situations to which the findings are generalized, subjects may not be forced to define their role relative to the behavior. For other situations, they may. Validity decreases as the role assumed in the research setting varies from the usual role present in comparable behavior beyond the research setting. Orne and his colleagues have provided compelling demonstrations of the magnitude of this variable's effect (Orne, 1959, 1962; Orne & Evans, 1965; Orne & Scheibe, 1964). Orne has noted:

> The experimental situation is one which takes place within context of an explicit agreement of the subject to participate in a special form of social interaction known as "taking part in an experiment." Within the context of our culture the roles of subject and experimenter are well understood and carry with them well-defined mutual role expectations. (1962, p. 777)

Looking at all the cues available to the respondent attempting to puzzle out an appropriate set of roles or behavior, Orne labeled the total of all such cues the "demand characteristics of the experimental situation." A study by Orne and Evans (1965) showed that the alleged antisocial effects induced by hypnosis can be accounted for by the demand characteristics of the research setting. Subjects who were not hypnotized engaged in "antisocial" activities as well as did those who were hypnotized. The behavior of those not hypnotized is traced to social cues that attend the experimental situation and are unrelated to the experimental variable.

The probability of this confounding role assumption varies from one research study to another, of course. The novelty of a test-taking role may be selectively biasing for subjects of different educational levels. Less familiar and comfortable with testing, those with little formal schooling are more likely to produce nonrepresentative behavior. The act of being tested is "more different." The same sort of distortion risk occurs when subject matter is unusual or novel. Subject matter with which the respondent is unfamiliar may produce uncertainty of which role to select. A role-playing choice is more likely with such new or unexpected material.

Lack of familiarity with tests or with testing materials can influence response in different ways. Responses may be depressed because of a lack of training with the materials. Or the response level may be distorted as the subject perceives himself or herself in the rare role of expert.

Both unfamiliarity and "expertness" can influence the character as well as the level of response. It is common to find experimental procedures that augment the experting bias. The instruction that reads, "You have been selected as part of a scientifically selected sample . . . it is important that you answer the questions . . ." underlines in what a special situation and what a special person the respondent is. The empirical test of the experting hypothesis in field research is the extent of "don't know" replies. One should predict that a set of instructions stressing the importance of the respondent as a member of a "scientifically selected sample" will produce significantly fewer "don't knows" than an instruction set that does not stress the individual's importance.

Although the "special person" set of instructions may increase participation in the project and thus reduce some concern on the sampling level, it concurrently increases the risk of reactive bias. In science as everywhere else, one seldom gets something for nothing. The critical question for the researcher must be whether or not the resultant sampling gain offsets the risk of deviation from "true" responses produced by the experting role.

Not only does interviewing result in role selection, but the problem or its analogues may exist for any measure. Thus, in a study utilizing conversation sampling with totally hidden microphones (a study that could raise serious ethical problems), each social setting elicits a different role selection. Conversation samples might thus differ between two cities, not because of any true differences, but rather because of subtle differences in role elicitation of the differing settings employed.

3. Measurement as Change Agent. With all the respondent candor possible, and with complete role representativeness, there can still be an important class of reactive effects—those in which the initial measurement activity introduces real changes in what is being measured. The change may be real enough in these instances and invalidly generalized to other settings not involving a pretest. This process has been deliberately demonstrated by Schanck and Goodman (1939) in a classic study involving information-test taking as a disguised persuasive process. Research by Roper (cited by Crespi, 1948) shows that the well-established "preamble effect" (Cantril, 1944) is not merely a technical flaw in determining the response to the question at hand, but that it also creates attitudes that persist and that are measurable on subsequent unbiased questions. Crespi reports additional research of his own confirming that processes leading to opinion development are initiated even for those who initially say "don't know."

The effect has been long established in the social sciences. In psychology, early research in transfer of training encountered the threat to internal validity called practice effects: The exercise provided by the pretest accounted for the gain shown on the posttest. Such research led to the introduction of control groups in studies that had earlier neglected to include them. Similarly, research in intelligence testing showed that dependable gains in test-passing ability could be traced to experience with previous tests, even where no knowledge of results had been provided. (See Cane & Heim, 1950, and Anastasi, 1958, pp. 190-191, for reviews of this literature.) Similar gains have been shown in personal "adjustment" scores (Windle, 1954).

Limitations on measurement because the act of measurement changes the phenomenon or object are not unique to social science. In fact, measurement in the physical and natural sciences often produces a permanent change in the object being measured. For example, engineers could not do an actual test of the load carrying capacity of a bridge because the test would destroy it. Assessing physiological and anatomical changes in laboratory animal specimens often requires destroying them so that one cannot, for example, do longitudinal studies of anatomical changes subsequent to brain injuries.

Although actual change in characteristics stemming from measurement operations is likely to be directly proportional to the intrusiveness of measurement, the possibility of analogous artifacts in unobtrusive measures must be considered. Suppose one were interested in measuring the weight of women in a secretarial pool, and their weights were to be the dependent variable in a study on the effects of a change from an all-female staff to one including men. One might, for this purpose, put free weight scales in the women's rest room, with an automatic recording device inside. However, the recurrent availability of knowledge of one's own weight in a semisocial situation would probably act as a greater change agent for weight than would any experimental treatment that might be under investigation. A floor-panel treadle would be better, recording weights without providing feedback to the participant, possibly disguised as an automatic door-opener.

4. Response Sets. The critical literature on questionnaire methodology has demonstrated the presence of several irrelevant but lawful sources of variance. Most of these are probably applicable to interviews also, although this has been less elaborately demonstrated to date. Cronbach (1946) originally summarized this literature, and evidence continues to show its importance (Wiggins, 1973).

Respondents will more frequently endorse a statement than disagree with its opposite (Sletto, 1937). This tendency differs widely and consistently among individuals, generating the reliable source of variance known as acquiescence response set (Cronbach, 1946). Although Rorer (1965) and Block (1965) have dissented from this point of view, the ubiquitous presence of direction-of-wording effects—to varying degrees depending on content—seems clearly demonstrated for a wide variety of scales when the effect is examined in the correlations between traits (Campbell, Siegman, & Rees, 1967).

Another idiosyncracy, dependably demonstrated over varied multiple-choice content, is the preference for strong statements versus moderate or indecisive ones. Sequences of questions asked in very similar format produce stereotyped responses, such as a tendency to endorse the right-hand or the left-hand response, or to alternate in some simple fashion. Furthermore, decreasing attention produces reliable biases from the order of item presentation.

Response biases can occur not only for questionnaires or public opinion polls, but also for archival records such as votes (Bain & Hecock, 1957). Still more esoteric observational or erosion measures face similar problems. Take the example of a traffic study.

Suppose one wanted to obtain a nonreactive measure of the relative attractiveness of paintings in an art museum. One might employ an erosion method, such as the relative degree of carpet or floor-tile wear in front of each painting. Or, more elaborately, one might install invisible photoelectric timers and counters. Such an approach must also take into account irrelevant habits that affect traffic flow. There is, for example, a general right turn bias upon entering a building or room. When this is combined with time deadlines and fatigue (Do people drag their feet more by the time they get to the paintings on the left side of the building?), there probably is a predictably biased response tendency. The design of museums tends to be systematic, and this, too, can bias the measures. The placement of an exit door will consistently bias the traffic flow and thus confound any erosion measure unless it is controlled. (For imaginative and provocative observational studies on museum behavior see Melton, 1933a, 1933b, 1935, 1936; Melton, Feldman, & Mason, 1936; Robinson, 1928.)

Each of these four types of reactive error can be reduced by employing research measures that do not require the cooperation of the respondent and that are "blind" to him. Although we urge more methodological research to make known the degree of error that may be traced to reactivity, our inclination now is to urge the use of compensating measures that do not contain the reactive risk.

Error From the Investigator

To some degree, error from the investigator was implicit in the reactive error effects. After all, the investigator is an important source of cues to the respondent, and he or she helps to structure the demand characteristics of the interview. However, in these previous points, interviewer character was unspecified. Here we deal with effects that vary systematically with interviewer characteristics and with instrument errors mostly independent of respondents.

5. Interviewer Effects. It is old news that the characteristics of the interviewer can contribute a substantial amount of variance to a set of findings. Interviewees respond differentially to visible cues provided by the interviewer. Within any single study, this variance can produce a spurious difference. The work of Katz (1942) and Cantril (1944) demonstrated the differential effect of the race of the interviewer, and that bias has been more recently shown by Athey, Coleman, Reitman, and Tang (1960). The bias does seem limited to race-sensitive issues, and then it operates in both directions, for example, white interviewers with black respondents and black interviewers with white respondents (Schuman & Converse, 1971). Riesman and Ehrlich (1961) reported that the age of the interviewer produced a bias, with the number of "unacceptable" (to the experimenter) answers higher when questions were posed by younger interviewers.

Religion of the interviewer is a possible contaminant (Hyman, Cobb, Feldman, Hart, & Stember, 1954; Robinson & Rohde, 1946), as is his or her social class (Lenski & Leggett, 1960; Riesman, 1956). Benney, Riesman, and Star (1956) showed that one should consider not only main effects, but also interactions. In their study of age and sex variables they report: "Male interviewers obtain fewer responses than female, and fewest of all from males, while female interviewers obtain their highest responses from men, except for young women talking to young men" (p. 143). These findings are amplified by an observational study of transactions in banks that revealed different times required for transactions depending on sex of teller and sex of customer (Larwood, Zalkind, & Legault, 1975). Generally transactions involving female customers were longer, and that was especially the case when tellers were male. On the other hand, transactions between female tellers and male customers were shortest. Probably it is the case that the teller has greatest control over transaction time. One of Dabbs's (J. M. Dabbs, Jr., personal communication, 1980) students has reported the same effect for library transactions. For a generally useful discussion of various effects on responses in interviews, see Sudman and Bradburn (1974).

The evidence is overwhelming that a substantial number of biases can be introduced by an interviewer (see Hyman et al., 1954; Kahn & Cannell, 1957). In fact, bias may be introduced even by the tone of voice in which a question is asked. In a study of reporting of health-related matters, a rising tone of voice elicited more symptoms than a falling tone but also produced greater reported interest in the interview (Cannell, Oksenberg, & Converse, 1977). Other investigators have found that even slight differences in the wording of questions or the order in which they are presented may lead to significant differences in the outcome of a survey (Turner & Krauss, 1978). Some of the major biases, such as race, are relatively easily controlled; other biases, such as the interaction of age and sex or specific question order effects, are less easily handled.

If we heeded all the known biases, without considering our ignorance of major interactions, there could no longer be a simple survey. The understandable action by most researchers has been to ignore these biases and to assume them away. The biases are lawful and consistent, and all research employing face-to-face interviewing or questionnaire administration is subject to them. Rather than flee by assumptions, the experimenter may use alternative methodologies that let him flee by circumvention.

6. Change in the Research Instrument. The measuring (data-gathering) instrument is frequently an interviewer, whose characteristics, we have just shown, may alter responses. In panel studies, or those using the same interviewer at two or more points in time, it is essential to ask: To what degree is the interviewer or experimenter the same research instrument at all points of the research?

Just as a spring scale becomes fatigued with use, reading "heavier" a second time, interviewers may also measure differently at different times. Their skill may increase. They may be better able to establish rapport. They may have learned necessary vocabulary. They may loaf or become bored. They may have increasingly strong expectations of what a respondent 'means" and code differently with practice. Some errors relate to recording accuracy, while others are linked to the nature of the interviewer's interpretation of what transpired. Either way, there is always the risk that the interviewer will be a variable filter over time and experience.

Even when the interviewer becomes more competent, there is potential trouble. Although we usually think of difficulty only when the instrument weakens, a difference in competence between two waves of interviewing, either increasing or decreasing, can yield spurious effects. The source of error is not limited to interviewers, and every class of measurement is vulnerable to wavering calibration. Suicides in Prussia jumped 20% between 1882 and 1883. This clearly reflected a change in record-keeping, not a massive increase in depression. Until 1883 the records were kept by the police, but in that year the job was transferred to the civil service (Halbwachs, 1930, cited in Selltiz et al., 1959). Archivists undoubtedly drift in recording standards, with occasional administrative reforms in conscientiousness altering the output of the "instrument" (Kitsuse & Cicourel, 1963).

Where human observers are used, they have fluctuating adaptation levels and response thresholds (Campbell, 1961b; Holmes, 1958). Rosenthal, in an impressive series of commentary and research, has focused on errors traceable to the experimenter. Of particular interest is Rosenthal's (1976) work on the influence of early data returns upon analysis of subsequent data.

Varieties of Sampling Error

Historically, social science has examined sampling errors as a problem in the selection of respondents. The person or group has been the critical unit, and our thinking has been focused on a universe of people. Often a sample of time or space can provide a practical substitute for a sample of persons. Novel methods should be examined for their potential in this regard. For example, a study of the viewing of bus advertisements used a time-stratified, random triggering of an automatic camera pointed out a window over the bus ad (Politz Media Studies, 1959). One could similarly take a photographic sample of bus passengers modulated by door entries as counted by a photo cell. A photo could be taken one minute after the entry of every 20th passenger. For some methods, such as the erosion methods, total population records are no more costly than partial ones. For some archives, temporal samples or agency samples are possible. For voting records, precincts may be sampled. But for any one method the possibilities should be examined.

We look at sampling in this section from the point of view of restrictions on reaching people associated with various methods and the stability of populations over time and areas.

7. Population Restrictions. In the public-opinion-polling tradition, one conceptualizes a "universe" from which a representative sample is drawn. This model gives little or no formal attention to the fact that only certain universes are possible for any given method. A method-respondent interaction exists—one that gives each method a different set of defining boundaries for its universe. One reason so little attention is given to this fact is that, as methods go, public opinion polling is relatively unrestricted. Yet even here there is definite universe rigidity, with definite restrictions on the size and character of the population that can be sampled.

In the earliest days of polling, people were questioned in public places, probably excluding some 80% of the total population. Shifting to in-home interviewing with quota controls and no callbacks still excluded some 60%—perhaps 5% inaccessible in homes under any conditions, 25% not at home, 25% refusals, and 5% through interviewers' reluctance to approach homes of extreme wealth or poverty and a tendency to avoid fourth-floor walkups.

Under modern probability sampling with callbacks and household designation, perhaps only 15% of the population is excluded: 5% are totally inaccessible in private residences (those institutionalized, hospitalized, homeless, transient, in the military, mentally incompetent, etc.), another 10% refuse to answer, are unavailable after three callbacks, or have moved to no known address. A 20% figure was found in the model Elmira study in its first wave (Williams, 1950), although other studies have reported much lower figures. Ross (1963) has written a general statement on the problem of inaccessibility, and

Stephan and McCarthy (1958), in their literature survey, show from 3 to 14% of sample populations of residences inaccessible.

Also to be considered in population restriction is the degree to which the accessible universe deviates in important parameters from the excluded population. This bias is probably minimal in probability sampling with adequate callbacks, but great with catch-as-catch-can and quota samples. Much survey research has centered on household behavior, and the great mass of probability approaches employ a prelisted household as the terminal sampling unit. This frequently requires the enlistment of a household member as a reporter on the behavior of others. Since those who answer doorbells overrepresent the old, the young, and women, this can be a confounding error.

When we come to more demanding verbal techniques, the universe rigidity is much greater. What proportion of the population is available for self-administered questionnaires? Payment for filling out the questionnaire reduces the limitations a bit, but a money reward is selectively attractive—at least at the rates most researchers pay. A considerable proportion of the populace is functionally illiterate for personality and attitude tests developed on college populations.

Not only do the demands of the task create population restrictions, differential volunteering provides similar effects, interacting in a particularly biasing way when the nature of the task is known (Capra & Dittes, 1962; Rosenthal & Rosnow, 1975). Baumrind (1964) writes of the motivation of volunteers and notes: "The dependent attitude of most subjects toward the experimenter is an artifact of the experimental situation as well as an expression of some subjects' personal need systems at the time they volunteer" (p. 421).

The curious, the exhibitionistic, and the succorant are likely to overpopulate any sample of volunteers. How secure a base can volunteers be with such groups overrepresented and the shy, suspicious, and inhibited underrepresented? The only defensible position is a probability sample of the units to which the findings will be generalized. Even conscripting sophomores may be better than relying on volunteers.

Returning to the rigidity of sampling, what proportion of the total population is available for the studio test audiences used in advertising and television program evaluation? Perhaps 2%. For mailed questionnaires, the population available for addressing might be 95% of the total in the United States, but low-cost, convenient mailing lists probably cover no more than 70% of the families through automobile registration and telephone directories. The exclusion is, again, highly selective. If, however, we consider the volunteering feature, where 10% returns are typical, the effective population is a biased 7% selection of the total. The nature of this selective-return bias includes a skewing of the sample in favor of lower middle-class individuals drawn from unusually stable, "happy" families (Vincent, 1964).

[The original article discussed the advantages and difficulties of acquiring data through telephone interviews. Since it appeared in 1981, however, the number of telephones and the new technologies have changed drastically. Although most households have telephones, many still choose to keep their numbers unlisted. With the proliferation of solicitation calls to sell products (the phone equivalent of the door-to-door salesman) telephone etiquette has changed somewhat. If the caller is not familiar, individuals may simply hang up without giving the caller an opportunity to explain the purpose for the call. Many households simply do not answer the telephone or have procured devices that identify the caller so that calls can be answered selectively. Answering machines and voice mail allow the caller to leave a message; however, the researcher is more likely to secure an agreement to participate if speaking directly to the potential respondent. While telephone interviewing is a convenient way of gathering information and the cost can be kept far below the cost of face-to-face interviewing, some groups may be overrepresented in the sample, such as the elderly, who spend more time in their homes yet may be less likely to acquire the new technologies to protect their privacy, or the poor who cannot afford them.]

Sampling problems of many kinds are certainly acute for the research methods considered here. Although a few have the full population access of public opinion surveys, most have much more restricted populations. Consider, for example, the sampling of natural conversations. What are the proportions of men and women whose conversations are accessible in public places and on public transport? What is the representativeness of social class or role?

8. Population Stability Over Time. When comparisons over time are the focus, the stability of a population restriction is more important than the magnitude of the restriction. Examine conversation sampling on a bus. The population represented differs on dry days and snowy days, in winter and spring, and by day of the week. These shifts would in many instances provide plausible rival explanations of shifts in topics of conversation. Sampling from a much narrower universe would be preferable if the population were more stable over time, as, say, conversation samples from an employees' rest room in an office building. Comparisons of interview survey results over time periods are more troubled by population instability than is generally realized, because of seasonal layoffs in many fields of employment, plus status-differentiated patterns of summer and winter vacations. An extended discussion of time sampling has been provided by Brookover and Back (1966).

9. *Population Stability Over Areas.* Similarly, research populations available to a given method may vary from region to region, providing a more serious problem than a population restriction common to both. Thus, for a comparison of attitudes between New York and Los Angeles, conversation sampling in buses and commuter trains would tap such different segments of the communities as to be scarcely worth doing. Again, a comparison of employees' washrooms in comparable office buildings would provide a more interpretable comparison. Through the advantage of background data to check on some dimensions of representativeness, public opinion surveys again have an advantage in this regard.

Any enumeration of sources of invalidity is bound to be incomplete. Some threats are too highly specific to a given setting and method to be generalized, as are some opportunities for ingenious measurement and control. This list contains a long series of general threats that apply to a broad body of research method and content. It does not say that additional problems cannot be found.

AN INTERLUDE:
THE MEASUREMENT OF OUTCROPPINGS

The population restrictions discussed here are apt to seem so severe as to traumatize the researcher and to lead to the abandonment of the method. This is particularly so for one approaching social science with the goal of complete description. Such trauma is, of course, far from our intention. While discussion of these restrictions is a necessary background to their intelligent use and correction, there is need here for a parenthesis forestalling excessive pessimism.

First, it can be noted that a theory predicting a change in civic opinion, due to an event and occurring between two time periods, might be such that this opinion shift could be predicted for many partially overlapping populations. One might predict changes on public opinion polls within that universe, changes in sampled conversation on commuter trains for a much smaller segment, changes in letters mailed to editors and the still more limited letters published by editors, changes in purchase rates of books on relevant subjects by that minute universe, and so on. In such an instance, the occurrence of the predicted shift on any one of these meters is confirmatory and its absence discouraging. If the effect is found on only one measure, it probably reflects more on the method than on the theory (e.g., Burwen & Campbell, 1957; Campbell & Fiske, 1959). A more complicated theory might well predict differential shifts for different meters, and, again, the evidence of each is relevant to the validity of the theory. The joint confirmation between pollings of high-income populations and commuter-train conversations is much more validating than either taken alone, just because of the difference between the methods in irrelevant components.

The "outcropping" model from geology may be used more generally. Any given theory has innumerable implications and makes innumerable predictions that are unaccessible to available measures at any given time. The testing of the theory can only be done at the available outcroppings, those points where theoretical predictions and available instrumentation meet. Any one such outcropping is equivocal, and all types available should be checked. The more remote or independent such checks, the more confirmatory their agreement.

Within this model, science opportunistically exploits the available points of observation. As long as nature abhorred a vacuum up to 33 feet of water, little research was feasible. When manufacturing skills made it possible to represent the same abhorrence by 76 centimeters of mercury in a glass tube, a whole new outcropping for the checking of theory was made available. The telescope in Galileo's hands, the microscope, the induction coil, the photographic emulsion of silver nitrate, and the cloud chamber all represent partial new outcroppings available for the verification of theory. Even where several of these are relevant to the same theory, their mode of relevance is quite different and short of a complete overlap. Analogously, social science methods with individually restricted and nonidentical universes can provide collectively valuable outcroppings for the testing of theory.

The goal of complete description in science is particularly misleading when it is assumed that raw data provide complete description. Theory is necessarily abstract, for any given event is so complex that its complete description may demand many more theories than are actually brought to bear on it—or than are even known at any given stage of development. But theories are more complete descriptions than obtained data, since they describe processes and entities in their unobserved as well as in their observed states. The scintillation counter notes but a small and nonrepresentative segment of a meson's course. [A meson is an unstable particle having a mass between that of the electron and the proton.] The visual data of an ordinary object are literally superficial. Perceiving an object as solid or vaporous, persistent or transient, involves theory going far beyond the data given. The raw data, observations, field notes, tape recordings, and sound movies of a social event are but transient superficial outcroppings of events and objects much more continuously and completely (even if abstractly) described in the social scientist's theory. Tycho Brahe and Kepler's observations provided Kepler with only small fragments of the orbit of Mars, for a biased and narrow sampling of times of day, days, and years. From these he constructed a complete description through theory. The fragments provided outcroppings sufficiently stubborn to force Kepler to reject his preferred theory. The data were even sufficient to cause the rejection of Newton's later theory had Einstein's better fitting theory then been available.

So if the restraints on validity sometimes seem demoralizing, they remain so only as long as one set of data, one type of method, is considered separately. Viewed in consort with other methods, matched against the available outcroppings for theory testing, there can be strength in converging weakness.

THE ACCESS TO CONTENT

Often a choice among methods is delimited by the relative ability of different classes of measurement to penetrate into content areas of research interest. In the simplest instance, this is not so much a question of validity as it is a limitation on the utility of the measure. Each class of research method, be it the questionnaire or hidden observation, has rigidities on the content it can cover. These rigidities can be divided, as were population restrictions, into those linked to an interaction between method and materials, those associated with time, and those with physical area.

10. Restrictions on Content. If we adopt the research strategy of combining different classes of measurement, it becomes important to understand what content is and is not feasible or practical for each overlapping approach.

Observational methods can be used to yield an index of black-white amicability by computing the degree of "aggregation" or nonrandom clustering among mixed groups of blacks and whites (Campbell, Kruskal, & Wallace, 1966). This method could also be used to study male-female relations, or army-navy relations in wartime when uniforms are worn on liberty. But these indexes of aggregation would be largely unavailable for Catholic-Protestant relations or for Jewish-Christian relations. Door-to-door solicitation of funds for causes relevant to attitudes is obviously plausible but available for only a limited range of topics. For public opinion surveys, there are perhaps tabooed topics (although research on birth control and venereal disease has shown these to be fewer than might have been expected). More important, there are topics on which people are unable to report but that a social scientist can reliably observe.

Examples of this can be seen in the literature on verbal reinforcers in speech and in interviews. (For a review of this literature, see Krasner, 1958, as well as Hildum & Brown, 1956; Matarazzo, 1962). A graphic display of opportunistic exploitation of an "outcropping" was displayed by Matarazzo, Wiens, Saslow, Dunham, and Voas (1964). They took tapes of the speech of astronauts and ground communicators for two space flights and studied the duration of the ground communicator's unit of speech to the astronauts. The data supported their expectations and confirmed findings from the laboratory. We are not sure if an orbital flight should be considered a "natural setting" or not, but certainly the astronaut and his colleagues were not overly sensitive to the duration of individual speech units. The observational method has consistently produced findings on the effect of verbal reinforcers unattainable by direct questioning.

It is obvious that secondary records and physical evidence are high in their content rigidity. The researcher cannot go out and generate a new set of historical records. He or she may discover a new set, but will always be restrained by what is available. We cite examples later that demonstrate that this weakness is not so great as is frequently thought, but it would be naive to suggest that it is not present.

11. Stability of Content Over Time. The restrictions on content just mentioned are often questions of convenience. The instability of content, however, is a serious concern for validity. Consider conversation sampling again: If one is attending to the amount of comment on race relations, for example, the occurrence of extremely bad weather may so completely dominate all conversations as to cause a meaningless drop in racial comments. This is a typical problem for index-making. In such an instance, one would probably prefer some index such as the proportion of all race comments that were favorable. In specific studies of content variability over time, personnel-evaluation studies have employed time sampling with considerable success. Observation during a random sample of a worker's laboring minutes efficiently does much to describe both the job and the worker (Thorndike, 1949; Ghiselli & Brown, 1955; Whisler & Harper, 1962).

Public opinion surveys have obvious limitations in this regard, which have led to the utilization of telephone interviews and built-in dialing recorders for television and radio audience surveys (Lucas & Britt, 1950, 1963). By what means other than a recorder could one get a reasonable estimate of the number of people who watch *The Late Show?*

12. Stability of Content Over Area. Where regional comparisons are being made, cross-sectional stability in the kinds of contents elicited by a given method is desirable.

Take the measurement of interservice rivalry as a research question. As suggested earlier, one could study the degree of mingling among men in uniform, or study the number of barroom fights among men dressed in different uniforms. To have a valid regional comparison, one must assume the same incidence of men wearing uniforms in public places when at liberty. Such an assumption is probably not justified, partly because of past experience in a given area, partly because of proximity to urban centers. If a cluster of military bases is close to a large city, only a selective group wear uniforms off duty, and they are more likely to be the belligerent ones. Another comparison region may have the same level of behavior but be less visible.

The effect of peace is to reduce the influence of the total level of the observed response, since dressing in civilian clothes is more common. But if all the comparisons are made in peacetime, it is not an issue. The problem occurs only if one elected to study the problem by a time-series design that cuts across war and peace. To the foot-on-rail researcher, the number of outcroppings may vary because of war, but this is no necessary threat to internal validity.

Sampling of locations, such as bus routes, waiting rooms, shop windows, and so forth, needs to be developed to expand access to both content and populations. Obviously, different methods present different opportunities and problems in this regard. Among the few studies that have seriously attempted this type of sampling, the problem of enumerating the universe of such locations has proved extremely difficult (James, 1951). Location sampling has, of course, been practiced more systematically with preestablished enumerated units such as blocks, census tracts, and incorporated areas.

OPERATING EASE AND VALIDITY CHECKS

There are differences among methods that have nothing to do with the interpretation on a single piece of research. These are familiar issues to working researchers and are important ones for the selection of procedures. Choosing between two different methods that promise to yield equally valid data, the researcher is likely to reject the more time-consuming or costly method. Also, there is an inclination toward those methods that have sufficient flexibility to allow repetition if something unforeseen goes wrong, and that further hold potential for producing internal checks on validity or sampling errors.

13. Dross Rate. In any given interview, a part of the conversation is irrelevant to the topic at hand. This proportion is the dross rate. It is greater in open-ended, general, free-response interviewing than it is in structured interviews with fixed-answer categories; by the same token, the latter are potentially the more reactive. But in all such procedures, the great advantage is the interviewer's power to introduce and reintroduce certain topics. This ability allows a greater density of relevant data. At the other extreme is unobserved conversation sampling, which is low-grade ore. If one elected to measure attitudes toward Russia by sampling conversations on public transportation, a major share of experimental effort could be spent in listening to comparisons of hairdressers or discussions of the Yankees' one-time dominance of the American League. For a specific problem, conversation sampling provides low-grade ore. The price one must pay for this ore, in order to get a naturally occurring response, may be too high for the experimenter's resources.

14. Access to Descriptive Cues. In evaluating methods, one should consider their potential for generating associated validity checks, as well as the differences in the universes they tap. Looking at alternative measures, what other data can they produce that give descriptive cues on the specific nature of the method's population? Internal evidence from early opinion polls showed their population biases when answers about prior voting and education did not match known election results and census data.

On this criterion, survey research methods have great advantages, for they permit the researcher to build in controls with ease. Observational procedures can check restrictions only for such gross and visible variables as sex, approximate age, and conspicuous ethnicity. Trace methods such as the relative wear of floor tiles offer no such intrinsic possibility. However, it is possible in many instances to introduce interview methods in conjunction with other methods for the purpose of ascertaining population characteristics. Thus, commuter-train passengers, window shoppers, and waiting-room conversationalists can, on a sample of times of day, days of the week, and so on, be interviewed on background data, probably without creating any serious reactive effects for measures taken on other occasions.

15. Ability to Replicate. The questionnaire and the interview are particularly good methods because they permit the investigator to replicate his own or someone else's research. There is a tolerance for error when one is producing new data that does not exist when working with old. If a confounding event occurs or materials are spoiled, one can start another survey repeating the procedure. Archives and physical evidence are more restricted, with only a fixed amount of data available. This may be a large amount—allowing split-sample replication—but it may also be a one-shot occurrence that permits only a single analysis. In the latter case, there is no second chance, and the materials may be completely consumed methodologically.

The one-sample problem is not an issue if data are used in a clear-cut test of theory. If the physical evidence or secondary records are an outcropping where the theory can be probed, the inability to produce another equivalent body of information is secondary. The greater latitude of the questionnaire and interview, however, permit the same statement and provide, in addition, a margin for error.

SCORES AS HYPOTHESES: A METAPHOR

We suggest here that any "score" on any measure is susceptible to a variety of explanations, one of which will usually be that it represents an accurate representation of a person or object's standing on a trait or dimension of interest. For example, an IQ score of 125 may be taken to represent the hypothesis that the person to whom it is attached is "bright." The radar reading of 78 miles per hour represents the hypothesis that the motorist is speeding. The six cigarettes in the ashtray suggest that the previous occupant of the room was "nervous." In each case there are rival hypotheses that would account for the score, and the rivals are more or less plausible depending upon a variety of factors.

Consider the IQ score of 125. How else might it be explained other than by the brightness of the test subject? Several possibilities come to mind:

The subject had been coached on the test.
The examiner made a serious error in arithmetic.
The subject was extremely ingratiating and the examiner was lenient.
The subject had taken the test several times previously.
The examiner was the subject's mother.

Now all these explanations are possible, and some of them may be plausible in a given case. What wise and careful psychologists try to do, of course, is to render the hypotheses rival to intelligence implausible by the manner in which the test is conducted: arithmetic is checked, examiners are trained to be objective, previous testing is looked for, and mothers are not allowed to report findings on their own children. These usual procedures tend to make the IQ score relatively robust against most rival explanations. Exactly the same strategies are adopted by experimenters to protect their findings against hypotheses that the findings are the result of miscalculations, experimenter bias, and so on. In addition, the socialization processes of science help to protect against the hypothesis that any given set of results might have been faked.

The radar speed score is not so easily protected against plausible rivals, it seems. A controversy in the traffic court in Miami has forced a reevaluation of the use of radar, and speed indicators are now thought susceptible to such plausible rival hypotheses as: The radar detected a stationary house or tree, the radar detected some surface of the patrol car in which it was mounted, the radar detected a truck moving up on a smaller vehicle, or the radar simply detected the wrong car in a string of cars. Radar is now under wide attack as a mechanism for detecting speeding violations, and new equipment may have to be designed and built before the plausible rival hypotheses can be laid to rest.

The cigarette butts in the ashtray pose other problems. Could there have been two people in the room? At least check to see whether all six cigarettes are the same brand. Was the ashtray cleaned before the room was occupied? Might the person actually have entered the room much earlier than was originally supposed? Did an absent-minded but quite relaxed person actually light a new cigarette with another left burning and thus produce what appears to be an indicator of heavy smoking? There may, in such cases, be no way of actually rendering all the rival hypotheses implausible, and the measurer—or detective— may be left with the job of selecting among the hypotheses on some other basis, for example, consistency with other information.

If measures are regarded as embodying hypotheses, the careful and alert scientist will often be led to plan measurement operations in such a way as to reduce the number of plausible rival hypotheses to as few as possible and, perhaps, to collect supplementary data that would cast doubt on those remaining as threats to his or her favorite.

EVERYMAN AND THE UNOBTRUSIVE MEASURER

George A. Kelly (1955) thought it interesting to examine the implications of regarding every person as his or her own scientist. Kelly did not think that scientists do anything so very special that everyone else does not do. Scientists form ideas (hypotheses) about the way things work, they run tests (experiments) to see whether their ideas are right, and they incorporate the findings into their ways of looking at things (theories) and go on to their next hypothesis. That, Kelly thought, is just about how everyone conducts his or her life.

Similarly, everyone engages constantly in a variety of measurement operations not much different from those of scientists. With respect to physical measurement, ordinary people often even use versions of the same instruments that scientists use, for example, thermometers, clocks, tape measures, litmus paper, speed or extent of chemical reactions, and so on. In contrast, ordinary people scarcely ever have available the customary measuring instruments of the social and behavioral scientists, for example, questionnaires and surveys. Probably when operating in the realms of social and behavioral science, ordinary people make use primarily of two measurement approaches, simple self-report and unobtrusive measures.

For many purposes self-report measures will do: Where are you going? Is that a mild cigar? Doctor, is it anything serious? Still, in a great many circumstances, ordinary people know that responses to direct inquiries are not to be trusted: What time did you get home last night? Do you love me? How do I look? Is this a good brand? Are you an honest tradesman?

What then do ordinary people do when they have need of information? They supplement direct self-reports with unobtrusive measures. Rodgers and Hammerstein, the marvelous song writing team, had a canny insight into the nature of unobtrusive measurement:

> Don't throw bouquets at me
> Don't please my folks too much,
> Don't laugh at my jokes too much,
> People will say we're in love.
>
> Don't sigh and gaze at me,
> Your sighs are so like mine.
> Your eyes mustn't glow like mine,
> People will say we're in love.
>
> Don't start collecting things;
> Give me my rose and my glove.
> Sweetheart, they're suspecting things.
> People will say we're in love.

The richness of the imagery is remarkable, and as will become clear later, several important types of unobtrusive measures are alluded to in the lyrics.

We are confident that such unobtrusive measurement is characteristic of us all. Moreover, at some level we are all aware of it, and we often attempt to control the image we present to those who would assess us. A young woman meeting her sweetheart's parents for the first time will be trying to create a particular impression (Goffman, 1959), and the parents will be trying to penetrate the obvious by less obvious measures. Hodgkinson (1971) discovered that some maitre d's apparently can predict the size of the tips they will receive from gauging the quality of the footwear worn by customers, and bank loan officers can size up prospective borrowers in only a few seconds. Money doth make careful measurers of us all.

Probably the feature that most distinguishes social scientists from ordinary people as they go about their measurement tasks is the self-consciousness of the social scientists about what they are doing. Like Moliere's character who never knew that he had been speaking prose, most ordinary people never know that they are engaging in unobtrusive measurement. The awareness of social scientists probably does make them somewhat more systematic about the assessment effort, so that they end up with, for example, veritable numerical counts of responses rather than impressions about how often something happened. But the processes are the same. Distrusting deliberate (and possibly self-serving or otherwise biased) reports, all of us, if we are wise, try to supplement our measuring capacities by identifying and observing responses not so susceptible to these biases.

So long as we maintain, as social scientists, an approach to comparisons that considers compensating error and converging corroboration from individually contaminated outcroppings, there is no cause for concern. It is only when we naively place faith in a single measure that the massive problems of social research vitiate the validity of our comparisons. We have argued strongly in this chapter for a conceptualization of method that demands multiple measurement of the same phenomenon or comparison. Overreliance on questionnaires and interviews is dangerous because it does not give us enough points in conceptual space to triangulate. We are urging the employment of novel, sometimes "oddball," methods to give those points in space.

OVERVIEW OF CHAPTER 8

————•◆•————

In the previous chapter, Campbell and others discussed a number of threats to validity that involve the respondent, the investigator, or access to content. The authors emphasized the importance of triangulation or multiple operationism, which requires two or more instruments measured with independent methods to characterize complex constructs. This chapter reviews indirect measures of social attitudes. These measures may be more valid than direct attitude tests in some instances, but more importantly, they provide another option when applying multiple operationism.

While these indirect measures can be extremely useful to the researcher, Kidder and Campbell suggest four negative aspects of which the reader should be aware. Invasion of privacy can be an issue if the researcher does not consider future uses of indirect measures and provide safeguards against improper uses. Second, researchers must take care when developing indirect measures to avoid taking advantage of the "gullible sucker." While the authors believe that the value of the research question can override the moral aversion to deception, investigators must take care not to betray the trust of those who would participate in the research. Third, more research should be done to demonstrate whether indirect tests avoid the problems inherent in direct testing while providing valid measures of the constructs. Finally, published reports of studies using indirect tests have shown only modest success, making it difficult to argue that the indirect test is superior to direct tests.

This chapter deals with testing that requires the cooperation of the respondent. However, the respondent may be deceived, since indirect measures may be used for an ulterior purpose. There are three dichotomies that define types of tests, and indirect tests are described in terms of these dichotomies. The first dichotomy is indirect versus direct. For the direct test, the respondent is informed of the purpose of the test; in an indirect test, the respondent is not aware of the real purpose of the test. The second dichotomy is voluntary versus objective. The voluntary test indicates that there are no incorrect answers. In objective tests, the respondent believes that there is a correct answer that is verifiable. In providing such "facts," individuals do not realize that they are giving their own view of the world. This idiosyncratic view actually projects the individual's own hopes, fears, prejudices, and beliefs. The final dichotomy is free response versus structured. Free-response items do not suggest answers and allow an open range of possibilities. Structured tests offer several alternatives from which the respondent chooses the most appropriate. From these dichotomies, four types of indirect tests emerge: (a) voluntary free-response, (b) voluntary structured, (c) objective free-response, and (d) objective structured.

For voluntary free-response tests, respondents are shown some ambiguous stimuli and are asked to provide structure by using their imagination. Examples of this type of test are the Thematic Apperception Test (TAT), doll-playing techniques, the Rosenzweig Picture Frustration Test, and sentence completion tests. All of these voluntary, free-response tests stress the freedom of the respondent to answer in any way he or she wishes. This can lead to new attitude dimensions not foreseen by the researcher. This is what recommends such tests, rather than their indirectness, since in many instances, the respondents are aware of the purpose of the tests.

While voluntary structured tests do not have the freedom of the tests described in the previous section, there are ways to disguise the tests so that they can be done voluntarily without the respondent being aware of the purpose. One such test is the semantic differential technique, which offers two adjectives that are polar opposites and asks respondents to indicate their attitude on the continuum between these two positions. These tests may be direct, but can also be used as an indirect measure, for example, testing racial attitudes with a test purported to be a study on colors. Other variations of the semantic and word choice techniques are the binary choice tests, where respondents are asked to relate a stimulus word with one of two response words, or the adjective checklist, in which the respondent rates photographs by checking off the adjectives that apply. Another form of voluntary, structured methods involves eliciting the respondent's preference for pictures or objects. Judgments about situations that are identical except for the specific persons or group involved offer another way of eliciting social attitudes. The authors suggest that the combination of a voluntary test that provides structured responses may be difficult to disguise as an indirect test. This may be the reason for the lack of success in differentiating among criterion groups or correlating significantly with measures of attitudes.

Objective tests differ from the volunteer type because the respondents are told that there are, indeed, right and wrong answers. Even in searching for a correct answer in an objective test, the respondent reflects his or her own attitudes.

Objective free-response tests involve auditory or visual interpretation tasks. Respondents are asked to identify what is being said on an indistinct recording or to identify words that are "spelled out" by a dot of light in a darkened room. The verbal content or the words recognized by the respondents actually come entirely from themselves. Another example of an objective free-response test would involve asking the respondent to judge a person's behavior or character while informing him or her that the researcher knows these characteristics through a personality inventory. The respondent is focusing on the external world, and it becomes more difficult to recognize that the researcher may be measuring anything other than the correctness of the response.

Objective structured tests are information tests in which respondents must guess a response if they do not know the answer. Their guessing tends to be biased in the direction of their attitudes. Some tests provide two answers, both incorrect, from which the respondent selects. The respondent's choice presents a systematic bias that reflects attitudes. Objective structured tests were used in the study of racial prejudice, although when the indirect tests were compared to direct tests, the direct tests were more reliable and valid. The authors question whether this is due to the fact that individuals are truly able to maintain an unbiased view of reality in spite of personal prejudices, or whether it might be due to irrelevancies or errors inherent in the items of an indirect information test. Other examples of objective structured tests are described and their shortcomings discussed. They include tests of ability to do critical thinking, tests employing bias in learning and memory, tests employing bias in perception, estimation of group opinion and social norms, tests involving miscellaneous abilities, tests involving ability to judge character, and tests involving miscellaneous judgments.

The indirect tests enumerated in this chapter generally have lower reliabilities than the direct tests. This comparison with direct tests may not be appropriate since there may be a concerted effort on the part of the respondent to be consistent when aware of the purpose of the test. In fact, the indirect test is most useful precisely because of the unselfconscious consistency. The authors suggest that the criterial measures used to validate direct and indirect tests may be tapping into social norms in much the same way that direct tests do. It is this freedom from social appearances that increases the value of indirect tests.

Instead of distinguishing attitudes by whether they reflect norms or processes, one socially acceptable and the other taboo, it might be helpful to scale the various expressions of attitudes in terms of their different thresholds. For example, on the lower end of the hierarchy would be an involuntary response, next a verbal report on some aspect of a topic, then a verbal report on one's own attitude toward the topic, and finally, an overt behavior response. One would expect that tests with similar thresholds would correlate more highly. This hierarchy should be considered when interpreting criterial correlations. Often criterial measures are positioned in the hierarchy closer to the direct than the indirect tests.

When using indirect tests, two things must be considered: their effectiveness and their ethical status. They should not be used to probe those areas that an individual considers private. The creator of indirect tests has a responsibility to investigate the applications of the instruments to be sure they are not used to discriminate against individuals. Perhaps the only way to avoid ethical questions for the tester is to guarantee absolute anonymity for the respondent. The authors advocate using anonymous forms wherever possible.

There are two benefits of indirect tests that justify their use. One involves the necessity of validating a measure by using the multitrait-multimethod matrix. Each method has irrelevant variance associated with it; therefore, different methods should be applied to determine the common variance due to the trait itself. Indirect methods provide widely differing methods. The second justification for using indirect tests is that they provide useful tools for examining the relationship between an individual's hopes and fears and the way in which that individual perceives reality. This knowledge may help to reduce bigotry by enlightening educators regarding the areas of information that are lacking or that need to be corrected if this goal is to be accomplished. Although indirect tests did not fulfill the hopes of their pioneers with regard to their statistical credentials, they should be recognized as novel, creative, yet fallible measures of attitude.

EIGHT

INDIRECT
ATTITUDE MEASURES

————•◆•————

his chapter, which appeared in 1970, updated a 20-year-old review of disguised and projective measures of social attitudes
(Campbell, 1950). Many of the reasons for positive evaluation of
indirect attitude measures still remain. At their best, they are admirably ingenious. They utilize and illustrate psychological laws to a greater degree than direct attitude tests, and are thus more characteristic of measurement in the successful sciences wherein yesterday's crucial experiments are today's routine
measurement procedures. And even if not better, they are different, thus fitting
in with multiple operationism, which attempts by using multiple methods of,
hopefully, independent biases to curb the inevitable biases to single methods
(Campbell & Fiske, 1959; Webb, Campbell, Schwartz, & Sechrest, 1966).

In studying interpersonal relations, certain issues should be kept in mind
as we discuss specific problems. Four points can be examined: (a) the invasion

Kidder, L. H., & Campbell, D. T. (1970). The indirect testing of social attitudes. In G. F.
Summers (Ed.), *Attitude measurement*. Chicago: Rand McNally.

of privacy issue, (b) the deceptive-deprecatory-exploitative attitudes of psychologists toward subjects, (c) the failure to do the research implied in the introduction of indirect tests, and (d) the disappointing nature of the research results.

Invasion of Privacy. As the atomic scientists discovered, creating tools and placing them in the hands of those apt to use them immorally involves moral problems for the inventor. It is not enough to say that his discovery is neutral, available for good and ill alike—if he can on scientific grounds anticipate the preponderance of likely use, he shares direct responsibility for that likely use. The atomic scientist was therefore responsible for the military use of atomic weapons, since that preponderance of use was clearly anticipatable. It is only the lack of success of the indirect attitude test movement that spared its inventors an analogous problem. If one looks at the applied uses of tests of any kind, the predominant use is supportive of the status quo rather than supportive of change. That is, the tests are used to fit people into the existing institutions. Insofar as tests offer channels of upward social mobility, it is by rewarding those who fit in, or have the potential of fitting in. This is true in a general way of test uses in school and clinic, and is, of course, particularly true of industrial psychology and personnel selection applications—here the uses are entirely on the side of management, never of labor. The indirect test designers should, therefore, have anticipated outcomes like that substantially rumored at the time of the appearance of the 1950 review, to the effect that a well-known applied psychology research institute had designed an attitude test disguised as an information test to weed out applicants with anti-management, pro-union attitudes.

The Deceptive-Deprecatory-Exploitative Attitude Toward "Subjects." While much of the ingenuity invested in indirect attitude measurement has been the result of competent scientists overcoming genuine obstacles to scientific research, some of it has been the expression of an unworthy attitude toward the subject on the part of the researcher. This excessive and sometimes sadistic glee at deceiving the gullible victim has also found expression in the ingenious deceptions and the write-ups of those deceptions in laboratory social psychology. This is not to rule out all deception in research. In all ethical problems, strong principles are in conflict. A most important ethical consideration is our duty to produce a relevant and accurate social science, and this value is frequently sufficient to override our moral aversion to deception, particularly in cases in which no harm or change-of-fate comes to the deceived respondent, and in which he remains essentially anonymous. Even where psychic damage is done, the value of the finding may still justify the study. The authors would agree that this is so in the Milgram (1963, 1964) studies. But in both experimental artifice and indirect test invention, sometimes the act of deception becomes an enjoyable end in itself, not only as an intellectual challenge but also from a sense of social superiority over the subject, the enjoyment of "taking" a gullible sucker. The very use of the term *subject,* the reference to both human collaborators and rats as Ss smacks of this implicit social distance and exploitativeness vis-à-vis a subordinate caste. (Much better is the old German *Versuchsperson,* which might best be translated as "researcher." Better, too, the anthropologist's informant or the sociologist's respondent, which we try to use in this chapter.)

How different this deceptive deprecatory approach is from truly leveling with one's volunteer collaborators, sharing with them the research purpose, and trusting them to serve those purposes as best they can. (As implemented through anonymous direct tests, this naive, trusting strategy works better than indirect measures in six out of the eight available validity comparisons that we review below.) Classification of measurement types is discussed in the subsequent section but we can note here that indirect attitude tests face this problem more than do unobtrusive measures (Webb et al., 1966) because, being tests, they demand the cooperation of the respondents and thus involve direct deception and the exploitation of another's goodwill.

With psychologists and psychological research becoming a standard part of the model college curriculum, our chronic dishonesty and our subsequent gloating over it contribute to the general degradation of interpersonal trust. The effects of this are beginning to be felt in the occasional refusal of a subject to participate. There may come a day when student activists take up the cry against involuntary servitude in psychological experiments.

Failure to Do the Implied Research. The concept of indirect attitude measurement was very much needed at a time when definitional operationism was implicitly claiming perfection for all measuring procedures. As such, the move toward indirect methods was part and parcel of a more general critical approach to research measures that also found expression in such concepts as demand characteristics (Orne, 1962), experimenter effects (Rosenthal, 1966), evaluation apprehension (Rosenberg, 1965, 1969), reactive measures (Campbell, 1957), guinea pig effects (Selltiz, Jahoda, Deutsch, & Cook, 1959), "Hawthorne" effects (Roethlisberger & Dickson, 1939), placebo effects, studies of the fakability of tests (Dicken, 1959, 1960), studies of social desirability (Edwards, 1957), studies of the biases introduced when questionnaires are signed, and so forth. All this provides favorable valence toward indirect measures. By and large, however, the designers have been content to assert the advantages of indirect measures and have made few efforts to demonstrate them. Thus after many years, this most basic research is still not done.

More specifically, we need research comparing direct and indirect tests in the effort to confirm that the latter are

a. less affected by experimental manipulation of demand characteristics;
b. less susceptible to manipulation of evaluation apprehension;
c. less likely to be reactive measures as judged by the main and interaction effects of testing as in the Solomon four groups design (Campbell & Stanley, 1966; Solomon, 1949);
d. less susceptible to placebo and Hawthorne effects;
e. less affected by instructions to fake a good impression;
f. less modified by the requirement to sign one's name (Cook, Johnson, & Scott, 1969, report no difference for direct and indirect tests);
g. less affected by the role setting of test administration (e.g., employment applicant, psychotherapy applicant, respondent for the sake of science).

We still need to know whether indirect tests can be evaluated positively to all of these while still demonstrating relevant diagnostic ability.

By and large, there has been no critical literature on indirect tests comparable to that on direct ones. While one might hope that indirect tests would have different method factors (Campbell & Fiske, 1959), there is no reason to expect them to have smaller methods variance. Response sets should be expected in indirect tests wherever there are repetitions of an item format, or where repeated similar guesses are required. Many indirect tests have even more chance of changing attitudes in the process of measuring them than direct tests do.

The Disappointing Nature of the Research Results. In the literature we review, the most common evidence of the adequacy of an indirect test is the fact that it correlates positively with a direct test designed for the same purpose. While such evidence provides some minimum comfort, it is hardly any argument for the superiority of the indirect. In these rare cases where there is a third variable or criterion against which both direct and indirect can be compared, the indirect is almost never the better—although it is true that there is a lack of data for settings that would lead to falsification of direct test responses.

The literature here reviewed shows only modest success, and yet considering the dynamics of publishing, this is almost certainly the most promising of the research that has been done. This is a literature to which low-budget entrepreneurs can freely contribute. For each, the zest with which he polishes, analyzes, completes manuscripts, endures one editor's contumely to resubmit to another, will all depend upon the exciting nature of the results. If these published reports represent the best of the disguised testing attempts, we may begin to lose faith in the refinement and reliability of these instruments. Of all our imperfect measures, these are apparently not the least impure.

A TYPOLOGY OF ASSESSMENT PROCEDURES

The title of this chapter identifies our realm as indirect *testing* rather than *assessment. Unobtrusive Measures* (Webb, Campbell, Schwartz, & Sechrest, 1966) deals with assessing attitudes by other than testing and interviewing techniques. In retrospect, all the 1950 survey [by Campbell] covered was testing, requiring the cooperation of the respondents either for the true purpose or for some ulterior reason. It is this reliance on cooperation that makes testing particularly vulnerable to distortion and by the same token makes the deception in indirect testing appear more blatantly exploitative.

In our concern with testing as opposed to assessment in general, we shall elaborate on three dichotomies defining types of tests and refer the reader to Webb et al. (1966) for a fuller discussion of the nontest procedures of attitude measurement. The questionable status of some supposedly indirect tests has led us to include them in our discussion, with the observation that they might better be classified as direct. If there is enough disagreement over the indirectness of some of these measures, it might be wiser to consider these classifications also to represent continua rather than dichotomies.

1. Indirect Versus Direct. In the direct test the respondent's understanding of the purpose of the test and the psychologist's understanding are in agreement. Were the respondent to read the psychologist's report of the test results, none of the topics introduced would surprise him. This is obvious in an achievement test given at the end of a course. It is equally evident for the typical public opinion poll. It is probably so for the usual preference tests and adjustment inventories. With some direct attitude questionnaires, it is true, the respondent might be surprised to find himself labeled a "segregationist" if he thought of himself as a "moderate." He might not have anticipated the extremity of his score, but he was probably quite aware of the content and direction of scoring.

In the indirect test the investigator interprets the responses in terms of dimensions and categories different from those held in mind by the respondent while answering. If a person tells stories to pictures under the belief that his thematic creativity is being measured and the psychologist then interprets the products as depth projections, the test is indirect. If a person judges the logical validity of statements and his responses are scored for race prejudice, the test is indirect. If he thinks his memory powers are being tested while his behavior is interpreted by the investigator in terms of attitudes toward Russia, the test is indirect. In general, whenever responses are taken as symptoms rather than as literal information, the test is indirect.

Characteristic of the indirect test is a facade. By this is meant a false assignment to the respondent that distracts him from recognizing the test's true purpose and that provides him with a plausible reason for cooperating. Initially the TAT had such a facade: "This is a test of your creative imagination." The objective test facade is used in an important class of indirect tests of social attitudes, wherein the respondent tries to show his knowledge of current events and is scored for the bias he shows in the directionality of his errors. The expression of aesthetic taste, estimates of public opinion, judgments of moral right and wrong, and judgments of logical consistency all have been used as facades.

2. Voluntary Versus Objective. In the voluntary test the respondent is given to understand that any answer is acceptable, and that there is no external criterion of correctness against which the answers will be evaluated. One is encouraged in idiosyncrasy and self-description. The test assignment may state "this is not a test of your ability," or "there are no right or wrong answers," or "answer in terms of how you really feel." In contrast, in an objective test the person is told, either explicitly or implicitly, that there is a correct external answer, for which the individual should search in selecting an answer. The concepts of accuracy and error are in the respondent's mind. One is describing the external, objective world, although in doing so is inevitably reflecting one's own idiosyncratic view of that world, and can be unselfconsciously "projecting." When the facade succeeds, the respondents believe that they are describing reality, speaking of facts and judgments that are verifiable. They exhibit a phenomenal absolutism, a conviction that what they say reflects the way things are. It does not occur to them that they are projecting instead their view of the world, their hopes and fears, their prejudices and beliefs. This absolutism is a product of the respondent's having taken such so-called objective tests in the past plus his belief in the tester's honesty. If either of these ingredients is lacking, the disguise may be shattered.

3. Free-Response Versus Structured. This dichotomy is already well established in the classification of personality and attitude testing procedures. The free-response format has the advantage of not suggesting answers or alternatives to the respondent. It neither limits nor artificially expands the range of possibilities. Projective tests have typically employed free, open-ended formats that enable the respondents to create their own organization and view of the world. Multiple choice TATs or Rorschachs, on the other hand, may impose a set of alternatives that the respondents would never have volunteered if left to their own devices. Structured formats are more frequently found with objective tests and have the advantage of a single uniform scoring system. They were typical of the personality and attitude measurement devices of the first flowering of such tests in the period from 1920 to 1935 and hence provide the tradition against which both the projective test movement and modern survey research techniques revolted.

The four indirect test types that emerge from the above dichotomies and around which we have organized our survey are as follows:

1. Voluntary free-response
2. Voluntary structured
3. Objective free-response
4. Objective structured

Voluntary, Free-Response

This category includes the classic projective techniques that capitalize on ambiguous stimuli and require the respondent to employ his own imagination to provide structure. Most of these tests were designed for clinical use but have found extensive application in the testing of social attitudes as well.

Approaches Based on the Thematic Apperception Test (TAT). Storytelling tasks such as the TAT are particularly useful in studying prejudice among children. For them the assignment is a familiar one and the facade and indirection are easily maintained. Vaughan and Thompson (1961) reported the successful development of a set of matched TAT-type cards to study the attitudes of white New Zealand children toward Maoris. The cards of each pair were identical except for the crucial figure, which was either Maori or white. Stories told by the children revealed a significant rise in unfavorable attitudes between the ages of 8 and 12 years. An earlier investigation (Johnson, 1949) also reports the successful study of Anglo-Spanish attitudes with a specially designed series of pictures. Johnson used six carefully selected conflict situations that were duplicated in three forms: with all Anglo characters (for use with English-American children); with all Spanish characters (for use with Spanish children); and with mixed Anglo-Spanish characters (for use with both groups). Attitudes were assessed by contrasting responses to identical situations when they involved Anglo-Spanish conflict and when depicted by their own group members only. Quantification was achieved by having two judges categorize individual responses on a number of dimensions. Reliability coefficients for six subgroups were over .90.

Rather than compare responses to pictures that were matched for scenes but differed on the race of the crucial figure, Radke, Trager, and Davis (1949) compared the responses of children to Barrier and Non-Barrier pictures in their Social Episodes Test. In the former, one child of a different race watched the others play, and in the latter all of the children were pictured playing together. Stories told in response to the Barrier picture referred to the social disadvantage of being black and contained expectations of being rejected. It should be noted that the Barrier pictures emphasized black minority group status by depicting one black child among many whites and there was no complementary set of pictures in which a white child stood outside the group. The interpretation would be more convincing if there had been this control.

Among projective tests of attitudes of adults, the most widely cited in previous surveys of the literature (Cook & Selltiz, 1964; Deri, Dinnerstein, Harding, & Pepitone, 1948; Krech & Crutchfield, 1948; McNemar, 1946; Williams, 1947) is that of Proshansky (1943). He intermingled ambiguous pictures of labor situations with the more usual TAT scenes. The pictures were presented to a group by means of slides, with instructions to write for 2½ minutes on what the slide represented. Each slide was shown for only 5 seconds. Proshansky found that ratings made from the resulting descriptions correlated .77 and .67 with a direct verbal scale of attitudes toward labor.

In examining attitudes toward blacks, other researchers such as Neel and Neel (1953) and Riddleberger and Motz (1957) added more structure to the tests. They asked their respondents such questions as, "Who are the people in the picture? What has led up to or caused this situation? How do the people in the picture feel about what is happening?" or "How might these people have met? What two words would you use to describe this person?"

Specially designed Thematic Apperception pictures were also used by Frenkel-Brunswik, Levinson, and Sanford (1947) in their extensive study of the personality correlates of prejudice. In this research the purpose was not so much to measure prejudice as to get a more detailed and qualitative picture of its expression. The complicated interrelationships they found qualify the use of such pictures as attitude measuring instruments. For example, many prejudiced women told warmer and more sympathetic stories to a picture of an elderly black woman than they did to pictures of an elderly white woman (Frenkel-Brunswik & Reichert, 1946-1947). While such a finding is consistent with personality theory, it points to the danger of an oversimplified one-to-one interpretation of such material. Problems of interpreting such projective data have been discussed at length by Campbell, Miller, Lubetsky, and O'Connell (1964).

Other problems related to the use and interpretation of the TAT have been investigated in a multitrait-multimethod approach to the study of attitudes toward authority (Burwen & Campbell, 1957). The reliability of the TAT, although low, compared favorably with the reliability coefficients of several other measures. The authority measures of the TAT had a reliability of .55, compared with .46 for a photo judging task, .56 for an autobiographical inventory, .59 for a direct attitude questionnaire, .75 for a sociometric questionnaire, and .24 for an adjective checklist. Technically, the study might better be called "multi-target" rather than multitrait. Favorable and unfavorable attitudes were studied toward generalized and specific familial and institutional superiors and subordinates. When "multitarget"-monomethod and monotarget-multimethod comparisons were made, the TAT appeared to be a victim of its own apparatus. Whereas the TAT responses to a symbolic authority correlated .49 with TAT responses to a symbolic peer, the correlation between TAT responses to symbolic authority and responses on other instruments to boss or father ranged from only .03 to .14. This warns that any attempts to use TAT-type tests should include not only other methods in order to establish the validity of a construct but also other attitudes in order to reveal the role of factors that are peculiar to that method. The correlation between two different measures of a single attitude should be not only significantly greater than zero but also significantly greater than the correlation between two different attitudes measured by a single method. In the language of Campbell and Fiske (1959), it is necessary to demonstrate not only the "convergent validity" of a construct but also its "discriminant validity." Before introducing a new concept or construct, in other words, one must demonstrate that it is indeed new and different. If, as in Burwen and Campbell's (1957) study, the TAT scores for authority and peer figures are more similar than are the scores for authority figures obtained from a TAT and a direct attitude survey, there is no justification for speaking of a generalized attitude toward authority.

The use of matched pairs of TAT cards is one step in the direction of meeting these requirements. If only one set of cards were shown, in which the critical figure was always black, for instance, it would be impossible to distinguish between responses that reveal hostility in general and responses that express race prejudice. Direct tests are also susceptible to such confounding (Sullivan & Adelson, 1954). Using matched pairs of cards amounts to the study of two attitudinal objects, or two traits. What remains to be done is the introduction of other methods as well.

Problems of another sort beset the projective tester who tries to use TAT-type materials in cross-cultural research. These problems have been treated extensively by Kaplan (1961a, 1961b), Atkinson (1958), Lindzey (1961), and Doob (1965; personal communication, 1968). There are many cross-cultural studies that have attempted to correct the cultural inappropriateness of the standard TAT pictures by using pictures appropriate to the specific culture. However, when these are then used in cross-cultural comparisons, it becomes equivocal whether the differences are due to differences in pictures or to the differences in culture.

Approaches Utilizing Doll Play Techniques. Because of their naturalness and self-sustaining interest, doll play techniques would appear to be a useful method of testing attitudes in children. Arnold Meier (College Study in Intergroup Relations, 1948) developed the "What Would You Do?" test in which cardboard dolls depicting white and minority group children are manipulated on background scenes of the home or school. Hartley and Schwartz (1948) manipulated the symbols and characteristics of the background rather than the appearance of the dolls in study of children's attitudes toward different religious groups. Identical sets of family dolls were employed against backgrounds containing symbols from the Jewish religion, Catholic religion, or no religion. The results indicated that children are able to identify the religious symbols with considerable accuracy and that their play reflects intergroup attitudes in a meaningful way. A similar approach called the "Movie Story Game" (Evans & Chein, 1948) measured not only the spatial patterning of black and white dolls but also the child's verbalizations when asked periodically what the identified doll would say. The results indicated effective disguise and general meaningfulness for the test.

Doll play techniques are by no means limited to use with children. As early as 1940, Dubin utilized toys to assess the attitudes of 10 adult respondents. He asked them to "construct on this table a dramatic scene or scenes of the world as you see it today" and later "make a dramatic scene or scenes of the world as you would like it to be." Utilizing these data, three judges were able to estimate answers on 21 direct attitude questions dealing with labor, blacks, internationalism, and so forth, with an average rank order correlation of .49. There was no evidence presented to support the discriminant validity of these attitudes.

A technique that has more modest aims but perhaps more rigorous measurement possibilities has been developed by Kuethe (1962a, 1962b, 1964). To test the feasibility of the method, Kuethe and Stricker (1963) studied the social schemata of male and female undergraduates by instructing them to place the following sets of figures on a felt field: two men and two women; two men and one woman; one man, one woman, and two rectangles; and so on. These sets were given separately in random order and after each was placed in the field the placement was measured with a ruler, the set removed, and the next set given. Both male and female respondents generally paired the man and woman figures rather than grouping them separately by sex. Ninety percent of the female and 91% of the male respondents placed the man and woman figures side by side and did not allow the rectangles to intervene. The difference between male and female respondents was revealed by the males generally forming one group of alternating man and woman figures and the females forming separate man-woman pairs or subgroups. This was predicted by the authors and presumably reflected the marriage orientation of the female respondents.

Evidence for the validity of the felt board tests comes from a second study by Kuethe (1964) that measured prejudice and aggression. In the first task 74 male undergraduates were given three groups of felt figures consisting of two black and two white men; two black men and one white woman; one white man, one white woman, and one black man. The respondents were instructed to place each set on a blue field in any manner they wished. The resultant organizations were classified in terms of whether black and white were subgrouped apart or grouped together with the figures alternating by color. A comparison of integrated and segregated groupings with the respondents' scores on the Negro subscale of the Ethnocentrism scale yielded a significant chi square. The validity of the test as a measure of aggression was similarly established.

Modifications of the Rosenzweig Picture Frustration Test. Rather than require persons to supply behavioral repertoires for a test character, this test requests them to fill in the dialogue in a series of cartoon drawings involving face-to-face intergroup contacts (Brown, 1947). This technique has been adapted by several investigators for use in studying social attitudes (Reynolds, 1949; Sanford, 1950; Sanford & Rosenstock, 1952). Sanford (1950) presented his respondents with scenes such as an auto accident with one man saying to the other, "It was all your fault." The respondents' replies to the cartoon character enabled judges to predict their approximate scores on the Authoritarianism-Equalitarianism test. Sanford recommended the use of such projective devices in door-to-door interviewing.

Sommer (1954) tested the susceptibility of the cartoon technique to censorship and distortion by trying to detect deliberate distortions. He employed

10 drawings with ambiguous quotations and asked the respondents to fill in the dialogue for the black individual. Following this a Likert-type scale was administered. One group of 18 respondents was given additional instructions—to try to distort their dialogue answers so as to appear very liberal and unprejudiced, but they were asked to answer the Likert scale honestly. Sommer selected the top and bottom quintiles from the Likert scores plus the 18 who distorted their answers and then tried to predict the respondent's Likert scale position by examining his dialogue responses. He was able to detect 12 of the deliberate distortions and among the rest he correctly predicted 85% of the Likert scale positions. These findings suggest that if persons do attempt to disguise their answers on such projective tests, their answers can be detected if the tester so desires.

Another variation on this technique that probably belongs within the limits of this category is the study by Fromme (1941). He presented to the respondents five political cartoons, each with four alternative captions, covering a wide range of pro and con opinion. The respondent was asked to pick the best caption, and this choice, plus the discussion resulting, was utilized in a qualitative analysis of attitude structure.

Sentence Completion Tests. These are perhaps the least disguised of the indirect measures since little effort is made to deceive in the majority of cases. Most stems make direct reference to the attitudinal object and thus make obvious the tester's intent. Occasionally neutral items may be interspersed among the critical items as in a modification of Rotter's test (Rotter & Willerman, 1947) used by Shirley Wilcox Brown at the Ohio State University. Examples of relevant and neutral items are as follows:

1. I feel . . .
2. Skin color . . .
3. I hate . . .
4. Maybe . . .
5. Some lynchings . . .
6. The K. K. K. . . .
7. It seems to me that segregation . . .
15. Negro body odor . . .
37. Racial intermarriage . . .

Even in this test, however, no effort is made to conceal its purpose. With instructions that ask the subject to "express your real feelings," without providing any other plausible assignment, he is not likely to miss the purpose of the test even if critical items are embedded among neutral ones.

Another twist to the sentence completion notion avoids all mention of minority groups but provides stereotypic statements that may be completed with names of various minority groups or others (Frenkel-Brunswik, Jones, Rokeach, Jarvik, & Campbell, 1946-1947). Examples of items are:

1. Are there some people who are mean? WHAT PEOPLE?
2. It would be better if more of a certain type of people were allowed to come into the United States. WHAT PEOPLE?
3. Some people are poor and it is their own fault. WHAT PEOPLE?

This test elicited mention of foreign and minority groups from about one third of the children to whom it was administered. From another third or so came one or more antiprejudice statements. A portion of the students made no responses classifiable in either way and were thus not effectively evaluated. Using a net score (subtracting antiprejudice responses from the total of prejudiced ones) corrected reliability figures ran around .6 to .8 and correlations with a highly reliable direct test were on the order of .5. The approach is most satisfactory for the comparison of groups of respondents, and for the evaluation of the relative salience and extremeness of attitudes toward different minority groups. In addition, unique data on the uniformity of stereotyping were provided.

As long as the task is presented in a voluntary framework, it is not too different from any free-response questionnaire on attitudes. Compare, for example, Zeligs's (1937) approach in which school children were asked to "write the most interesting true sentence" they know about each group within a one-minute limit. A different set of instructions, however, could perhaps impart a degree of disguise. Getzels and Walsh (1958) used a third-person sentence completion task and presented it as a test of verbal speed. To compare public and private racial attitudes, for instance, they used the following two items: "If Negroes began being admitted to the club, Bill . . ." and, "If Negroes began being admitted to the club, I . . ." The latter item conformed more to socially desirable answers. This finding, plus the observation by Hanfmann and Getzels (1953) that in retrospect their subjects admitted that the third-person completions referred to themselves, would argue in favor of discarding the first-person stems in order to achieve a greater degree of disguise. Cook (1968), however, reports that although answers to first-person stems do conform more to socially accepted patterns, the eta coefficients for the first-person completions were slightly higher than those for the third-person stems.

In a multitrait-multimethod study of attitudes in a prison population Maher, Watt, and Campbell (1960) compared a relatively thinly disguised sentence completion test with a direct structured attitude scale on attitudes toward family and law. The validity coefficients showed the two tests to be mutually validating, with values of .50 and .51 for the two attitudes studied. In terms of discriminant validity, these values were distinctly higher than the heterotrait-heteromethod values, and methods factors were surprisingly low. Biserial correlations of the test scores with crime committed, however, showed the direct test to be slightly superior, although the difference was not great. The finding that both methods produced the same pattern of correlation with crimes was also regarded as mutually validating.

The virtue of this entire category of voluntary free-response tests lies not so much in their indirection, which is doubtful in many instances, but rather in their freedom. Although the tester does not label the test as an attitude measure, his invitation to the respondent to answer in any way he sees fit the obviously "loaded" questions may be interpreted by the respondent in many ways. While some of the persons may complete their assignments unaware of the experimenter's interest, in a tense situation one could hardly expect to get unconscious or uncensored expressions from unwilling or suspicious respondents. It is, then, the voluntary quality of the responses that leaves open the way for the respondent to question the tester's purpose and to suspect the worst. And it is the freedom of the answers that provides the opportunity for noting novel attitude dimensions unanticipated by the author and justifies the use of these projective techniques.

Voluntary Structured

In light of the evaluation of projective techniques offered in the preceding section, this category would seem to suffer from the faults of voluntary tests without the benefit of free responses. The picture is not entirely bleak, however, for there is considerable leeway for persons to respond voluntarily with-

out their sensing the test as a direct probe, and there are advantages to the unambiguous character of structured responses.

Semantic Differential Techniques. Perhaps the most frequently used innovation in attitude measurement since the 1950 review has been the "semantic
differential." In most cases the semantic differential rating scales are applied
directly to the attitude object, and analyzed in terms of total scores on the
evaluative component. We shall not review this voluminous literature, classifying it as direct attitude measurement, the modern substitute for Remmers's
(1934, 1954; Remmers & Silance, 1934) generalized attitude scales, a set of
items ready for use with regard to any attitude topic.

Even in such instances, the semantic differential probably achieves some
minimum of indirection. Diab (1965) found that with semantic differential ratings of the concept of "Arab Unity" he could differentiate pro- and anti-unity
students with more success than could the Hovland-Sherif method of accepting or rejecting a series of statements about Arab unity. He contended that the
use of adjectival pairs evoked less conscious censorship than did the use of
complete sentences. When the stimuli are presented in such bald terms, however, for most purposes the test could be classified as direct. Persons who rated
Nixon and John Kennedy (Stricker, 1963) or "myself" and "my ideal self"
(Babbitt, 1962), for instance, were probably very aware of the intent of the investigators. Hicks (1967) also made no attempt to hide the object of investigation from his respondents who rated "Negro," "Peace Corps," and "Journalism" on 14 semantic rating scales. This unmasked form of testing did not suffer
from any pressures toward social desirability, however, since the correlation
between semantic differential scores for "Negro" and an indirect (Objective
Judgments) test of attitudes toward blacks was equal to the correlation for
"Peace Corps" (.47) and was greater than the correlation for "Journalism"
(.06). Hicks argued that the testing situation might have seemed sufficiently in-
nocuous to prevent distortion of answers. In the absence of convincing data to
show that the indirect "Objective" test was not also susceptible to distortion,
however, the interpretation is equivocal.

Perhaps the most indirect of the semantic differential approaches to studying racial attitudes is an investigation of the connotations of color names by
Williams (1964). His respondents were asked to rate the color names on 12 semantic scales with heavy loadings on the evaluation, potency, and activity fac-

tors. The experimenter made no reference to race but said instead that he was conducting a research project on colors. After the respondents rated each color, Williams analyzed the data by comparing the ratings given by white and black respondents to race-related colors (white, black, brown, yellow, red) and control colors (blue, green, purple, orange, gray). Using those two groups of respondents as criterion groups, he found an interesting interaction—Caucasians gave significantly higher "bad" scores to black and brown than did blacks.

In another attempt to achieve indirection with the semantic differential, Eisenman, Bernard, and Jannon (1966) had their respondents rank 10 Rorschach cards according to the degree to which they symbolize God. Then they rated each card on six benevolence and six potency scales. Just as Williams assumed that in rating the word *black* his respondents were rating something akin to the concept of "Negro," so Eisenman et al. presumed that when respondents rated the cards on the semantic differential they were rating some aspect of "God." The results showed the cards rated most like God were also rated most benevolent and least potent, with a significant negative correlation between the benevolence and potency scores (rho = −.51).

Other Semantic and Word Choice Techniques. In a modification of the free-association technique, Havron, Nordlie, and Cofer (1957) developed a binary choice test to measure religious and political-economic attitudes and to test radicalism-conservatism and authoritarianism-equalitarianism as well. The respondents were presented triplets of words and told to "Associate the stimulus word with the response word you find easiest to associate with it by drawing a line between the stimulus word and that response word." To maintain a degree of disguise, neutral items were interspersed among the attitudinally relevant triplets. The following are examples of the triplets employed:

            ethical
(a) Become
            forceful

            understand
(b) Law
            obedience

Test-retest reliability was .81 for 57 cases and .87 for 74 cases. Criterial correlations based on the Allport-Vernon study of values and a conservatism-radicalism opinionnaire for the religious-political items and for the radicalism-conservatism items were .81 and .42, respectively (both significant beyond the .01 level). For the authoritarianism-equalitarianism triplets, however, the correlation with the F-scale scores was only .18, which may be the result of a markedly skewed distribution of F-scale scores. There were not enough data reported to assess the discriminant validity of attitudinal traits.

Another variation on the word association technique was devised by Campbell and Shanan (1958) to study attitudes toward authority. Ostensibly, the aim of the task was to have Air Force cadets rate 50 photographs on an adjective checklist of 30 items. The variable of interest to the investigators was the coapplication of the word *strict* with two favorable (*loyal* and *intelligent*) and two unfavorable (*trouble-making* and *scheming*) adjectives. Coapplication was measured by tetrachoric correlations between absence of *strict* and presence or absence of a favorable or unfavorable adjective. Such coapplication was regarded as a functional measure of synonymity. Additional tests and reputational measures relevant to the dimension of authority showed no relationship to the connotative evaluations the word *strict*. The authors concluded that these findings pointed to the invalidity of the construct under examination and did not negate the merit of the semantic analysis.

Tests Involving Preferences for Pictures and Objects. These studies, like many already discussed, depend upon the demonstration of a judgment differential of which the respondent is presumably unaware. They are voluntary insofar as judgments are required in situations wherein there is no "objective" right answer. At the same time they retain the advantage of having the respondent (a) work on a task presumably less threatening than the experimenter's primary problem, and (b) report upon external values or realities, rather than upon himself directly.

Murphy and Likert, in *Public Opinion and the Individual* (1937), utilized a wealth of techniques that anticipated the projective testing movement. Among these was the "Ratings From Photographs." Following the general framework of Rice's classic study on stereotypes, they provided labeled pictures of a union president, a railroad magnate, a pacifist, and a black civil rights champion. Respondents were asked to judge from these labeled photographs the character of the pictured person, in terms of courage, selfishness, intelligence, conceit, sympathy, practicality, and sentimentality. Contrary to expectation, they found no relationship between attitudes, as measured in a variety of paper-and-pencil tests, and these picture ratings. Such a test could be made "objective" by using a label such as "social intelligence test" or the like.

Hsü (1949) had three female graduate students sort photographs of males for handsomeness, and 10 days later for judged membership in the Communist party. The correlations were negative (−.50 and −.21) for the two women who were anticommunist, and positive (.51) for the one woman who was relatively procommunist. After reading a *Time* report on the blockade of Berlin, the correlations for sorts on a second set of photographs were negative for all three women.

Green and Stacey (1966) used a multiple-choice projective technique to study the self-images of a sample of London voters. They presented eight photographs of men and asked their respondents to indicate which of the men he would most like to be. Later each was asked to indicate which of the photos he thought were Conservative and which were Labor supporters. The judged affiliation of the respondent's most preferred photo was significantly related to the respondent's actual political affiliation. Although Green and Stacey used this technique for measuring the self-images of their respondents, it also offers possibilities for assessing likes and dislikes by comparing the judged affiliation of a photograph with the respondent's own affiliation.

Cook (1968) attached a photo of a black, a white, or a Japanese-American to one of a trio of personality descriptions. These descriptions had been shown in previous work with persons similar to be equally favorable (or unfavorable) when presented without photos. The personality descriptions were formed by varying the persons' occupation, sociability, dependability, and ambitiousness. In order to relieve the respondents of the notion that this was an attitude test, the instructions stressed the relevance of this task to many real-life situations where persons must be evaluated on the basis of such scant information. The subjects were thus motivated to perform well and their attention was focused on the personality descriptions rather than the physical features of the photos. They rated each photo with its accompanying description on semantic differential and social distance scales. Racial attitude scores were derived by taking the difference between ratings of matched white and black descriptions. These scores successfully differentiated members of attitudinal criterion groups ranging from strongly equalitarian to antiblack.

Tests Involving Miscellaneous Judgments. In Watson's (1925) "Moral Judgments" subtest, judgments of approval or disapproval are made about a variety of situations, sets of these situations being identical except for the specific persons or groups involved. For example, unwarranted search is made of a suspected "radical" headquarters on the one hand, while in a parallel item the same type of search is carried out on a business corporation suspected of dishonesty (Watson, 1925). Scoring is done on the basis of discrepancy of judgments between the parallel situations.

Similar in title and in plan to Watson's test was the ingenious approach to black-white attitudes devised by Seeman (1947). While he used equated comparison groups, the technique could be modified for diagnosing bias in individuals. He selected six items from a standard test of moral evaluations on marriage and sexual matters. To one group, the episode items were illustrated by pictures of white couples, to the other with black couples. Both groups were made up of white college students. Contrary to expectation, the judgments were more lenient—less disapproval—with the black illustrations. Furthermore, when the two groups were subclassified according to scores on the Likert scale of attitudes toward blacks, the major part of the differential was contributed by the more tolerant persons rather than the more antiblack persons in the two groups. The intolerant extremes in this sample were more consistent, less "biased." These results are important and meaningful, but further indicate the danger of oversimplified interpretations in indirect approaches.

Sherriffs's (1948) Intuition Questionnaire is an example of a test that could be presented with an objective facade but has been used to elicit voluntary judgments instead. His subjects were instructed to, "Give a probable explanation for the behavior indicated in each of the following excerpts from life stories taken from a random sample of the population. Include the motivation underlying the behavior and the origins of the motivation." If the subjects could be convinced that the tester had accurate information about the motivations and explanations for the behavior samples, this would qualify as an objective measure.

A variety of other judgments tests have found disappointingly low or insignificant correlations. The readiness with which judgments of literary merit can be manipulated by the substitution of fictitious authors has been demonstrated by Saadi and Farnsworth (1934) and Sherif (1935). Prestige seems to be one of those forces that can bias the performance on a judgmental task and therefore gives promise as a basis for inferring attitudes. Frenkel-Brunswik, Jones, et al. (1946-1947) tried to utilize the prestige effect to measure attitudes toward five minority groups. Instead of literary passages, proverbs or mottoes were used. The adage was attributed to the group as a whole, rather than to individual authors (e.g., "American pioneer saying" or "old Jewish motto"). Eighth- and ninth-grade students were asked to evaluate the quality of each motto separately—there being 10 mottoes attributed to each group. The test yielded a general prejudice score that correlated only .30 with a direct test. Scores on attitudes toward particular outgroups were worthless. It is quite possible that in the form given the task was trivial and the disguise thin.

As Wolff, Smith, and Murray (1934) have shown, reactions to group disparagement jokes are correlated with group membership. Gordon (1947) tried to utilize this phenomenon in the assessment of social attitudes. Twenty-four jokes, both antagonistic and sympathetic, dealing with blacks and Jews were rated as to their funniness on a 5-point scale. Five groups of college men were used: a Protestant fraternity, a Catholic fraternity, a black fraternity, a Jewish fraternity (non-Zionist), and a Zionist club. The groups differed in their responses to these jokes but not as anticipated in all instances. With regard to individual differences within the various groups, the ratings of the jokes showed no relationship to attitudes toward blacks or Jews as revealed in a direct attitude test or a test of symbol endorsement.

Employing a battery of materials that are more true to life than many projective tests, Campbell and Mehra (1958) had a group of Air Force cadets observe a sound film of community leaders discussing problems of juvenile delinquency and also had them read a transcript of Air Force officers discussing the reservists' curriculum. The subjects' task was to evaluate specific features of the leader's and group members' performance. The superior-subordinate orientation score looked to whether leaders' actions were evaluated more favorably than group members' reactions, or whether the leaders or group members were blamed for ineffectiveness. This score had a reliability of .45. The test failed to show expected correlations with a wide variety of other efforts to measure "superior-subordinate orientation." The general invalidity of measures in this study supports the notion that it may be a case of a nonexistent construct rather than a poor method.

Cook (1968) has reported promising results with a judgments test that involves predicting the relative effectiveness of alternative social policies. He constructed descriptions of alternative remedial programs for minority group progress and varied two factors—the degree of educational opportunity offered and the degree of legislative assurances for equal opportunity. Respondents were asked to predict the effectiveness of the various programs. The expectation was that antiblack persons would favor the black self-improvement programs and equalitarians would favor programs that stressed legislative controls. His results suggest that this may prove to be the case. Scores on the judgment measure correlated .61 with a previously validated self-report inventory based on preference between the two remedial programs.

A unique measure of social attitudes has been developed by Laughlin and Laughlin (1968) in their study of source effects in the judgment of social argot [phraseology peculiar to any class or group]. Ten expressions were selected from the jargon of pickpockets and Ozark mountaineers, such as "in the gales" and "misbobble." Each item was given one of four different definitions and attributed to either a Nobel prize-winning physicist, a deep sea diver, an organizer for the Black Panthers, or an underworld pickpocket. The following definitions of "misbobble" gave the flavor of the test:

> physicist: "failure of an experiment due to a careless oversight."
> diver: "unsuccessful dive due to faulty equipment."
> organizer: "failure at a rally to sway the audience, use of a poor tactic."
> pickpocket: "an unsuccessful attempt to fleece a victim."

The persons rated each item, as attributed to only one of the four sources, for its expressiveness, creativity, acceptability for adoption into the conversation of a learned person, and acceptability for adoption into formal communications such as speeches or journals. Analysis of variance of the ratings showed that for expressiveness there were no differences for the various sources—the pickpocket's use of "misbobble" was considered as expressive as the physicist's. On the other three scales, however, the source to whom the expression was attributed was a significant factor. Ratings for the physicist and diver were all significantly higher than those for the Black Panther and pickpocket, which did not differ from each other. It appears that persons consider the argot of a lower-status individual expressive, but are not willing to use it themselves. The failure to find a difference between ratings for the Black Panther and the pickpocket may have reflected the racial tensions of the period—summer 1967. The authors made no analyses of individual differences in their study but suggest that this may be a potential indirect measure of ethnic attitudes.

The failure of the majority of these tests to demonstrate clear differences between criterion groups of subjects or to correlate significantly with other measures of attitudes may be attributed to many different factors in the various studies. Campbell and Mehra's findings may be the result of testing a homogeneous population where individual differences would not appear. Frenkel-Brunswik et al.'s (1946-1947) low correlation may have been a function of the task, having little relevance to ethnic attitudes. In general it appears that finding judgment tests that are both indirect and relevant to the attitude under investigation is difficult. The tests requiring character judgments from photographs, for instance, and the "show me the prettiest" approach seem capable of differentiating persons with different attitudes, but they are so thinly disguised that one wonders whether they really qualify as indirect measures. Of the semantic and word choice tests, the semantic differential seems to be open to charges of being either too direct or bizarre a task to succeed as a disguised test. These negative evaluations are not intended to imply that work with voluntary structured tests is a fruitless endeavor. In general, however, the combination of voluntary judgments and a structured format militates against constructing a test that will be both disguised and relevant to the attitude in question.

Objective Tests—Free and Structured

The approaches that we will consider below differ from the above mentioned ones perhaps only in degree or in relative emphasis. Yet the distinction involved is important. The characteristics of these disguised, nonvoluntary tests can be stated in a number of different ways.

The respondent participates in an objective task in which he seeks right answers. The voluntarism of the usual projective technique is lacking. To the respondent the situation is similar to that of an achievement or ability test. All respondents have a common motivation in taking the test. All, we may assume, are seeking to perform adequately on the same objective task. Attention is focused on a common goal, oblique to the experimenter's purpose. Rather than capitalizing on freedom and lack of structuring, there is an attempt to diagnose attitudes from systematic bias in the performance of an objective task. The test may be highly structured (directly scorable) and still offer opportunity for the unconscious operation of bias to distort behavior in a systematic and diagnosable manner.

Here is a simple formula for constructing such a test. Find a task that all your respondents will take as objective and in which all will strive to do well. Stress the importance of accuracy and emphasize the fact that there are right and wrong answers. Make the task sufficiently difficult so that answers will not reflect differential knowledge on the part of the respondents. At the same time, tell the subjects that the test is admittedly hard and they may have to guess when they are in doubt. Load the test with content relevant to the attitude under study. Look for systematic error or for persistent selectivity of performance. If such be found, it seems an adequate basis for the inference of an attitude.

Objective Free-Response

These tests employ an objective facade by focusing the respondent's attention on the external world, but they allow him to supply his own answers or perceptions in an unstructured situation.

Auditory and Visual Interpretation Tasks. The oldest and most used of the projective tests in this category is the "Verbal Summator" or "Tautophone" (Grings, 1942). A recording of indistinct vowel sounds is presented with instructions such as, "This is a recording of a man talking. He is not speaking very plainly, but if you listen carefully you will be able to tell what he is saying. I'll play it over and over again, so that you can get it, but be sure to tell me as soon as you have an idea of what he is saying." To the authors' knowledge, this technique has been used only for personality assessment. It seems well suited to testing attitudes as well, however, and certainly qualifies as an objective test. The facade is almost always accepted without question and persons manage to produce intelligible verbal content without being aware that it comes entirely from themselves.

A visual variation of the Tautophone is Rechtschaffen and Mednick's (1955) Autokinetic Word Technique. In the normal autokinetic illusion, a single dot of light in an otherwise darkened room appears to move. The subjects were instructed that the light was spelling out words that they were to read and report. All of the respondents "saw" words, and when told about the nature of the experiment were shocked to learn that they themselves had fabricated the content. The test was totally unstructured and the answers were interpreted as personality indicators. The instructions could just as easily limit answers to some particular topic by telling the persons that the words related to communism or religion, and the answers could become diagnostic of attitudes.

A "phony language examination" developed by Nunnally and Husek (1958) offers possibilities for projective testing. Randomly chosen foreign words were scattered throughout English sentences and respondents were instructed to guess the meanings of the words and then decide whether they agreed or disagreed with the sentences. The authors were interested in the influence of sentence structure and the tendency for persons to accept or be suspicious of causal relations. This test could readily be converted into a test of social attitudes by introducing either foreign words or nonsense syllables into sentences that refer to the attitudinal object and asking for a translation of the foreign word. Under the guise of a "test of language ability" this could perhaps pass as an indirect attitude measure.

Tests Requiring Judgments of Behavior and Character. The assignment to judge the character of persons presented in photographs can also be presented as an objective task. Common statements in psychology texts as to the impossibility of making valid judgments of this kind may create a problem, although with a properly prepared set of materials (e.g., Campbell & Burwen, 1956) the phenomenological validity of the task is great enough so that even college students will accept it as a legitimate objective task. Campbell and Burwen employed five photographs of men and five of women from each of four age levels in an attempt to investigate trait judgments as a function of age and sex. The respondents, Air Force personnel, were led to believe that information on the personalities of the photographees had been collected prior to the experiment. The task was thus an apparently objective one. The subjects were told to judge the individuals from their pictures and their accuracy would be determined by comparing their judgments with the actual personality information. Responses were obtained on both a free-response format and a structured adjective check-list of 30 traits. Efforts to relate a differential favorableness to older males as opposed to younger males, or a differential favorableness to weak versus strong middle-aged males were so unrewarding as not to have been reported.

Examples of the objective free-response category are apparently hard to come by not because of the impossibility of devising suitable techniques, but rather because of the rarity with which projective tests are masqueraded as objective tasks with right and wrong answers. All that would be required to turn a TAT question such as, "How did the people in this picture meet?" into an objective test would be to inform the respondent that the tester knew how the persons had met. The voluntary character of the test would then vanish. There may, however, be an interaction between structuredness and apparent objectivity.

A conversion of voluntary tests into objective types would seem to be in the spirit of a movement to develop better disguised measures of social attitudes. Since the indirectness of a test is only as good as its facade, the aim must be to develop more convincing facades that focus the respondent's attention elsewhere. The guise of a test of creative imagination has the effect of focusing the respondent's attention upon himself, and in the process of wondering whether he is being sufficiently creative he may also begin to wonder how the tester will interpret his creative endeavors. The practice of "interpreting" a creative work, whether it be a short story, a poem, or a response to an ink blot is familiar to most persons. Thus, the respondent might not be terribly surprised to learn that the tester was really interested in measuring his attitudes toward minority groups. The objective facade is much less susceptible to such a cracking of the code, since the respondent's attention is focused on the external world and there is no popularized tradition of interpreting motives or prejudices from factual, right and wrong answers.

Objective Structured

While employing many of the same facades as the tests discussed in the previous section, these tests restrict the responses to a set of alternatives specified by the multiple choice format or by the tester's instructions.

Information Tests. The reader has probably commented at one time or another upon the inextricable interrelationship between people's attitudes and what they take to be facts. Newcomb (1946) has dramatically portrayed the nonrandom character of right and wrong answers on an information test in his study of "The Effect of Social Climate Upon Some Determinants of Information." He comments with regard to the difficult information items, "the direction of guessing is altogether likely to be weighted toward the subject's attitude. If this reasoning is correct, the . . . test tends to become itself an attitude test." Coffin (1941) and G. H. Smith (1947) have found beliefs of factual type statements to correlate highly with related attitude tests. This correlation is particularly interesting where the "facts" are difficult to ascertain. The relationship is then a result not only of selective exposure but also of selective "creation."

Hammond (1948) made perhaps the first deliberate effort to measure attitudes through biased guesses on an information test, measuring attitudes toward labor-management and Russia. His work is worthy of some detailed comment here. We have mentioned that not only guessing behavior but also differential patterns of information may be diagnostic of attitudes. Hammond eliminated the latter by the error choice technique, in which the respondent was forced to choose between two alternative answers, each of which was, by intent, equally wrong, but in opposite directions from the correct answer. Such items were: "average weekly wage of the war worker in 1945 was (1) $37, (2) $57" and "financial reports show that out of every dollar (1) 16¢, (2) 3¢ is profit." Scoring these information guesses as attitude items gave total scores on 20 such items that differentiated a labor union group from two business clubs with almost no overlap.

What we have here is an objective test situation (which could be made more so by using more alternatives and including a correct one) in which people's errors are not random, but systematic. The presence of biased performance clearly necessitates the influence of some underlying process, which we choose to call attitude. The claim for face validity on such a test might even be judged stronger than the claim that can be made for either the direct or unstructured test. Systematically biased performance in dealing with environmental actualities is an essential practical meaning of attitude.

Cattell and colleagues (Cattell, Heist, Heist, & Stewart, 1950; Cattell, Maxwell, Light, & Unger, 1949) attempted a large-scale exploration into the "objective" measurement of attitudes using a rationale very similar to the one presented here for nonvoluntary attitude tests. Two of the methods may be classified with information test approaches. A sample item from his "False Belief (Delusion)" measure reads: "During the war church attendance increased greatly and since V-J day it has: declined slightly; tended to increase still more; stayed at its high peak; returned to its pre-war level; fallen to its lowest since 1920." Applied to a religious attitude, 10 such items gave a Spearman-Brown reliability of .53 and correlated .33 with a paired-comparisons preference test and .10 with records kept of time and money expenditures.

In a study of the effects of pro- and anti-Kuomintang propaganda, Parrish (1948; Parrish & Campbell, 1953) used an information test, a public opinion estimate test, and a direct Likert scale. The following item appeared in the information test:

> Chiang Kai-shek and the Kuomintang gained control of China in 1927 by what means: (a) popular election, (b) representative election, (c) replacement of a deceased leader, (d) political party split, (e) armed revolution.

The alternatives were weighted in terms of pro-Kuomintang attitudes as: $a = 5$, $b = 4$, $c = 3$, $d = 2$, $e = 1$. Indicative of the presumptions involved in such tests, and of the differences between 1948 and 1968 in student attitude climates, is the assumption that "armed revolution" was the most unfavorable alternative. The direct test of attitudes demonstrated higher reliability than the other two—it yielded a Kuder-Richardson coefficient of .87 as compared with .57 for the information test and .50 for the public opinion test. Intercorrelations among the three tests averaged .47, .51, and .53, indicating that the two indirect tests shared as much with the direct test as with each other. The information test was superior in the degree to which it reflected propaganda differences, as evidenced by a point-biserial correlation between test scores and the type of propaganda (pro- versus anti-). Corrected for attenuation, this value was .71 for the information test compared with .54 and .59 for the other two. Since, however, the messages were communicated by way of particular information, this is not purely a validity feature.

Some practical applications of the information test format have been reported by Gatty and Hamje (1961) and Westfall, Boyd, and Campbell (1957). The latter investigated opinions about hot cereal by asking for estimates of the average cost of a bowl of hot cereal and several cold cereals, or for the estimates of the vitamin, protein, and caloric contents of hot and cold cereals. The heavy users of oatmeal believed it cheaper and more nutritious.

In view of the social desirability of appearing unprejudiced, an "objective" test of information about minority groups would appear particularly appropriate in place of direct questioning. An early form of such a test is reported in Rankin (1951) and Rankin and Campbell (1959) and was used in the unpublished master's thesis of Kremen (1949). These appeared to be bona fide information tests, but in fact the authors had not done the research to determine the right answer. With the assistance of Miss Florence Simon these beginnings were revised and expanded into a 50-item test with a specific right answer and a bibliographical source for each item. This was done both in order to backstop the facade and to make available actual data on the state of the respondents' information. Considerable unpublished research has been done with this test. Campbell, in 1951, collected data from 500 respondents at four universities, black and white, Northern and Southern.

In examining the "definition of the situation" or the stereotype of the person hostile to blacks, and the views held by those who are favorably disposed, it was felt that these eight paradigms, among others, are to be found:

1. Negroes are (are not) inferior, different, in a. intelligence, b. culture, c. physical traits, d. morality
2. Negroes do (do not) get a fair chance in America. a. restriction of social freedom, b. income differential, c. education, d. housing
3. Majority persons like myself are (are not) hostile toward Negroes.
4. Removal of segregation does not (does) improve the situation.
5. Negroes are (are not) threatening, dangerous, powerful.
6. Prejudice is (is not) and has (has not) always been with us.
7. Negroes do (do not) prefer segregation.
8. Miscegenation is (is not) bad.

All of these are essentially factual, or are "beliefs" rather than "valuations" in Myrdal's (1944) terms. In designing test items we were essentially spelling out these paradigms in more detailed form. Some items of fact may imply more than one paradigm. Where these are conflicting in implication, the item probably lacks diagnostic value.

The items were presented in both multiple-choice and free-response forms. The multiple-choice form of the test has a number of obvious advantages over the free-response form. Foremost among these is the ease of answering on the part of the test taker and the ease of scoring on the part of the research person. The disadvantages are in part peculiar to the purposes and content area of this particular study. First there is difficulty in selection of alternatives. If improperly selected, a large proportion of the respondents will concentrate their choices on some single alternative while some will receive no use. A correlated disadvantage of the fixed alternatives is that they provide a perspective for the persons taking the test or give some minimal information if, in fact, they do center around the correct answer and restrict themselves to popularly used items. The perspective or frame of reference thus provided could, in a test like this, have a propagandizing or educative effect upon some of the persons taking the test. Inasmuch as the popular range of expectation on many of the items will tend to be unfavorable to blacks, however, a test based upon fixed alternatives might have an undesirable effect upon the attitudes of the test taker. It is for these reasons that items requiring answers in percentage terms were given in free-response form.

Examples of some of the free-response and multiple-choice items are as follows:

> In 1948 what percentage of all persons arrested for drug violations were colored?

> Intelligence tests given to the soldiers during World War I indicated that the blacks of Ohio as compared to the whites of Kentucky tested on an average: (1) much lower, (2) slightly lower, (3) the same, (4) slightly higher, or (5) much higher.

Since the correct answers were included among the alternatives and were obtainable in the percentage estimates, two methods of weighting the answers were possible. A uniform weighting approach included the correct answers and gave them a weighting of zero, and the wrong answers on either side were given plus and minus weights in accordance with their distance and direction from the right answer. In the second item above, for instance, number four was the correct answer. Numbers one, two, and three would thus be weighted minus 3, minus 2, and minus 1, and answer number five would be weighted plus 1. For all practical purposes the correctness of the answer has been disregarded and it has been used just as the other alternatives. This would be a small matter if it were certain that everyone was guessing and that no one came into the test-taking situation sufficiently well informed to be able to pick out the correct answer on the basis of neutral objective information. It could also be justified, particularly for those items in which the correct answer is at one or another extreme, by the argument noted above that a person's attitudes may be diagnosed by the kinds of correct facts that he accumulates.

The alternative approach to scoring has been called the preponderance score. In this computation the items that a person scores correctly are disregarded for attitude diagnosis. Instead, the percentage of his error points in a problack or antiblack direction is computed. If we were to meet a test taker who was very well informed, we would have relatively few items on which to diagnose his attitudes. Nonetheless, we would use the few items on which he had made errors and study the preponderant direction of errors in this small sample. In the research done by Campbell these two scoring methods were compared by correlating the indirect test scores with a direct test. The correlations showed no consistent superiority of either method. The trend, however, was most strongly in favor of the uniform weighting approach. Of 28 comparisons available, the uniform approach was superior in 23. Thus, while the logical purist may very well continue to favor the preponderance method, and while it would be definitely preferable for studies based upon populations that had special training in this area, the statistical analysis would seem to favor the employment of the uniform method of scoring. The two methods of scoring correlated.

Several sets of data comparing the indirect information test with a direct test of racial attitudes seem to indicate that the direct test has higher validity as well as reliability. Kremen (1949) used an early version of the information test along with a direct test in an attempt to evaluate the effect of student role-playing of a discrimination episode upon attitudes toward blacks, using a multiple-choice information-type indirect test and a direct test. While neither test reflected the role-playing in mean scores, her findings have importance for attitude measurement, inasmuch as role-playing lowered the relationship between the direct and indirect test. The results from 10 sociology classes (five pairs in which the instructor and subject were the same) are presented below:

	Correlation Between Direct and Indirect Test				
Role-Playing Classes:	.39	.36	.20	.53	.38
Paired Control Classes:	.54	.70	.35	.58	.60

For all classes combined, the direct test had a reliability of .89, the indirect test .42 (Kuder-Richardson, Formula 14). The explanation of this phenomenon is not obvious from her data insofar as analyzed. She does not report reliability values separately for the 10 classes.

Where lie the faults and weaknesses of information tests as attitude measures? Are facts and attitudes indeed as unrelated as rational man would like to believe? The consistently lower reliabilities and validities of the information test when compared with direct tests might be taken as evidence of man's ability to maintain unbiased views of "reality" in spite of his personal prejudices and values. Or, they may reflect instead some confounding of the test scores with other irrelevancies and errors. One possible source of error lies in the seemingly nonmonotonic functions to which some items might give rise. The same answer to a given question might mean two different things to two different respondents. Underestimating the number of black students in American colleges, for instance, might mean that "black people don't have the ability to become doctors" or that "white society continually refuses to provide equal opportunity." By the same token, overestimating the proportion of black students receiving national awards could be the response of a poor white who feels threatened and feels that more than enough has been done in the way of programs for minority group progress, or could be the response of a middle class "liberal" and sponsor of civil rights legislation who believes that the programs must have accomplished something. Even if the full content of a respondent's thought could be ascertained, it is not clear that one view is pro-black and the other anti-black, one favorable and the other unfavorable. The view that "white society continually refuses to provide equal opportunity," for instance, could reflect condescension as well as a pro-black or favorable attitude. Thus, not only are the items likely to be nonmonotonic, but the dimensions along which the responses fall may be multiple.

Tests of Ability to Do Critical Thinking. The syllogism approach was anticipated by Goodwin Watson's *Measurement of Fair-Mindedness* published in 1925. By fair-mindedness, Watson seems to have meant something roughly equivalent to tolerance, critical thinking, or open-mindedness. His tests were designed to measure this trait, but in the process Watson recognized that the "errors" or lapses from fair-mindedness contained clues as to the biases or attitudes of the respondents, and a secondary "analytic" scoring was made in those terms. The Inference Test provided statements of fact followed by several conclusions that might be drawn, only one of which was logically justified, the others offering opportunities for the intrusion of personal biases in various directions. This test has been expanded in the Watson-Glazer Tests of Critical Thinking (Glazer, 1941) that could be scored for various prejudices although they have not been so used as far as the authors are aware. Gilbert (1941) also made use of the same technique in a study in which high school children were given hypothetical racial problems for which they could choose strictly logical conclusions or conclusions showing bias.

Morgan (1943, 1945; with Morton, 1944) developed an objective test that presented the same syllogisms in two forms—impersonal or abstract (e.g., "No A's are B's. Some C's are B's. From these statements it is logical to conclude: No C's are A's . . .") and with content ("A trustworthy man does not engage in deceitful acts. The bombing of Pearl Harbor by the Japanese was a deceitful act. From these statements it is logical to conclude: No Japanese are trustworthy. . . ."). By studying the shift in the popular response from the nonsense to the meaningful form, Morgan attempted to diagnose group attitudes.

Morton (1942), a student of Morgan, also compared the distortion of reasoning on abstract and concrete emotional materials. He varied not only the content of the syllogisms but also their form, paying particular attention to atmosphere effects. A concrete item with a particular-negative atmosphere is as follows:

Some large empires do not exploit the people under their control; since Japan is not a large empire:

1. Japan will exploit the people under her control
2. Japan may exploit the people under her control
3. Japan will not exploit the people under her control
4. Japan may not exploit the people under her control
5. None of the given conclusions seems to follow logically

This is an invalid syllogism, and its particular-negative atmosphere would lead a person to accept conclusion number 4. Most persons tended to answer, however, with number 1 or 2, and only one person said Japan would not exploit persons under her control. Morton concluded that persons reason differently when confronted with syllogisms phrased in abstract and concrete terms, and the direction of change is generally in accord with the popular opinion publicized by the press and radio. Lansdell (1946) utilized the same technique for studying covert attitudes toward marriage, attempting to apply it for the diagnosis of the attitudes of a single individual.

Several investigators have devised syllogisms tests in which no choice of conclusions is offered but rather the persons are required to judge the validity of the complete syllogism as stated (e.g., Feather, 1964; Janis & Frick, 1943; Thistlethwaite, 1950; Thouless, 1959). Thistlethwaite (1950) investigated a variety of attitudes in a test that contained syllogisms dealing with blacks, Jews, women, and various nationalistic themes. Embedding the critical items in a nest of neutral items probably facilitated the guise as a test of reasoning ability. His results supported the hypothesis that attitudes distort logical performance since he found that criterion groups of students from the North and South differed significantly in their performance. A weakness in his method, however, lay in the fact that all items were designed so that prejudiced persons would make more errors than the nonprejudiced. It would seem advisable to design items such that persons with pro and con attitudes would both make errors, though in opposite directions or on different items.

This rule was followed by Thouless (1959). He used items such as the following: "Slave labor was inefficient because of the lack of incentive to individual effort. Competitive civilizations have prospered because they have provided incentive to individual effort but under socialism such incentives would disappear. We see, therefore, that *socialism is a form of slavery.*" His subjects were instructed first to read only the underlined conclusion, ignoring the rest, and indicate whether they thought the conclusion alone was true or false. After this they read the entire argument for each and decided whether it was "sound" or "unsound," logical or not. Using both sound and unsound syllogisms for both pro- and anti-socialism statements, Thouless computed each person's score by obtaining the difference between the number of times he made an error in the direction of his prejudice and the number of times he erred in the opposite direction. With a sample of adult students, ranging in age from 23 to 58, he found 40% erroneous judgments, and of these 78% were in the predicted direction, yielding a chi-square of 24, which was significant beyond the .000001 level. With a sample of university students, however, there were only 10% erroneous judgments and the direction of those errors did not conform to the subjects' attitudinal biases. The failure of the syllogisms test to measure attitudes with this sample could perhaps be attributed to the higher education and intelligence of the university students, making them less susceptible to distortions in reasoning; or, as suggested by Thouless, they may have approached the test with greater suspicion and thus made conscious efforts to hide their views. These problems encountered by syllogisms tests will be discussed in greater detail below.

Feather (1964) also employed both valid and invalid pro- and anti-religion syllogisms and predicted that pro-religion persons would err more often in the direction of accepting invalid pro-religion statements and rejecting valid anti-religion statements, and that anti-religion respondents would err likewise on the two other types of items. Examples of his syllogisms are as follows:

> *Pro-religious valid:* People who are without religion are spiritually devoid and need the Christian teachings to show them the true way of life. Atheists and agnostics are people without religion and devoid of spiritual life. Therefore, atheists and agnostics need Christian teachings to show them the true way of life.

> *Pro-religious invalid:* A charitable and tolerant attitude towards mankind helps to bring people together in love and harmony. Christianity always helps to bring people together in love and harmony. Therefore, a consequence of Christianity is a charitable and tolerant attitude towards mankind.

His hypothesis was confirmed by his pro-religion respondents, who made significantly more pro- than anti-religion errors ($p = < .001$). But for the anti-re-ligion subjects there was no significant difference in the direction of their errors. Furthermore, whereas persons with strong pro-religion attitudes made more pro-religion errors than did persons with weak attitudes, the opposite was found for anti-religion respondents—the stronger their attitudes, the fewer their errors. These contradictions can be resolved by taking into account the critical abilities scores of both sets of subjects, as measured by their performance on neutral syllogisms. The anti-religion subjects had significantly higher critical ability scores than the pro-religion respondents, and the stronger their opinions against religion, the higher their critical abilities. These findings suggest that the usefulness of the syllogisms test as an indirect attitude test may be limited by such factors as education, training in logic, and general critical abilities. At one extreme, it is likely that an uneducated person might not even grasp the distinction between the logical soundness of an argument and its empirical validity. For him, the instructions to judge the soundness of an argument may be no different from asking him whether he agrees or disagrees with the conclusion. Under such conditions the test loses all disguise. If, on the other hand, the subjects possess a high degree of education and training, and can easily distinguish between the logical and descriptive truth of an argument, the test may again fail not because it lacks disguise but because it does not tap attitudes at all. In addition to the evidence from Thouless (1959) and Feather (1964), Shelley and Davis (1957) report that a class of logic students made fewer errors in judging the validity of syllogisms than did a control class.

If this analysis is correct it suggests an inverted U-shaped function relating the usefulness of the syllogisms test as an indirect attitude measure to the level of education of the respondents. For persons with very little training, the test measures attitudes, but it is hardly disguised; for persons with a great deal of education and training in logic, the test is neither a direct nor an indirect measure of attitudes because they make almost no errors. Only for the middle range of respondents, who know enough about the distinction between logical and descriptive truth to follow the instructions but who still make errors, is the test both an attitude measure and a disguised one at that.

Tests Employing Bias in Learning and Memory. The use of learning and recall errors in the diagnosis of individual attitudes epitomizes the disguised, structured, and nonvoluntary approach. Pioneers in the use of this technique are Horowitz and Horowitz (1938). In their study of the development of social attitudes among the children of a Southern community they invented a number of techniques. While designed to portray group differences, many of them should be appropriate to individual testing. Their Aussage Test involved exposing a complicated picture for two or three seconds, following which they tested for recall through a series of standardized deliberately leading questions. For example, the question "who is cleaning up the grounds" to Picture 10 brought answers referring to a nonexistent black in some 70% of the cases. To Picture 4 the misleading question "what is the colored man in the corner doing" brought a steadily increasing proportion (in reports from higher age groups) of menial activities for the nonexistent character.

Their Perception-Span Test involved a series of posters each having pictures of 10 items mounted upon it. These were exposed for 10 seconds and the children asked to "tell all the pictures you can remember." While there were difficulties with perseveration and blocking, some age group differences were noted, with the younger children failing to note blacks and the older ones showing a selective awareness for them. A Recall Test asking for the reproduction of 10 words used earlier in a word association test seemed also to indicate that in the younger years the word "Negro" was less well remembered than would be expected. The Pictorial Recognition Test, involving the recognition of faces previously viewed, finds the faces of whites more frequently recognized than the faces of blacks.

In a preliminary investigation Murray Jarvik (Frenkel-Brunswik et al., 1946-1947) attempted to utilize memory distortion as an indicator of attitudes. Sixth-, seventh-, and eighth-grade students were read 5-minute stories and then were asked to write down all they could remember of the story. The stories had simple dramatic plots but were full of confusing detail and omissions with regard to specific names, characteristics, and ethnic identities. Opportunity was given for memory distortion in the direction of common stereotypes. The results were essentially negative. However, motivation and literacy were both low in this sample of respondents. Using a similar method with a sample of college students, Alper and Korchin (1952) tested for recall of a letter about coeducation that was generally unflattering to women. Their male subjects recalled significantly more than the females did, and the females made more distortions in recall.

Cattell and colleagues (1949, 1950) utilized three techniques involving memory and learning biases. His test of "Immediate Memory" was based upon selective recall for attitude-relevant statements from sets of 12 presented at one-second intervals. In the total there were over 500 statements. Spearman-Brown reliability figures for 11 eleven attitudes ranged from .13 to .86, averaging .50. Correlations with other measures were essentially zero. In the scoring both "facilitating" and "frustrating" statements relative to the attitude were pooled. Cattell recommended that in future research these be separated. Taft (1954) did note the differential recall of favorable items from a passage about, "One of the greatest Negro baseball pitchers in America . . ." He read the story aloud to two groups of black and white boys and tested for immediate and delayed recall. On delayed recall, 3 days after the story, the blacks recalled favorable items best and the whites recalled unfavorable items best.

Cattell's "Distraction" method involved the exposure for 10 seconds of statements related to attitudes. Around the statement were scattered 12 or 13 nonsense syllables. Subjects were held responsible for recalling the statement and nonsense syllables. The original hypothesis was that the stronger the attitude the poorer the nonsense syllable learning because of distraction. Actually, the opposite effect was found. Contrary to these findings, however, Burtt (1942) found that greater distractibility was associated with stronger interest.

Another demonstration of the effect of attitude strength on memory has been reported by Doob (1953). On the first day of testing his subjects were given a questionnaire in which five paragraphs dealt with controversial subjects—advertising, religion, the Tennessee Valley Authority, the function of a liberal arts education, and war between the United States and Russia. Their task was merely to read the items and indicate their agreement or disagreement with the paragraph on a 5-point scale. Two days later the memory test was administered by reminding the respondents that, "The day before yesterday you read through some statements on various topics. In the space below, please LIST the topics you remember at this time." In addition, they were told "for each topic you have listed above, please recall as many of the arguments and ideas as you can which were advanced in the original statements." The results suggest that the quantity and quality of recall are determined by different factors. Quantity of recall was associated with attitude intensity: items with which persons fully agreed were recalled more than items with which they merely agreed, and a similar pattern appeared for disagreement. Quality of recall, on the other hand, was associated with congruence of attitudes and items: paragraphs with which the respondents agreed were recalled more accurately.

In addition to attitude intensity, the incentive provided for memory is another factor that must be considered in interpreting the results of tests of memory. Jones and Aneshansel (1956) instructed their pro-segregation subjects that they would be asked to provide counterarguments to pro-segregation statements later in the experiment. Under these conditions pro-segregation subjects learned the anti-segregation items better than anti-segregation subjects did. These results warn against applying a uniform rule of interpretation to such indirect attitude tests.

A third variable, the plausibility of the statements, also has complex effects upon learning and recall. Jones and Kohler (1958) report that persons learn plausible statements supporting their beliefs and implausible statements opposing their beliefs better than they learn implausible-favoring or plausible-opposing items. Attempts to use this as an indirect test of attitudes needs further confirmation, however.

It often happens that disconfirmation of a widely accepted hypothesis is regarded as failure rather than success. Witness the title used by Waly and Cook (1966), "Attitude as a Determinant of Learning and Memory: A Failure to Confirm." Since that "failure," there have been others (Brigham & Cook, 1969; Greenwald & Sakumura, 1967). These more recent experiments, which have both replicated the conditions used by Jones and Kohler (1958) and elaborated the design and number of conditions, report no relationship between attitude, plausibility, and memory. Greenwald and Sakumura (1967) suggest that another variable—information novelty—might be more facilitative than is covaluant information. An ironical extension of this suggestion, noted by Brigham and Cook (1969), predicts the opposite of the Jones-Kohler work—namely, that plausible-contravaluant or implausible-covaluant information may be more novel and thus more easily remembered. No explicit tests of this hypothesis have been made, but the contradictory and sometimes confusing outcomes of experiments in this area present a strong case for further testing.

Tests Employing Bias in Perception. Distortion in accordance with beliefs and attitudes has been demonstrated not only in memory but also in immediate visual perception. Binocular rivalry tests are an innovation in attitude testing that have found successful application in some settings. Bagby (1957) used a series of 10 stereogram slide pairs of similar scenes in Mexico and the United States. With both Mexican and American respondents he found that the person's own cultural content predominated in reports of what was seen. Pettigrew, Allport, and Barnett (1958) turned this into an index of racial attitudes. In a test that could be subtitled "nothing's either black or white but thinking makes it so," they presented pictures of four racial groups to respondents in South Africa. The four groups were African, Colored, Indian, and European. These terms for describing the races were the common parlance of these respondents. Because of the greater apprehensiveness of the Afrikaaner population, it was predicted that they would show either excessive vigilance or defense and report "white" or "black" more often than "colored" or "Indian." Their results confirmed this prediction—Afrikaaners reported seeing significantly more European and African faces whereas the English, Colored, Indian, and African respondents gave more "fusion" reports such as "Indian" and "Colored." This finding was "in line with the bifurcation hypothesis, i.e., highly involved subjects generally require a minimum number of categories and ignore small differences between stimuli" (p. 276).

Reynolds and Toch (1965) attempted to use similar binocular rivalry techniques by presenting biracial stereograms to an American sample. They expected unprejudiced persons to report more black-white fusions and prejudiced persons to experience more rivalry. In their first study they found no significant differences in the number of fusion and rivalry reports by high- and low-prejudice subjects. In a second study, using a liberal criterion of fusion, the results reached significance. Because of the strong constancy effects the authors felt the stereogram method was weak and inappropriate for demonstrating the effects of prejudice. It may be that tests of binocular fusion are particularly suited to a setting where "fusion" reports such as "Indian" or "Colored" are part of the vocabulary, as in South Africa. Doob (personal communication, 1968) reports that attempts to use binocular rivalry techniques in Jamaica were singularly unsuccessful, though the failure appeared to be due to faulty equipment.

A unique demonstration of errors in the perception of social objects is that of Kuethe (1962a, 1962b). He presented a pair of male and female figures placed 30 inches apart. After 5 seconds he removed the figures and instructed the respondents to replace them in the same locations. The next respondent viewed the figures as they had been placed by the previous person, and the procedure was repeated. The serial reproduction by 30 respondents showed a significant tendency for the male and female figures to be placed closer and closer, whereas a pair of rectangles was maintained at the original separation of 30 inches, without any systematic distortion. In the elaboration of this technique, Kuethe (1962a, 1962b) concluded that it was the specific content of the figures that determined both the direction and magnitude of the distortion. Two men facing away from each other were replaced with greater distance between them while two figures facing each other were replaced closer together. The distortion apparently occurs at the time of reconstruction rather than during the original perception or during retention, for when subjects viewed two rectangles and were then instructed to place male and female figures in the places where the rectangles had been, they showed the systematic errors associated with the man-woman schemata.

In contrast to the traditional social distance tests, this method approximates what could be called a "Social Distances of Third Persons" test. Like Getzels's third-person sentence completion stems, this task requires the respondent to guess or reconstruct the distance between two others, without being aware of his own contribution or intervention in the process. This method could be expanded to test other social schemata, by varying the racial, religious, or other characteristics of the figures.

Estimation of Group Opinion and Social Norms. As Travers (1941) and Wallen (1943) and others have demonstrated, there is a persistent correlation between a person's own attitude and his estimate of group opinion. While a few persons may perceive themselves as unrepresentative of the population and chronically underestimate the popularity of their own views, as in the sample of college professors studied by Lana (1964), the prevailing tendency is to overestimate the size of the group agreeing with oneself.

The technique is by no means entirely new. In 1929 Sweet, using a test designed by Goodwin Watson, found boys' estimates of group opinions valuable in diagnosing adjustment problems. Katz (1947), Murray and Morgan (1945), and Newcomb (1943) all used percentage estimates of group opinion, although some of their data are not reported in terms of the responses of individuals. It might be pointed out that the correlation involved in these studies is not necessarily to be interpreted as projection. In a group of any size, the respondent has an uneven acquaintanceship, and probably associates more with those having tastes like his own. Basing his estimates of group opinion upon his own experience in the group, his error may be in part a sampling bias as well as biased perception. Furthermore, the causal relation may be from belief about group opinion to formation of own attitude, as seen in bandwagon effects (see Lipset, Lazarsfeld, Barton, & Linz, 1954).

Parrish (1948, and Parrish & Campbell, 1953) used a public opinion estimate test with items dealing with United States opinion on China, the opinion of Americans with experience in China, and the opinions of the Chinese. Only the first type are directly comparable to the Travers and Wallen situation, and these did not fare very well in item analysis. An item from the public opinion test reads as follows: "In April, 1948, the Gallup Poll asked the American public the following question: 'Do you approve or disapprove of the U.S. giving the Chiang Kai-shek (Nationalist) government more military supplies, goods, and money?' What percent answered 'approve'? (a) 13 percent, (b) 28 percent, (c) 40 percent, (d) 56 percent, (e) 71 percent." The public opinion test had an average reliability of .50, compared with .87 for a Likert scale of attitudes toward the Kuomintang. The public opinion test correlated .51 with an information test of attitudes and .53 with the Likert scale.

A test of group opinion was used in a study of morale among submarine officers conducted by Campbell (1953, 1956). The respondents first completed an anonymous direct "Secret Ballot" test of ship morale. This was followed by an indirect test of group opinion with instructions that read,

> You and the other members of the ship's company have voted on the "Secret Ballot." Your job on this test is to guess the results on that ballot. We want your judgment or guess as to how your own ship voted and your guess as to how the whole squadron voted. . . . Some people are much better at this sort of thing than are others. It has been said that good leaders are better at knowing what the group thinks. This is one of the problems we are trying to study.

The results that follow compare the direct questionnaire and the estimates of own ship since estimates of squadron opinion correlated negatively with almost all critical measures.

	Direct	*Indirect*
Reputation for morale with other ships	.75	.49
Reputation for morale with squadron headquarters (officers)	.70	.37
Reputation for morale with squadron headquarters (enlisted)	.93	.71
Reenlistment rate	.26	.15
Total offenses	.39	.18
Strictness	.55	.44
Requests for transfer	−.19	−.56
Reputation for efficiency	.62	.45

Although the differences between the direct and indirect tests are not significant since the values are based on an N of 10 ships, the consistent superiority of the direct test leaves little room for doubting its relative strength over the public opinion test.

Test Involving Miscellaneous Abilities. Another of the tests in the Horowitzes' study (1938) was labeled the Categories Test. This test was modeled directly upon a typical intelligence test item. Five pictures were presented and the question was asked, "Which one does not belong?" As they adapted it, the item could be answered in more than one way, the choice presumably showing something about those social categories important for the child. For example, a page might contain pictures of three white boys, one white girl, and one black boy. In this instance, the child could use either sex or race as the dominant category. Other items provided opportunities to categorize by age and socioeconomic status as well. Hartley (1946) also used the categorization of photographs as a measure of ethnic salience. The task was presented in a voluntary framework, however, with instructions reading, "You can classify them on any basis you want to!" and as such could not qualify as a test of "abilities."

In the Murray and Morgan (1945) "Study of Sentiments," several of the indirect methods employ an ability test facade. The "Sentiments Examination" Section A, Part 1, asks for the "most descriptive adjectives" for 48 stimulus words, "the S [subject] being led to believe that the examiner is interested in testing the range of his vocabulary." In Part 3 "the S is led to believe his verbal ability is being tested with a simile completion test" (e.g., "As pathetic as a . . ."). In the "Arguments Completion Test" the respondent is asked to continue and finish an argument, the beginning of which has been described. "Being led to believe his powers of argumentation are being tested, the subject quickly becomes involved in the controversy he or she is inventing, and ends by exposing more of his own sentiments than he might otherwise have done" (pp. 58-60).

Cook (1968) has proposed several tests of classification and clustering that are analogous to the categories test though in different sensory modes. A verbal free recall test of a list of names of well-known persons could be presented as a test of memory. He suggests as an example a list containing the names of four baseball players, four musicians, four political figures, and four actors, with one name in each category referring to a black individual. The clustering in free recall would indicate which categories the respondent employs. And a test of auditory clustering could be devised using methods of dichotic listening.

A multiple-choice TAT test disguised with a facade that claims it is a test of detective abilities has also been used by Cook (1968). Each picture used in the test is presented in five stages, ranging from very little information in the initial stage to a complete (though still ambiguous) picture in the final stage. Respondents are told that detective skill is reflected in correctly diagnosing the situation as early as possible in the series of pictures. To reinforce this idea the test is speeded. Half of the pictures have white characters only; half contain black and whites. This permits the use of a difference score.

Each stage of each picture is accompanied by questions such as:

1. Are A and B friends? (a) Yes (b) No
2. (a) A and B planned to meet (b) A and B preferred not to meet

Cook's failure to obtain significant results with this test may be a function of insufficient disguise. With pictures of persons who differ only in racial features and with questions dealing exclusively with A and B's reactions to one another, the supposed detective nature of the task may not have been convincing.

A more successful demonstration of systematic bias in "abilities" has been reported by Clarke and Campbell (1955). The study dealt with the effect of the common stereotype of black intellectual inferiority on judgments of the academic achievements of specific blacks. In several integrated seventh- and eighth-grade classes, the students were asked to predict one another's test scores prior to objective examinations. Comparisons of predicted and obtained scores revealed a tendency for the white students to underestimate the scores of their black classmates. The mean standard score of the black students was −.78 while the mean standard score as estimated by the whites was −.97. This discrepancy in the predicted direction was significant at the .01 level.

Tests Involving Ability to Judge Character. As mentioned earlier in relation to free-response tests, the assignment to judge character can be given as an objective task. Such objectivity was approached in the "Faces Game," originally developed by Radke (Rose, 1948, pp. 50-51) and modified by Chein and Schreiber (Commission on Community Interrelations of the American Jewish Congress, 1947). In this test children were told, "Let's see how good you are at telling what people are like just by looking at their faces." Thirty-four sets of four pictures (two white and two black for all but four sets) were presented, each with questions such as "one of the girls in this row is very lazy and never bothers to do anything" or "one of the boys in this row is the best sport in his class; which one?" Two scores were provided: one the *white salience* score (the total mentions of white children for items either good or bad), and the other the *prejudice* score (the ratio of unfavorable choices of faces of the other group to total choices). The test produced significant individual and group differences, and showed retest reliabilities over a 6-month period of .50 and .36 for white and black children, respectively, on the prejudice score. For the white salience score the values were .32 and .16.

In another study (Radke & Trager, 1950) grade school children were asked to identify which of two houses the black and white dolls lived in, which houses the dolls preferred, and which set of clothing belonged to each doll. The choices were between a lower class and middle class house, and between servant's dress and street clothes. In another instance (Radke, Sutherland, & Rosenberg, 1950), they were asked to choose from a series of pictures to show which "is the smartest in the school," "which is very mean," and so forth. In both cases their choices reflected a comprehension of social differentiation and revealed prejudices and stereotypes with regard to blacks.

Tests Involving Miscellaneous Judgments. There is a fairly extensive literature on the effects of attitudes on ratings of the favorability of statements. Although most of these studies have not employed instructions that would encourage the subjects to believe that the test was tapping their attitudes, the testers have not taken care to put up an objective facade, either. In an exploration of a multitrait-multimethod matrix, Hicks (1967) did try to create an indirect test by asking subjects to rate the favorability or unfavorability of statements, with instructions reading, "Remember, we want your OBJECTIVE JUDGMENT about each statement as it stands." Three methods—a Likert scale, semantic differential, and the "objective" judgments—were used to measure three attitudes—toward blacks, the Peace Corps, and journalism. Corrected Spearman-Brown reliability coefficients were high for all three methods and three attitudes, ranging from .82 to .95, with no obvious differences for the different methods. In this case, then, the reliability of the indirect measure matched that of a direct test. The validity coefficients showed the semantic differential correlating higher with the Likert than with the indirect test, ranging from .53 to .69 in the former and .06 and .47 in the latter case. Hicks accounts for this difference by noting that the objective judgment instructions are incompatible with evaluative attitudinal responses, and to the extent that the objective judgments prevail, one would expect the correlation with another attitude measure to decline. A comparison of monomethod and monoattitude value also showed the Likert scale to be superior, yielding slightly less methods variance than the "objective" judgments. Hicks does not rule out the usefulness of this indirect test, however, since problems of social desirability might not have been operating strongly enough to make an indirect test particularly valuable.

There is a variation on the theme of making objective judgments of statements that Waly and Cook (1965) have found useful as an indirect attitude test. They had their respondents rate the plausibility of statements by instructing them as follows:

> We are interested in arguments for segregation and for integration to be used in the construction of a psychological test. . . . Imagine that you are judging a debate between two teams on the topic of segregation vs. integration. Acting as an impartial judge, you are to rate each argument presented by either side in terms of its effectiveness.

The subjects were presented with statements that prior ratings had shown were judged to range from clearly effective to clearly ineffective on both sides of the argument. The four types of statements were ineffective pro-segregation, effective pro-segregation, ineffective pro-integration, and effective pro-integration. The respondents also answered a self-report questionnaire that correlated significantly ($r = .84$) with the plausibility ratings. This approach was first used by Watson in his Arguments Test in 1925.

As with the syllogisms tests, it might be helpful to analyze the various interpretations that the subjects might make of the instructions. In a task that merely instructs persons to judge the "strength" of an argument, without specifying whether it is the logical or empirical truth or the linguistic eloquence that they are to judge, the results may be difficult to interpret since different subjects may perceive the assignment in different ways. Some might try to judge the elegance of the statements, or the descriptive truth of the premise, or the internal consistency of the argument, or the empirical truth of the intervening arguments. If they interpret the instructions to mean "tell me whether you agree or disagree with the conclusion" this amounts to no more than a direct attitude test. If, on the other hand, the subjects accept the assignment to rate the "effectiveness" of the statements much as a debate judge would do, then the various items must be matched for elegance and consistency so that the only variable that could determine the subject's answer would be the extent to which one's views agreed with the content of the argument.

Less objective in appearance and more in the tradition of the studies of attitudes as anchors, Ager and Dawes (1965) had their subjects perform a paired-comparisons task in which the pairs were statements about science that came from six categories of favorability in a previous ranking by other respondents. Instead of recording the relative ratings of favorability, however, the authors were interested in the error patterns (errors being defined as discrepancies from a consensus ordering of the statements obtained in a previous study). In line with the findings of Hovland and Sherif (1952; Sherif & Hovland, 1953), they predicted that persons would not only lump together the statements that were at the opposite pole from their own attitudes but would also be unable to discriminate among them. Thus, the number of errors should be a positive function of the distance of the judged categories from the subject's own position. A significant interaction of criterion groups by pairs of statements confirmed this prediction.

GENERAL CONSIDERATIONS AND CONCLUSIONS

The reliability coefficients reported for the indirect attitude tests reviewed here are probably among the highest of their kind, since they have passed through the selection processes of publication procedures. Still, they generally fall below the levels considered respectable, and where comparisons between direct and indirect tests are available, the latter clearly come out in second place. A comparison with direct tests might not be entirely appropriate, however, in light of what consistency on the two different measures signifies. It is highly probable that the desire to appear consistent, even on anonymous questionnaires, may inflate the reliability ratings for direct tests. Such self-conscious and possibly superficial consistency is hardly comparable with the unplanned systematic biases revealed in errors on an information test or in judgments of logical validity. It is, moreover, this unselfconscious consistency that is more in keeping with the notion of attitude and that gives vitality to current usage of the concept.

Validity of Indirect Tests. Indications of the validity of an instrument come in at least two general forms. One form consists of "validity correlations" of the instrument with criterial measures. The other—trans-situational validity—consists of evidence that the test produces the same results in a variety of circumstances and is not buffeted about by various irrelevant demands. The validity evidence of either form that is available for indirect tests is no more flattering than the evidence for direct attitude tests.

Two studies were conducted to compare the trans-situational validity of direct and indirect tests by subjecting them to anonymous or signed conditions. Kidder (1969) found that responses on a direct test of opinions about military training on campuses were unmoved by the normative demands of signing one's name or the informational demands of seeing how "other students" answered. An indirect test of "Knowledge About ROTC," on the other hand, was significantly influenced both by seeing how "others" answered and by an interaction of that variable with the demand of signing. The author concluded that persons were willing to present the same "self" under private and public conditions when the direct test asked for such presentations and the items were unambiguous and almost stereotypic. On a more ambiguous task, however, which required difficult estimations and reports about external facts, answers were skewed to conform to "others'" answers and signing increased the distortion.

Cook, Johnson, and Scott (1969) also found that of three instruments covering 14 attitude topics, the direct test and one of the indirect tests were not significantly affected by identified and anonymous conditions, while a second indirect test showed more counter-norm responses under anonymous than under identified answering. These results can be interpreted in two opposite fashions: (a) the counternorm responses represent the superior validity of the anonymous indirect test (as suggested by Cook et al.), or (b) the robustness of the direct test and the first indirect test reflect their superior trans-situational validity. This tie is broken at least partially by the criterial correlations of each test with friends' ratings of the respondents. The mean correlation of the direct self-report instrument was significantly greater than that of the two indirect tests. Validating tests by examining criterial correlations is often a delicate operation, however, as is described in the following sections.

Where comparisons of the criterial correlations of direct and disguised measures are available (e.g., Campbell, 1953, 1955; Campbell & Damarin, 1961; Green, 1954; Rankin & Campbell, 1959), the indirect test fails to reach the levels of the direct tests. In order to evaluate these findings, it might be helpful to delineate some of the factors involved in such criterial correlations to determine whether the direct and indirect tests are tapping different attitude universes or just different levels of the same universe.

The most obvious distinction between the direct and disguised measures is the extent to which they are sensitive to the operation of social norms. This distinction indeed provides the rationale for developing and using indirect measures. Indirect tests, it was hoped, would elude the respondent's censorial eye and be free from normative pressures. They were intended to reflect underlying processes that represent a person's "true" feelings, not distorted by concerns with social appearances. The notion that attitudes are found and expressed in misperception, in memory biases, in selective learning, in faulty logic, and in many other cognitive and behavioral processes is consistent with a theory of social attitudes developed by Campbell (1963). That theory contends that a host of seemingly unrelated terms such as acquired drive, belief, conditioned reflex, fixation, judgment, stereotype, and valence, to mention only a few, are all functionally synonymous with the concept of attitude. All describe the residues of past experience, which are the stuff of which attitudes are made. They are the underlying processes, or the behavioral manifestations of underlying processes, which are products of learning. In contrast to such "natural" manifestations of attitudes, the verbal reports obtained by direct attitude questionnaires may seem artificial and molded by social considerations. Rather than say what he honestly thinks and feels, a person may say what he thinks he ought to say or what he thinks the tester would like to hear. If these two types of measures are tapping different realms of attitudes, one characterized by norms and the other by processes, it might be reasonable to expect the validity criteria of the two to be drawn from similarly diverse realms. Reputational measures, then, would be classified in the "normative" category since they are also derived from behavior in social situations, and as such would be expected to correlate more highly with the direct tests. Similarly, the distinction between

Northern and Southern whites might involve a large "normative" component insofar as open expression of race prejudice is less sanctioned by the norms of colleges in the North than in the South.

If one were to search for suitable criterial measures for indirect tests, one might look for other measures that tap "processes," unencumbered by normative influences. Two indirect tests, in other words, should correlate more highly with each other than with a direct test. The few studies that have employed multiple indirect and direct methods have not substantiated this (e.g., Campbell, 1955; Hicks, 1967; Parrish & Campbell, 1953). Reasons for this failure may lie in the contamination of the indirect tests by other factors, not normative factors but irrelevant abilities or judgments. The syllogisms test, for instance, is influenced by education and training in logic; binocular rivalry tests contain constancy factors; and TAT measures have their own peculiar methods variance.

Perhaps this distinction between the operation of norms and processes, while useful, should not be so overdrawn. Rather than try to distinguish between two attitude realms—one overt and the other covert, one public and one private, one socially acceptable and the other taboo—it might be more useful to try to scale the various expressions of attitudes in terms of their different thresholds.

The notion of a hierarchy of responses with successively higher thresholds is familiar in the verbal learning tradition. If one considers the learning of paired associates, for instance, it is apparent that different tests will reveal different degrees of learning, depending upon the thresholds for the responses required by each. A hierarchy of tests with progressively lower thresholds is as follows (Campbell, 1963):

Recall
Recognition
Savings in relearning

Similarly, in diagnosing social attitudes, each test involves responses with different thresholds, such that one measure indicates the existence of an attitude under study while another seemingly denies it. A hierarchy of attitude tests might be as follows (Campbell, 1963):

1. Autonomic response
2. Verbal report on perceived character of the stimulus
   e.g., "The average I.Q. of blacks is lower than that of whites."
3. Verbal report on own response tendency
   e.g., "I would not let a black move onto my block."
4. Overt locomotor response
   e.g., refusing to serve black patrons

One could imagine situations in which some of the relations would be reversed. For instance a person might refrain from verbal expressions of prejudice but his overt behavior may go so far as refusing to rent his house to blacks, or organizing a parents' group to protest school desegregation. Whereas the hierarchy of tests for nonsocial behavior, such as paired-associate learning, is relatively stable, the ordering of thresholds for social behavior varies with the incentives and prohibitions of the moment.

If the concept of a hierarchy of tests with different thresholds is accurate, one would expect tests with similar thresholds to correlate more highly than those with different thresholds. In choosing criterial measures for validation, in other words, it is meaningless to say that one test has higher "validity" coefficients without considering the positions of the tests and criterial measures in such a hierarchy. A look at the various criterial measures that have been used in the literature reviewed here suggests that many of them occupy positions in the hierarchy that are closer to the direct than to the indirect measures. Reputational measures, for instance, are derived from social interaction and are more likely to share the thresholds of overt locomotor responses and verbal expressions of response tendencies than the thresholds of statements of belief.

The issue of comparative validity is not easily resolved. One might speak of a test as being a valid measure of something, but a reasonable question might be "valid for what?" The answer "for prediction" is a nonanswer unless one specifies what it is that the test is supposed to predict. Since we are considering social attitudes, it seems intuitively reasonable that the test would be used to predict social behavior. If this is the case, then the direct tests, which are influenced by normative factors and considerations of social desirability, are probably the more valid predictors. If, however, one were interested in studying stereotypes and ethnocentric belief systems, the indirect information tests may well be the more valid instruments.

From a less practical, more theoretical point of view, the concept of construct validity calls for correlation with as many dissimilar methods as possible rather than with one other related measure. Every measurement technique, be it direct or disguised, involves certain irrelevant factors that do not properly belong to the construct under consideration. Likert scales contain response biases, syllogisms tests tap logical abilities, and estimates of public opinion depend upon the respondent's perception of himself as belonging to the majority. The demonstration of construct validity requires that the correlation between two such different methods measuring the same trait be significantly greater than zero and also greater than the correlation between two different traits measured by the two different methods. The more dissimilar the different methods, the more impressive and convincing the validity coefficients are. Any construct that survives the triangulation of various irrelevancies of different tests has earned the name by which it goes. Indirect tests thus have an important role in such triangulation processes, since they involve different methods and irrelevancies.

Relation of Attitude Testing to Attitude Theory. The operational definition of an attitude, as evidenced by the requirements of reliability and reproducibility coefficients, is consistency of response to social objects. Spearman-Brown reliabilities, Kuder-Richardson coefficients, and Guttman's reproducibility coefficient all demand such consistency of response, and in order to qualify as an attitude scale, a test must meet this minimal requirement. Such consistency at a molecular level, among responses on a single instrument, finds a parallel at a molar level. Validity coefficients require consistency across measuring instruments and across modes of responding. This means that different modes of expression are intersubstitutable, as cosymptoms of the same underlying disposition to respond.

Evidence of response consistency is a requirement that is not peculiar to the study of social attitudes. It is the sine qua non of all studies of learning, the most elementary datum of psychology. Any test of a habit, a set, a preference, a cognitive map, or a motive requires evidence of a consistent tendency to respond. It is by no means coincidental that the experimental psychologist studying rat learning and the social psychologist studying attitudes should use similar criteria. They are both engaged in a diagnostic venture, trying to identify what has been learned.

Most contemporary attitude theorists would say that attitudes are learned, whether they conceive of them as dispositions to respond or to perceive or feel, or think. Operationally, in fact, it is impossible to distinguish between an attitude and a habit. This does not imply a narrowness of definition, however, but rather a breadth and scope that some readers might find unimaginable. Campbell (1963) has sought to demonstrate the functional synonymity of terms as diverse-sounding as *anticipation, cognitive structure, life space,* and *attitude.* All of these terms refer to the fact that something has changed, some residue has been left, as a function of past experience. They all represent attempts to identify some underlying process, though with slightly different connotations and concomitant slightly different methods of approach. A psychologist interested in life space may record the gross locomotor activity; another, interested in motives and intentions, may ask his respondents directly what they would do in certain situations; one interested in beliefs and stereotypes might pose direct questions or use indirect tests of "information," and so on. None of these methods is clearly superior to the others in tapping the true processes. No one of them is free of systematic irrelevancies that are of little interest to the student of social attitudes. It is rather their use in combination, in a triangulation of knowledge processes, that contributes most to the understanding of acquisition and expression of attitudes.

RECOMMENDATIONS FOR
THE USE OF INDIRECT TESTS

Suggestions for the use of indirect tests must be tempered by considerations of their efficacy as well as their ethical status. The ethical problems surrounding the application of disguised tests in administrative settings (see Weschler, 1951) may serve to inhibit the use of methods designed to probe those levels of feeling and belief that a person considers private. At the same time, the benefits obtained from the judicious use of these ingenious instruments encourage their further use and development in certain prescribed manners and areas.

Cautions Concerning Indirect Testing. There was a rumor circulating among labor leaders in the 1950s that came to the attention of one of the authors and that deserves mention here. The rumor had it that certain personnel managers were employing indirect tests of labor-management attitudes in order to identify persons with strong pro-labor sentiments and prevent them from entering the firm. A "Test of Your Information About Industry" might well seem like a reasonable entrance exam and could, if well written, deceive many an eager applicant. Feeling practically defenseless in the face of hidden weapons such as these, it is not surprising that union leaders should have protested. The potential power of such instruments threatens not only the privacy of a person's mind but also the security of his job. If there is resistance and resentment against the direct questions of census takers (e.g., do you have a flush toilet in your house?), it should come as no shock to an industrial psychologist or personnel manager that disguised tests would infuriate the unsuspecting job applicant or employee. Census data, at least until now, have not been used to discriminate against anyone in matters of hiring or promotion. And if employers began to use such direct data there would be little to prevent a person from answering in ways that would not jeopardize his chances. The plausible facades of indirect attitude tests effectively prohibit self-defense and permit testing in many administrative settings where attitude scores might otherwise be unobtainable.

If a psychologist has devised an instrument that permits such invasions of privacy to occur, does he/she not also share in the responsibility for its use? The authors venture to argue that one does, and that one might consider it part of one's ongoing research to investigate the applications of one's instruments.

The ethical problems that arise from administrative applications of indirect attitude tests do not disappear entirely in the pure research laboratory. Although no crucial decisions hinge upon a person's systematic errors on an information test or his stories told to TAT cards, the invasion of privacy and the use of deception may well arouse the anger of the respondent and raise ethical questions for the tester. Perhaps the only means of avoiding these problems while still obtaining the desired information is to guarantee absolute anonymity to the subjects.

Anonymity, although sounding like a well-defined condition in itself, comes in varying forms and degrees. Sampling the studies reviewed in this chapter reveals that most investigators made no reference to assuring their respondents of anonymity (e.g., Ager & Dawes, 1965; Alper & Korchin, 1952; Burwen, Campbell, & Kidd, 1956; Campbell & Damarin, 1961; Campbell & Shanan, 1958; Doob, 1953; Feather, 1964; Getzels & Walsh, 1958; Hammond,

1948; Hsü, 1949; Janis & Frick, 1943; Jones & Kohler, 1958; Kuethe, 1964; Newcomb, 1943; Proshansky, 1943; Rokeach, 1952: Shelley & Davis, 1957; Sherriffs, 1948; Sommer, 1954; Thistlethwaite, 1950; Waly & Cook, 1965). One pair of investigators tried to assure the participants of "practical" anonymity by telling them that even though they signed their names the information would not become part of their permanent records (Burwen & Campbell, 1957); and some guaranteed absolute anonymity by using unsigned tests (e.g., Himmelfarb, 1966; Jones & Aneshansel, 1956; Parrish & Campbell, 1953; Rankin & Campbell, 1959; Weschler, 1950; Williams, 1964).

We advocate using anonymous forms wherever possible. Some indirect tests might admittedly benefit from having subjects sign their names in the belief that their "information" scores will be taken seriously as measures of knowledge or ability. Some criterial correlations, as with reputational measures, might also require identifiable papers. Whenever the facade will not suffer from anonymity, however, and criterial measures can also be obtained, it would seem advisable to avoid identifying respondents and the concomitant criticism that indirect testing bears.

It might be pointed out that indirect assessment (e.g., Webb et al., 1966), unlike testing, does not encounter the same problems of deception and personal prying when it relies on group data, physical traces, and simple observation of public behavior. Many of these measures are anonymous of necessity, and others are part of the public domain of observable behavior and constitute no more an invasion of privacy than does one person's watching another (although even this may be considered a breach of good faith by some, e.g., Webb et al., 1966, p. vi).

CONTRIBUTIONS OF INDIRECT TESTING

If we find that anonymous data from indirect attitude tests suffice, may we not also be satisfied with unsigned direct attitude questionnaires? Moreover, if guaranteed anonymity reduces or eliminates distortion on direct tests, why bother with the oddball measures and uncertain gimmicks at all? Quite aside from the intrinsic rewards of creating and using an ingenious instrument, there are at least two benefits from indirect tests that, in the minds of the authors, justify their use.

Multitrait-Multimethod Matrices. This procedure for establishing construct validity by using at least two traits and two methods has been advocated elsewhere by Campbell and Fiske (1959). Briefly, the design requires that the correlation between two measures of a single trait be not only greater than zero but also greater than the correlation of two different traits measured by two different methods. In addition, it is desirable for that validity coefficient to be greater than the correlation between two different traits measured by a single method. The necessity for at least two traits and two methods derives from the imperfections and irrelevancies that inevitably adhere in any measurement effort. Single operations are thus better construed as approximations to knowledge rather than as definitions, and multiple operations are advocated in their stead. The interpretation of results obtained from any single measure is equivocal, for there is no way of distinguishing between variance contributed by the trait and variance attributable to the method. "Halo effects" and response sets are examples of methods factors that contaminate data and make interpretation problematic. They must be extracted as completely as possible in order to demonstrate the validity of the trait under study. Elimination of methods factors cannot be achieved by looking for a "pure" instrument, however, since none is perfect. Rather, we may take account of the imperfections and employ multiple measures with heterogeneous irrelevancies so that what is shared is not methods variance but the trait.

It is in this context that indirect tests, with their novel methods and heterogeneous irrelevancies, can contribute to the discovery of constructs. High correlations between widely different methods provide convincing evidence of the existence of a trait. Low correlations, however, may suggest one of several other alternatives. Neither method may measure the trait with any degree of precision. One method may fail to measure a particular trait but succeed in measuring another. Or both may be tapping different aspects of a trait, leading to theoretical developments that would not have occurred had the trait been assumed to exist as a unified element (Campbell & Fiske, 1959).

Some of the studies reviewed here do suggest that direct and indirect tests are tapping different aspects of attitudes. The distinction lies not only in the dimensions of public versus private or overt versus covert processes, but might be expressed in terms of the difference between beliefs and valuations. Tests of information, or public opinion, or syllogistic reasoning all seem to be measuring what Myrdal (1944) has called the "belief" component of attitudes. This aspect of indirect methods relates to the second justification for using these tests.

A Sociology of Knowledge of the Man-on-the-Street. The information test format is perhaps best suited for studying what men believe, what they take to be truth, about other men. Direct tests containing items such as "I believe all Englishmen are snobs: fully agree, agree, don't know, disagree, fully disagree," may also tap the belief system of the respondent but they do not play upon the phenomenal absolutism of men's beliefs and perceptions. An objective facade and a stress upon facts and accuracy are better able to explore the relationship between men's hopes and fears and their perceptions of reality.

The interplay between facts and attitudes is a topic of profound theoretical and practical significance. In the words of Solomon Asch (1952), "That there can be disagreement about facts is a matter of the greatest consequence. For facts have a special status; the world is built on them. It is therefore pertinent to ask: What forms of interaction take place between an existing attitude and a fact relevant to it?"

The interaction seems to work in complex ways. Beliefs are undoubtedly products of experience—results of contiguity between stimuli or between stimuli and responses—and these experiences evoke certain evaluations of the attitudinal objects. If a child, for instance, is exposed only to minority group children who rank at the bottom of his class, his beliefs about those children are likely to be tinged by negative evaluations. However, negative and positive evaluations predispose a person to seek particular kinds of verifying information in order to justify his judgments. His beliefs then become convenient rationalizations for his feelings; and beliefs that justify deeply felt prejudices are no less real or true for the beholder than are the more neutral beliefs about the weather or the shape of the earth.

Studying the beliefs and knowledge systems of social groups serve at least two functions. First, a revelation of a man's beliefs is a revelation not only of his thoughts but also of his feelings about and response tendencies toward others. An enlightened student of social science might argue that negative valuations do not follow logically from a belief that blacks receive lower grades than whites. And he may be right. But in fact our beliefs are accompanied by judgments of right and wrong, good and bad, and only the blandest observations pass through our perceptual filters without positive and negative tags. By studying these beliefs that rationalize men's biases and prejudices, we may come to understand, predict, and perhaps control some of the bigotry that now prevails.

The second function of a sociology of knowledge of the man-on-the-street is closely related to the first. As suggested by Myrdal (1944), a study of misinformation and selective ignorance has educational implications. Admittedly, filling in blind spots or correcting errors in belief is more difficult with attitudinally relevant topics than it is with spelling and simple arithmetic. The same skills and processes that created the distortions in original learning can create interference for educationally corrective programs. Nonetheless, new experiences may be provided, new contiguities established, and new belief systems may begin to emerge.

Neither of these functions violates the code of anonymity that is advocated here. Rather than a study of individual differences, a study of group beliefs and attitudes is in order. Item analysis should reveal the particular areas of information that are distorted and in need of change. And group data on shared backgrounds and experiences may suggest which variables are important in the creation of the beliefs and which may be manipulated in the educational venture.

Supported in part by National Science Foundation Grant GS 1309. We [Kidder and Campbell] are grateful to the American Psychological Association for permission to reprint edited fragments of Campbell, D. T., "The Indirect Assessment of Social Attitudes," *Psychological Bulletin,* 1950, *47,* 15-38; and Campbell, D. T., "A Typology of Tests, Projective and Otherwise," *Journal of Consulting Psychology,* 1957, *11,* 207-210. Our appreciation goes to Stuart W. Cook for providing reports of his extensive research in indirect attitude testing and to Miles L. Patterson and Patricia S. Gilbert for help in locating and abstracting the literature. This manuscript [the original article from which Chapter 8 was excerpted] was prepared especially for Summers, Gene F. (Ed.), *Attitude Measurement,* Rand McNally & Company, 1970.

OVERVIEW OF CHAPTER 9

————•◆•————

K idder and Campbell, in Chapter 8, discussed the importance of triangulation when attempting to measure a construct. They considered several classes of indirect methods, more in terms of their contribution to the multimethod approach rather than because of gains in validity over direct methods. In this chapter, Campbell, Kruskal, and Wallace once again emphasize the importance of using multiple methods to rule out the systematic, but irrelevant, aspects of any single method.

One unobtrusive measure for the degree of acquaintance or friendship between members of different races is called aggregation. Aggregation is the amount of voluntary mixing of the races, and one way of measuring it is through seating arrangements in classrooms. As with all measures, this, too, can be distorted by factors unrelated to prejudice, such as the tendency to sit with prior acquaintances who happen to be of the same race. To examine the usefulness of aggregation as a measure of prejudice, the authors discuss it in the context of a study on race relations conducted in 1963 and 1964. Using an aggregation index, observations were made at two schools that drew from the same community but had divergent attitudes regarding racial issues. Downtown U. had very liberal views while students at Normal U. had more traditional nonintegrationist attitudes.

The aggregation index is based on the number of pair-wise adjacencies of black and white students in a classroom. This alone does not provide a valid measure, since it is dependent on several factors, such as the number of students and available seats, and the proportions of black and white students. For this study, a baseline was established based on the number of expected adjacencies and the standard deviations based on what would occur if seats were chosen totally at random, without regard to race. Also, seating charts from prior years were examined to see if any trends were present. All observations were made by a single observer who posed as a student. If possible, several observers should be used, since this would allow an assessment of inter-observer variation.

The results showed that both schools had a negative mean index, which means that there were significantly fewer black-white adjacencies than would be expected by chance. There were significant differences in the aggregation indexes of the two schools. These were in the expected direction, confirming the researchers' hypothesis that this index may provide a measure of prejudice.

The differences in the aggregation measure of Normal U. and Downtown U. in 1963-1964 were much smaller than the differences found 12 to 13 years earlier through a questionnaire on attitudes toward blacks. These questionnaires from 1951 provided the only measure against which to compare the aggregation index, even though they were completed years apart, different classes were used, and only attitudes of whites toward blacks were measured. The smaller differences noted with the aggregation index suggest that actions tend to be less prejudiced than attitudes measured with an anonymous questionnaire.

The aggregation index for Normal U. did not change significantly from 1951 to 1964. While attitude test data for these two periods were not available, national trends showed a decrease in prejudiced attitudes. The index appeared to be counter to this national trend.

Further analyses were done to determine if there was a joint effect between sex and race. There were fewer adjacencies when both sex and race were involved; however, the aggregation index for the sex-race factor was not significantly different from the indexes based on race alone or sex alone.

The researchers also conducted control analyses to determine whether other factors, such as the proportion of blacks, class size, or the number of empty seats, affected the aggregation index. Only class size seemed to be significantly related in one situation. The authors suggested further study to take into account the number of aisle seats for which no adjacency is possible.

While the aggregation index is not extremely precise or pure, it does offer a supplementary method to the self-report tests of prejudiced attitudes. It might be used to gauge before-and-after attitudes in a class aimed at improving race relations. This index may also be a useful tool to examine shifts in the degree of mutual trust among the races.

SEATING PATTERNS
AS AN ATTITUDE INDEX

———·◆·———

he social sciences are overdependent upon voluntary verbal self-description by questionnaire or interview. This method is subject to weaknesses, such as voluntary or unconscious distortion, self-consciousness, reactive effects upon attitudes, and awkwardness of administration. More important, even though voluntary verbal self-description may eventually be judged the best of all methods, every method contains systematic irrelevancies that can only be ascertained through a strategy of joint application of methods as different as possible (Webb, Campbell, Schwartz, & Sechrest, 1966). It is in the service of developing such other measures that this study of seating aggregation is presented.

Where seating in a classroom is voluntary, the degree to which the blacks and whites present sit by themselves rather than mixing randomly is a presumptive index of the degree to which acquaintance, friendship, and prefer-

Campbell, D. T., Kruskal, W. H., & Wallace, W. P. (1966). Seating aggregation as an index of attitude. *Sociometry, 29,* 1-15.

ence are affected by race. Such voluntary clustering by race will be termed *aggregation,* as opposed to the enforced separation connoted by the term *segregation.*

Just as an attitude questionnaire has its irrelevant components such as response sets, social desirability factors, social class differences in willingness to use hostile vocabulary for any purpose, and so forth, so such a measure as seating aggregation is distorted by factors irrelevant to the concept of interest. Observation of the high degree of racial clustering or aggregation at the typical annual banquet of a society dedicated to removing racial barriers reflects no doubt the biased opportunities for prior acquaintance rather than the racial attitudes of the persons involved. So too in a classroom, the tendency to sit with friends from one's neighborhood and previous schools provides a bias perhaps more directly reflecting acquaintance opportunity than lack of goodwill. None the less, if within a classroom there are marked shifts in aggregation from time to time, these might reflect shifts in interracial fear and goodwill superimposed on the baseline provided by prior acquaintance opportunity. Or if two schools drawing from the same community provide markedly different aggregation indices, these differences might be attributed to attitudinal factors. The illustrative data of the present study are primarily of this latter case.

The Aggregation Index. Among the many possible ways one might measure aggregation, we chose to base a measure on the number of black-white seating adjacencies, that is, the number of pairs of row-wise adjacent seats, one of which is occupied by a black student, the other by a white student. (Seats separated by an aisle, and seats with empty seats in between, are not considered to be adjacent.) The number of adjacencies by itself, however, is not suitable as an index. For one thing, it is clearly influenced by the total number of students and by the proportions of black and white students. Some kind of baseline and yardstick are necessary. In principle, a realistic stochastic model for the seating of students should be used, but not enough is known about the phenomenon to warrant work on such a model. Instead, we have used a baseline and yardstick corresponding to expected number and standard deviation of adjacencies derived from a randomness assumption, namely that the seats were randomly chosen as regards race, but that the pattern of occupied seats was fixed. [For the interested reader, the development of the aggregation index is presented in an Appendix in the original article.]

The index used was

$$I = (A - EA)/\sigma_A,$$

where

A $\quad$ = observed number of adjacencies

EA $\quad$ = expected number of adjacencies under randomness

σ_A $\quad$ = standard deviation of number of adjacencies under randomness.

The expressions for EA and σ_A are in terms of

$\qquad$ N $\quad$ = total number of students in a class

$\qquad$ M $\quad$ = number of black students

$\quad$ M − N $\quad$ = number of white students

$\qquad$ K $\quad$ = number of groups of row-wise contiguous students

$\qquad\qquad$ (including isolates)

$\qquad$ K_1 $\quad$ = number of students with no one next to them (isolates).

In these terms

$$EA = 2\,\frac{M(N-M)}{N(N-1)}\,(N-K)$$

$$\sigma_A^2 = 2\,\frac{M(N-M)}{N(N-1)}\,(2N - 3K + K_1) + 4\,\frac{M(M-1)(N-M)(N-M-1)}{N(N-1)(N-2)(N-3)}\,(N-K)^2.$$

$$[(N-K)\,(N-K-1) - 2\,(N - 2K + K_1)] - 4\,\frac{M^2(N-M)^2}{N^2(N-1)^2}\,(N-K)^2.$$

Figure 9.1 shows a typical seating chart from the study. In this case

$$N = 22,\ M = 6,\ K = 10,\ K_1 = 4,\ A = 1,\ EA = 4.99,\ \text{and}\ \sigma_A = 1.51.$$

$$I = \frac{1 - 4.99}{1.51} = -2.64.$$

Negative values of I indicate more aggregation than under randomness, and positive values indicate less aggregation than that under randomness.

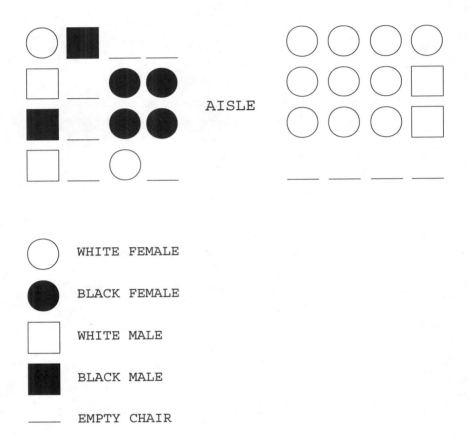

Figure 9.1. Sample Seating Chart From Normal U., 1964

Data Sources. The data of major interest come from classrooms observed at two colleges in the fall of 1963 and 1964. These two colleges had in a previous unpublished study provided the two extremes of most prejudiced and least prejudiced white students in a comparison of five colleges scattered over the nation, including one southern white college. Both were located in the same northern metropolis. Both consisted entirely of commuter students. Both had substantial minorities—as colleges go—of black students. Both had unbiased administrative policies and black faculty members. One, which we shall call Downtown U., was by reputation militantly liberal on the race issue. The other, which we shall call Normal U., attracted primarily students seeking teaching credentials, and apparently of predominantly traditional, nonintegrationist attitudes. Also available were seating charts for classes from Normal U. in 1951 and for 1963 from a Junior College that was located in this same northern metropolis. The basic data pool is described in Table 9.1. In this table the 1963-1964 data have been pooled. Inspection showed no trends within this period.

The 1963-1964 data were collected by an observer who entered the classroom as though a student and from a convenient vantage point prepared the seating chart. The 1951 observations were made by the administrator of a test while the test was being taken by the students, no record being made of the sex of the students. It must be noted that the observations on any one class were collected by a single observer. Consequently, difficulties in observer identification of black and white students present an unchecked source of error. Although it is presumed this problem produces a negligible error, it would be desirable to have several observers in each classroom to assess inter-observer variation, and if possible to check these against self-identification.

Any errors of identification almost certainly lead to underestimation of the number of blacks present, given the current U.S. norms of the time. This would make the expected number of adjacencies too low in classrooms where blacks are in the minority. The number of observed black-white adjacencies would be overestimated where a black-black adjacency was recorded as a BW, and underestimated where a BW was recorded as a white-white adjacency. If aggregation occurs to the same degree among the potential passers on whom errors have been made, the net error would probably be one of overestimation of black-white adjacencies, which, when combined with the downward error of expected adjacencies, leads the computed indices to be underestimates of aggregation. There is no reason to believe that in the present data such errors have been distributed in any systematic manner. (The dichotomous recording made should be more accurately described as black and nonblack, as there were a few oriental students who were classified as white.)

Table 9.1 Basic Data Pool

	Number of Classes			of Blacks		of Whites		Percentage	
	Total	All of One Race	All of One Sex	Male	Female	Male	Female	Black	Female
Downtown U. 1963-1964	23	2	1	34	24	335	160	10	33
Normal U. 1963-1964	20	0	0	49	103	164	215	29	60
Junior College 1963	12	1	0	59	79	106	23	52	38
Normal U. 1951	19	0	?		89		435	17	?

Table 9.2 Racial Aggregation Indices

	Downtown U. 1963-1964	Normal U. 1963-1964	Junior College 1963	Normal U. 1951
Mean index	−0.81	−1.50	−1.41	−1.05
Standard deviation	0.81	0.98	1.46	1.53
t from zero index	4.50	6.82	3.20	3.00
Number of classes	21	20	11	19
Number of classes with positive indices	3	1	2	6

NOTE: Differences in numbers of classes from Table 9.1 reflect discarding of classes with M or N − M equal to zero.

The courses sampled covered a variety of liberal arts classes. The selection of classes was haphazard but not random. During a class hour the experimenter observed as many classes as he could, selecting the classes to be observed systematically on the basis of their location, for example, the second class sampled in a given hour would be one located near the first class sampled. This selection method was judged to be sufficiently unrelated to observed characteristics that statistical procedures based on randomness might be tentatively used. Approximately three class hours were needed for the collection of the data from each school. This gives rise to the possibility that some students may have been observed in more than one classroom. The possibility of some dependence between classrooms thus cannot be ruled out, but is judged to be of minor importance. Observations at both schools were made within a week of each other in both 1963 and 1964, with no incidents of racial relevance occurring during the period of observation.

RESULTS

The Generality of Aggregation by Race. Table 9.2 shows the basic results for the class indices. (Classes not having members of both races have been omitted.) All schools have a negative mean index, indicating fewer black-white seating adjacencies than would be expected by chance. Using the *t* test, all of these means are statistically significantly different from zero at the $p = < .01$ level. Most individual classes show negative indices, although there are a few that do not.

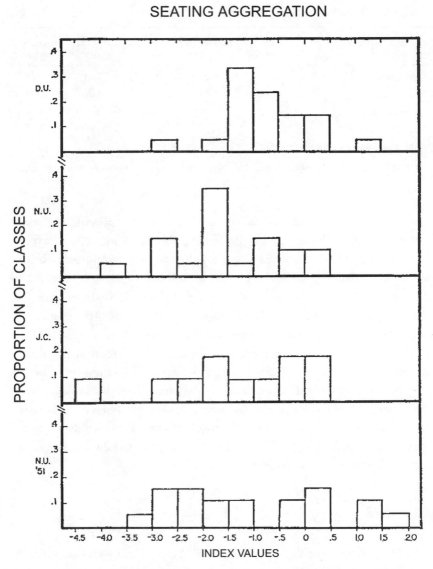

Figure 9.2. Distribution of Index Values for D.U., N.U., J.C., and N.U., 1951

School Differences in Aggregation. The distributions of the aggrega-
tion-index values for each school appear in Figure 9.2. In Figure 9.2, D.U. refers to the Downtown U., 1963-1964 samples, N.U. refers to the Normal U.,

1963-1964 samples, J.C. refers to the Junior College, and N. '51 refers to the Normal U., 1951 sample. The two schools of major interest show a statistically significant difference in aggregation indices in the expected direction. The Downtown U. mean of $-.81$ was significantly less negative than the Normal U. mean of -1.50 with a t of 2.46, 39 degrees of freedom, $p = < .02$ (a two-sided test of significance). The difference was in the same direction and to about the same degree in the 1963 and 1964 data taken separately. The utility of the index as a measure of attitude thus receives some confirmation.

The degrees of differentiation that the index provides is, however, by no means as sharp as that provided by the earlier unpublished questionnaire data. In 1951, anonymous questionnaire data on attitudes toward blacks were collected from six classes at Downtown U. and nine at Normal U. When means are computed for the white students in each class, the two schools show no overlap on either a direct attitude scale or a multiple choice information test scored for anti- and pro-black bias in the alternatives selected. The t ratios for the difference between the two schools, computed for an n of classes, were 5.74 for "direct" scores and 8.62 for "indirect" scores, these values being much larger than the t of 2.46 for the aggregation index even though fewer classes were involved. Different years, different classes, and different constructs are involved. It is, of course, presumptive to assume that had anonymous questionnaire data been collected in 1963-1964 the differences would have remained as large as they were in 1951, but this is the only comparison available. Since no measures of anti-white attitudes were taken from the 1951 black students, only the white data have been examined. The aggregation index is presumably a joint product of the dislikes and fears of both blacks and whites. (In more refined data collection, the total sequence of seat-taking might be examined in such a way as to isolate actions symptomatic of white attitudes from those symptomatic of black attitudes.) The lesser degree of prejudice-differential for the aggregation index might be regarded as another illustration of a recurrent observation in northern settings that overt actions are less prejudiced than anonymous questionnaire responses.

Aggregation Changes Over Time. For Normal U. the difference between the 1951 data and that for 1964 was not statistically significant. Corresponding attitude test data from the school for the time trend is not available, although general public opinion surveys show a decrease in prejudice for this decade

Table 9.3 Aggregation Indices for Sex

	Downtown U. 1963-1964	Normal U. 1963-1964	Junior College 1963
Mean index	−0.90	−1.36	−0.77
Standard deviation	1.36	0.98	1.18
t from zero index	3.10	6.18	2.26
Number of classes	22	20	12
Number of classes with positive indices	4	2	4

(Hyman & Sheatsly, 1964). The direction of shift for the index is counter to this national trend. While the proportion of blacks attending Normal U. increased between 1951 and 1964, this proportion seems, as shown below, to be unrelated to bias.

Aggregation by Sex. As is commonly noted, classroom seating shows aggregation by sex. The computation of indices for sex aggregation was thought to be of value both as a check on the index and to provide a comparison for the racial aggregation indices. Table 9.3 shows the basic values for the indices of aggregation by sex. (Sex was not recorded in the 1951 data from Normal U., and classes have been omitted that did not have members of both sexes.) The general finding is one of significant sex aggregation in all schools.

Within the classrooms there is significant aggregation by sex and there is significant aggregation by race. However, the difference between sex and race aggregation is not statistically significant when computed by a paired-sample t test on the 51 classes for which both indices were available (Race mean = 1.20, Sex mean = .99, $t = 1.24$, df = 49, $p = < .25$). Since pooling across schools may be inappropriate, the analyses were repeated considering each school separately. None of the resultant t's approached statistical significance.

Joint Effect of Sex and Race. The following analysis asks whether or not the number of adjacencies is particularly low when the adjacency crosses both race and sex. That is, do adjacencies between black men and white women or between black women and white men occur still less frequently than do adjacencies between persons differing on race alone, or on sex alone. No ade-

Table 9.4 Aggregation Indices With Fragmented Classes

	Cross Race & Sex		Cross Race		Cross Sex	
	MB-FW	MW-FB	MB-MW	FB-FW	MB-FB	MW-FW
Mean index	−1.20	−1.26	−0.66	−1.21	−0.60	−1.34
Average subclass size	15.00	17.59	14.82	17.76	9.47	23.12
Number of classes	17	17	17	17	17	17
Number of classes with positive indices	1	4	6	3	5	2

quate approach to this problem was found. What has been explored are fragmented indices, paying attention only to the two subgroups involved, and treating all other persons as though they were empty seats. This analysis has been limited to those classes providing persons in all four race-sex subgroups. Table 9.4 shows the results of this analysis. While the two indices crossing both race and sex average lower (more negative) than either of the other pairs, they both fall within the range of indices provided by the other subgroups. Using class-by-class paired-sample t's for the averages of these pairs, no significant differences were found (cross Sex & Race vs. cross Race. $t = 1.85$; cross Sex & Race vs. cross Sex, $t = 1.53$; cross Sex vs. cross Race, $t = .20$, df $= 16$ in each case). Thus while a slight trend toward a joint effect was present, it did not approach usual standards for statistical significance. This approach has inadequacies on logical grounds, and a better approach is being sought.

Control Analyses. It is very difficult to achieve descriptive indices of degree of effect that are comparable with assurance across heterogeneous conditions of size and proportion. For this reason, certain control analyses have been done. It is possible that the index might not be comparable between two classes varying widely in the proportion of blacks present. Computing the correlation between this proportion and the resulting index for each of the four samples, the following correlation coefficients were obtained: Downtown U., 1963-1964, $r = -.21$; Normal U., 1963-1964, $r = +.37$; Junior College, $r = -.13$; Normal U., 1951, $r = +.13$. None of these coefficients reached a usual level of statistical significance.

Class size is somewhat more problematic. The correlations between the aggregation index and class size for the four samples were as follows: $r = -.18$ for Downtown U., 1963-1964; $r = -.17$ for Normal U., 1963-1964; $r = -.75$ for the Junior College; and $r = -.14$ for Normal U., 1951. Of the above correlations, only that in the Junior College reached statistical significance ($p = < .01$, df = 10). All of the correlations were negative, which suggests that larger classes show more racial aggregation. Larger classes probably come from freshmen and sophomore courses, and the correlation may thus indicate improved race relations as a function of maturity, familiarity, and the like. Unfortunately, course levels were not recorded. The class size correlations with aggregation by sex did not approach statistical significance ($r = +.01$ for Downtown U., 1963-1964; $r = -.11$ for Normal U., 1963-1964; $r = -.18$ for the Junior College). These latter results do not support an interpretation that the aggregation index is artificially influenced by class size. In any event, the class size correlation does not affect the interpretation of the Downtown U.-Normal U. aggregation differences, as the 1963-1964 mean sizes for these two are 26.33 and 26.55, respectively, and the class-size correlations within these schools did not reach an acceptable level of statistical significance.

In some respects the index neglects features that might artificially affect the number of black-white adjacencies. Thus no use is made of the number of vacant seats nor their possible location so as to buffer black-white adjacency. Undoubtedly in many instances a shortage of seats increases black-white adjacencies in a manner not reflecting the preferences of the persons involved. As a partial check on this, the proportion of empty seats was correlated with the race aggregation index. The resulting correlations were +.12 for Downtown U., +.24 for Normal U., 1963-1964, and +.55 for the Junior College. The correlations are not statistically significant and are in the opposite direction from that expected, showing the larger the proportion of empty seats, the less aggregation. For sex aggregation, these correlations were −.04, +.18, and −.49 for Downtown U., Normal U., 1963-1964, and the Junior College, respectively. None of these correlations reached statistical significance. Thus neglect of empty chairs does not in these data appear to have produced misleading effects. Another feature that an ideal index might attend to is the number or proportion of row ends where no adjacency is possible. Thus an arrangement of the same number of chairs into a pattern of many short rows reduces the opportunities for adjacency in comparison with an arrangement of fewer longer rows. This attribute varied so little in the present study that no control correlation has been computed. Even though empty seats and row ends probably do not distort the present data, the development of a more complex index that would take these into account seems desirable.

DISCUSSION

While there is no indication that the index is of high precision or purity, the results do encourage further exploration. The index might be used, for example, as a before-and-after measure in studies of class presentations designed to improve race relations. One of the most needed studies is the examination of shifts in the degree of mutual trust. A cooperating group of instructors could easily produce a daily series of seating charts in classes in which written classroom work takes place. The index can also be applied in any other situation in which unidimensional adjacency can be noted. One recurrent class of situations of this type is in the waiting lines for cafeterias, theater tickets, time clock punching, and so forth. For waiting lines, the formula is simpler, as K becomes 1, and the number of adjacencies becomes one less than the number of runs, a much studied topic (Brownlee, 1965; Wilks, 1962).

The adjacency index is but one of a larger class of potential aggregation indices. Consider a school playground in which many of the pupils can be identified as participating in activity groups, be they baseball games, hopscotch, penny-pitching, and so on. Utilizing children so classified, one could examine racial composition in terms of a contingency table in which columns were black and white, and in which each play group constituted a row. In a similar way, ethnic bias in isolates versus group-involved could be computed. A time-series of such indices from multiracial school yards might provide an index of changing tensions.

Another way of conceptualizing aggregation is in terms of the steepness of the interracial boundary—and note that the schoolroom and school yard indices must come from essentially boundary conditions; they are not available for either all white or all black schools. If one considers, for example, the residences, sidewalks, stores, and public services on a street that crosses the black-white boundary at right angles, the more aggregation there is, the "steeper" the racial boundary, that is, the narrower the transition area in which there is mixed racial presence, the more nearly the shift is from 100% black to 100% white, without blocks, stores, sidewalk segments, and the like, that have both blacks and whites present. For presences for which daily decisions and changes are possible, such as shopping for groceries, an increase in the steepness of the boundary might indicate an increase in tension, as blacks feel reluctance to shop in predominantly white stores and as whites feel reluctance to shop in predominantly black ones. Such considerations move us close to the sociological literature on city indices of segregation computed from census data (Duncan & Duncan, 1955; Duncan, Cuzzort, & Duncan, 1961; Freeman & Pilger, 1964, 1965).

The contributions of Donald T. Campbell and William P. Wallace to the preparation of this paper were supported by Project C998 Contract 3-20-001 with the Media Research Branch, Office of Education, U.S. Department of Health, Education and Welfare, under the provisions of Title VII of the National Defense Education Act. William H. Kruskal's work was carried out in the Department of Statistics, University of Chicago, under partial sponsorship of the Statistics Branch, Office of Naval Research. Reproduction in whole or part is permitted for any purpose of the United States government.

PART III

QUALITATIVE AND
ETHNOGRAPHIC APPROACHES

————•◆•————

*I*t is generally well known that Donald Campbell advocated quantitative methods, especially experimentation, for measuring the effects of social programs. Many are not aware, though, of his support for qualitative or humanistic methods. While he acknowledged the limitations of these methods, he recognized also that all quantitative measurement is based on qualitative assumptions, which he refers to as "commonsense knowing." This includes shared language, motives, and subjective judgments. Both physical and social scientists use qualitative knowledge regularly to interpret the results of their empirical data. It is this function of qualitative methods that Campbell sees as extremely valuable, and he expresses a wholehearted desire to promote even more integration between the two types of methods. He does not recommend supplanting quantitative methods with qualitative methods when inferring causality. Yet, he would argue that if quantitative results disagree with the findings of a qualitative study, then it is most likely the quantitative study that is in error.

Case studies, ethnographies, participant observation, and process evaluation are all methods of acquiring qualitative data. Qualitative approaches serve several functions. They can be a prelude to empirical studies by describing the characteristics and processes that merit further examination. Qualitative studies advance our understanding of quantitative results, and should be used for cross-validation. When using multiple methods is impossible or impractical, qualitative studies might even be used to test hypotheses if appropriate comparisons are made. This can be done by comparing the descriptions and judgments of two ethnographers, preferably from different cultures, studying the same two cultures. Even in the one-shot case study, validity can be increased if the ethnographer increases the degrees of freedom by testing the multiple implications of a hypothesis on various aspects of a culture. As always, Campbell warns that qualitative methods should be examined with regard to threats to validity, just as quantitative methods are. Successful replications can increase our confidence in the validity of a study, and the chances of replicating a study are more likely if standardized guidelines are used for fieldwork.

Campbell's experience with cross-cultural research gave him a closer view of qualitative methods. He first worked with Melville Herskovits and Marshall Segall examining the role of learning and cultural factors in visual perception in a study that included data from 20 anthropologists. Later, he worked with Robert LeVine in a cooperative cross-cultural study of ethnocentrism. This latter experience resulted in a fieldwork manual, which was formulated to increase the comparability of data collected from disparate cultures.

Campbell's involvement with these cross-cultural studies and his awareness of the role of method factors in social measures induced him to examine the biases that result when comparing different cultures. He identified several; for example, the researcher's choice of informant or the inferiority of translations to the target language of interviews or questionnaires. He then addressed ways to eliminate these biases. Finally, he believed that studies involving varying cultures would be strengthened by standardizing the methods through which the fieldwork is carried out. These issues are discussed in the chapters to follow.

In Chapter 10, Campbell discusses the complementary nature of quantitative and qualitative studies. The next chapter, "The Qualitative Case Study," revisits Campbell's assessment of the one-shot case study. He concludes that such studies can be validity-seeking when degrees of freedom are increased by testing numerous implications of a theory on various features of a culture.

Chapter 12 considers the use of the informant in cross-cultural studies and the biases that can be introduced in this way. The chapter includes suggestions on how to choose informants so this bias that might be reduced or eliminated. In his early cross-cultural work, Campbell became aware of how questions that are translated from a foreign language might be misunderstood. In Chapter 13, Werner and Campbell suggest decentered translation, which involves using back translations in an iterative process. This method is more effective for improving the quality and comparability of instruments in a target language than when translations are anchored on the ethnographer's language. Finally, Chapter 14 contains LeVine and Campbell's argument in favor of a fieldwork manual to increase the validity of cross-cultural studies.

——— •◆• ———

OVERVIEW OF CHAPTER 10

————•◆•————

In this chapter, originally published in 1978, Campbell discusses the trend in the social sciences to move away from experimental methods toward the methods of the humanities. He uses the terms *quantitative methods* to describe the scientific method and *qualitative methods* to describe the humanistic methods. *Action research* refers to the evaluation of social innovations. As developed by Kurt Lewin and his associates, action research utilizes both quantitative and qualitative methods. Another important feature of action research is that it involves those who are members of the action group in the evaluation of their own progress. Campbell wishes to present a unified perspective for both quantitative and qualitative methods. He begins this analysis with a discussion of some of the developments in the philosophy of science.

Social science produces theories. These theories can never be proven; they are merely better than other theories. Everything we "know" is based on presumptions. We must accept the majority of unproven presumptions while examining small subsets of them. In order to justify scientific inquiry, one must find a center path between being skeptical of all knowledge or blindly trusting all research outcomes. Evolutionary epistemology provides such a justification, because it alleges that commonsense knowing, while based on presumptions, is winnowed through biological and social evolution. Scientific theories, which are still more presumptive, are winnowed through competitive selection among various theories. Through this process of competitive selection, the methodologist can take some comfort in knowing that science can lead to more valid knowledge. If there are data to support a theory, the theory can be invalidated only if there are equally plausible or better explanations of those data.

Scientific knowledge often goes beyond commonsense knowledge or may even contradict it, but in order to come to such a conclusion, the bulk of commonsense knowledge must be trusted. Yet, even the most basic of commonsense knowledge is based on presumptions. There are no facts against which to test theory; even the so-called facts are theory-laden. Using optical illusions, we can demonstrate that even visual perceptions may lead to incorrect conclusions. When we accept this, it is easy to speculate how much more "theory-laden" scientific facts are.

Kuhn's interpretation of a scientific revolution assumes that all facts are tied up in a single integrated theory. When that master theory changes, all the facts change as well. Campbell suggests that there is a hierarchy of trusts-presumptions-theories. For example, commonsense knowledge is depended upon both before and after a revolution.

Another aspect of evolutionary epistemology is its emphasis on patterns rather than details. To demonstrate this concept, think of trying to identify a picture in a newspaper by seeing only a single dot. This is an impossible task; it is only after familiar patterns emerge that the picture can be identified. Unlike the epistemological orientations that seek certainty in particles, Campbell suggests that it is the knowing of wholes and patterns that allows the interpretation of the particulars. Science depends on commonsense knowing, because it is this knowledge that is used to validate scientific theories. Scientists use qualitative knowledge to confirm their quantitative data. Campbell would like this practice to extend to the social sciences. He stresses the importance of applying both types of knowledge to social problems.

There sometimes appears to be a dichotomy in the social sciences. Quantitative social scientists, using their numbers, forget about the qualitative underpinnings of their data. For example, shared language, motives, and subjective judgments underlie all quantitative data. Qualitative social scientists tend to criticize quantitative data collection and refuse to participate. While there is some movement toward blending quantitative and qualitative methods, Campbell would like to see even more integration.

The evaluation of social programs depends on qualitative knowing. Decisions to stop, retain, or expand programs are based on recorded experiences of the participants. These experiences may be assembled through site visits, participant observation, nonparticipant observation, or informant interviews, to name a few. They may even be transformed into quantitative data in the form of counts or rating scales. While some distinguish qualitative data from quantitative collations of qualitative experience, Campbell feels both should be categorized as qualitative.

There are several types of qualitative evaluation. Process evaluation summarizes the way in which the program was implemented and the experiences of the participants. Since this type of evaluation is not a dependable way to determine causal relations, Campbell sees it as a supplement to experimental design. Formative evaluation is done concurrently with the program and is intended to point out aspects of the program that are ineffective. Formative evaluation should precede a full-scale process evaluation or quantitative experimentation. Systems analysis in social program evaluation is a qualitative approach that examines, in detail, the functioning of the organization and how it relates to other systems. In this type of evaluation, the treatment is given special attention. Some social programs use anthropologists and their fieldwork methods for the evaluation. While Campbell sees these ethnographies as useful tools prior to experimental studies, he stands by his conviction that experimental design is still the best method for demonstrating a program's effectiveness. An ethnography might offer more interpretable results if there was a basis for comparison. There are several suggestions as to how this can be accomplished: Two similar units, one with and the other without the program, can be studied simultaneously; information on the treatment unit can be documented for the year or two prior to the implementation of the program; or two anthropologists can study the same program independently to see if there is agreement as to the impact of the program.

Campbell stresses the importance of replication, not only of qualitative studies, but of quantitative studies as well. If a quantitative and qualitative study are done simultaneously, he believes it likely that they will be in agreement. If they disagree, it is probably the quantitative evaluation that is in error.

Case studies are useful for uncovering program implications that can be examined further; however, they are a weak design for demonstrating causality. Replication is important to increase the validity of the results, and chances of replicating a case study will be improved if the guidelines for anthropological and sociological fieldwork are followed.

As mentioned earlier, action research includes in the evaluation of a program those who benefit from it. These participants are an excellent source for qualitative information about the program's activities and effectiveness. Participants should be allowed to meet together to pool their judgments, make group statements, and vote on them. Others associated with the program, such as teachers, social workers, and interviewers, should be given an opportunity to speculate on the effectiveness of the program. These qualitative data can be used to validate quantitative results and to point out unanticipated effects.

Both quantitative and qualitative methods should be examined with regard to the threats to validity. Finally, the politics of program evaluation should be considered, since quantitative and qualitative evaluations will be affected differently.

TEN

QUALITATIVE RESEARCH METHODS IN PROGRAM EVALUATION

————•◆•————

*I*n program evaluation methodology, there is a vigorous search for alternatives to the quantitative-experimental approach. In academic social science there is renewed emphasis on the methods of the humanities and increased doubts as to the appropriateness of applying the natural science model to social science problems. There appears to exist a qualitative versus quantitative polarity. These terms are shorthand for a common denominator among a wide range of partially overlapping concepts: For *quantitative* read also scientific, scientistic, and *naturwissenschaftlich*. For *qualitative* read also humanistic, humanitistic, *geisteswissenschaftlich*, experiential, phenomenological, clinical, case study, fieldwork, participant observation, process evaluation, and commonsense knowing.

Campbell, D. T. (1978). Qualitative knowing in action research. In M. Brenner, P. Marsh, & M. Brenner (Eds.), *The social contexts of method* (pp. 184-209). London: Croom Helm.

While initially my discussion of these issues will involve epistemology and the social sciences in general, the target focus is on the evaluation of the outcomes of deliberately introduced novel social innovations. The phrase *action research* is particularly appropriate to research centered around deliberate efforts at social action. As developed by Lewin and his associates in the heroic Committee on Community Interrelations it involved a wise integration of qualitative and quantitative approaches (Chein, 1949, 1956; Chein, Cook, & Harding, 1948a, 1948b; Cook, 1962; Harding, 1948; Lewin, 1946, 1947; Lippitt & Radke, 1946; Marrow, 1969, pp. 191-218; Selltiz, 1956; Selltiz & Cook, 1948). It also had an important feature for this chapter: the development of procedures whereby action groups can assess their own progress—program self-evaluation.

The analysis that follows starts out with epistemological considerations, aspiring to a unified perspective for both quantitative and qualitative knowing, consistent with the modern uprootings in the philosophy of science. It reaches the conclusion that quantitative knowing depends upon qualitative knowing in going beyond it. This dependence is poorly represented in much of quantitative social science. Subsequently, the qualitative grounding of quantitative social sciences is discussed, and the role of qualitative knowing in program evaluation.

SOME DESCRIPTIVE EPISTEMOLOGY

Nonlaboratory social science is precariously scientific at best. But even for the strongest sciences, the theories believed to be true are radically underjustified and have, at most, the status of "better than" rather than the status of "proven." All commonsense and scientific knowledge is presumptive. In any setting in which we seem to gain new knowledge, we do so at the expense of many presumptions, untestable to say nothing of unconfirmable in that situation. While the appropriateness of some presumptions can be probed singly or in small sets, this can only be done by assuming the correctness of the great bulk of other presumptions. Single presumptions or small subsets can in turn be probed, but the total set of presumptions is not of demonstrable validity, is radically underjustified. Such are the pessimistic conclusions of the most modern developments in the philosophy of science (Feyerabend, 1970; Goodman,

1955; Hanson, 1958; Kuhn, 1962, 1970; Lakatos, 1970; Polanyi, 1958; Popper, 1959, 1963, 1972; Quine, 1953, 1969b; Toulmin, 1961, 1972).

Yet science is much better than ignorance and, on many topics, better than traditional wisdom. Our problem as methodologists is to define our course between the extremes of inert skepticism and naive credulity. An evolutionary epistemology may help because it portrays commonsense knowing as based upon presumptions built into the sensory/nervous system and into ordinary language, presumptions that have been well winnowed, highly edited, and thus indirectly confirmed through the natural selection of biological and social evolution. For scientific theories, still more presumptive, the natural selection process is continued through the competitive selection from among existing theories (Campbell, 1959a, 1960a, 1966, 1970; Caws, 1969; Popper, 1959, 1963, 1972; Quine, 1969b; Shimony, 1970; Toulmin, 1961, 1972).

The concrete activities of "methodology" can be subsumed under such a perspective, and in a way somewhat comforting for those in the social sciences, where so much must be presumed in order to come to any conclusions at all. When a scientist argues that a given body of data corroborate a theory, invalidation of that claim comes only from equally plausible or better explanations of those data. The mere existence of an infinite number of logically possible alternatives is not in practice invalidating. As we have known since Hume, scientific inductions are unproven, deductively or inductively. We must now allow our critics to point out specific examples of this general scandal of induction as though it were peculiar to our study or to our field.

The Dependence of Science
Upon Commonsense Knowing

We must not suppose that scientific knowing replaces commonsense knowing. Rather, science depends upon common sense even though at best it goes beyond it. Science in the end contradicts some items of common sense, but it only does so by trusting the great bulk of the rest of commonsense knowledge. Such revision of common sense by science is akin to the revision of common sense by common sense, which, paradoxically, can only be done by trusting more common sense. Let us consider as an example the Müller-Lyer illustration (Figure 10.1).

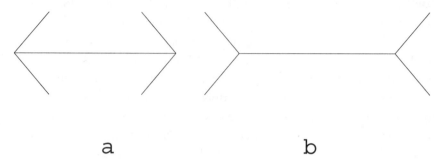

a   b

Figure 10.1.

If you ask the normal resident of a "carpentered" culture (Segall, Campbell, & Herskovits, 1966) which horizontal line is longer, a or b, he will reply b. If you supply him with a ruler, or allow him to use the edge of another piece of paper as a makeshift ruler, he will eventually convince himself that he is wrong, and that line a is longer. In so deciding he will have rejected as inaccurate one product of visual perception by trusting a larger set of other visual perceptions. He will also have made many presumptions, inexplicit for the most part, including the assumption that the lengths of the lines have remained relatively constant during the measurement process, that the ruler was rigid rather than elastic, that the heat and moisture of his hand have not changed the ruler's length in such a coincidental way as to produce the different measurements, expanding it when approaching line a, contracting it when approaching line b, and so on.

Let us take as another example a scientific paper, containing theory and experimental results, demonstrating the quantum nature of light, in dramatic contrast to commonsense understanding. Were such a paper to limit its symbols to scientific terms, it would fail to communicate to another scientist in such a way as to enable him to replicate the experiment and verify the observations. Instead, the few scientific terms have been embedded in a discourse of prescientific ordinary language that the reader is presumed to (and presumes to) understand. This language is demonstrably incomplete, elliptical, metaphorical, and equivocal. In addition, in the laboratory work of the original and replicating laboratory, a commonsense prescientific perception of objects, solids, and light was employed and trusted in coming to the conclusions that revise the ordinary understanding. To challenge and correct the commonsense understanding in one detail, commonsense understanding in general had to be trusted.

The Doubt-Trust Ratio

These two illustrations introduce the theme of continuity between commonsense and scientific knowing and the doubt-trust ratio. If we opt for total scepticism or solipsism, we give up "knowing" or science. If we opt for total credulity, as some versions of phenomenology and "direct realism" seem to, we give up consistency, simplicity, and the expansion or perfection of "knowledge." Ordinary knowing and science are in between these extremes, and somehow combine a capacity for focused distrust and revision with a belief in a common body of knowledge claims. One aspect of the process that makes the cumulative revision of science possible is the practice of trusting (tentatively at least) the great bulk of current scientific and commonsense belief ("knowledge") and using it to discredit and revise one aspect of scientific belief. The ratio of the doubted to the trusted is always a very small fraction. This is expressed in the metaphor Quine (1953) borrows from von Neurath: We are like sailors who must repair a rotting ship at sea. We trust the great bulk of the timbers while we replace a particularly weak plank. Each of the timbers we now trust we may in its turn replace. The proportion of the planks we are replacing to those we treat as sound must always be small.

The presumptive character of even the most ordinary and basic instances of perception and commonsense knowing is currently being referred to through the truism that there are no hard facts that speak for themselves and against which theory may be checked. Instead, the so-called facts are themselves "theory-laden" (Feyerabend, 1970; Hanson, 1958; Kuhn, 1962, 1970). This is a point worth emphasizing. The Müller-Lyer illusion used above may very well be due to an implicit "theory" of environmental relations built into the nervous system by learning or genetic heredity to the effect that obtuse and acute angles in the plane of vision are most likely generated by rectangular solids (Segall et al., 1966; Stewart, 1973). The Duncker (1929) dot-and-frame illusion may be more convincing. In an otherwise totally dark room is a large luminous frame with a luminous dot within. The frame is moved several inches to the right. The observer instead perceives the dot move several inches to the left. The perceptual system has built-in preconscious decision-trees that convert the evidence of relative motion into an inference of absolute motion. The "presumption" or "theory" used is this: In case of doubt, it is the small fragment of the visual field that has moved, the large bulk that has remained still. This is an excellent general rule, but wrong in the ecologically atypical setting of Duncker's laboratory. This is theory-ladenness at the natural knowing level. When we come to reading a galvanometer of a scintillation counter, the theory-ladenness of the resultant facts is still more obviously "theoretical" because explicit scientific theories must be trusted in order to interpret the meter readings.

This emphasis can acquire a misleading connotation. In Kuhn's (1962) usage, when speaking of scientific revolutions, he seems to assume that all of physical knowing is tied up in one single integrated theory, one single equation, and that the "facts" against which this theory is checked are all laden with, and only with, this one encompassing theory. When this master-theory is changed, then it is supposed that all of the "facts" change simultaneously. Hanson (1958) and Feyerabend (1970) are similar on this point.

This assumption of a single overreaching theory is wrong. The actual situation of science is much less "integrated" or "unified" than this. The theory-ladenness of "facts" involves many deep-seated presumptions not overthrown by a specific scientific revolution. Instead, there is an elaborate hierarchy of trusts-presumptions-theories in which the simpler commonsense levels are for the most part depended upon in an unchanged fashion both before and after the revolution. The same trust is also true for 90% of the laboratory-level, instrument-dependent "facts" in the course of a scientific revolution. Indeed, some of these prerevolutionary facts provide the anomalies that are the principal leverage for overthrowing the old paradigms.

This is not to deny the relevance of the duck-rabbit ambiguous figure made famous by Jastrow (1900), Wittgenstein (1953), Hanson (1958), and Kuhn (1962). Facts are seen in (or from) a different perspective after the shift in the "theory" of duck to the "theory" of rabbit. But there is a continuity of the paper pigment pattern for which the duck or the rabbit is the changed solution or interpretation. The pigment pattern represents a continuing shared restraint on possible interpretations. Duck or rabbit are the "incommensurable" interpretations of a shared puzzle. There are very few such acceptable interpretations

Figure 10.2. Do you see a duck or a rabbit? Illusion on left from Jastrow (1900, p. 295); illusion on right from Wittgenstein (1953, p. 194). Jastrow credits *Harper's Weekly,* who credit *Fliegende Blätter.* Wittgenstein credits Jastrow, but uses his own casual freehand drawing, making one wonder why he provides a citation, the only one in his book.

Figure 10.3. Hanson's Antelope-Stork figure (Hanson, 1958, pp. 13-14)

practically available, perhaps only these two. Moreover, the pigment pattern that seems a common base of "fact" underlying these two "theories" is itself a theory-laden perception. When examined in microscopic detail, its solid linearity disappears into discrete specks of pigment and these, in turn, into organizations to which attributes of color or pigment are inappropriate. But this lower-level theory-laden presumptiveness that produces the line pattern is not changed in shifting from duck to rabbit, although the perception of some specific angles or other linear relationships may be (see, for example, Figures 10.2 and 10.3).

The Priority of Pattern Identification
Over Knowledge of Details

Another aspect of this descriptive epistemology is an emphasis on the epistemic priority of patterns rather than particles (Campbell, 1966). Consider

the task of identifying "the same" dot in two prints of the same newspaper photograph. Let each picture be covered with a large sheet of paper with a small
hole in it. When this reduction screen exposes only one dot at a time, the task is
impossible—the particle in isolation is nearly totally equivocal. When a square
centimeter or a square inch is exposed, the task becomes more possible because patterns become identifiable—the larger the pattern, the more certain the
identification. Insofar as an identification of corresponding dots is achieved, it
is because of a prior identification of the patterns. This is an obvious truism, yet
epistemological orientations still abound that seek certainty in particles, be it
definitions of terms or particulate sense data. All knowing of atoms or minute
details is at least as context-dependent and as presumptive as is the knowing of
larger or more encompassing patterns. Atomic particles or sense data are the
very reverse of dependable building blocks. Qualitative, commonsense knowing of wholes and patterns provides the enveloping context necessary for the
interpretation of particulate quantitative data.

Commonsense Cross-Validation of Science

Not only does science depend upon commonsense knowing as the trusted
grounding for its elaborate esoteric instrumentation and quantification, in addition many products and achievements of this esoteric science are cross-
validated in ways accessible to common sense. The mysteries of trigonometry
are visibly confirmed when the two ends of a tunnel or bridge meet. Faraday's
invisible flows of electrical currents produced visible sparks and visible mag-
netic movement of bars of iron. Thus even nonscientists have the capacity to
perceive evidences of the validity of esoteric science in commonsense terms.
Engineering achievements visible to the naked eye do thus validly validate science in the public mind.

Among laboratory scientists themselves, this commonsense cross-
validating is in continual use, and is a fundamental component in that identification and expectation amalgam that justifies their rejecting much of their meter readings as in error (due to faulty calibration, misconnections, or whatever).
This cross-validation of the quantitative by the qualitative is today usually
missing in the social sciences, or appears as hostile criticism, discussed below.
In well-used scientific laboratories there emerges another fusion of the qualitative with the quantitative, in which mechanical, quantifying instruments be-

come such familiar appendages that they become incorporated into qualitative knowing, like the blind man's cane. Whether we will ever achieve this state in the social sciences is moot, but it will never emerge without an intense prior interaction of commonsense and scientific knowing on the same problems.

QUALITATIVE KNOWING IN QUANTITATIVE PROGRAM EVALUATION

The qualitative underpinnings of quantitative data can be discovered by tracing back to its sources any numerical value on a computer printout. Behind the test scores in a Head Start Program lie the verbal and demonstrational instructions to the test administrator, the verbal and demonstrational explanations given by the test administrator to the children, the children's qualitative comprehension of the questions, and so on. Qualitative knowing on someone's part is also basic to identifying these tested children as the same individuals who participated in the prior Head Start sessions. The Head Start curriculum instructions were conveyed by ordinary language, and if the loyalty of their execution has been checked, it has been by qualitative observations. If interviews with parents have been used, a commonsense trust in shared language and shared motives has undergirded the interview conversation. Recording of responses and the coding of free-response answers achieve quantification only as the end product of a qualitative judgmental process. Most of this underpinning of commonsense knowing is so ubiquitous and so dependable that we fail to notice it. But I believe that such a base underlies all quantitative knowing in the social sciences just as in the physical.

It is usually so dependable we fail to notice it, yet the dependence on the qualitative is there even when unwarranted. Critique of the qualitative base is needed and this turns out to depend upon a qualitative knowledge of the more complete context. At the present time we have an unhealthy division of labor in this regard: On the one hand, we have quantitative social scientists who use census data, monetary records, and crime rates, forgetting their qualitative judgmental base. On the other hand, we have qualitative sociologists who do critiques on how the numbers get recorded—for example, analyzing the social dynamics of a census interview, the incommensurable understandings of the participants, and the fears and pressures lying behind the answers. Because of the scepticism thus generated, these qualitative sociologists refuse to participate in quantitative analyses.

Particularly in the area of quantified administrative records, a vigorous critical literature has emerged, the flavor of which can be caught from titles such as " 'Good' Organizational Reasons for 'Bad' Clinic Records" (Garfinkel, 1967), "A Note on the Uses of Official Statistics" (Kitsuse & Cicourel, 1963), "Police Misreporting of Crime and Political Pressures" (Seidman & Couzens, 1972), "Nixon Anti-Crime Plan Undermines Crime Statistics" (Morrissey, 1972), "Downgrading of Crimes Verified in Baltimore" (Twigg, 1972). (See also Beck, 1970; Becker, 1970; Becker, Geer, & Hughes, 1968; Blau, 1963; Douglas, 1967; Etzioni & Lehman, 1967; Ridgeway, 1956.)

Similar studies are needed for the achievement test situation. If multiple independent anecdotes are to be trusted, the computers too often have been processing in stolid seriousness worthless data produced by children who were staging mass boycotts, or deliberately sabotaging the process, or making jokes out of their answers. Anecdotes of similar scandals are available for questionnaires, attitude scales, and interviews (Vidich & Bensman, 1954). We need such critique to be integrated with quantitative study. These two approaches are integrated somewhat, although not enough. Some of this integration is at least called for in the methodology of field experimentation, under the headings of "threats to validity" or "plausible rival hypotheses" (e.g., Campbell & Stanley, 1966; Cook & Campbell, 1979). A qualitative consideration of the differing contexts of measurement often generates hypotheses as to how differences between pretest and posttest, or between experimental group and control group, are due to differences in the respondent's or researcher's understanding of the measurement process, rather than to changes in the attribute that the measure is intended to reflect. Some of these rival hypotheses can be ruled out by formal aspects of design, but many of them must remain qualitative even in the most thorough report: in the mode of generating the rival hypotheses, in seeking out other evidence of that hypothesis' validity, and in the overall judgment as to its plausibility. Where the social interactions producing measurement are concerned, this is at least as great a problem for randomized "true" experiments as for quasi-experimental ones.

For many experimental program evaluations, especially quasi-experimental ones, a major category of threats to validity are the many other events, other than the experimental program, that might have produced the measured changes. Generating these specific alternative explanations and estimating their plausibility are matters of commonsense knowing and require a thorough familiarity with the specific local setting.

While these rules regarding the use of qualitative knowing are clearly present in the quantitative methods books, they are rarely exercised. The researcher is apt to feel that presenting such content undermines the appearances of scientific certainty, or that weaknesses on these points are evidence of his own incompetence. The field experimenter's defensiveness vis-à-vis his laboratory colleagues leads to further minimizing of this content and still more so when he is earning his living as a contractor in program evaluation.

In current quantitative program evaluations, qualitative knowing is also regularly present in the narrative history of the program, as well as in the description of the program content, the measures and means of data collection, and in the verbal summary of program outcomes. The numerical evidence would not be interpretable otherwise. Yet such qualitative content is often an unplanned afterthought.

This sketch of the present role of qualitative knowing in the quantitative evaluation of action programs has already implied the need for increasing explicit cognizance of that role at several points. In what follows, this theme will be expanded. There will also be some grudging consideration of qualitative program evaluation in the absence of quantitative measures. Before getting to that, it seems well to look at the types of qualitative knowing that might be or have been proposed.

Types of Qualitative Evaluation

Tribes, governments, and voluntary groups have for centuries instituted new programs, which have been stopped, retained, or disseminated. From a social-evolutionary perspective (Campbell, 1965), such program fates are evaluations and the decision processes involved constitute evaluation mechanisms. Some of these mechanisms are matters of organizational survival, a social-evolutionary natural selection. But more often, the decisions, and certainly the borrowing decisions, have involved human judgments serving as vicarious representatives of potential survival value. These vicarious judgmental processes are themselves products of biological and social natural selection.

The raw material for such evaluations is the remembered experiences of participants transformed into an institutional decision by some formal or informal political process. Remembered experiences of participants will be treated as the most primitive and pervasive of qualitative knowing relevant to program evaluation. Since memory of the past is continually readjusted by current context and recent experience, an important variant becomes *recorded participant experience,* as through writings and recorded votes. For action research, there are other relevant groups of lay observers, persons well placed to observe, incidental to other social roles. These include the program staff and those groups of citizens who come into regular contact with the recipients.

Qualitative evaluation by evaluation experts (by social scientists) can take many forms. It can involve the social scientist's own qualitative experiences, as in a single time sample in the *site visit,* or over an entire social action experience, including a preprogram period, as in *participant observation* and *nonparticipant observation.* But still more common in qualitative social science is the expert's role in recording and collating the participant's experiences, as through *informant interviews, opinion surveys,* or the *experience interview.*

In the political processes in which groups transform the remembered experiences of participants into evaluative decisions, voting may be used, a kind of quantification of the qualitative for the purposes of pooling subjective judgments. Similarly, the social scientist's role in collating participant experience may involve quantification, as in coding free-response interviews, or in counting the number of participants who had generally negative evaluations of the program, or in providing rating scales and structured questions on which participants can quantify their own subjective experience. Indeed, much of what we think of as experimental measures, recorded on the occasion of pretest and posttest for both experimental and control groups, are in fact quantifications of subjective judgments. The qualitative social scientist may also use quantitative translations in recording or summarizing his own direct experiences. In what follows I shall try to distinguish qualitative from quantitative collations of qualitative experience, but shall treat both under the overall category of qualitative.

Process evaluation has been offered as a supplement (Freeman & Sherwood, 1970) or alternative to quantitative experimental program evaluation (e.g., Guttentag, 1971, 1973; Weiss & Rein, 1970). One founding statement presents this challenge in exaggerated form:

> The reason we require "control groups" in experimental science is that the processes presumably go on in the famous "black box." So we cannot observe the significant middle state of "throughput." We can only ascertain the input and measure the output. But where it is possible to observe the throughput—the process—then the need for the crude experimental model is bypassed. (Bennis, 1968, p. 231)

In practice, process evaluation has meant qualitative consideration of the specific events in program implementation, including the typical experiences of participants. Process evaluation may be done by the program implementation staff themselves, or by process evaluation specialists whose full-time job it is, or conceivably by getting participants to keep diaries. Narrative histories of program experience may be a typical product. Such are referred to as the extensive database for Kaplan et al.'s (1973) summary Model Cities evaluation (see also Gilbert & Specht, 1973). While we as yet lack classic examples and critical reactions, we may be sure that the clairvoyant visibility of causal relations anticipated by Bennis is lacking. Nonetheless, a well-planned and conscientiously executed process description seems a desirable feature in any program evaluation as a cross-validation and as a critique of the measurement process and the experimental arrangements. (The usual assignment to the process evaluator should be explicitly extended to cover these latter activities.)

If we were to see develop a widespread practice of process evaluation and if process evaluators were to criticize each other and argue about assessments of program effects, their mutual criticisms would almost certainly lead them to reinvent aspects of experimental design. That is, a need would be felt for similar process records prior to the innovation, and for a record of the process stream for comparable social units experiencing the same historical events except for the program. Experimental design can be separated from quantification. The equivocalities of inference that experimental design seeks to reduce are present for qualitative evaluation fully as much as for quantitative.

Formative evaluation has been distinguished from the *summative evaluation,* the measurement of program impact that is the goal of the typical quantitative experimental program evaluation. Formative evaluation refers to a continuous monitoring of a new program designed to support immediate revisions in aspects of the program that prove to be unworkable or obviously ineffective. While conceivably some of this could be done by quantitative experiments on these features, the cumbersomeness resulting, the need for immediate reaction, and the fact that many of the errors in planning are visible to the naked eye, make formative evaluation primarily a matter of commonsense knowing. It is an obviously desirable precursor to quantitative experimentation or full-scale process evaluation, since these expensive procedures should not be wasted on programs that the program implementor would not want to see repeated and disseminated in that form. Where feasible, such a debugging formative run of a program should precede program evaluation. The need for formative evaluation needs emphasizing and scheduling. Otherwise, the project may defensively implement a program designed only on paper, and in so doing, may blind itself to available qualitative evidence of implementation failure.

Systems analysis is a frequently recommended alternative/supplement to the quantitative experimental approach (Baker, 1968, 1970; Schulberg & Baker, 1968; Schulberg, Sheldon, & Baker, 1969; Weiss & Rein, 1970). While in biology, and engineering (e.g., Jones, 1973), this is a highly quantified utilization of experimental findings, it has come to represent in social program evaluation a generally qualitative approach typified by an attention to organizational functioning, relationships to other systems, and close attention to the actual processes involved in the treatment. In this, it certainly avoids the narrow blindness of many quantitative evaluations. Awaiting the day when we have some full-scale systems analyses of new programs and their impact, I will not try to distinguish this approach from process evaluation or the fieldwork methods to be described below, and will repeat the recommendation that it would seem a valuable adjunct to quantitative evaluations.

The use of *anthropologists* as program evaluators has been undertaken in the Experimental Schools Program of the National Institute of Education in the United States. While this is not to the total exclusion of quantitative measurement, the anthropological fieldwork represents the one dominant research expense in several expensive program evaluations.

Prior to Malinowski, most anthropological research represented the compilation of the experience of informants, often with the aim of reconstructing a picture of the local culture prior to contact with Europeans. Since Malinowski, the typical goal has been to describe the current lived culture of a specific village, without regard to its historical sources or cultural typicality. With this has come an emphasis on the anthropologist as a direct observer, as fully a participant in the collective life of the community as possible, learning the local language thoroughly, and living the local life 24 hours a day for some 2 years or more. It is this latter anthropological model that has been dominant so far in program evaluation. Particularly influential has been one nonparticipant-observer study of a school superintendent's office (Wolcott, 1973), although this study was not itself focused on a program evaluation. The fieldwork methods of the qualitative sociologists have also been used as models (Nelson & Giannotta, 1974a, 1974b).

A few preliminary samples of this approach in the U.S. Experimental School Program are available (Nelson, Reynolds, French, & Giannotta, 1974). There is also available a methodological essay stemming from a similar experience (Everhart, 1975). Already I am willing to affirm that they provide a background that will help the interpretation of quantitative evaluations, if and when the latter are forthcoming. There is a richness of detail on how things happened and what went wrong that would occasionally lead one to throw aside a quantitative evaluation as not worth reading since in the end no real changes were made, or because so many stronger extraneous forces impinged on the scene that the experimental program's impact had no chance of showing. But it does not seem to me yet that these ethnographies can stand alone as evidence of program effectiveness, replacing a good quantitative experimental evaluation.

The anthropologists had never studied a school system before. They had been hired after (or just as) the experimental program got under way, and were inevitably studying a mixture of the old and the new. Under such conditions, it is easy to make a mistake of attributing results to the program that would have been there anyway. It would help in this if the anthropologists were to spend half of their time studying another school that was similar, except for the new experimental program. This has apparently not been considered. It would also help if the anthropologists were to study the school for a year or two prior to the program evaluation. (This would be hard to schedule, but we might regard the current school ethnographies as prestudies for new innovations still to come.)

All knowing is comparative, however phenomenally absolute it appears, and anthropologists are usually in a very poor position for valid comparison, as their own student experience and their secondhand knowledge of schools involve such different perspectives as to be of little comparative use. The perceptual position of the lay program participants is in fact superior to that of the anthropologists, as we shall discuss below. (In the Southeast Minneapolis studies [Nelson et al., 1974], the several anthropologists working with the different schools did have the advantage of comparing notes with each other.)

In its prior uses, anthropological and sociological field observation methods have not usually been focused on the causal impact of a single factor or new institution. Instead, the goal has been that of describing things as they are without causal imputation. Indeed, the methodological orientation often includes a denial of the relevance or possibility of attempting to infer causal relationships. In accepting the assignment of evaluating the effects and effectiveness of a program, the anthropologist or sociologist has lost a significant freedom, and has reentered the more traditional scientific arena of causal inference. The ambiguities of this task may often lead the anthropologist to abandon the focus on program impact, and instead, justify the effort in terms of the value of having some thorough ethnographies of schools. However well-tested observational fieldwork methods are for their usual purposes, they are untried for program evaluation.

There are no reliability or validity studies of observational fieldwork that I am aware of. I believe that if two ethnographers were sent to study the same culture, or two participant-observer sociologists to study the same factory, considerable agreement would be found. But when you propose such studies, it turns out that qualitative social scientists would be more interested in differences than in congruences. They would not necessarily expect agreements, since each observer is recognized to have a unique perspective or since there is believed to exist no social reality except as constructed by the observer. Such a perspective on diversity of product can hardly be tolerable to a government agency or a volunteer group trying to decide on expanding or terminating a new program. The degree to which two anthropologists working independently agree on institutional program description will certainly be tested. I myself believe that there is some firm social reality there to be described and that considerable agreement will be found. But an anthropologist's idiosyncrasies will also be present (Campbell, 1964), and I am not sure the agreement will extend to the usually low-contrast details of program effectiveness.

But it is not only for qualitative evaluations that such replicability needs demonstrating. Quantitative experimental studies involve so many judgmental decisions as to mode of implementation, choice and wording of measures, assembly of data in analysis, and so on, that they too should be done in replicate. Our big evaluations should be split up into two or more parts and independently implemented. When the results agree, the decision implications are clear. When they disagree, we are properly warned about the limited generality of the findings. If qualitative and quantitative evaluations were to be organized on the same programs, I would expect them to agree. If they did not, I feel we should regard it possible that the quantitative was the one in error.

For qualitative program evaluation, historians should also be considered. Political scientists are already involved (e.g., Greenstone & Peterson, 1973, although they eschew estimates of impact). If qualitative program evaluation is to become a frequent procedure, the methodologies of humanistic studies should be reassembled and reassessed for this purpose. The most frequent methodological package is the "case study," combining all available evidence from informants, news reports, documents, archives, and firsthand observations. Standards of evidence exist that not all process evaluations and program ethnographies as yet live up to. There is the anthropological and sociological fieldwork requirement of field notes, written up each day, and subsequently used to check attempts at generalization. In the anthropology department at Berkeley, Lowie and Kroeber used to require all myths and histories to be obtained independently from at least two informants. Greenstone and Peterson (1973), in a report that boldly names names and events in recounting off-the-record program history, are able to assert: "In all cases, reports of the participant's behavior are based . . . on evidence obtained from several actors speaking from various perspectives" (p. 7). Such a requirement is certainly apt to increase the replicability of a study.

In past writings (1961b, 1963, 1970) I have spoken harshly of the single-occasion, single-setting (one-shot) case study, not on the grounds of its qualitative nature, but because it combined such a fewness of points of observation, and such a plethora of available causal concepts, that a spuriously perfect fit was almost certain. Recently, in a quixotic and ambivalent article, "Degrees of Freedom" (1975), I recanted, reminding myself that such studies regularly contradict the prior expectations of the authors, and are convincing and informative to skeptics like me to a degree that my simple-minded rejection does not allow for. My tentative solution is that there must exist many "degrees of freedom" in the multiple-implications attribute space, giving such a study a probing and testing power that I had not allowed for. It is possible that specific examples of case studies focused-program effects might eventually convince me that they had the power to evaluate programs. Particularly, they might validly pick up unanticipated effects missed by more structured approaches. But I have not yet seen specific examples.

Acquaintance with events and persons extended across time and settings provides even the quantitative scientist with qualitative knowledge that enables one to catch misunderstanding, error, and fraud in the data. Where the same person runs the treatment program, collects the data, and analyzes the results, the qualitative support for the quantitative results is apt to be strong. Much or all of this acquaintanceship base can be lost in large-scale modern quantitative program evaluations. At its worst, four different teams under four separate contracts collect pretreatment data, administer the program, collect posttreatment data, and analyze the results. Even on single-contract studies the division of labor within the project produces a similar split. The belief that external evaluators are more objective further prevents the sharing of qualitative experience. Undoubtedly the computer printouts often provide a pseudoscientific facade that gullibly uses data for which the qualitative basis of the quantitative is in fact invalid. A project anthropologist, sociologist, or historian, assigned to the task of commonsense acquaintance with the overall context including the social interactions producing the measures, could often fill in this gap.

PARTICIPANT EVALUATION

Participants, as we have noted, will usually have a better observational position than will anthropologists or other outside observers of a new program. They usually have experienced the preprogram conditions from the same viewing point as they have the special program. Their experience of the program will have been more relevant, direct, and valid, less vicarious. Collectively, their greater numbers will average out observer idiosyncrasies that might dominate the report of any one ethnographer.

While participants are asked to generate a lot of data in program evaluations, rarely are they directly asked to evaluate the program, to judge its adequacy, to advise on its continuance, discontinuance, dissemination, or modification. Rather than evaluating programs, participants are usually asked about themselves and their own adequacy. We are thus wasting a lot of well-founded opinions. Course evaluations are one exception to this, and at their best confirm the competence of participants as observers (Frey, 1973).

In a Head Start program, many of the mothers have the experience of older children to compare to their Headstarters. In the New Jersey Negative Income Tax Experiment, the participants have gone through 3 years of a very special income subsidy system. They have both their own prior experience and the concurrent experiences of their equally poor nonexperimental neighbors as comparison bases. They know they've been in an experiment, and must have a variety of impressions about its effects on their lives.

We should start trying to assemble these participant judgments. In the spirit of qualitative compilations of qualitative judgments, we should probably let the participants pool their judgments in face-to-face meetings, perhaps first in small groups with recording secretaries and then in delegate groups, buzz-session style. The group's meetings could generate conclusion statements and vote on them, but usually verbal statements of unquantified consensus would result.

Should the control group participants meet with the experimentals to add that comparison base? If one wanted to use such evaluation methods, would it not be desirable to have alternative programs tried out adjacent to each other, so that the participants could compare notes on the alternatives all during the course of the study? In any event, it would seem a fruitful way of generating informed qualitative comparisons to have the participants of differing alternative programs brought together in conferences.

In Head Start programs, there are other competent observers whose evaluations go unrecorded: the Head Start teachers, the first-grade teachers, the Headstarters themselves. In the Negative Income Tax Experiments, the regular community social workers, the interviewers, and next-door neighbors all suggest themselves as competent qualitative observers, well worth listening to.

Robert L. Wolf (1974), in an impressive, detailed, speculative dissertation, proposed that judicial procedures, adversary hearings, with witnesses such as Head Start parents, teachers, and pupils, with attorney cross-examination and an expert jury, be used to generate the integrated decision. He presented a very persuasive case for the extra validity provided by judicial procedures, especially cross-examination, citing Levine (1974) among others.

But qualitative compilation procedures do not seem to me to be essential. Group opinion, if a mature consensus exists, has a stubborn reality that will show through a variety of methods. Thus I think much of the value of participant evaluation could be obtained by direct interview questions on the effects of the program, and the like, which could then be statistically summarized. Occasionally subtleties would be missed that the participants would discover and agree upon in a group discussion. Equally often, however, the minutes of the group discussion would be dominated by a single participant and lack the averaging-out of errors achieved by a statistical summary.

For institutions and groups that will be continuing sites of program changes, such as the welfare system and schools, Gordon and I (Gordon, Campbell, Appleton, & Conner, 1971) proposed that all participant groups (social workers and clients, pupils, parents, and teachers) fill out an "Annual Report for Program Evaluation" that would provide the pretests and time series for the quasi-experimental evaluations of changes.

We need to try out a variety of such procedures. As described so far, these would represent methodologically independent cross-validations of the quantitative results. They would have the chance of discovering program effects on topics not anticipated in the formal measurement devices. They would be likely to confirm the major findings on shared dimensions. If they did not, as I've said, we should consider the possibility that the quantitative procedures are in error. If I will concede all this, why would I be reluctant to see the qualitative procedures used without the quantitative? It is because I believe that the quantitative, when based on firm and examined qualitative knowing, can validly go beyond the qualitative, and can produce subtleties that the qualitative would have missed.

The issue may be made clearer by considering a second valuable role for participants, or for qualitative social science observers, that is, as critics of the quantitative results. If our program ethnographers or historians and the participant discussion groups were to be presented with the major results and allowed to criticize them, an important kind of validation would be achieved. Some of the findings they would concur with. Other results they would disagree with and explain away as artifacts due to aspects of the situation that the quantitative measurers had missed. Still, other results would surprise them, but stand up under their cross-examination, and eventually appear valid to the qualitative observers. It is these latter instances in which the quantitative would have gone beyond the qualitative in a valid manner.

Before this analysis is completed, it should go on to make use of our century of research on human judgment and its biases. It should go over the lists of threats to validity of experiments and measures, comparing the susceptibility of qualitative and quantitative on each. It should look to the special threats coming from the politics of evaluation, the internal project politics, and the intrusion of the politics of the external setting: In what ways do these political pressures impinge differently on the quantitative and the qualitative?

In summary, the polarity of quantitative versus qualitative approaches to research on social action remains unresolved, if resolution were to mean a predominant justification of one over the other. Social knowing, even more than physical knowing, is a precarious and presumptive process. However approached, there is much room for valid criticism. Each pole is at its best in its criticisms of the other, not in the invulnerability of its own claims to descriptive knowledge.

Accepting my own continued identification with the quantitative experimental approach to action research, I cannot recommend qualitative social science, nor group process lay participant consensus, as substitutes for the quantitative. But I have strongly recommended them both as needed cross-validating additions.

More than that, I have sought to remind my quantitative colleagues that in the successful laboratory sciences, quantification both builds upon and is cross-validated by the scientist's pervasive qualitative knowledge. The conditions of mass-produced quantitative social science in program evaluation are such that much of this qualitative base is apt to be lost. If we are to be truly scientific, we must reestablish this qualitative grounding of the quantitative in action research.

OVERVIEW OF CHAPTER 11

————•◆•————

In certain fields, such as anthropology, comparative political science, and comparative sociology, the researcher tends to study a single foreign setting. The product of this study, whether carried out by the trained scientist or an amateur observer, is called "commonsense knowing" for comparative social science. When a quantitative multinational study is performed, it is based on a large number of these individual case studies. It is still, however, dependent on commonsense knowing.

Campbell views the single case study in the following way. An observer notes an unusual characteristic of a culture and then finds an explanation for it by examining all the differences on all other variables. This observer will always find an explanation that seems to fit perfectly. This is not good science.

One type of case study is more acceptable—the type in which the researcher examines the multiple implications of the theory on other aspects of the culture. The theory is not accepted unless the expected pattern holds up. Intensive case studies may find that prior beliefs and theories were wrong. By documenting these instances, researchers can be assured that the case study method does not accept merely any explanation that appears to fit. The quality of the ethnographer, based on his or her knowledge of and familiarity with the culture, may be the best indication of the quality of the work produced.

Campbell recognizes that the single-culture case study will continue to be the method for comparative social science. He offers some suggestions to improve the ability of this method to probe for theory. First, a field-worker should use all available observations to see if each new observation supports the theory. Records should be kept of all observations and the multiple implications of proposed theories, and these records should be made available to other scientists to offer dissenting or affirming arguments. Second, theories posited prior to the observations, when affirmed, have more credibility than theories offered after the observations have been collected. Also, sites should be chosen blindly, and not because the culture exhibits characteristics that would have to be present to confirm a theory. Another suggestion deals with error rate experiment-wise, which can be problematic for qualitative studies, just as it is for quantitative studies. This issue involves making statistical conclusions about multiple hypotheses by using the rules of significance that apply when testing only a single hypothesis. For example, at the .05 significance level, 1 of 20 tests of hypotheses may appear to be significant due simply to chance. To handle this problem for qualitative studies, the field-worker must keep a record of all hypotheses, the multiple implications of those hypotheses, and the frequencies with which those implications are borne out or disputed. Campbell's final suggestion involves triangulation through the use of independent observers and multiple objects of study—ideally, two observers from different cultures studying a third and fourth culture. This avoids labeling a new culture as strange or puzzling, simply because it differs from one's own culture, which is accepted without question.

Campbell supports using experimental and quasi-experimental designs to probe theories, yet he recognizes that qualitative commonsense knowing cannot be replaced by quantitative knowing. Instead, quantitative knowing is rooted in commonsense knowing, and a validity-seeking epistemology must integrate both of them.

ELEVEN

THE QUALITATIVE CASE STUDY

———•◆•———

*T*he dominant mode of study in anthropology, comparative political science, and comparative sociology remains the intensive
study of a single foreign setting by an outsider for whom this is
the only intensively experienced foreign culture. Such studies may be written
by "trained" social scientists or by "amateur" observers (such as missionaries,
diplomats, newspaper reporters, businessmen, soldiers of fortune, or tourists)
whose observations and leisure may provoke them to write on the for-
eign-to-them culture. Even when these amateur observers do not write, they
participate strongly in enculturating the social scientist into the foreign culture, or into the expatriate accommodation to that culture (Kidder, 1971). Another similar genre are descriptions of one's own country done while or after
being a resident in another, as Kenyatta (1938) describing the Kikuyu while in
England as a student of Malinowski. Such knowing written or unwritten, I will
use to represent "commonsense knowing" for comparative social science. If

Campbell, D. T. (1975). "Degrees of freedom" and the case study. *Comparative Political
Studies, 8*(2), 178-193.

we achieve a meaningful quantitative 100-nation correlation, it is by dependence on this kind of knowing at every point, not by replacing it with a "scientific" quantitative methodology that substitutes for such knowing. The quantitative multination generalization will contradict such anecdotal, single-case, naturalistic observation at some points, but it will do so only by trusting a much larger body of such anecdotal, single-case, naturalistic observations (Campbell, 1974b).

This is not to say that such commonsense naturalistic observation is objective, dependable, or unbiased. But it is all that we have. It is the only route to knowledge—noisy, fallible, and biased though it be. We should be aware of its weaknesses, but must still be willing to trust it if we are to go about the process of comparative (or monocultural) social science at all. First, let me try to correct some of my own prior excesses in describing the case study approach. The caricature of the single case study approach that I had in mind consists of an observer who notes a single striking characteristic of a culture, and then has available all of the other differences on all other variables to search through in finding an explanation. He may have very nearly all of the causal concepts in his language on which to draw. That he will find an "explanation" that seems to fit perfectly becomes inevitable, through his total lack of "degrees of freedom." (It is as though he were trying to fit two points of observation with a formula including a thousand adjustable terms, whereas in good science, we must have fewer terms in our formula than our data points.)

While it is probable that many case studies professing or implying interpretation or explanation, or relating the case to theory, are guilty of this fault, it now seems to me clear that not all are, or need be, and that I have overlooked a major source of discipline (i.e., of degrees of freedom if I persist in using this statistical concept for the analogous problem in nonstatistical settings). In a case study done by an alert social scientist who has thorough local acquaintance, the theory he uses to explain the focal difference also generates predictions or expectations on dozens of other aspects of the culture, and he does not retain the theory unless most of these are also confirmed. In some sense, he has tested the theory with degrees of freedom coming from the multiple implications of any one theory. The process is a kind of pattern-matching (Campbell, 1966; Raser, 1969) in which there are many aspects of the pattern demanded by theory that are available for matching with his observations on the local setting.

Experiences of social scientists confirm this. Even in a single qualitative case study the conscientious social scientist often finds no explanation that seems satisfactory. Such an outcome would be impossible if the caricature of the single case study as presented earlier were correct—there would instead be a surfeit of subjectively compelling explanations. While I have no doubt that there is a statistically significant bias in favor of drawing conclusions rather than holding belief in abeyance in the face of essentially random evidence (Campbell, 1959b; demonstrated for animals by Tolman & Krechevsky, 1933; and by B. F. Skinner's research on superstition in pigeons), this cannot be a dominant bias, as both biological and social evolution would have eliminated such credulity in favor of more discriminating mutants. That is, our common-sense mechanisms of knowing must have had a net adaptive value, at least for the ecology in which they were evolved.

Becker (personal communication, 1970; see also Becker, 1970, pp. 25-38, 39-62) assures me that almost invariably the social scientist undertaking an intensive case study, by means of participant observation and other qualitative commonsense approaches to acquaintance, ends up finding out that his prior beliefs and theories were wrong. If so, this is an important fact, and one worth systematic documentation. If so, it shows that the intensive cross-cultural case study has a discipline and a capacity to reject theories.

Naroll (1962), one of the arch quantifiers of anthropology, acquires a powerful tool for data quality control in quantitative studies from classifying the "quality" of the ethnographer. It is noteworthy that the criteria of quality come not from the use by the ethnographer of any special tools of quantitative social science (such as random sampling procedures, structured interview schedules, psychological tests, etc.), but rather from superior qualitative acquaintance with the culture described, for example, through longer residence and better knowledge of the local language.

Since single-culture case studies will continue to be the major form of comparative social science, it may be well to offer a few suggestions for improving the discipline such studies offer as probes for theory. These suggestions are based on analogues from quantitative studies. Quantitative studies, as published, are not by any means immune from these problems, as we shall see. But quantitative studies lead to efforts to set significance levels that in turn lead to awareness of subtle aspects of the problem. In what follows, the major general recommendation is that the researcher doing a single-site case study keep more explicit records on the analogous aspects of his problem-solving activities.

The best-known problem regarding degrees of freedom in tests of significance is the number of observations against which the hypothesis is checked. For similar replications within a culture site, the field-worker is usually already alert to this, for example, the number of observed villages in which the leadership pattern holds and the number in which it does not. What is here being suggested is that an analogous record be kept for the box score of implications of the theory, aspiring to a full record of all of the theory-testing thoughts and investigations that take this form: If theory A is true, then B, C, and D ought to follow. Where these implications have motivated him to active search, recording will be easy. Where the test has been adequately completed in the thought process alone, much of the implication count will be lost. But even for these thought trials, a self-conscious attention to the problem can result in much more complete recording than case study monographs now present. Much of this puzzle-worrying is no doubt literally unconscious and/or during sleep, as Poincaré (1913) argues. Thus a full record will not be achieved. Probably the most common omission would be the neglect of implications that do not fit, particularly by the more theory-driven observers. The cumulative literature of other studies and of criticism provides a slow and partial curb to this. We need a tradition of deliberately fostering an adversary process in which other experts are encouraged to look for other implications of the theory and other facts to contradict or support it. Some of this is now done, but not in a form that would generate a box score of hits and misses. A further curb on the inevitable residual ethnocentrism of social scientists would be a practice of inviting local social scientists to present dissenting and affirming footnotes and commentaries along with the original publication of the regional monographs. This would also help to expand the box scores of hits and misses. For almost every classic theory-relevant case study there are as yet unused predictions on which to cross-validate them. If it is an important study, it is worth a confirmatory case study.

A second degrees-of-freedom, test-of-significance issue worth borrowing is the distinction between one-tailed and two-tailed tests. This can perhaps be translated into the case study setting as a distinction between the confirmatory value of an agreement between implication and facts when the theory has been chosen in light of those facts versus the higher confirmatory value when the theory has been chosen without knowledge of these confirmations. Certainly, the box score should keep these two types separate. Moreover, when the theory correctly predicts a fact that would be very unexpected from the point of view of common sense or other theories or other cultures, for example, the confirmation is correctly a lot more convincing than when the prediction is banal. This point is not easily recognized in the tests-of-significance tradition (Meehl, 1967), but is in the history of science as in Galileo's use of the phases of the moons of Jupiter. A Bayesian orientation could probably be used to focus on comparison of prior probabilities, given theory A, as opposed to the prior probabilities given other theories. This does not seem typical of Bayesian applications, which are more apt to treat for one theory at a time the prior probabilities and the probabilities after data collection. However this may be, one can certainly recommend the attention of a Bayesian statistician-epistemologist to the theory-testing case study problem. This problem should also be elaborated separately for each one of Lijphart's (1971) six types of case study (e.g., hypothesis-generating, theory-confirming, theory-infirming, etc.) with particular attention to the difference in the degrees of freedom when one has chosen, for example, the site expecting it to be confirmatory after an implicit or explicit search of many cultures for such an instance, versus going in blind and happening on a confirmation. Prior knowledge of extremity on one of two variables of relevance, or on both, or on neither, all affect the problem of degrees of freedom, that is, of capitalization on chance. Lijphart's analysis is very relevant here, although he neglects testing from multiple implications with a single case.

A final degrees-of-freedom problem is not well represented in published statistical studies, but is of increasing concern. This is the issue of doing tests of multiple hypotheses and then writing up as conclusions those that are "statistically significant" by a significance test that assumes that one went into the inquiry with only this one hypothesis. Thus if one's data had been generated in fact solely from random numbers, if one studies all of the interrelationships among 15 variables, generating 105 hypothesized two-variable relationships, 1/20 of these or 5+ would be found "significant" at the 5% level. The problem emerges in the literature as the "error rate experiment-wise" (Ryan, 1960) and the "problem of multiple comparisons" (Scheffé, 1953) or of "data dredging" (Selvin & Stuart, 1966). Combined with the problem of number of observations, it can be noted in a form particularly acute for political science studies correlating dimensions of nations: If one has as many variables as nations, then the multiple correlation relating any one variable to the others will be 1.00, even if all data are random numbers.

To handle this problem in the hypothesis-generating case study, one should keep a record of all of the theories considered in the creative puzzle-solving process. To represent the degrees of freedom from multiple implications, one should also keep a record of the implications against which each was tested, and the box score of hits and misses. I am personally convinced testing the implications of a single theory is better than the pseudo-perfect multiple correlation arising from exhausting one's degrees of freedom by testing too many hypotheses on too few cases or implications. I am also convinced that case studies can be improved in their theory-testing value in this regard. When one also recognizes the reality of higher-order interaction among variables (e.g., the relation of variables A and B being different for different levels of C, D, E, etc.), one must recognize that the plethora of plausible hypotheses and the fewness or costliness of instances create real limits for a comparative social science. But the recognition of instances in implication-space, to supplement the instances of persons, villages, nations, eras, and so on, alleviates the problem at least a little.

One more suggestion for improving the case study is offered. The single case study, as presented above, is in reality a comparison of two cases: the original culture and the foreign culture. But this is a very asymmetrical comparison, asymmetrical on a number of important parameters: One culture is learned as a child who had no alternative, and is learned concomitant with acquiring the local presuppositions and language of social knowing. The other culture is learned as an adult foreigner. The details of the new culture under study are focal and specified. The own-culture comparison base is left implicit. Had the features of the own-culture been made equally focal and explicit, had they been "studied" directly, the implicit comparison would often have been negated. But although this would be an improvement, the features of the own-culture would still seem more sensible, reasonable, intuitively comprehensible, and moral. Those of the foreign culture would tend to seem arbitrary, strange, puzzling, if not immoral. To correct this, in an earlier paper I made the following suggestion:

Triangulation through the own-culture bias of observers. The achievement of useful "realistic" constructs in a science requires multiple methods focused on the diagnosis of the same construct from independent points of observation, through a kind of triangulation. This is required because the sense data or meter readings are now understood as the result of a transaction in which both the observer (or meter) and the object of investigation contribute to the form of the data. With a single observation at hand, it is impossible to separate the subjective and the objective component. When, however, observations through separate instruments and separate vantage points can be matched as reflecting "the same" objects, then it is possible to separate out the components in the data due to observer (instrument) and observed. It turns out that this disentangling process requires both multiple observers (methods) and multiple, dissimilar, objects of study.

Applied to the study of the philosophy of a culture, this implies that our typical one-observer one-culture study is inherently ambiguous. For any given feature of the report it is equivocal whether or not it is a trait of the observer or a trait of the object observed. To correct this the ideal paradigm might be as shown in Figure 11.1(a).

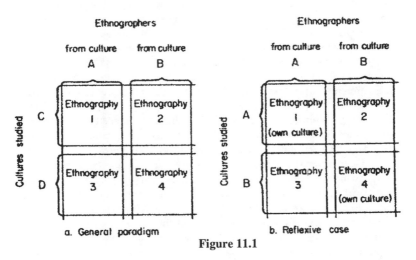

Figure 11.1

In the most general model, two anthropologists from different cultures would each study a third and fourth culture. Of the four ethnographies resulting, the common attributes in ethnographies 1 and 3 not shared with 2 and 4 could be attributed to ethnographer A, the common attributes in 2 and 4 not elsewhere present to ethnographer B. Looking at row consistencies in the figure, the common attributes in ethnographies 1 and 2 not present in 3 and 4 could be attributed to culture C as "objectively" known. Attributes common to all four ethnographies are inherently ambiguous, interpretable as either shared biases on the part of the ethnographers or shared culture on the part of the societies studied. Note the desirability in this regard of comparing ethnologists with as widely differing cultural backgrounds as possible. Insofar as the ethnologists come from the same culture, the replication of results becomes more a matter of reliability than validity, as these terms are used in discussions of psychological tests. Were such a study carried out by using four ethnographers, two from each ethnographer cultures A and B, studying separate villages of cultures C and D to avoid interference and collusion, then the attributes unique to any one of the ethnographies would be attributable to an equivocal pool of village specificities within its culture, to personality specifics of the ethnographer, and interaction of specific ethnographer culture and studied culture. (If only one ethnologist were used from each culture, and if each of the two studied in turn the same village in the target cultures, then the features unique to any one of the four ethnographies would be equivocally due to ethnographer-culture interactions, time-order effects in which the ethnographer reacted differently to his second culture, time-order effects in which the society reacted differently to the second student of it, historical trends, and interactions among these.) The presence of these indeterminacies should neither be suppressed nor be allowed to overshadow the great gains in understanding which such multiple ethnographer studies would introduce.

While multiplicity of both ethnographer-cultures and cultures studied is ideal, it would also be a great gain to achieve only the upper half of Figure 11.1(a), i.e., two ethnographer-cultures focused on the study of a single target culture. In all such triangulations, we again face the paradox of inability to use differences when these so dominate as to make it impossible to match the corresponding aspects of the reports being compared. The necessity of this common denominator provides one justification for Hockett's advocacy of including material and behavioral cultural details even in ethnographies focused on the determination of the philosophy of the cultures.

Another version of the multi-ethnographer, multiple-target design is that in which two cultures study each other, as diagramed in Figure 11.1(b). Usually the focus is on ethnographies 2 and 3, A's report on B and B's report on A. Implicitly, however, A's description of A and B's description of B are contained as bases of reference. There is probably some scientific value to be gained from such reports, even at the level of mutual stereotype sets or of reputational consensus from neighboring peoples. Once the evaluative component (each tribe viewing itself as best) is removed, such mutual stereotype sets show remarkable agreement in confirming the direction of group differences. (Campbell, 1964, pp. 331-333)

In line with the present discussion, I would now expand the requirements by asking that in a second phase of fieldwork, each ethnographer be asked to cross-validate, and invalidate, the other's interpretation of the culture they had studied in common.

CONCLUDING COMMENTS

This chapter is obviously exploratory, an extreme oscillation away from my earlier dogmatic disparagement of case studies into another extreme equally one sided. While it will not appreciably affect my own teaching about quasi-experimental designs and research methods, it does for the moment ring true. After all, man is, in his ordinary way, a very competent knower, and qualitative commonsense knowing is not replaced by quantitative knowing. Rather, quantitative knowing has to trust and build on the qualitative, including ordinary perception (Campbell, 1974b). We methodologists must achieve an applied epistemology that integrates both.

This paper is based on a presentation to the SSRC Workshop on Comparative Methodology meeting at Harvard University, August 1970. Its preparation in this form has been supported by NSF Grant SOC-7103704-03.

OVERVIEW OF CHAPTER 12

———•◆•———

In previous chapters, Campbell emphasized the importance of using qualitative methods to aid in the interpretation and understanding of quantitative findings. In this chapter, he considers the informant, and discusses a study that offers some guidance on how to select optimal informants.

There are two ways in which an informant can be chosen. First, when the culture is homogeneous, any one participant in the society can substitute for another. The other way of choosing an informant is to seek an individual who is very familiar with the group being studied, but also speaks the language of the scientist and understands the scientist's frame of reference. The problem with this latter method is that the individual who is able to look critically at his or her own culture, and then express those observations in terms the scientist will understand, may be different from the general populace. This may introduce a bias, although this bias may be reduced somewhat by using several informants.

Campbell used informants in a study of the quality of leadership in a U.S. Navy squadron of 10 submarines. One way to evaluate leadership is to examine the morale of the enlisted men on the submarines. The good informant for this project would be a person who is not an officer and who is familiar with all 10 ships. Such individuals were available in the squadron headquarters, because they had the opportunity to spend time on all 10 ships when they were in port.

Three yeomen were selected for this study, and the average ranking of the three yeomen provided a measure of the "happiness" of the ships' crews. Along with their ratings, the yeomen related specific stories and events and offered their opinions as to why morale might be poor. There are two ways in which the information provided by an informant can be quantified. The first way is to take the information they provide and categorize, code, and count. Another way is to ask the informant to provide some quantification at the outset, as for example, in this instance, where the yeomen were asked to rank the ships from happiest to least happy. Informants can also use prepared rating scales provided by the researcher.

Another measure of morale was provided by having the ships' enlisted personnel complete a questionnaire dealing with possible sources of dissatisfaction. The questionnaire was completed off the ship with no officers present. The results of this questionnaire were not used to judge whether the informants were accurately describing the morale on the ship, but, rather, they simply provided another source of information. It must be recognized that these surveys, too, may be subject to bias and error.

When the relationship between the two methods of judging morale was tested, the correlation between the enlisted informants and the surveys was an impressive .9. Officer informants and survey results correlated at .7. The difference in the correlations between these two groups was mainly due to a difference on one ship. Officers tended to underestimate the morale of the enlisted men. Still, Campbell felt that the overall correlation between officer and enlisted informants shows that there is a substantial degree of communication across these two groups.

One final method of judging morale was used, in which the survey respondents were asked to indicate the ship that they would most like to be assigned to during peace time. This method of rating morale also correlated highly with the data from the informants.

The comparison of the three methods for judging morale demonstrate that informants provide useful and valid information. This method has advantages over other quantitative methods because it is less costly and, at times, it may be the only option if ballots are out of the question.

TWELVE

USING THE ANTHROPOLOGIST'S INFORMANTS

———·◆·———

mong the several contributions of anthropology to general social science methodology, the technique of utilizing informants has received relatively little systematic attention. The
present report deals with an exploratory use of informants in research focused
upon the evaluation of morale as an adjunct to a study in naval leadership.

There are at least two ways in which the use of the informant may be interpreted as a general social science tool. On the one hand, it may be considered as
a sampling technique, in which any normal participant in the society could substitute for any other. The use of only one or a few individuals is justified where
the culture is homogeneous and where there are no relevant individual differences in the knowledge or behavior in question. Were this interpretation of the
technique to be generalized for rigorous application to complex Western cul-

Campbell, D. T. (1955). The informant in quantitative research. *The American Journal of Sociology, 60,* 339-342.

tures, it would take the form of opinion-survey procedures with methodological emphasis upon representativeness of the sample employed and statistical
sampling techniques employing randomness as the most feasible means of
achieving representativeness on all possible relevant grounds. This interpretation seems implied by Margaret Mead (1953) in her paper on "National Character."

In contrast, an alternative interpretation of the technique of the informant
seems to offer something new to the other social sciences in the way of explicitly formalized methodology. As understood in the present study, the technique
of the informant means that the social scientist obtains information about the
group under study through a member who occupies such a role as to be well informed but who at the same time speaks the social scientist's language. It is
epitomized by the use of one or a few *special* persons who are extensively interviewed and upon whose responses exceptional reliance is placed and, thus,
is to be most clearly distinguished from randomly or representatively sampled
interviews. The requirement that the informant speak the language of the social scientist epitomizes this difference. For the general public opinion survey
there is typically no procedure for placing special credence upon the answers
of those who intelligently understand the interview questions; rather there is an
attempt to describe the state of information and opinion among a universe that
includes those who comprehend and can verbalize adequately as well as those
who lack comprehension or expressive skill. By the requirement of speaking
the scientist's language we mean not only the literal sharing of a common
tongue (which can, of course, be the informant's native tongue if the social scientist is so trained) but also the capacity to share, in some degree at least, the
scientist's frame of reference and his interest in abstract generalized and comparative aspects of culture. As Paul (1953), for one, has pointed out, more often
than not the informant is himself an amateur or self-developed social scientist
with a genuine curiosity about cultural phenomena and the capacity to verbalize his observations.

But the seeking-out of the exceptionally observant and communicatively
gifted person as an informant raises a number of methodological problems.
The very backgrounds that would stimulate in the potential informant an interest in observing social custom and would develop perspectives making verbal-
ization possible are likely also to produce eccentricities of personality and

asymmetries of social locus that are possible sources of bias. To quote Paul: "Those who are willing to enter into novel relationships rather than to remain within familiar grooves, to examine culture rather than express it in action, are likely, almost by definition, to diverge from the normal." While to some extent bias can be reduced by using several informants, the danger cannot be corrected by recourse to representative sampling without at the same time losing the special character of the technique. If the use of informants as a social science research tool is to be developed, it seems likely that principles for optimal selection will have to be developed. Paul has made suggestions along this line, and the present study can be considered as a small contribution in this direction.

The problem was the ranking of 10 ships in a squadron of submarines in terms of their morale, for the purpose of helping evaluate the quality of leadership. A good informant for this purpose had to be one who had access to all 10 ships. Such could be found in the personnel of the squadron headquarters. For each of the major types of billet aboard the submarine there were parallel numbers in the squadron headquarters. Thus there were officers and enlisted men with responsibilities for engine maintenance on each submarine and in the squadron headquarters. The same held for other functions such as communication, electronics, supply, and so on. The personnel from the squadron headquarters had opportunity to visit with their parallel numbers from the ships when the latter came in to the headquarters office, and they frequently took short cruises with them or at least found an opportunity to eat with them when they were alongside dock. The squadron headquarters personnel had all had extensive and recent shipboard experience. Thus within the personnel of the squadron headquarters there were some at least who had the opportunity to be expert informants in the comparison of the ships.

Morale, for the purposes of this study, was considered primarily as an attribute of the enlisted personnel, that is, the 90% of the crews who were not commissioned officers. For this reason the best informants would probably come from the enlisted personnel in the squadron headquarters, if one assumes some barrier to communication between officers and enlisted personnel. In addition, the ideal informants had to be observant of the symptoms of morale and be willing and able to talk of them. This latter requirement would tend to rule out some of the enlisted personnel of the more mechanically oriented specialties, many of whom found it hard to speak with any confidence about social-psychological intangibles. For such reasons, as well as for reasons of expediency, the informants were selected from the yeoman (rated enlisted personnel performing secretarial duties) of the squadron headquarters company. Three of these men were willing to rank the 10 ships in terms of which were the "happiest." A ranking based upon the average of the three individual rankings was the basis of our elementary quantification.

Similar rankings of the ships were obtained from officers of varying duty in the squadron headquarters. None of them was in the direct line of command, and none had in the normal course of his duties the administrative responsibility of making comparative evaluations of ships or their personnel.

In addition to the rankings of the ships, the informants provided anecdotal material about specific episodes and persons, guesses as to the source of poor morale, and so on. These materials are perhaps more characteristic of what would be obtained in the typical anthropological use of informants, but they are not the aspects of the data receiving emphasis here. In the quantification of material from informants, two basic procedures seem to be open. First of all, the free-response verbal material provided by them may be coded, categorized, and then counted, as in public opinion surveys. Second, the informant may agree to participate in a procedure that provides some quantification at the onset. Of the possible ways of achieving this, the method of ranking here employed is probably the most flexible; it is one that probably could be employed for informants at any degree of civilization. While the level of quantification is primitive by mathematical or physical standards, it does provide that rudiment of quantification necessary for checking the data against other sources of information. In some situations the use of rating-scale procedures, which have been elaborately evolved by psychologists, would also be possible.

The study employed several other techniques for the evaluation of the relative morale of the 10 ships, the most expensive and extensive of which was a "morale ballot." This was a questionnaire containing prepared statements to be answered "Yes" or "No" and administered anonymously to the enlisted personnel in rooms off the ship, none of the ship's commissioned officers being present. It contained 30 questions dealing with a variety of potential complaints or expressions of dissatisfaction. Representative questions are:

Will you ship over and request duty on the same ship when your present enlistment is up?

On the whole, does everyone get a square deal aboard this ship?

Is there a better bunch of fellows here than aboard most ships?

Is the commanding officer aboard this ship a better leader than most skippers?

Do the officers play favorites and give certain fellows the breaks?

Do all hands get enough information on ship's plans?

Would you like to see more recreational activities aboard this ship?

While there is considerable topical variation among the 30 items, statistical analysis showed that they shared enough variance in common to justify the computation of an overall morale score for the ship, based upon the total of answers in the direction of high morale. Although this questionnaire is the most direct approach to morale used, it should not necessarily be regarded as a "criterion," inasmuch as it, like any other approach, is potentially subject to error. For example, it might have been that the questions employed did not cover the actual sources of discontent, although their development from earlier interviews had attempted to achieve this. It might also have been that the research setting did not provide convincing anonymity and that the degree of distortion due to distrust and caution varied significantly from ship to ship. While probably not the case, such possibilities must be kept in mind.

A Spearman rank order correlation has been used to describe the degree of agreement between the various approaches used to rank the ships in terms of morale. With only 10 observations, a high degree of correlation is required before we can be certain that the relationship is other than a chance sampling error. A rank order correlation of .6 is required before the 5% level of confidence is reached. That is, through sampling error alone the value of .6 would be reached in a series of samples of 10 cases less than 5% of the time if the "true" correlation in the universe of samples was zero. The value of .8 is required for significance at the 1% level. The small number of cases must make the study exploratory rather than definitive from the statistical point of view.

The correlation between the ranking of the ships by the enlisted informants and the ranking of ships by morale ballot is .9, showing an impressive amount of agreement, considering the independence and dissimilarity of the two methods. The correlation between the officer informants and the morale ballot is .7. The correlation between these two groups of informants is .8. These values, all substantially high, serve collectively to reinforce our confidence in each of the techniques. While it is impossible to claim that the superiority of the enlisted informants over the officer informants in degree of correlation with the morale ballot is statistically significant, it is certainly in the anticipated direction. The major advantage of the enlisted over the officer informants turns out upon more detailed inspection to involve the placement of a single ship, rated relatively high in morale by the enlisted personnel and low in morale by the squadron headquarters officers. The commanding officer of this particular ship had a cavalier and arrogant manner that made him unpopular with his junior officers and with the squadron headquarters officers (except possibly his immediate superiors) but that apparently did not create discontent among the enlisted personnel. The ship had recently been assigned to a new duty. There had also recently been a concentration of requests for transfer from the personnel of the ship. The squadron officers tended to interpret this flurry of requests for transfer as reflecting on the morale of the ship and the adequacy of its leadership. The alternative interpretation in terms of the kind of duty involved and the likelihood of the ship remaining in its home port was overlooked by them, although utilized to explain away similar increases of requests for transfer on other ships of the squadron. Probably because of the increased contact with the enlisted personnel of the ship, the enlisted headquarters informants were not misled by these superficial symptoms of discontent. While the difference gives some slight evidence of the anticipated barrier to communication between officer and enlisted strata in the naval service, the correlations also provide clear evidence of substantial communication across it. It seems probable, considering the conditions of service in the submarine study, that the barrier to communication is slight in this setting.

One other approach to the comparative morale on the ships seems worthy of attention. This is the ship's reputation for morale with other ships. At the time of taking the secret ballot, each enlisted crewman of the 10 ships of the squadron was given the opportunity to name other ships in answer to the question, "which of the ships in this squadron would you most like to serve on for peacetime duty?" The ships were ranked in terms of the number of times mentioned by the personnel of other ships. This may be described as an opinion survey on a reputational topic or as the utilization of informants in an exhaustive and nondiscriminative fashion. It should be pointed out that, while all the ships were in the same squadron and had roughly the same kind cf duty, they were on separate annual schedules that kept them out of their home port for periods up to 2 or 3 months during the year. At the moment of the survey, all the ships were in the home port, but some had only recently arrived from extended tours. In addition, a great bulk of the men were married and went directly from ship to home, thus not availing themselves of the opportunity for mass recreational intermingling that might have characterized the personnel of such a squadron in a foreign port. The ranking of the ships on reputation for morale correlated .8 with the morale-ballot ranking. In this instance, at least, such exhaustive sampling of opinion proves inferior to the careful selection cf a few informants. Reputation for morale with other ships correlates with the data from both enlisted informants and officer informants at the level of .7.

It seems fair to conclude from these data that the use of the informants in quantitative studies may be successfully carried out and may produce findings of validity and generality. Further methodological research seems justified on a number of grounds. From a standpoint of research cost, the expense of obtaining ship rankings and of securing data by the morale ballot might easily be in the ratio of 1 to 100. In addition, there will be many situations in which procedures for the morale ballot will be out of the question but in which informants might be effectively used.

This study was supported by a contract from the Office of Naval Research to Ohio State University, N6ori-17 T. O. 111 NR 171 123. It has been more fully reported in the research report issued by the Personnel Research Board, Ohio State University, "A Study of Leadership Among Submarine Officers" (1953).

OVERVIEW OF CHAPTER 13

———•◆•———

Any social scientist who wishes to conduct cross-cultural research is faced with the difficulties of working with an unfamiliar language. The researcher must be sensitive to the risks involved when making judgments based on translations. In this chapter [which is a portion of an article written by Werner and Campbell], Campbell offers recommendations to researchers on how to improve the validity of their findings on unfamiliar cultures when language is not shared.

The authors propose the use of back-translation, which requires the services of two translators. One translates the first half of the interview from English into the target language, while the second individual translates the second half. The translator of the first half then takes the target language translation of the second half and translates it back into English, and vice versa. When the back-translations provide a reasonable rendering of the original English version, the researcher can place more confidence in the newly created versions. When there are inconsistencies, a three-way conference with the researcher and the two interpreters may be necessary. This helps the researcher understand the equivocalities in the translations. It is suggested that this method be used even when there is not a preset interview. The activity itself gives the interviewers a set of local-language translations that may be useful in free-flowing interviews.

Another use of back-translation is to provide insights into the local language taxonomy. That is, it illustrates the ways that the social scientific terms of interest can be understood or misunderstood in the target language. For all its power, however, back-translation is not foolproof, and items may still be translated incorrectly. This may be due to errors in English-to-local language dictionaries. This can be avoided by employing translators who received less formal schooling in the language, but, instead, learned it by participating in the culture. For detecting errors, it is useful to see the words in context, perhaps in the form of descriptive narratives. It is much more difficult to detect errors in short answer form and almost impossible with yes or no answers.

The collective experiences of those using back-translations has already provided a number of common errors that occur when writing English versions to be translated. The authors recommend more research on back-translations, and recommend that a history of the method be recorded so that researchers are aware of its existence.

When standardized tests are used, an unfortunate tendency to provide exact translations may cause fundamental asymmetry in which common English terms become exotic or awkward in the target language. In intelligence tests, for example, individuals with the same intelligence do more poorly on the target language version. It is difficult to determine the direction of the effect on other types of tests. To avoid this problem, the authors suggest that the original English version be revised to make it equivalent with the target-language version. This new English version may be more banal and less valid and reliable, but it is preferable to have a comparison with such a test rather than to have two versions that are noncomparable because of asymmetrical translation. For the most valid comparison, the target-language version should be compared to new data collected using the revised English version. Ideally, a multistage iterative process should be used in which the original version is translated back and forth until a monolingual judge decides that the last two versions in the target language are equivalent. This process, in which both English versions and the target language are revised, provides an ideal conceptualization of decentered translating.

When doing cultural comparisons, imperfect translations will always be a plausible rival hypothesis to explain noted differences. If the cultural difference occurs on each item of a multi-item test, then this hypothesis ceases to be plausible. Each concept should be presented using two items that do not share key words, and analysis should be done on an item-by-item basis rather than simply the total score. Another way to confirm the equivalence of the versions is to have bilinguals respond to items in both languages. The goal is to have equivalent means and variances and appropriate correlations between the two versions. The authors demonstrate, however, that even tests that have similar validity, reliability, and factor structure may include ambiguities when a version is created through unicentered anchoring on an English version. They suggest that factor analysis should be carried out in both language versions, and only items showing upon the same factors in both cultures should be used to compute factor scores.

A problem could also arise when, to avoid having respondents choose the socially desirable alternative among two or three statements, the statements in each culture are scaled for social desirability using the values for the particular culture for which they are intended. While such tests will demonstrate differences within a culture, this procedure is not the appropriate one for comparing two different cultures.

While some researchers of cross-cultural differences support nonverbal tasks to avoid the translation problem, it should be recognized that nonverbal tasks, too, have their own irrelevant and misleading components. The authors advocate using such methods to supplement and support verbal methods, but warn against supplanting verbal methods with nonverbal ones. It is further pointed out that nonverbal tasks also require translation; however, the art of translating is not developed to the point to which verbal translation is. Even with gestures, there are differences among cultures.

Cross-cultural research can shed light on myriad social issues by uncovering the universality of or the variations in specific behaviors or attitudes. The researcher must be aware of the possibility that noted differences may exist simply because of inadequate translations. Back-translations and decentered translations are tools that the researcher can use to render this hypothesis implausible.

THIRTEEN

THE TRANSLATION
OF PERSONALITY
AND ATTITUDE TESTS

———·◆·———

*T*ranslation of a source language into a target language is a crucial undertaking for anyone interested in cross-cultural research. The purpose of this chapter will be to make specific recommendations of how some of the difficulties might be overcome, at least in part. The ideas and techniques that we propose are far from being thoroughly tested. While they are offered here as advice, they are also presented in the spirit of hypotheses, and as a call for systematic research into the translation problems faced by social scientists.

Werner, O., & Campbell, D. T. (1973). Translating, working through interpreters, and the problem of decentering. In R. Naroll & R. Cohen (Eds.), *A handbook of method in cultural anthropology* (pp. 398-420). Garden City, NY: Natural History Press.

USES OF BACK-TRANSLATION IN
FIELDWORK WITH INTERVIEWERS

The social scientist who finds himself needing to interview through interpreters while knowing little or nothing of the target language is in a relatively helpless situation, utterly dependent upon his interpreters, unable to judge their skill, and unable to instruct them in the quality of translation he requires. In this setting, the technique of back-translation offers him some degree of discipline. After the investigator has prepared an interview schedule in his most translatable English, he sets two interpreters to work, one translating the first half into the local target language, the other the second half. This completed, each then works with the translated local-language versions of the other, translating these back into English. (These can be written translations, if interpreters are literate in both languages, or spoken into tape recorders, copying so as to produce a monolingual tape in the local language for the back-translator to work on.) The investigator thus ends up with two versions in his language, and through them a triangulation on to the local-language version, which almost certainly must be adequate if the two English versions are.

The investigator immediately gains some insight into the quality of his translators. Both are validated where the back-translation is adequate. Where not, a three-way conference about each item, discussing the into-translations and back-translations, will achieve a consensus as to the specific problems. These will cumulate into evidence of general ability that the interpreters themselves will accept as valid. There is probably no better way of selecting among a surfeit of candidates for the job of interpreting.

The results of such first-round back-translations are usually distressingly poor, as Phillips (1959) reports in one of the very few published discussions of the method, and as our experience confirms. Unlike Phillips, however, we accept this usually poor quality as something the investigator needs to be confronted with and as a testimony to the value of back-translation rather than a reason for avoiding it. Certainly the more informal ways of having one translator check the translations of another give the investigator more confidence in the translator's competence, but this is probably misleading. The investigator has no control over shared misconceptions, professional reluctance to criticize another professional, local loyalty in exploiting a rich outsider, and the like.

Back-translation gives him a very considerable (although, to be sure, not complete) control over quality even when he knows nothing of the local language.

Back-translation will instructively inform the investigator of what part of his content can be successfully asked and what part of his social science interest is uncommunicable, at least with the translation talent available. It will force a realistic abandonment of many subtle distinctions that cannot be communicated. It will further an active revision of the English language "original."

Back-translation is the most powerful tool available to the investigator in training his interpreters. Teaching requires the ability to note errors, and only through back-translation can the investigator do this unless he is exceedingly expert in the local language. A week or so spent in back-translating in the whole range of the investigator's area of interest produces a great advance in interviewer sophistication and willingness to discuss the equivocalities of specific translation problems. Without this, the interpreter uses the face-saving posture of dogmatic professional certainty.

Even for that majority of anthropologists who use no preset inquiry schedule but who use interpreters in extempore interviewing, which follows the respondents' leads—and for the bulk of fieldwork this is undoubtedly the best method—the discipline of back-translation seems desirable for the reasons given above. Dependence upon interpreters without such checks undoubtedly leads to a great deal of self-deception as to the translation quality. Even if the back-translation effort produces no standard questions for use in interviewing, it produces an appropriate set of local-language translations of the investigators' key concepts.

Another specific use of back-translation is as a shortcut approach to ethnotaxonomy in a given domain (LeVine & Campbell, 1965). The investigator prepares a list of terms and near-synonyms in a given domain (e.g., interpersonal aggression). One bilingual generates as many as possible local-language translations for each term. Another bilingual generates as many as possible English-language translations of each local-language term. The investigator then has his original English-language taxonomy plus the heterogeneous sets of English back-translations, which he seeks to make sense of by hypotheses about the local-language taxonomy.

Back-translation, for all its power, is not foolproof. Even after an inquiry schedule item has successfully been back-translated, later use in the field will turn up ludicrously mistranslated items. It is instructive to consider how these are noted. One depends upon context and assumptions of already achieved knowledge and consistency to judge a given response bizarre, off the subject, irrelevant. When tracked down, these errors often turn out to be due to established translation-dictionary equivalents that have been used both in the into-translation and the back-translation.

These translation-dictionary rules come from standardized schoolroom and Bible-reading "solutions" to difficult but recurrent translation problems. Such errors are avoided by the less-schooled interpreter who has never seen a translation-dictionary, who has learned each language by participation rather than instruction, and who thus translates English-to-local-language. Note that the greater the context and redundancy provided, the more chance to note interpreter errors. Coherent descriptive narratives are best for this, short-answer questions poorer. Yes-no answers provide so little opportunity to verify respondent comprehension as to be worthless in work through interpreters.

More research is needed on the whole technique of back-translation, and more detailed collecting and reporting of existing experience. The records in any such collection of research should include, as a minimum, the English original and the first English back-translation, with errors marked as "into" errors or "back" errors. From a large sampling, recurrent "into" errors would add to our principles of writing maximally translatable English. Our experience to date recommends simple sentences, repetition of nouns rather than use of pronouns, avoiding metaphor and colloquialisms, avoiding the English passive tense, avoiding the hypothetical phrasings of the subjunctive tense, avoiding questions in which an abstract category concept is used to elicit specific instances in the response (such questions assume ethnotaxonomic universals, which misleading assumption may explain the widespread belief that local languages lack abstract terms typical of European ones). A list of frequently mistranslated English words would also result, for which words like "like" (affection or similarity), "kind" (considerate or variety), "people" (persons or ethnic group), would be included.

A history of the method is also needed. It has undoubtedly been several times independently invented. Anthropologists guiding opinion polls in Japan for the U.S. military government were using it by 1946 (John W. Bennett, personal communication). Stern and D'Epinay (1948) provide the earliest published description we have encountered. It has been frequently used, although without much methodological discussion (Almond & Verba, 1963; Cantril, 1965; Duijker, 1955; Ervin & Bower, 1952; Jacobson, 1954; Mitchell, 1965; Schachter, 1954). Phillips (1959) has provided the only anthropological discussion of the method of which we are aware.

TRANSLATION OF PERSONALITY, ATTITUDE, AND ABILITY TESTS

Cross-cultural research using psychological instruments has been greatly hampered by the concept of "standardized tests," that is, the belief that there are well-developed all-purpose comparison instruments for which valuable "population norms" have been collected. This notion of "standardized tests," the almost magical assumption that psychological tests could measure directly and perfectly what they claimed to measure, has led to a most unfortunate ethnocentric asymmetry in the translation of such instruments. The version in the investigator's language (e.g., English) has been regarded as inviolable. A mischievous brand of logical positivism has even regarded it as the operational definition of the scientific construct intended (Campbell, 1966; Campbell & Fiske, 1959; Webb, Campbell, Schwartz, & Sechrest, 1966). As a result, all of the translation effort has been directed toward representing it loyally in the target language. Figurative, metaphoric translation, in which target-language idioms have been substituted for analogous idioms in the original, has been avoided due to fear of losing an item-by-item identity. Illustrative referents have been retained even though they represented familiar objects in the original language but exotic objects in the target language. Thus a fundamental asymmetry has resulted in which familiar, colloquial, accessible test items in English become exotic, awkward, and difficult items in the target language.

For intelligence tests, it becomes obvious that equivalently able persons will do more poorly on the target-language version. For other types of tests, the direction of distortion cannot be specified without considering their specific content, but is no doubt equally important. The cure requires treating the original-language version as itself up for revision. Such revision and item-selection processes will no doubt produce an original version that is more banal, less subtle, more explicit, less colloquial, less idiomatic, less metaphorical, and with less extreme items. This may produce a test that is less reliable and less valid for original-language use. It will require collecting new original-language comparison groups on the new instrument. But certainly it is better to have comparable data on two banal tests, than to have noncomparable data because only one is banal.

The prevalence of the unconscious assumption of the unmodifiability of the original-language version is shown in a discussion by Berrien (1967) in a generally excellent article:

> Iwahara was faced with another complicating problem when translating the Edwards (Personality Preference Schedule) statements into Japanese. The items pertaining to heterosexual interest were too crude and blatant for the Japanese sensibilities. He, therefore, wrote new statements which pertained to heterosexual interests that were more acceptable in that culture. Under those circumstances, is it still more legitimate to compare the Japanese results with those of Americans? (Berrien, 1967, p. 39)

In his extended answer to this question, involving suggested solution of bicultural construct validation, he fails to consider the solution of collecting new United Statesian data on well-translated versions of the milder Japanese items.

Back-translation provides a most useful technique for suggesting revisions of the original, as well as revisions of the first translation effort. It also provides an epistemological model for the difficult process of decentering. Consider an original test, its first translation, and the first back-translation. We now have two original-language versions. Which should we use in our original-language data collation? The researcher, comparing the original and the first back-translation, will certainly prefer the original. But which is more comparable to the target-language version? Undoubtedly the back-translation— because of its comparably poor quality, for one thing. If translation is possible, then the researcher should be willing to collect data using the back-translation. Any qualms he has about this he should have about the translated version too.

The back-translation concept considered as multistage iterative process provides an ideal conceptualization of decentered translating. In addition to a large supply of competent bilingual translators, ideally some with each first language, there would be monolingual translation-judges in each of the languages. These judges would have the power to say when any double-translation

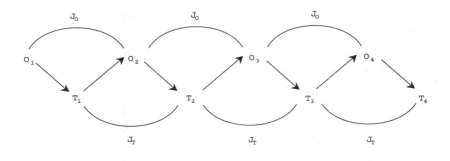

O₁, O₂, etc. = Original language versions 1, 2, etc.
T₁, T₁, etc. = Target language versions 1, 2, etc.
⟶ = Translation
⌒⌣ = Comparison of two same-language versions

J₀, J_T = Monolanguage judges in O and T languages

Figure 13.1. An Iterative Sequence of Back-Translation

was adequate by comparing the two versions in his language. Translation revision efforts would be made until he was satisfied. Figure 13.1 illustrates such a process. Essential to the decentering process is the monolingual judge in the target language. Without him, with only the judge in the original language (usually the investigator himself), the process would still produce a unicentered product, although less so than if the first original-language version were kept unmodified.

The strategy of cultural comparison has to be one of competitive interpretation of obtained differences, in which differences in culture attitude or personality are only one of the possible explanations. Imperfections of translations will ubiquitously appear among the plausible rival hypotheses. As with such rival hypotheses in general (Frijda & Jahoda, 1966; Segall, Campbell, & Herskovits, 1966), studying the effects of deliberate variation may help rule this out. Thus, if for a multiple-item attitude test, the same cultural difference occurs on each item, translation-imperfection ceases to be a plausible hypothesis. Note here two recommendations: first, in favor of multiple items over single items, and second, analysis of results by item rather than solely by total score. So strong is the likelihood of translation-imperfection, that even in the public-opinion survey format, where typically a single item represents a concept, one should use at least two items per concept, each pair sharing no key words but by intention as identical as possible in meaning.

A suggested tactic for confirming the equivalence of translation is to have bilinguals respond to the items in both languages (e.g., Schachter, 1954). Used as a formal statistical approach, the goal should not be identity at the item-by-item level, but rather equivalence of means and variances, plus appropriate correlations between scores on the two forms. Bentz (1955) and Lonner (1968) report translations of standard personality and interest scales that approximate these requirements. In Bentz's study, using 60 bilingual Latin American executives, the cross-language correlations after a 5-month delay averaged .57 for the six scales of the Allport and Vernon Study Values, in contrast with the test-retest values for the original scale after 3 months' delay (on an unspecified population) of .74. Parallel values for the Kuder Interest Scales were .75 versus .90 (over 2 months). In Lonner's study the average cross-language correlation of 62 scales on the Strong Vocational Interest Blank, administered in German one month later in English to 18 European psychologists, was .80, in comparison with English test-retest correlations over one month on a much less homogeneous group that averaged .91. Both Lonner and Bentz write as though optimal translation would bring the cross-language correlations up to the same level as test-retest values. But surely this is unreasonable, for as we have emphasized, a translation at best can be no more similar than a paraphrase in the same language. If one has constructed an original-language paraphrase for each item, and if these are then separated into a Form A and Form B, the cross-language correlation of Form A should be at best as high as the within-language correlation of Form A with Form B across a comparable time delay. This latter correlation will certainly be lower than an ordinary test-retest correlation. Lacking the deliberate preparation of paraphrase pairs, an odd-even split of items could be used for the same purpose. (To complicate the epistemological problem, Ervin, 1964, presents a plausible case for bilinguals showing appropriately different personalities in each of their languages [see also Anderson, 1967].)

Most commonly, claims for adequacy of test-translation are based upon finding similarity in reliability, validity, factor structure, and other statistics for the forms in both languages. This is fine when successful, and can be quite unequivocal evidence for both the universality of the trait and for the adequacy of translation. Gough (1966a, 1966b) has provided quite impressive parallel validations. But even in these, the disadvantages of a unicentered anchoring on the United States version of the test create ambiguities. Thus while the "Femininity" scale was designed for use as a personality trait within sexes, sex differences are relevant to its validity. For the U.S. form, the sex difference is indicated by a point biserial correlation coefficient of .71. For other countries, the values were significant, but lower: France, .52; Italy, .47; Norway, 62; Turkey, .47; Venezuela, .58. If the instrument had been decentered (with the U.S. version as subject to editing as the others, with items being suggested equally from the commonly observed sex differences in interests in each country, with statistical item selection being done jointly for all countries, etc., and with multicentered back-translation editing), then we might interpret this finding as demonstrating that sex differences in interests were the greatest in the United States, and were the least in Italy and Turkey. What we know anthropologically leads us to believe the reverse to be true, and that the .71 value reflects merely the cultural bias of the test, it having been constructed just so as to maximize sex differences within the United States; naturally this did less well in dissimilar cultures.

Where procedures such as factor analysis or item selection are involved, in a decentered test development procedure, these should be carried out in both languages, and only those items showing up on the same factors in both cultures used in computing factor scores (Gordon & Kikuchi, 1966; Kikuchi & Gordon, 1966). The unwillingness to revise the United States version again stands in the way of this getting done. The unicentered biases may be very subtle and hard to root out. While Gordon (e.g., Gordon & Kikuchi, 1966) has written very sensitively on such problems, and has pointed to the dimensions that get left out when value studies start only with United States forms ("none of the published American tests would measure the very important Japanese value *Giri* or 'filial piety'"), he has in a later study (Gordon, 1967) made the error of concluding that Chinese personalities were in fact more homogeneous than United Statesian ones, using a translation of Q-sort items designed for the purpose of maximizing United Statesian individual differences. Until he has reversed the process, developing Q-sort items in China to maximize Chinese differences and then translated these for the United States administration, no such conclusion is warranted.

Special problems emerge with special features of tests, which are perhaps only metaphorically translation problems, but are illustrative of fundamental problems in cross-cultural equivalence. The Edwards Personality Preference Schedule, like many of the better personality tests, is designed to avoid meaningless self-flattery through forcing the respondent to choose among pairs or triads of statements equated for social desirability. Berrien (1966), in building a Japanese version, had the translated items scaled for social desirability in Japan, and then used these quite-different values to assemble the items into different pairs. This was undoubtedly the correct thing to do if one wanted a test for use in making differentiations among Japanese. But for developing a test to compare the United States and Japan, it was wrong, for had the procedure been perfectly executed there would have been no value or need differences between the cultures (and within each culture, the mean of each value or need would have been the same [Kikuchi & Gordon, 1966]). His intermediate-stage data on Japanese and United States differences in social desirability ratings of the items were the relevant facts for describing cultural differences in personality. Similarly, Cantril's (1965) self-anchoring scales, supposedly an improvement in cross-cultural comparability, are no doubt useful for within-country comparisons, but by making all comparisons relative to the local adaptation level and frame of reference, they obscure the differences that would otherwise be found.

There has recently been emphasis on the importance of nonverbal indicators of attitude (e.g., Webb et al., 1966) and advocacies of increased use of nonverbal tasks in cross-cultural research as a method of avoiding the translation problems that verbal materials present (Frijda & Jahoda, 1966). Along with the latter is an emphasis on the desirability of using tasks that can be communicated by gesture. Construed as advocacy of avoiding an overdependence on verbal methods by supplementing and cross-validating them by alternate means, this is to be strongly supported. Nonverbal and observational methods have imperfections that are different from those of verbal procedures, and this makes possible a methodological triangulation that filters out the systematic irrelevancies associated with any one method (Campbell & Fiske, 1959; Webb et al., 1966). But any advocacy of nonverbal tasks and observation as a substitute for (rather than a supplement to) verbal methods must be rejected, for these nonverbal procedures have their own irrelevant and misleading components, just as serious as those of verbal procedures (Webb et al., 1966).

Particularly should the notion be rejected that no translation is required for nonverbal tasks and gestural instructions. The actual status is the reverse—

such instruments require fully as much translation as do verbal materials, but the art of translating them is nowhere near as fully developed. Nonverbal intelligence test items are in general not more independent of culture than are verbal ones—usually they are more culturally specific, more unicentered. In the TAT personality test in which pictures are used to which stories are told, the pictorial content is very culture-bound. Efforts to cure this by making new pictures appropriate to specific cultures have not helped the problem of comparison, for the possibility remains that the differences in response are due to the differences in the pictures (Doob, 1965; Lindzey, 1961). In the end, a projective personality test with the verbal instruction, "Tell me a story about a little boy and his mother" is more translatable than the TAT technique stimulating such stories by means of a picture stimulus. (This is claimed in full recognition of the difficulties that even this simple example would encounter.) Gesture surely often works for simple communication between persons sharing no languages—yet, gesture too is culturally specific, with some New Guinea groups pointing with eyes and not understanding pointing with fingers, with Bulgarians indicating assent with the side-to-side head motion we use to indicate negation, with Tibetans indicating approval by sticking out their tongues, and so on.

This research was in part supported by grant MH-10949-3 from the National Institutes of Health, and by the Council for Intersocietal Studies, operating at Northwestern University under a grant from the Ford Foundation.

OVERVIEW OF CHAPTER 14

——————•◆•——————

In the early days of social anthropology, researchers used comparative methods, reporting on all aspects of the cultures of interest. Now the field has become specialized, and anthropologists are more likely to examine one specific aspect of a culture. Partly, this is due to the high standards required in ethnographic reporting. Another reason for the trend toward specialization is that the goal of the research has shifted from descriptive studies to hypothesis testing. The authors, Campbell and LeVine, warn that examining a single culture, or even comparing two cultures, provides equivocal results when used for hypothesis testing. Rather, studies such as these should be used to generate hypotheses for future research.

Those doing fieldwork control many decisions regarding methods, hypotheses, and content. When using comparative studies, it is difficult to determine whether noted differences reflect actual differences between the cultures or occur simply because of the different methods utilized by the individual researchers. The authors believe it is important to investigate methods that would increase the validity, and therefore encourage comparisons in ethnographic research.

One method by which ethnographers can produce more valid comparisons is through coordinated full-time research in which ethnographers dedicate a full year to comparable fieldwork. Unfortunately, quantitative tests cannot be used to test hypotheses since there are a limited number of cultures to be studied. Also, the necessary adherence to early research decisions, some of which may be inappropriate to a culture, is burdensome for the field-worker. This method discourages the spontaneity that may lead to the discoveries that are so rewarding for the anthropologist.

These problems can be addressed through collaborative research, in which a field-worker devotes a small amount of time replicating another study. This can be done by employing a number of anthropologists who spend several weeks on a specific research topic or by using dissertation teams in which each member devotes a month of fieldwork to the topic of each of the other members of the team. While this is costly, these types of cooperative research should be encouraged to provide more explicit comparable material so vital to the field.

With the need for more comparable data also comes the need for a technology that can guide the research from a distance so as to maximize comparability. The authors offer such a technology under the term *field-manual anthropology.* Similar manuals have been used in the past in the form of questionnaires sent out to missionaries to collect comparable data from numerous cultures. In the original article from which this chapter was extracted, Campbell and LeVine give an example of a field manual they used for the Cross-Cultural Study of Ethnocentrism. The remainder of this chapter discusses some of the methodological considerations associated with the field-manual approach.

In examining ethnocentrism, the authors chose to study traditional rather than current group relations. They explain that in order to test hypotheses about a social process such as ethnocentrism, it is important to include many cultures with as vast differences as possible. At the time of their study, almost all cultures experienced colonialism by European powers. Once colonialism had begun, a common pattern of anticolonialism made the cultures more homogeneous, and the traditional local jealousies tended to be eliminated. For this reason, the study placed its focus on the pattern of intergroup relations as they might have existed prior to European contact. The authors chose to include as large a number of ethnic groups as possible.

For this anthropological study, it was suggested that the field manual interview be conducted with two to five informants. By comparison, survey researchers suggested that as many as 30 to 50 interviews be done.

The researchers defended the option of interviewing fewer informants for several reasons. First, the cost was prohibitive. Second, less than half of the collaborators were able to perform even the four replications requested by the researchers. Finally, they believed that if the correlation between two interviews within a single culture demonstrated high reliability, then the emphasis should be on adding other cultures rather than adding interviews within cultures.

Although uniformity is desirable for comparisons, the interview had to be applied in different languages in different cultural models. While the field-manual method enforced more uniformity than usually found in anthropological research, it would inevitably be less than that found in survey research. The uniformity issue has two sides. Strict adherence to an interview schedule may reduce, rather than enhance, the interpretability of the data. Further, matching information obtained from two different interpreters or with two different definitions of the term would be more trustworthy than a retest of a rigid interview with the same individual. On the other hand, systematic deviations from the interview by one ethnographer or in one culture may lead to spurious results. Another source of bias can be introduced through the interpreter, and therefore, several interpreters should be used.

In order to avoid a bias in the data due to the field-worker's commitment to a particular hypothesis, the researchers provided a host of competing theories. This encouraged the ethnographer to record relevant observations that may not have been in the field manual and to warn the researchers if some of the data might appear misleading.

Another methodological issue involves the degree to which the procedures are specified by the researcher. In their field manual, the present authors suggested questions but made it clear that they were interested in the information, no matter how it was obtained. While they reject the demand for explicit observations, they do argue for methodological explicitness, since it could help rule out one needless source of differences in cross-cultural comparisons. They admit that an explicit field manual can be very fatiguing for the field-worker and for the informants. First, the topics are those of interest to the researcher rather than the informant. Also, the field-worker must ask questions rather than simply listen. Another factor that makes this approach more difficult is that the absence of a trait must be established. This can be frustrating since the field-worker and informant can never be sure if they are understanding one another.

Even with these drawbacks, the authors were advised not to relax their standards or efforts to attain comparability.

In a cross-cultural study, the observations must be carried out by different field-workers with varying degrees of experience and acquaintance with the culture. When differences occur between the field-worker's own observation of behaviors and the informant's account of those behaviors, the experienced field-worker may be in a better position to assess the accuracy of the informants' accounts. In any event, these dissimilar versions should be viewed separately, and an independent source should be obtained to verify the responses.

Whenever collaborative projects are carried out, problems may arise as to publication rights. The authors recommend that there be explicit recognition of the rights of ownership for those designing the study and for those who carry it out.

The authors recount the difficulties in recording and transcribing field notes. They suggest that on-the-spot translations should be done to guide the inquiry, but taped versions of informants' responses should be transcribed by several interpreters. Another option is to have the ethnographer prepare an essay on the field notes. While this simplifies the coding process and may give a more accurate portrayal than field notes, the resultant delays would make it unfeasible.

The final issue involves translating the anthropologist's field experience into the coding categories relevant to theory. One possible suggestion is that the ethnographer in the field be provided examples of the dimensions of interest and how they might be coded. The individual would then do whatever fieldwork was required to provide a code for each dimension requested.

Throughout his career, Campbell was constantly searching for methods that would make data about social processes more interpretable. In this chapter, he and LeVine directed this quest for validity to anthropological research in the hopes that new and better methods will continue to be explored.

FOURTEEN

FIELD-MANUAL
ANTHROPOLOGY

————·◆·————

*T*he title refers to an emerging solution to the growing problem of data comparability in anthropology. The use of comparative method in social anthropology, whether in enumerative cross-cultural surveys like those of Murdock (1949) and Whiting and Child (1953) or in more qualitative controlled comparisons (Clignet, 1970; Eggan, 1954), has depended heavily on published ethnographic reports that attempted to describe "the whole culture." The current trend among anthropologists, however, is toward specialized fieldwork that produces publications on a narrower range of cultural materials. One reason for this change is that standards of ethnographic reportage have risen. Even with the average period of fieldwork moving toward 2 years, only a few aspects of a culture can be thoroughly detailed by modern standards. Another and more questionable reason for the shift to specialization is the newer goal of attempting to test a behavioral sci-

Campbell, D. T., & LeVine, R. A. (1970). Field-manual anthropology. In R. Naroll & R. Cohen (Eds.), *A handbook of method in cultural anthropology* (pp. 366-387). Garden City, NY: Natural History Press.

ence hypothesis framed in terms of specific variables rather than remain at the level of descriptive ethnography. Ironically, the attempt to be scientific in this manner sometimes reduces the scientific value of the end product, for single case studies or even two-culture comparisons are hopelessly equivocal for hypothesis testing (see Campbell, 1961b; Campbell & Stanley, 1966) and can only be viewed as generating hypotheses for future research unless a large sample of subgroups or individuals is studied (see LeVine, 1970); whereas the narrowed scope of ethnographic coverage diminishes the potential utility of the data for future comparative analyses on unanticipated topics.

Each student doing fieldwork for his dissertation goes into a unique area, studies it with a unique set of methods, to which his own unique personality contributes heavily, and now must focus upon a unique hypothesis and a unique content. The resulting idiosyncrasy in an ethnographic report has as a result little chance of being interpretable as due to differences in culture. Were there consensus as to the scientific hypotheses most needing testing, so that several replications were available for each hypothesis, the situation would be more encouraging. But the narcissistic demands for originality, characteristic of all of the underdeveloped sciences, ensures that almost every study be of a different hypothesis. The result is that current ethnography is doing less to improve the Human Relations Files than the advances in methodological sophistication and ethnographic detail would suggest, and is not providing the needed new statistical degrees of freedom for cross-validating the discoveries made in our continual resorting of the old cases. From the point of view of comparative social science, the situation is chaotic. We must seek out and further those mechanisms that provide ways for getting comparison back into ethnographic research.

One alternative is coordinated full-time research as exemplified by Whiting's Six Cultures study (Minturn & Lambert, 1964; Whiting, Child, Lambert, & Whiting, 1963; Whiting et al., 1966) and Watson's (1963) four-culture micro-evolution studies in the New Guinea Highlands. In these, ethnographers dedicate a full year or so to coordinated, comparable fieldwork. While this may remain an ideal, it provides no general solution to the problem. On the one hand, the number of cultures is too small for the quantitative testing of hypotheses with an N of cultures. For another, if comparability is rigidly adhered to, the work itself becomes unpleasant both through its rigid control and through the very large commitment to a number of inevitably inappropriate research decisions made prior to acquaintance with the local scene. When the researchers did not participate in making these wrong decisions, the impositional burden is even greater. Furthermore, this approach tends to inhibit the exploratory quality of fieldwork.

The most generally available solution of this problem would seem to be part-time collaborative research, in which the field-worker devotes a small part of his time to doing research designed to replicate or parallel that of another. There are several possible arrangements for these. A single research project can solicit cooperation from numerous anthropologists. In the Cooperative Cross-Cultural Study of Ethnocentrism, directed by the present authors, some 20 to 30 cooperating anthropologists are subsidized for an extra 2 months' stay in the field devoted to collecting comparable data.

Many more modes of securing part-time commitment to collecting explicitly comparable data are needed. At the low cost end, one could consider five-man dissertation teams, each member of which agreed to spend 4 months toward the end of his stay collecting data at the rate of 1 month each for his four teammates. Each student would end up with profound acquaintance with his own area, plus explicit comparison data on his own topic for his own culture and four other areas.

So extreme is our need for comparable data that such developments are bound to increase in frequency and extensiveness. With them should come a technology of guiding research at a distance so as to maximize comparability. This technology we are tentatively designating under the term "field-manual anthropology." In this chapter, we illustrate possible approaches and raise some anticipatory problems.

Field manuals, at least in the sense of questionnaires to Europeans residing among exotic peoples, go back into the last century. Morgan (1871) sent a questionnaire on kinship to missionaries and administrators around the world. Allen (1879, pp. 204 ff), studying color vocabulary, asked correspondents in Asia, Africa, America, and the Pacific Islands, "Can they distinguish between [e.g.] blue and green?" and "Have they separate names for blue and green?" Magnus (1883) sent both a questionnaire and color samples to traders and missionaries.

Notes and Queries (Royal Anthropological Institute, 1874; 6th edition, 1951) might possibly be regarded as a field manual, for certainly it has had as its goal increasing the interpretable comparability of fieldwork, even though it partakes of the foregone goal of "complete" ethnographies. The field manual most widely available and most useful as a model is that used in the six culture study on child rearing (prepared in 1954, published as Whiting et al., 1966). While of limited topical focus, it is designed to cover over one year of field-work. A very narrowly focused field manual covering five types of optical illusion has also been published (Herskovits, Campbell, & Segall, 1969). Widely distributed is the 248-page *A Field Manual for Cross-Cultural Study of the Acquisition of Communicative Competence* (Slobin et al., 1967). These are no doubt but a sample of a much larger range of "field manuals" that have been employed in various studies.

The goal of the Cross-Cultural Study of Ethnocentrism was to collect data descriptive of precolonial indigenous intergroup relations, including such specific topics as history of intergroup conflict, intergroup cooperation and economic exchange, social distance, stereotypes, and intergroup hostility, and as potential predictors, data on social structure, child-training methods, and so forth (see Campbell, 1965, 1967b; Campbell & LeVine, 1961, 1965; LeVine, 1965). [The Ethnocentrism Field Manual used for this study was included in the original version of "Field-Manual Anthropology," cited on the first page of this chapter.]

METHODOLOGICAL CONSIDERATIONS

1. Indigenous Instances and the Retrospective Focus. Casual observations of daily events offer convincing evidence that there is no foreseeable shortage of material for the student of intergroup hostility. Why then this strenuous effort to get data under the expensive conditions of anthropological field-work, and with a focus upon traditional rather than current group relations? The answer is comparable to that motivating all cross-cultural work. For testing hypotheses about social process and group structure, the maximum heterogeneity of cultural forms is needed. Furthermore, the greater the independence among the instances, the more powerfully do the data probe the theory. The westernization of the world brings with it new and powerful ethnocentrisms. Both through processes of diffusion and through reactions to a common outgroup, we may soon have available only widespread replications of two or three basic cultural forms of intergroup imagery. Thus through reaction to a similar pattern of domination, a common pattern of anticolonialism is absorbing more and more of the ethnocentric energies of peoples in the underdeveloped areas. For historical reasons, this pattern is fused with anti-Western-Europeanism, anti-Caucasianism, anticapitalism, and (from our point of view) anti-democratic-blocism, since the white Western-European capitalistic democracies have been the colonial powers. Europe's traditional class warfare ideology (containing many ethnocentric features) has been diffused to become one base for new-nation nationalistic ethnocentrism, since indigenous peoples with colonial domination have for years found their most accessible allies in the labor movements of the colonial nations ruling them. Moreover, a dominant diffusion item has long been the European model for the national state. With these powerful and highly relevant foci for ingroup-outgroup identification, the currently irrelevant and obstructing traditional local jealousies will be under strong acculturation pressure, and their elimination will become a major goal of all educational systems. While the dynamics of ethnocentrism will no doubt remain, the researcher may be soon faced with but one or two universally diffused instances, a trivial numerical base upon which to build empirical generalizations. It is thus the intent of the present study to place its major focus upon the pattern of intergroup relations such as might have existed prior to European contact. While there is also an interest in the most salient current ingroup-outgroup orientations, the interview is oriented toward a retrospective recall of traditional patterns.

There is correspondingly an emphasis upon obtaining large numbers of ethnic groups. It would be desirable, for example, to have as many as one hundred groups as a basis for the study of relationships. The numbers employed in many cross-cultural studies are very small numbers, [and] coupled with the very large number of hypotheses tested (cross-tabulations made), allow for very striking relationships to appear that are purely the product of capitalization upon chance. The problem is the same whether qualitative interpretations or quantitative scores are used. For tests of hypotheses dealing with individual differences or life history variables in rats or men, the supply of instances is so great that the science will never exhaust its ability to test hypotheses. For the sciences of culture and social organization, this is not the case, however, and every unique culture is needed in the record before it disappears.

2. *Number of Respondents: Anthropological Versus Survey-Research Standards.* In the very first draft of the inquiry schedule distributed to a large number of interested social scientists (Campbell & LeVine, 1961, p. 82) for comments, we suggested that it be used "as an informant interview to be administered to as few as two to five individuals." This phrase drew no comment from the anthropologists responding, presumably because it was within the normal bounds of fieldwork practice (although crowding the upper limits of redundancy). It did draw criticism from experienced survey-researchers and psychologists with cross-cultural fieldwork experience who insisted upon larger numbers of interviews within each group, with perhaps 20 to 50 as a minimum. We do, of course, endorse the desirability of as many interviews as possible if other equally important values are not sacrificed. The other values almost certain to be sacrificed are: first, the number of ethnic groups studied, and second, the number of topics about which ethnographic data are collected. With the expense of anthropological fieldwork and with interviews proceeding at a rate of two or three per month, we have asked for four replications of each part of the schedule, conducted through several interpreters if possible. Less than half of our collaborators have actually met this standard. Some have stopped after one very good informant, requiring urgent persuasion to get up to our practical minimum, two.

The choice point of more reliable data on fewer instances or less data on more instances is one that correlational field studies of all types face, and is one for which in some instances a mathematical solution of optimal strategy is possible. Transposed to the correlational study of individual differences it becomes the relative advantage of increasing the number of questions dealing with the same attitude asked of each respondent (and thus increasing the reliability of the attitude score) versus using the same energy to increase the number of persons interviewed. The increase in reliability will increase the magnitude of correlations obtained, thus increasing one's confidence in (or the statistical significance of) the relationship. Increasing the number of cases upon which the relationship is based, even though it does not affect the magnitude of the correlation, has a similar effect upon confidence (or statistical significance). Neither relationship is linear. Estimating the reliability of the measure and the magnitude of the "true" correlation, the optimal strategy can be determined for the specific instance.

In our situation, the "reliability" of relevance becomes the correlation across the population of cultures of data supplied by two interviewers (technically, the intraclass correlation). The higher this reliability, the less the gain from duplicating interviews within a culture. With regard to this, we tentatively make the assumption that this reliability is greater when the respondent takes the role of "informant," reporting upon the group consensus, than when the focus is upon his "own opinions" and upon individual differences in attitude within the culture. This assumption is potentially open to empirical check.

To put the argument another way, the greatest increment in knowledge occurs when we shift from zero informants to one informant. From there on, there is diminishing utility or informational increment for each new informant. While some similar diminishing utility function holds for the social scientist in adding new cultures, this latter resource is so much scarcer as to be much more precious. Looking at the present achievements of cross-cultural correlational study, we note that striking relationships have been established upon the basis of data much less systematic and reliable than that called for in our suggested four-informant interviews. Furthermore, the need for more data, which one feels when conducting such a study, is preeminently for cross-validation upon a new set of cultures as opposed to better data within each of the cultures already studied, although admittedly both needs are felt.

3. Uniformity of Interview Administration and Confounded Error. Another place where survey procedures and anthropological fieldwork traditions may be at cross-purposes has to do with the rigidity or the uniformity with which the inquiry schedule is administered. With each ethnic group introducing both a different language and a different cultural model into which the informant interview is interpreted or rationalized, it is of course recognized that interviews will be inevitably less uniform than in survey research work within the United States. At the same time, our schedule asks for more uniformity between ethnographers than is now the case in anthropological fieldwork. In guiding the inevitable compromise it seems well to make explicit some of the issues, the values, and the hazards involved.

On the side of flexibility for the ethnographer to re-ask, restate, explain, and cross-examine informants, and to eliminate questions that the informant has already answered incidentally, we have these arguments: The communication problems involved are tremendous. There is no point in collecting data that the ethnographer does not trust, answers to questions that he believes are evasive or deceitful. Insistence upon a very rigid adherence to a schedule, requiring an exact usage of the printed words whenever an English-speaking interpreter is used, and so on, might easily defeat its purpose in providing data that the ethnographer himself believes to be worthless. Uniformity may in some instances reduce rather than enhance the interpretability. For instance, suppose we learn that the As regard the Bs as "greedy" in the course of a garrulous monologue elicited by some tangential question—a monologue that an opinion pollster might shut off by saying, "We'll come to those topics later." We would be more certain of this item in such a case than if it had been only later elicited by the taciturn naming of Bs in a routinized response to "greedy" in the long list of traits. Similarly, consider that two respondents have alleged Bs to be greedy—we will have greater confidence in this result in the case in which two different interpreters were used, or in which two different translation terms for "greedy" have been used, than for the case in which exactly the same procedures have been employed. This preference is an extension of that by which we would feel greater confirmation from agreement between two separate informants than from agreement between repetitions of the interview with a single informant. The principle involved may be designated that of "heterogeneity of irrelevancies," or the "diversification of biases" (LeVine, 1966). The more irrelevant factors have been randomized, the less likely we shall mistake the effect of one of them for the effect of the factors we seek to investigate.

Such encouragements of diversity must not be confused with the perhaps greater danger that systematic deviations from the interview schedule (e.g., deviations running through all of the interviews done in a given culture, or all done by a given ethnographer in several cultures) could generate spurious relationships. Thus if the ethnographer always gives the same concrete illustration to a too abstract question, the effects of this illustration may systematically bias the results, giving the interviews a higher consistency and reliability, but one that is spurious. Heterogeneity within the interviews of a single ethnographer are thus no necessary threat to validity and may even lead to gain, while heterogeneity between ethnographers when systematic within any one ethnographer will be a source of decreased validity. The systematic idiosyncracies of the interpreter are probably an even more likely source of bias than are those of the ethnographer, and the use of several interpreters is essential.

4. The Ethnographer's Awareness of the Purpose of the Study. There is increasing awareness of the possible bias in fieldwork of strong commitment to preobservational hypotheses, or of knowing the study designer's purposes (e.g., Rosenthal, 1966). These considerations might have led us to keeping the ethnographer uninformed of our hypotheses. They did not, and in fact we went to the other extreme of providing each collaborator with a 200-page review of competing theories on ethnocentrism and intergroup conflict. We justified this as follows:

> The following chapters attempt an assembly of propositions from a number of social science theories, applicable to the general content area of ethnocentrism, particularly as testable with anthropological data. These chapters in their present form are far from being polished or definitive analyses and employ a variety of expository styles. They should, nonetheless, be of use to collaborators in the Cross-Cultural Study of Ethnocentrism in illustrating some of the potential range of issues and modes of analysis to which the data being collected are relevant.
>
> One function should be to increase the ethnographer's sensitivity to relevant observations not specifically covered in the field manual. Another utility is that through knowing the interpretative use to which the data are to be put, the ethnographer should be in a better position to note misleading aspects of the data collected and to provide warnings as to their interpretation. In addition, it is also hoped that this overview of a number of theories might result in a type of enlightened objectivity. The problem of bias is always present whenever an observer goes into an ambiguous situation as a strong partisan of a single theory. One control for this sometimes employed is to keep the field worker in the dark as to the purposes and hopes of the study designers. This approach is not judged to be feasible in the present study and would, we believe result in a poorer quality of data, a mechanical collection of answers to questions often misleading or uninterpretable in that form. Instead, it is hoped that the recognition of multiple competing theories will create a theoretically motivated concern for collecting those data that will help decide among them, an objectivity resulting not from ignorance of theoretical issues, but rather from an awareness of a multiplicity of competing theories, with no one of which is the investigator so emotionally identified that disconfirmation becomes personally ego-deflating. We believe that the effort of preparing this analysis has helped move us from being defensive partisans of a single theory to more of an objective concern for the comparison of competing theories in the adequacy with which they fit the data. (Campbell & LeVine, 1965, pp. 1-2)

All field-manual studies we know of, including the one on optical illusion (Segall, Campbell, & Herskovits, 1966), have taken a similar position concerning informing field-workers about hypotheses, but the Whiting et al. Field Guide does not include competing hypotheses. In that study the field teams and senior investigators constituted a research group with a single theoretical orientation that could have biased the research, but part of their shared viewpoint was a strong skepticism about the empirical validity of their own hypotheses that was considered an adequate antidote to the apparent theoretical bias.

5. *Degree of Specification of Procedures.* Most of the field manuals specify the information wanted rather than how to go about getting it. The Whiting et al. Field Guide is divided into sections on cultural data, where the information desired is specified, and sections on individual measures where methods are made more explicit. Our field manual also eliminates specific instructions on data collection techniques when it comes to those classes of information that are professionally central to social anthropology, as on sociopolitical structure, territorial units, household organization, leadership, and societal complexity. We definitely do not aspire to the degree of specification typical of the public opinion surveys of sociologists. This is seen in our apology for suggesting specific questions, in our statement that these specific second-person wordings are intended to inform the ethnographer as to the content we want, and in our emphasis that it is the information we want, no matter how obtained.

Nonetheless, the degree of specification is extreme, and it is probably on this issue that the major future methodological controversies will center. Epistemological issues are involved. On the one hand is the demand for completely explicit operations, and with this the search for certainty in explicit particulars. This extreme we certainly reject and recognize that the matching of particulars across cultures must certainly depend upon a prior, context-dependent matching of whole patterns. Ludicrously useless would be a cross-cultural comparison of yes-no answers to an isolated single question administered by a stranger who had just arrived. We acknowledge our context-dependence by requiring that our inquiry be done by an anthropologist thoroughly familiar with the area, and that he not accept answers he believes are wrong or based upon a misunderstood question.

Favoring methodological explicitness is a general perspectival relativism that most anthropologists would accept. A given object will be seen differently from different perspectives, and we gain increased comparability when we are able to maximize perspectival comparability. Ideally we would use several independent methodological perspectives in every setting (the use of the anthropologist's wife as a field-worker is a recurrent example), but where we cannot, to specify the perspective used, and to attempt parallel perspectives, perhaps removes one needless irrelevant source of differences in cross-cultural comparison.

Our collaborators uniformly report that working with our field manual is much more fatiguing, both for them and for the informant, than is ordinary fieldwork. Most of them advise us, however, not to relax our standards or efforts for comparability. Why should the fatigue be so much greater? The answers are very revealing for the whole approach. An important feature is whose agenda of interests sets the course of conversation. In ordinary fieldwork, as in friendly discussion in general, the local informant's interests predominate, the anthropologist willingly learning of those topics seeming most interesting to his newfound friend. In field-manual ethnography, the ethnographer (or more properly, the field-manual designer) sets the agenda. While in our field manual, we have tried to relax this rigidity, the contrast with ordinary fieldwork becomes great. A second reason for field-manual fatigue comes from a distinction between listening and asking. Many topics and content areas are best and most validly learned of by listening, not asking—by passively waiting for the topic to come up incidentally and indirectly. The field-manual approach is just not suited for such topics, and cannot claim to be an all-purpose tool. A third and most important reason has to do with the method of establishing the absence of a given trait. In the quantitative cross-cultural studies based on the Human Relations Area Files or other ethnographic reports, absence is determined sometimes by the ethnographer's report on the trait's absence, but more often on his failure to mention it. Even where the ethnographer explicitly states an absence, his evidence may essentially be a failure to see or hear mention of the trait. Granted the incompleteness of all ethnographies, there is great ambiguity about absences. The field-manual approach, at least as used by us, asks directly about presence or absence. This is fine where the trait is present, and often brings up interesting features that might never have spontaneously emerged. But where the trait is absent, the interview becomes very frustrating, with the informant and ethnographer unable to be sure they are understanding each other.

The fatigue of field-manual ethnography sets very real limits on the amount of it that can be scheduled. Our 2-month commitment is probably at the upper limit or beyond.

6. *Variations in Data Quality and the Observational Base.* Even with the most realistically designed field manual and the most dedicated professional field-workers, there is likely to be considerable variation among field-workers in their levels of acquaintance with and experience in the cultures and communities studied, and this is bound to affect the quality of the data they produce. In terms of Naroll's (1962) criteria of ethnographic data quality, field-workers will vary in the total length of time they spend in the field, their mastery of the local language, and their exposure to the cultural behavior of comparative interest. The more experienced and knowledgeable field-worker who has undergone a more thorough socialization into the culture of the group can bring a more complete contextual understanding to the tasks the field manual demands of him and, theoretically, obtain a more valid set of data for comparative analysis. For a project like the Cross-Cultural Study of Ethnocentrism, in which the focus is on past history to be reconstructed from informant interviews, data quality can be largely controlled. For projects with a contemporaneous focus like the Six Culture Study, however, in which observational data and informant accounts are combined, special problems arise: What relative weights does the field-worker assign to what he has actually witnessed as opposed to what he has been told about by informants? Does not the field-worker with a longer and more intensive field experience have a greater observational base from which to assess the accuracy of his informants' accounts and on which to build more searching and meaningful interviews? A reading of the field-workers' comments in the Field Guide by Whiting et al. (1966) leaves no doubt that these issues arise and must be faced by the comparative analyst. We raise these problems not to solve them, but because they must be taken seriously into account by any designer of a field manual dealing with contemporary patterns of cultural or individual behavior. Insofar as the field manual is simply a set of instructions for administering a psychological test, like the optical illusion study of Segall et al. (1966), this type of problem is of little urgency, but when the manual is an attempt to make conventional ethnography more comparable, like the cultural part of the Six Cultures Field Guide, then it demands detailed attention in the manual's instructions. Current trends in ethnographic data collec-

tion would seem to recommend treating ethnographic observation in a given behavioral domain, and the recording of informants' views of behavior patterns in that domain, as separate tasks and independent data source to be checked against one another.

7. Publication Rights and "Ownership" of Data. Collaborative projects present special problems in regard to publication, around which there have been serious conflicts and frustrations. Occasionally there are bitter misunderstandings about "ownership" of the data, or about the relative importance in the collaborative product of the study designer or the data collector. More frequent are frustrating delays due to the bottleneck of unified or joint publication.

Our recommendation in this situation is an explicit recognition of ownership of dual rights, with the field-worker free to publish what he has collected. Such a policy has been applied without noticeable harm in the optical illusion study (Segall et al., 1966), in which several of the cooperators published on their own data prior to the major report, one scooping the project by as much as 7 years. In that study the collaborators donated their own time, but even where they are salaried research associates, this seems to be an optimal solution.

In most collaborative comparative studies, as in our own, there is a natural division of labor furthering this decision. There is the intensive specialization on a specific culture, which we can conceptualize as a vertical dimension of concern and the primary focus of the ethnographer. Orthogonal to this is the horizontal interest of the field-manual designer, a comparison across cultures on a narrow band of data. [In the original version of this article, the authors include a contract that spells out the rights of the study participants.]

8. Recording and Transmitting of Field Notes. The most common mode of recording the field notes has been by paper and pencil during the interview with the ethnographer filling out and transcribing as soon as possible afterwards. This initial note-taking is in English if the ethnographer is working with an interpreter. If he is working directly in the local language, his field notes may be in English by on-the-spot translation, or are more likely in the local language and require translation later.

The use of a tape recorder during the interview produces ampler notes, not necessarily more coherent, and adds listening and transcribing time to an already tedious process. A technique used in one instance for obtaining rather full records in work through interpreters is as follows: In the interview itself, the interpreter made on-the-spot oral translations, which the ethnographer then used to guide further inquiry. The whole interchange in both languages was taped. Later, the interpreter played the tape back step-by-step, writing out a more detailed translation of the informant's responses. This written translation process takes 4 or 5 hours for every hour transcribed, and is best undertaken with a staff of two or three interpreters. It is reasonable field work investment where such resources are available, and would probably now be our recommended procedure where the ethnographer is to work through interpreters, and perhaps even where not. Rough though these translations may be, they are usable. Postponed translating, to be done by the ethnographer himself, is certainly the most expensive of all.

There are ethnographers with a capacity for working 16 hours a day, who get their field notes into presentable form by editing and typing them each night while their informants sleep. Such ethnographers are ready to turn over their field notes to us as soon as the fieldwork is done. We have encountered one or two of these, but most have found it necessary to postpone the editing and translating, often for years. We should have scheduled a 1- or 2-month salaried period, augmented with secretarial funds, for editing the 2 months of fieldwork, and for supplying the information requested in the noninterview parts of the field manual.

The form in which the data are turned over to the project need not, of course, be as field notes. They could also be in the form of integrated ethnographic essays addressed to the questions raised, and based upon all of the information at the ethnographer's disposal. The specification of field notes was made primarily in an effort to avoid the long delays that ethnographic writing entails. By and large, our coders would find essays easier to code than field notes, because an essay is consistent, integrated, and interpreted. The essay may very well be argued to be a more accurate portrayal than the more voluminous field notes upon which it is based, and with some of which it disagrees. To regard the field notes as a firmer scientific base is perhaps like looking for greater clarity by examining the details of the television picture with a magnifying glass.

Not only are field notes weaker in their particularity and consistency, they are also less interpretable to coders for other reasons—they are framed in perspectives and reference levels unknown to the coder, in a language that is only superficially shared. The language and perspectives of the ethnographer's essay is much more certainly shared by the coders. The translation process has been carried one step further.

We are not seriously suggesting that ethnographic essays be substituted for field notes as the mode of data exchange. The increased delays in delivery would make that utterly unfeasible. But if it were to turn out that the field-manual approach were to be less effective in establishing cross-cultural correlations than are the published ethnographies of the Human Relations Area Files, this issue would be focal.

Field-manual anthropology must continue to explore alternatives in the means of communicating between the anthropologist's field experience and the coding categories relevant to theory. Tangentially it may be remarked that our big expansion of the field manual used in the field in 1931 and 1964 was due to the inclusion of content specifically related to our propositional analysis of competing theories. Much of this proposition specific content produced extremely awkward interview questions that were then eliminated in our fall 1964 revision conference, moving the schedule back to a more general content-area focus.

One alternative is to let the ethnographer do the coding. Questionnaires to anthropologists asking them to be informants after they have returned from the field have met with only mixed success, and are not what we are suggesting. Suppose one sent coding instructions to the ethnographer in the field, as a kind of field manual. This would include for each dimension clear-cut illustrations of each coding category or of extreme and intermediate points on a rating scale. These illustrations would be extensive excerpts from published ethnographies, providing context as well as specifics. The ethnographer's assignment might then be to do enough inquiry of his own devising to make a decision on each dimension—or he might do this as a supplement to a focused inquiry schedule such as presented here.

The preparation of this chapter [by Campbell and LeVine] has been supported in part by a grant from the Carnegie Corporation of New York to Northwestern University.

PART IV

THE USE OF
ADMINISTRATIVE RECORDS

————·◆·————

*I*n this section, Campbell discusses an important yet underutilized source of data for program evaluation. Government agencies, institutions, hospitals, insurance companies, and the like, collect information regularly on matters that could be useful to the social scientist conducting evaluations. There are several well-known instances in which such data were used, including the Connecticut Crackdown on Speeding of 1955, the British Breathalyser Crackdown of 1967, and the effect of Medicaid on the number of contacts with doctors, 1963-1969. Campbell feels that administrative data from governmental sources should be utilized and information from private institutions should be made available, providing certain precautions are taken by those who collect and house the data and by the researcher who wishes to use them.

There are several advantages to using administrative or archival records. First, the information has already been collected and is often in machine-readable form. The cost of retrieval would far undercut the cost of initial data gathering. Since those providing the data are not aware of how this information might be used in an analysis, the measures are nonreactive, thus eliminating one known source of bias. With appropriate precautions, the privacy of the individuals who provide the data can be protected. Finally, data are available on individuals who do not participate in the program, and this information can be used to construct control groups to increase the validity of the study.

Campbell also offers some cautions for those using available records. The researcher must always be aware of the ways in which the data are collected and coded, including policy changes or events that may have influenced the numbers. In an ideal situation, the data would be collected regularly and consistently in intervals that are useful to the evaluator's purpose. It would also be useful to have data for a period before and after the "treatment" being evaluated to allow an examination of trends prior to the treatment. When data collection procedures are changed, overlapping data should be collected using both the old and new methods to allow an analysis of the change's effect on the data. Protecting the privacy of those providing the data may require that special methods be used to prevent an individual from being identified through the information in the files. In many instances, where confidential information is not relevant to the study, the use of social security numbers as identifiers would simplify any attempt to merge files to other sources of data. However, the U.S. Privacy Act of 1974 precludes the use of social security numbers when evaluating certain programs, such as a medical rehabilitation program or a nonpaying job training program.

As mentioned earlier, certain agencies collect data regularly on program participants. Often these data consist of information about the clients themselves and the changes effected by the program. Campbell suggests that these agencies also provide regular information on the amount and types of services they provide. He also advocates collecting stakeholder comments, that is, using the welfare recipients, clients, social workers, and other well-placed individuals to report on their experiences with the services and to offer their opinions on whether the program is effective. Information of this nature should be provided to a source other than the agency being evaluated to eliminate biases that may occur if these informants fear retaliation for negative evaluations.

In Chapter 15, Campbell presents his case for the use of administrative records, with guidelines on how they might be most useful to the social scientist. Included in this chapter are brief excerpts from another article that describes how archival measures, such as those collected in Sweden, can be used for program evaluation, making Sweden a type of social polygram. Chapter 16 is included in this volume because Campbell wished to stress the importance of using "expert judgments" of program recipients and social workers in program evaluation. Since this matter does not appear often in the published literature, he wished to present some illustrations of data collection forms to be used for this purpose, which were developed by Andrew C. Gordon and himself.

————•◆•————

OVERVIEW OF CHAPTER 15

———•◆•———

S ocial indicators may be used to assess the impact of social reforms. This chapter discusses some of the problems evaluators face when indicators are used for this purpose.

Often, demonstration programs are initiated in smaller units before being disseminated nationwide. This is useful for program evaluation providing that the time prior to complete implementation is used to compare the "experimental" to the comparison regions. This requires consistent information for all of these regions. A number of social indicators, such as deaths, days hospitalized, traffic accidents, and so on, are collected regularly and can be used for this purpose if they can be broken down by local units. When using records of earnings, unemployment, insurance, and health services to establish the impact of ameliorative governmental actions, a government can be considered a social polygram. Sweden, with its centralized records and governmental health services, provides an example.

Subjective social indicators, in which people report on the quality of their lives, can also be used for program evaluation if they are collected before and after a new program in both the experimental and comparison regions.

Since experimental methods cannot be used to evaluate most ameliorative programs, the best quasi-experimental method available is the interrupted time series design with comparison series. For this type of study, many data points are needed for smaller time units, such as months or weeks. Administrative records that are already being collected can provide this type of information. Sweden is poised to do such studies since the records are available, and many of its programs are locally implemented within *Landstings* (similar to states) before complete implementation.

It is most helpful to evaluation if global indicators can be broken down to statistics related to the topic at hand. For example, for traffic accidents, it would be helpful to have data on driver fault or blood alcohol levels. A hospital is a record-rich environment in which data are collected in a number of areas useful to program evaluation. Further, a hospital has well-placed observers, such as nurses, orderlies, and even patients, who can provide informed opinions of benefits and side effects. Because of the number and variety of observations, the statistical quality is enhanced, making hospitals a social polygram with a number of recurrent indicators.

Interrupted time-series methodology is promising for program evaluation, although more work is needed by statisticians on appropriate models for tests of significance. The following are Campbell's methodological recommendations for legislators and administrators using time-series methods. Introduce the program decisively and be sure there is advanced publicity. Hold the record-keeping systems constant, or if changes are necessary, keep old and new styles for an overlap period. Be aware that ameliorative programs for chronic programs are more easily evaluated than programs responding to flare-ups. Recognize that there is a cost associated with assembling comparison statistics. And finally, allow time for preprogram data to be collected if administrative records are unavailable.

So far, social indicators have been discussed in the context of program evaluation. The interrupted time-series method evaluates changes in programs rather than ongoing programs. Social indicators can be used to monitor ongoing programs if averaged data for specified persons are made available. This can be done in a way that protects individual privacy. To interpret such studies, it is important that the assignment of applicants to ameliorative programs be done in a systematic way, with admissions hinging on a quantified eligibility score.

Using administrative records for evaluating ongoing social programs is an inexpensive alternative to interviews and avoids the problem of different mortality rates for experimental and control groups. This type of program evaluation can be used whenever there are more eligible applicants than the program can service. It is important however, to have access to relevant information, including private files, such as medical insurance and educational testing service files. It is also important to keep records on those rejected as well as those accepted.

The United States should carefully scrutinize the privacy legislation to be sure that certain types of evaluations are not needlessly precluded. For example, social security numbers accompanying names on a list would decrease the cost of data retrieval and reduce the number of errors. Yet, under the U.S. Privacy Act of 1974, this means of identification would be precluded for many types of program evaluation. While Campbell does not support the notion of a unified national data bank, he proposes that existing files be kept separate with the capacity for "mutually insulated" negotiation with other files (discussed in Chapter 17). The use of social security numbers should not be confused with a unified data bank. They do not make it easier to retrieve private information on individuals, but they do facilitate mass statistical retrievals. Their use for evaluating social programs outweighs the very slight increase in the danger of their misuse.

FIFTEEN

ADMINISTRATIVE RECORDS AS CONTINUOUS EXPERIMENTAL LABORATORIES FOR EXPERIMENTAL INNOVATIONS

————•◆•————

f the many uses to which social indicators may be put, perhaps the most important in the long run will be in evaluating the impact of specific social reforms, ameliorative programs, changes in laws, pilot programs, demonstration programs, and the like. Such use raises many problems and requirements not met with when social indicators are employed to assess the status of a whole nation.

Campbell, D. T. (1976). Focal local indicators for social program evaluation. *Social Indicators Research, 3,* 237-256.

Campbell, D. T. (1984). Hospital and landsting as continuously monitoring social polygrams: Advocacy and warning. In B. Cronholm & L. von Knorring (Eds.), *Evaluation of mental health services programs* (pp. 13-39). Stockholm: Forskningsraadet Medicinska.

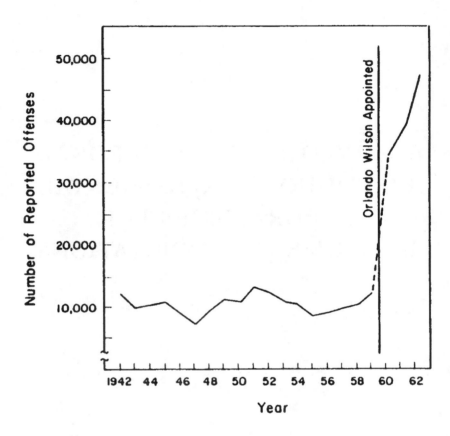

Figure 15.1. Number of reported larcenies under $50 in Chicago (data from *Uniform Crime Reports for the United States,* 1942-1962). Presumably the jump in crime rate represents a change in reporting quality rather than a crime increase (Campbell, 1969).

It seems useful to begin with a number of concrete illustrations of this use of social indicators, and Figures 15.1 through 15.7 have been provided for this purpose. It is hoped that the captions are sufficiently informative to make these disparate studies comprehensible.

LOCAL

Most programs that call for evaluation are applied to social units smaller than a nation as a whole. This is particularly true for demonstration programs, and for

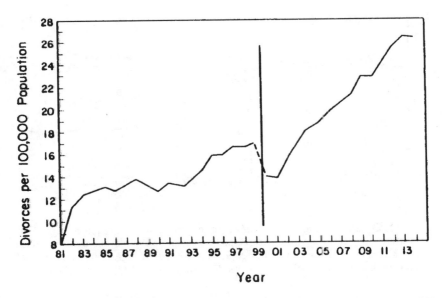

Figure 15.2. Divorce rate for the German Empire, 1881-1911. Does the law of 1899 make divorce less frequent. but also a poorer indicator of marital stability? (Glass, Tiao, & Maguire, 1971)

programs initiated by or in cooperation with city, county, state, or provincial governments. Even national programs are better evaluated if the introduction can be staged so that some regions get it a year before others, providing during that year the differences between the "experimental" region and comparison regions are examined. For program evaluation purposes, a federal system has the advantage that single states or provinces often try out new programs, with adjacent provinces available as comparisons. In a more centralized nation, these effective quasi-experimental designs might be precluded. (See Figures 15.3 and 15.4 for actual illustrations.) Thus we need *local* statistics, available on the unit receiving the new program and on comparable units not receiving it.

The kinds of social indicators that might be useful are as varied as the social programs our local. provincial, and national governments generate. Statistics on deaths, days hospitalized, days lost from work, traffic accidents, unemployment, achievement test scores, and crime illustrate the kinds of indicators that can be useful when made available by schools, census tracts, police districts, city, county, or province.

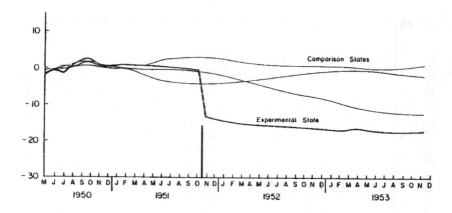

Figure 15.3. Effect of introducing a law in the experimental state requiring repayment of welfare costs from the deceased recipient's estate on the old age assistance case loads. Monthly data have all values expressed as a percentage of the case load 18 months prior to the change of the law. (Modified from Baldus, 1973, p. 204, Figure 1).

Potentially, the computerization of administrative records should make such regional breakdowns readily available. Not only should relevant government administrative records be made research-retrievable, it is also in the public interest that this capacity be created for records of insurance companies (hospitalization, medical, automobile, life), major educational testing firms, hospitals, schools, and the like.

One can envisage governmental records of earnings, utilizations of unemployment insurance, health services, police records, and the like, as a governmental level social polygram, providing well-established time-series records lying ready to reflect the impact of social changes and intentional governmental actions (Campbell, 1969b, 1976).

Sweden could be a social polygram, with its variety of recurrent indicators, its conscientious record keepers, centralized records, and governmental health service. Sweden could be the first experimenting society, with pioneering efforts to try new ways of doing things combined with a stability of record keeping with which to evaluate them. There are devices available to control the threats to individual privacy (Campbell, Boruch, Schwartz, & Steinberg, 1977). After all, it is programs, policies, and treatment modalities that we want to evaluate, not persons. For health policy and treatment-modality changes, the

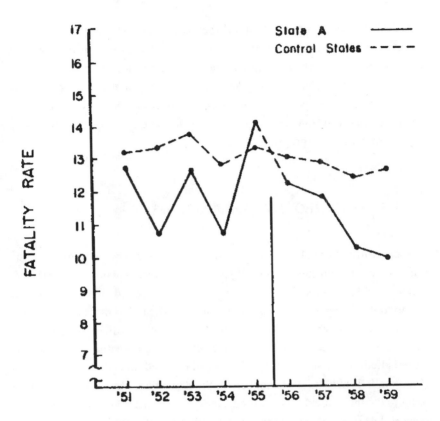

Figure 15.4. Traffic fatalities per 100,000 of population in State A prior to and after a strong crackdown on speeding initiated in 1956, compared with the average of four neighboring states (Campbell, 1969, p. 419, Figure 11). The fact that the crackdown was in response to the unprecedented rise in fatalities in 1955 complicates the interpretation. The 1957-1959 trend is more clearly indicative of genuine impact.

semi-autonomy and diversity of programs among the 26 *Landstings* (translating to provinces or what we call "states") is an advantage, creating ideal settings for control series, in which one Landsting's records provide a comparison base for another's experimental innovations, a potentiality that has already been used (Lindholm, 1983).

The social indicator movement is rightly spending a great deal of effort in the development of subjective social indicators in which people report on the quality of their lives as they see it, achieved through public opinion survey methods. These face special problems when used for program evaluation. Surveys designed to monitor national well-being do not provide useful local data. It is a frustrating statistical reality that one needs as large a sample (e.g., 2,500) to document an improvement in morale in Silver Springs, Maryland, as one does for the whole United States. However, the instruments designed for national surveys can be specially administered to local samples before and after a new program is tried out, and at the same time to some appropriate comparison region not getting the program.

FOCUSED ON FREQUENT TIME PERIODS

The real world of social ameliorative efforts is an imperfect laboratory at best. If a change is noted, there are usually many alternative explanations for the effect not ruled out by the data collection effort. Planning and improved research methodology can greatly improve this situation. The randomization of assignment to treatment that provides optimal clarity of results will usually be impossible, certainly for changes in laws that affect all persons within a governmental jurisdiction. For such settings, reviews of nonrandomized research designs (Campbell, 1969b, 1979; Campbell & Stanley, 1966; Riecken et al., 1974) point to the interrupted time-series design with comparison series as the most powerful of quasi-experimental designs. For tests of significance to be used, many time points are needed (Box & Tiao, 1965; Glass, Willson, & Gottman, 1975). For most reforms and legal changes, monthly or weekly data are needed; annual data do not provide enough degrees of freedom. Because of strong weekend effects, and because months vary from each other and from year to year in how many weekends they have, weekly data (even if combined into 4-week units) is much superior to monthly data (e.g., Ross, 1973; Ross, Campbell, & Glass, 1970). When as in Figure 15.5, the crackdown starts in the middle of the month, analytic "months," differing from calendar months, are desirable. Thus to our computer retrieval capacities for administrative records, public needs for program evaluation would be best served by retrieval capacity providing fine-grained time detail and flexible alternative aggregation units.

The desirability of fine-grained time series on local units accents the special usefulness for program evaluation of administrative records, which are being collected anyway, and on complete populations rather than samples. We

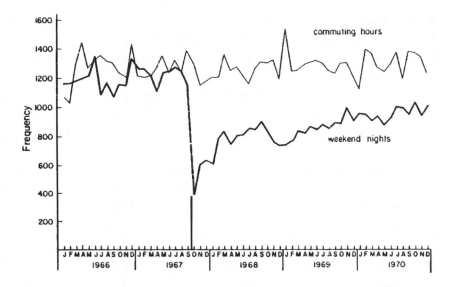

Figure 15.5. British traffic casualties (fatalities plus serious injuries) before and after the British Breathalyser crackdown of October 1967, seasonally adjusted (Ross, 1973, Figures 10 and 11 combined). Bars were closed prior to and during commuting hours.

cannot hope to achieve such local and frequent observations using subjective social indicators.

TOPICALLY FOCUSED

Ideally, for evaluating any new program, there would be a range of social indicators representing both the benefits expected by the advocates of the program and the harms expected by its opponents. We can move in this direction, but we must remember that all indicators are imperfect and that all are composite products of many causes, many of which are irrelevant to program impact. We can make social indicators based on administrative records more useful if we can break down global indicators into topically specific statistics more focally related to the topic at hand. Thus in evaluating the impact of the British Breathalyser Crackdown of 1967, shown in Figure 15.5, it would have been useful to have separate data on driver fault, blood alcohol of driver, and fatalities separate from nonfatal serious accidents. It added tremendous power to the

analysis that the data were retrievable by time of day. For crime statistics, details of type of crime should be retrievable; for hospital records, details of illness and medication, and so forth. Improving the topical specificity of retrievable administrative records is an urgent public need if we are to achieve the
ability to learn the effects of our new governmental programs.

A hospital is already a record-rich environment, already something like a
potential social polygram, available as a quasi-experimental laboratory with
numerous indicators at least partially relevant to a wide variety of changes in
mode of treatment. New indicators of potential relevance should be set in place
for a wide variety of future program changes. The valuable opinions of a large
number of well-placed observers are going unrecorded. Institutions should
provide an "annual report from program evaluation" from all staff and clients
(Gordon, Campbell, Appleton, & Conner, 1971). Nurses, social workers, at-
tendants, custodians, wardens, caretakers, and even the patients are often
well-placed observers who see programs come and go, see treatment modalities change, and who generate informed opinions of benefits and undesirable
side effects, opinions that are, as a rule, never recorded. The statistical quality
of such indicators is enhanced by the larger numbers of judges whose ratings
would be pooled.

It seems clear from Figures 15.1 through 15.7 that the interrupted time-
series methodology has great promise for program evaluation. More work is
needed by statisticians on appropriate models for tests of significance. For example, the flux-type models (Glass et al., 1975) fail to show significance in
Figure 15.7, perhaps because they weight the most recent observations too
heavily. Handling seasonal trends and combining experimental and control series in tests of significance remain problems. Public needs for hard-headed information on program effectiveness require further methodological research in
these areas.

Methodological considerations also provide recommendations to legisla-
tures and administrators for the optimal use of this method. Here are five.

1. Introduce a new program decisively with adequate advance publicity.
If a new program is gradually introduced, the gradual effects are apt to be indis-
tinguishable from the ordinary kinds of trend changes that would be apt to occur anyway. Delayed starting dates may facilitate this. Figure 15.5 provides a

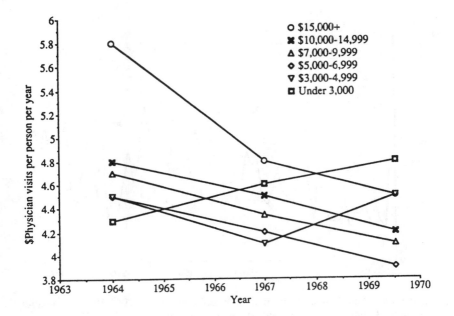

Figure 15.6. Possible evidence for the effect of Medicaid on the contacts with doctors of persons in low-income families. The first data set is based on weekly surveys carried out between July 1963 and June 1964. The second set comes from July 1966-June 1967. The third wave is entirely within 1969 (Wilder, 1972, p. 5, Table B).

good example. The bill was passed in May for a September starting date that was well publicized (Ross, 1973).

2. Keep the record-keeping systems constant, if they are any good at all. Too often the new reform also reforms the data system, resulting in changes that are uninterpretable as program effects. Figure 15.1 illustrates the problem, although in a setting where it was probably unavoidable. Dual record-keeping, old style and new, would be recommended for an extended overlap period.

3. Legislative and administrative actions attacking chronic problems are more easily evaluated than quick responses to acute problem flare-ups. This is due to a complex problem in statistical inference, illustrated, if not explained, in Figure 15.2 (Campbell, 1969b; Riecken et al., 1974).

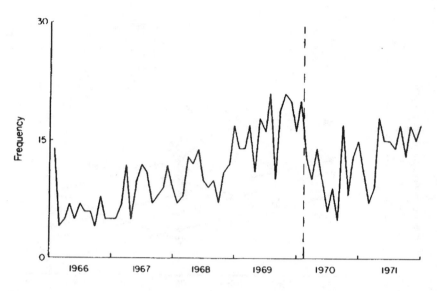

Figure 15.7. Gun homicides by month, Washington, D.C., 1966-1971. "Operation Disarm the Criminal" operated January-June, 1970 (Zimring, 1975, p. 189).

4. Evaluation money should often be invested in assembling comparison statistics from other neighboring governments, as other provinces in evaluating one province's legislation, or in Canadian statistics for evaluating United States programs and vice versa.

5. Where available administrative records are inadequate for the evaluation of major program goals, and where evaluation of the program has high priority, as in pilot programs, the enabling legislation should provide one-year delays in program start-up so that preprogram data can be obtained on newly developed social indicators specifically designed for the program.

FOCUSED ON PERSONS

Figures 15.1 through 15.7 and the preceding sections bear an obvious relation to "social indicators" as commonly understood. In the present section we pick up the theme of *administrative records used for program evaluation,* and move into an application that may be outside of the social indicator movement as usually delineated, but is of such high potential that it needs mention in any program evaluation context.

The interrupted time-series method described so far is available only for program *changes;* it cannot be used to evaluate ongoing programs. However, if administrative records can be made available as averaged data on lists of specified persons, then these records can be used as social indicators of program effectiveness on a wide range of *ongoing* social programs.

So great are contemporary concerns with individual privacy, with a corresponding abhorrence of combining individual data from two record systems, that it seems important to start out by making clear that this use of administrative records can be done, and done effectively, without breaching individual privacy, without releasing any individual data to anybody from any record file. The details are available in the U.S. National Research Council report of the Committee on Federal Agency Evaluation Research (Rivlin et al., 1975. See especially Campbell et al., 1977). [A discussion of "mutually insulated" statistical linkage between data files is presented in greater detail in Chapter 17 of this volume.] This process is achieved without file merger, that is, without expanding either file's data on individuals.

Let us use as a concrete illustration a U.S. Job Corps training program, eligibility for which is determined by a variety of requirements such as age, unemployment, family income, and the like. When there is a surplus of eligible applicants, priority is given to those with the lowest per-person family income. The Job Corps training center classifies applicants on this basis, among others, filling up its training class from the most needy among the eligible, using randomization to break ties, and keeping records also on those applicants above the cutting point for use as a comparison in measuring program effectiveness.

As illustrated in Figure 15.8, these applicants, admitted and rejected, are grouped into lists of 10 or so persons each, each list homogeneous on per-person family income. Each list is randomly given a meaningless code letter or number, for example, A through U in Figure 15.8. These lists of names are then sent to the U.S. Social Security Administration research retrieval staff, which randomly deletes one name from each list, retrieves for the other names the desired information (such as earnings subject to social security deductions or withholding tax and unemployment compensation claims for various time periods), statistically combines these data into statistical composites (such as averages, standard deviations, numbers of cases for which data are available,

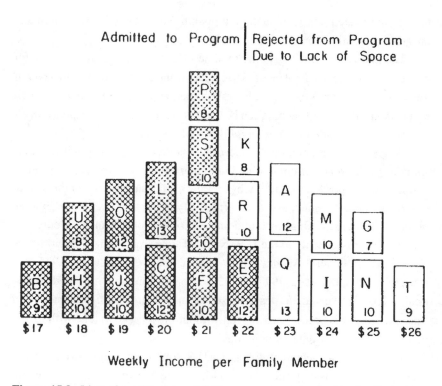

Figure 15.8. Lists of applicants to a Job Corps program organized by family income, producing an approximate frequency distribution (imaginary data). The lists have been randomly labeled by letters A through U. The number below the letter indicates the number of persons in the list. The cross-hatched lists are to receive the program, priority being given to those of lower income. There is space for only 12 of those persons at $22.00 per week. These 12 are chosen at random from the 30 available at $22.00, making up list E, the remainder going into lists K and R. (The design is also usable in the absence of tied cases and tie-breaking randomization.)

etc.), and returns only these statistical products for each list code to the local Job Corps evaluation staff. The evaluators then reassemble the lists in meaningful order, pooling the statistics for lists of the same income value, producing results such as shown in Figure 15.8. The Job Corps Staff would have learned nothing about individual earnings, nor the SSA have learned anything about individual training status or reported family earnings.

The general feasibility of such procedures has been demonstrated by Heller (1972) and Fischer (1972), but unfortunately, not where the assignment of applicants to programs had been done in a systematic way that made program effects estimable. Under normal operating procedures, the grounds for admission are imprecise, variable, unrecorded, and with no records kept on those rejected. Formalizing eligibility requirements, with the admission decision hinging (for some subgroups at least) on a quantified eligibility score (such as family income, reading skill scores, the sum of admission interviewers' ratings on several priority dimensions, or even time of application), makes possible the "regression discontinuity design" just illustrated (Campbell, 1969b; Riecken et al., 1974). (If it is feasible, randomized admissions of eligibles for the whole pool rather than just for tie-breaking cases at the cutting point is, of course, still better from the standpoint of statistical inference, particularly for estimating program effects for the whole range of income levels.)

No manpower program has as yet been as well or as validly evaluated as by the method illustrated in Figures 15.8 and 15.9. If it went no farther, settling just for administrative records unaugmented by follow-up interviews, it would be extremely inexpensive also. Heller (1972) reports retrieval costs of $1.00 per person. But even if it were 10 times that, it would still be cheap, as interviews will run $100.00 or more per person. Rate of follow-up contact by interviewers in manpower studies has run as low as 50%, and with more cases lost from the control group than for the trained group. SSA retrieval would probably be much better than this, and certainly less biased. Thus such use of administrative records would be a valuable low-cost adjunct even for a follow-up evaluation study employing interviews.

This type of program evaluation is potentially available wherever ameliorative programs have more eligible applicants than they are funded for. This is certainly the case for most federal and local programs targeted to special needy groups. It is usually only by failing to give these opportunities proper local publicity that program administrators avoid a surplus of applicants. Such programs are very expensive, and can be carried out in a wide variety of ways. It is in the highest public interest that we create the capacity to evaluate such programs by these means. To do so we must expand the research retrieval capacity of our major administrative files relevant to program evaluation, including again such private files as medical insurance and educational testing services. To do so we must also (when evaluation is wanted) formalize program admission procedures and keep records on those rejected as well as those accepted.

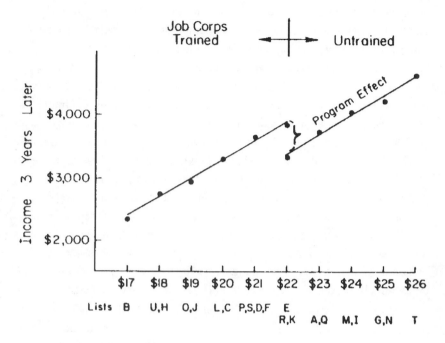

Figure 15.9. Subsequent income as a function of training and pretraining family income (same imaginary study as Figure 15.8). Training increases income by an estimated $500 per year, estimated with most confidence for those applicants near $22.00 per week in per-person family income.

Does present or proposed privacy legislation in the United States and elsewhere jeopardize such program evaluation? Certainly privacy legislation should be carefully scrutinized to determine whether or not it needlessly precludes such procedures. For example, in the case of Figures 15.8 and 15.9 it would certainly decrease the cost of retrieval and reduce the frequency of errors in the United States if Social Security numbers accompanied names on the lists. The U.S. Privacy Act of 1974 would not preclude this in the Job Corps case, since salary or subsistence payments are being made to the trainee. But the language of the bill would seem to preclude the use of Social Security numbers if we were evaluating a medical rehabilitation program or a nonpaying training program, for example. In the Job Corps case it might well preclude the retention of social security numbers for applicants for whom there was no space and thus got no funds, thus making the analysis impossible, needlessly.

A unified national data bank would jeopardize privacy through increasing the payoff to a blackmailing employee. Like most program evaluation methodologists, the present author opposes such a superfile. What is proposed instead is that all existing files be kept separate, or even split up further, but that each have the capacity for "mutually insulated" negotiation with other files in ways precluding the transfer of individual data from one file to another.

The use of a universal identifying number, such as the U.S. Social Security number almost is and could become, must not be confused with a unified data bank. The latter can be prohibited directly, as can all kinds of sharing of individual data between files. Social Security numbers do not as a rule facilitate the misuse of data in files, and have not been involved in the bad examples of using files to invade individual privacy. They add little to the convenience of retrieval of private information or gossip on a single person, but greatly facilitate mass statistical retrievals in which individuals are anonymous. Their social value for program evaluation greatly outweighs the very slight, if any, increase in the danger of misuse they incur.

OVERVIEW OF CHAPTER 16

———•◆•———

This chapter was written by Andrew C. Gordon, Don Campbell, and others at the Center for Urban Affairs at Northwestern University, for two specific social programs that were operating in Illinois in 1970. The recommended accounting procedures, however, can be used in the evaluation of many governmental programs that are undergoing change. Two questions are posed when evaluating change: Did the change have the desired effect? Are there undesirable side effects? Social indicators and social accounting procedures can be used to document changes within a program. The problem facing evaluators is that the program is not necessarily responsible for noted changes. To rule out a multitude of other events that might account for the observed results, control groups are a necessity. The authors recommend the interrupted time series design.

Input data about the implementation of the program should be gathered, as well as output data, such as counts of new jobs or diseases cured. The authors also recognize the importance of customers and other program participants in providing useful output data. They suggest that satisfaction reports from customers and needs assessments from potential customers should be collected. All these criteria should be used for budgeting decisions and decisions on agency expansion, reorganization, or elimination.

In Illinois, the community rejected the research procedures needed to obtain their opinions. They felt that the public opinion polls were more helpful to the researchers than they were to the community, and that the polls were an invasion of privacy, focusing on the shortcomings of the respondent. Their concerns might be addressed with the following four statements. First, the focus of the surveys will be to assess the quality of service available in the community rather than asking personal questions. Second, they will address the specific concerns of the community. Third, the respondents will have complete and immediate access to all results. Finally, the respondents will always be told who is sponsoring the survey. The authors suggest that efforts should be made to employ as interviewers residents from the affected areas where jobs are scarce. It is also important to educate the community so that they understand that the questions must be asked again and again to determine the best way to spend welfare funds.

There are a number of ways in which surveys could be conducted. Each method is listed along with the problems associated with it.

Election-type procedures can be set up as a ballot in which people go to a neighborhood polling place to vote. This can be expensive, and results may be reflective of "who" votes rather than of shifts in the opinion of the community. Still, the authors believe this may be one of the best procedures for assessing community opinion, except for the prohibitive cost. While this option was not seriously considered for the Illinois programs, the authors suggest that the feasibility of this procedure be studied.

Residential interview samples involve standard public opinion polling of a representative sample of the community. There are a number of problems associated with this method, including the perception that door-to-door interviews are intrusive, distrust of results by those not asked to participate, and the expense of interviewing. It should be done only if there are no alternative means and the value gained is real.

Telephone interviews are a major alternative to door-to-door interviewing. Refusal rates may be high, especially in this time of rampant telephone advertising. Anonymity is not ensured, and there may be more distrust regarding who the interviewer is. Fear of retaliation may be a problem, as well as problems of honesty and verifiability.

Mailed questionnaires have many weaknesses, yet this is the method recommended by the authors since each of the problems can be overcome if carefully addressed. The main weakness is the low and selective return rate. Ballot-box stuffing or ballot substitution becomes easier with this method. Campaigns by community organizations might be waged to tell individuals how to complete the survey. Open-ended questions may present a problem where writing fluency is a problem. Defining the sampling frame may also pose a difficulty.

Another option involves questionnaires delivered by a special staff member. While this method might solve a number of the problems associated with the mailed questionnaire method, the cost would increase. Also, the procedure faces the problems of intrusiveness, fear of retaliation, excess guidance by the interviewer, and ballot-box stuffing.

Agency-distributed questionnaires can provide a great deal of information from customers. For this method, each agency has clients complete a brief questionnaire evaluating the agency's services. This method does not provide any information on those who are not presently receiving the services but should be. If questionnaires are filled out immediately, clients might fear retaliation for negative evaluations. There is also the temptation for agency personnel to complete the questionnaires to give their agency a good report.

Other forms of distributions include questionnaires printed in community newspapers or distributed in local stores or on street corners.

One must be cautious when gathering community opinions. Individuals might portray their situation as worse than it is so that they might get more services. Frustration might occur because of raised expectations, which can be particularly problematic in the control areas. Access to survey results may affect respondents' answers in subsequent rounds. Finally, a program might appear more successful than it is simply because fewer questionnaires are completed due to boredom.

The authors provide several recommendations for customer and potential customer evaluation. State agencies will do their best to respond to the needs of their clientele if they are put in competition with private agencies. All agencies, in both experimental and control areas, should be required to supply monthly reports on services rendered. Giving recipients of services the opportunity to confirm the reports and evaluate the services should prevent inflated reports from the agencies. Forms should be provided to customers for this purpose, such as Introduction Cards or letters for "Certified Satisfied Customers Accounting." These forms, however, cannot help those who should be receiving services but are not getting them.

To monitor the implementation of the program, agencies from the experimental and control areas should be required to supply monthly reports on customers served, beginning 3 months prior to the start of the program. The forms sent to recipients should be approved by state government agencies and pilot tested. Both quantitative and qualitative items should be analyzed, although open-ended questions might be analyzed for a random sample. Reports should be provided to all interested parties and available to the public through newspapers, libraries, and community organizations.

A hypothetical outcome is given to demonstrate what a successful result might look like when graphed. To measure the effect of including customer feedback, one might include a second comparison area that instituted customer feedback at a later time. It should be recognized that a single graph will not provide the entire picture; multiple indicators should be used. An event log should record any potential causes for change in an indicator, such as temporary office closings, general changes in unemployment, or campaigns by local organizations.

Finally, Gordon and Campbell discuss the importance of recording the perceptions of the agency personnel as a part of program evaluation. These individuals are in an excellent position to observe the recipients of the services and to judge whether their needs are being met. They will also be aware of problems with the program and can offer suggestions as to how they might be addressed. The authors include a draft of a form that can be used for these purposes.

SIXTEEN

WELFARE RECIPIENTS AND SOCIAL WORKERS AS JUDGES OF THE EFFECTIVENESS OF THE PROGRAM

———•◆•———

*T*he recommendations contained in this report are focused primarily on the Woodlawn Service Program (WSP) of the Illinois Institute of Social Policy, and to a lesser degree the Peoria Program. The recommendations, however, are for procedures that might become permanent statewide additions to government record-keeping, thus providing a continuous base for evaluating future program changes anywhere in the state.

The general goal is to provide bases for judging whether the specific changes made in the mode of delivery of state services have had the desired effects, and have been free from undesirable side effects. Like all modern efforts

Gordon, A. C., Campbell, D. T., Appleton, H., & Conner, R. F. (1971). *Recommended accounting procedures for the evaluation of improvements in the delivery of state social services*. New York: Russell Sage Foundation; Springfield: Illinois Institute of Social Policy.

at evaluation of new government programs (e.g., Wholey, 1970; Williams & Evans, 1969) there is recognition that many well-intentioned reforms have failed to have the intended consequences, and that in such cases, government should continue to try alternate approaches until some genuinely effective procedure is found. But the means of measuring such effects are usually unavailable. Hence the need for social indicators and social accounting procedures designed for these purposes (Bauer, 1966; Freeman & Sherwood, 1970; Sheldon & Moore, 1968; Suchman, 1967). For a change in any given indicator, there are often a dozen other events in addition to the change in state service delivery that might account for the change. To render such changes interpretable often requires control comparison, that is, data from other areas or on other topics.

To analyze these data we recommend the "Control Series" version of the "Interrupted Time-Series Design."

PROBLEMS AND POSSIBILITIES IN REPRESENTING COMMUNITY JUDGMENTS

The typical content of government welfare records and progress reports has in the past been mainly limited to input data, how many persons were on the staff, how many new offices were opened, total money spent, and so on. The demand now is for output data, measures of results (Wholey, 1970; Williams & Evans, 1969). Some of these results may be in things countable such as jobs found, diseases cured, rats killed, number of persons per room (or hopefully, number of rooms per person), and so on. But for the most part, output measurement will have to involve some kind of reports from observers about how things are going, what has been achieved, what needs to be done.

One of the first and most important commitments of the Woodlawn Service Program, under its Director Clinton McKay, was that reports from the system's customers and potential customers be given a major role in judging program effectiveness. Furthermore, such reporting was seen not only as a means for measuring the effects of new programs, but also as an effective and important part of the new program itself.

This point is important enough to take space to restate McKay's argument. The natural inclination of the staff in any public office is to adjust to the demands of their fellow staff members. Clients, customers, the public, interfere as strangers with the ingroup social system that develops among the staff. There arises an unconscious tendency to define the agency's mission narrowly so that there are as few clients as possible. In case of doubt, an applicant is sent to some other agency, or is told there is no agency for his needs. The customers accepted are given the type of service most convenient for the staff member, not most needed, and the like.

These same pressures exist in business enterprises. Many of us have felt like unwanted intruders in some fancy department stores. But in the business world there is a powerful feedback system from us customers. Stores that have no customers go out of business. No such feedback exists at the present time in most government service agencies. It is McKay's goal to create such feedback, and to achieve a situation in which agencies compete for satisfied customers, and go out into the street to dig up new business, people who are entitled to services they may not know exist.

His proposed mechanisms for doing this are (a) Units-of-service-delivered accounting; asking all state service agencies to report each month who they have served and how many units of service they have delivered. (b) Putting government service agencies into direct competition with private agencies whom the government will contract with for delivery of specified amounts of service. (c) Initiating customer satisfaction reports and unsatisfied need statements from needy potential customers. (d) Using all three of these productivity criteria as basis for decisions on budgeting, agency expansion, reorganization, elimination, and more.

At the present time, governmental decision making on the adequacy of programs is based on the judgment of those employed to run the program, or those still higher up and still more removed from the actual situation. There is no machinery available at present to let those served give their judgments. We might expect, therefore, that the plans of the Woodlawn Service Program to provide such a voice would be welcomed by the community. Unfortunately, many of the means by which these judgments might be obtained are similar to research procedures now rejected by the community. We must understand these objections and attempt to correct the evils to which they point.

The people of Woodlawn, and no doubt people in other urban communities, are fed up with being researched by public opinion polls or questionnaires. Such research is seen as exploitative, as providing jobs for white middle-class researchers using money that would be better spent on helping poor folks. Such research is also seen as helping the researcher through the articles and theses that get written. In contrast, surveys are only a burden to the community respondents. As to "making the community's needs known," this has been done for Woodlawn again and again and nothing helpful ever comes of it. Rarely, if ever, are the results reported back to the community.

Furthermore, community public opinion surveys, like the case work interviews, usually contain humiliating invasions of privacy. The focus seems always to be on what is wrong with the respondent rather than what is wrong with government services. Even in terms of the respondent's needs, it is assumed that he doesn't know his own needs, a specialist must pry them out and tell him.

While we cannot hope to meet all of these objections, we must keep them in the forefront and only counter them when there are strong reasons, understandable by the community. As a start, here are four statements of intent:

1. The community opinion surveys will focus upon agency performance and the quality of service available in the community rather than asking personal questions. They will provide a convenient means of expressing complaints, and of mobilizing them so that they get heard.

2. In order to be of service to the people, the surveys will cover topics that the people want to sound off on, even when these involve problems not under the control of the state.

3. The people will have complete and immediate access to all the results. They will not be exploited by being excluded from information created by their own cooperation. The local communities will be allowed to follow shifts in their own local opinion just as, at the national level, we follow Gallup Poll results and election returns. The state should cooperate in this regard with all groups claiming to represent the community or segments of it. It is to be anticipated that the government will thus be providing strong ammunition that will be used in pressing community claims against the government. This is not to be avoided, but instead will be the clearest evidence that the opinion research activity has not been exploitative, but has instead provided a real service to the community.

4. The people responding will be told explicitly whom they are talking to. The sponsorship of any opinion interview or questionnaire will not be dis-

guised or attributed merely to some survey agency such as NORC, Gallup, or Harris Poll. It is commonly believed in both commercial and political polling that the responder knowing who the sponsor is will bias the results (presumably in the direction of being more favorable to the sponsor than is accurate). If so, this is a bias we must live with if we are truly to level with the public. Every statement from one person to another occurs in conversation, and is inadequately interpretable without the context of that conversation. The public opinion survey respondent is entrapped and betrayed if he does not know what conversation he is in, who he is talking to.

These recommendations do not meet all of the objections. The research activity will continue to be dominated at the administrative level by middle-class persons, although with a greatly improved representation of blacks. Because it must cover control areas as well as experimental, because it must eventually go statewide, and to avoid challenges of bias, the information collection activity cannot become a monopoly of any one community nor even give preferential employment to residents of any one area, although staffing procedures should certainly give high priority to employing those now unemployed and underemployed, and to creating jobs in areas where jobs are scarce.

As to the challenge that adequate information on community needs is already at hand, we must attempt to educate the community to the fact that welfare funds can be spent in quite different ways, and that in order to choose the best way we need to repeat the same questions again and again.

Possible Ways of Conducting the Surveys

We are recommending that somehow the judgments and preferences of the people get assembled so as to become a part of government decision making processes. Something more official than newspaper reports of Gallup Poll surveys would seem desirable. The more important the role of such community opinion becomes, the more it must be able to stand up to challenges and the more it must have safeguards against inadvertent or deliberate bias.

As a background for recommending specific procedures, it seems well to lay out the range of possible techniques, and to inventory the recurrent problems or sources of bias. (In what follows we will interweave a list of issues and problems, A, B, C, D, etc., with the list of ways of conducting surveys, 1, 2, 3, etc.)

1. Election-Type Procedures. A survey of community opinion, judgments, and complaints could be set up as a ballot, on which people "voted" in a neighborhood (precinct) polling place. Such a procedure would be (A.) very *expensive,* but not necessarily more expensive than door-to-door interviewing. It would be (B.) *representative-in-opportunity* to participate, but (C.) *unrepresentative-in-participation,* in that the indifferent, incompetent, too busy, and totally alienated would be underrepresented. It might be more biased in this regard than some public opinion surveys. If there were (D.) *stability-in-representation* bias, then shifts in votes from time to time would be interpretable as a shift in public opinion. It would be possible for a shift to occur due just to a shift in who votes, without a shift in opinion, although this is not likely, and the number of voters would usually in itself be a symptom of community discontent. However, a record of (E.) *campaigns to get out the vote* would be essential in interpretation, as would also campaigns to get people to vote in specific ways.

The specific voting procedures now in use are the result of a long historical process in which features were added to correct previous problems. These problems occurred because voting was important in governmental decision making. If the community judgments we collect become important in governmental decision making, as we intend they should, similar problems will emerge. (The history of voting procedures should be studied in detail for our present guidance. We have not actually done this yet.)

(F.) *Anonymity* is insisted upon in modern voting procedures, although absent in the town-meeting democracy of our past. It is instituted to avoid (G.) *fear of retaliation* that would lead people to vote as others wanted them to rather than as they actually felt. These others feared were usually, but not always, the government in power. To prevent (H.) *people filling out other people's ballots,* the voting is done alone and in the polling place (except for those few qualifying for assistance in voting, and this assistance must be given by a family member, or by two judges of opposing parties. For such assistance, special affidavits are filed). Anonymity creates problems as well as solves them. It makes (I.) *ballot-box stuffing* easier, by persons who vote twice, by persons who come in from other areas to vote, and so on. To curb these biases there are prepared (J.) *registration lists of eligible voters,* and (K.) *signed records of who did vote.* To prevent ballot-box stuffing by substituting false ballots for the true ones, (M.) *poll watchers* from competing political parties are required. To make possible meaningful challenges to the validity of the process, there is (N.) *public accessibility of the records,* public verifiability for a period of time long enough to allow for challenge, perhaps a year, and the possibility of re-counts. These procedures are probably adequate, if vigorously implemented, to ensure honest elections. That we do not always have such is due to lack of vigilance in removing dead and gone persons from the registration lists, lack of verification of the identity of the voters, poll watchers all of whom are in actu-ality from the same party or political machine, and so on. It probably would not help to add still further precautions. Much less adequately handled in our sys-tem is genuine (O.) *public representation in the design of the ballot.* The public power to decide is limited by the alternatives that get on the ballot to be voted on. These, whether candidates or issues, are often decided upon by quite unrep-resentative procedures and omit what would have been the most popular public choice.

We have discussed voting primarily to raise issues for other procedures, rather than as a procedure to be seriously considered. But perhaps it should be. While we must not regard *any* procedure as ideal, and must be on the alert for misleading results from each, it might be judged that precinct voting on a "Community Problems Inventory" would be the best procedure if it were not for cost. These costs would be greatly reduced if such a survey could be added as an additional ballot at elections scheduled for other purposes. This would slow up such voting, and require additional booths and space just for that pur-pose, but would probably not involve more than a 20% increase in cost. As in other voting, sample ballots in local newspapers and the like could ready the voter for the polling place decisions. Much of the ballot would be highly struc-tured questions that could be electronically (optical scanner) tallied, an ade-quate procedure as long as the ballots remained available for more traditional verification. (Space for written comments and suggestions for future invento-ries would also be included, but probably only analyzed for samples, and impressionistically.) Even though we are not seriously considering this proce-dure, we should at least find out if it is legally and financially feasible.

2. Residential Interview Samples. By this heading we mean to designate the now standard public opinion survey procedures, where a representative (often random) sample of the community is selected to be interviewed in their homes. For many reasons this is the social scientists' first recommendation, as shown in the Woodlawn Base Line study. This was rejected by the Woodlawn Service Program Community Advisory Board for several reasons, at least one of which is intrinsic to the method. One objection was that personal questions were to be asked. This could have been cured by eliminating those questions and retaining the many excellent questions calling for judgments of community agencies. Another important objection we can label (P.) *intrusiveness*. Interviewers intrude like bill collectors, police, and public welfare workers in a poor neighborhood. Their very presence is a burden, an invasion of privacy no matter what questions are asked. Door-to-door interviewing is on these grounds to be avoided if other adequate means are available and unless the values to be achieved are real and can be made clear to the community.

Interviewing is also expensive. With typical rates for interviewing and analyzing results running near $100 per respondent, with 1,000 respondents being a reasonable number to provide sampling stability, with interviews required in equal numbers for control areas, and with repeat surveys needed at least each year, the annual budget for Woodlawn could run $200,000, and that for Peoria the same. (We must bear in mind that public opinion surveying has achieved enough experience to do realistic budgeting, unlike most of the other procedures we suggest. Also, much of the $100 per interview cost comes from coding free responses. Were the interview to use highly structured questions amenable to mechanical tallying, as do many of our other suggestions, costs could be greatly reduced, perhaps as low as $15.00 per interview.) Representative samples can be drawn up, but interviewers will find 25% not at home. Call backs can reduce this but are expensive. Another 25% may be expected to refuse. Nonetheless, overall, opinion surveys are likely to be more representative than any other procedure, since representativeness is increased through preventing procrastination, and through not requiring the effort of reading and writing. We meet here, however, the new problem of (Q.) *perceived representativeness*. The public is apt to distrust a survey in which they were not asked to participate, and they are apt to not believe that randomization and stratification can provide representativeness, or have actually been done. That is, it may be assumed that only those known to be favorable were asked. Thus procedures that give everyone a chance to respond may be perceived as more validly representative than those that use a small proportion of the community randomly selected (even though a statistician might decide the opposite if there were a small turnout on the all-invited procedure). Anonymity is not provided in that the interviewer knows or can know who the respondent is, and name, address, and telephone number are often requested to make interview verification easier. Depending on whom the interviewer is, fear of retaliation may operate. (The interviewers should be powerless outsiders rather than local officials with power over the respondents.)

Interviewers can easily guide respondents to preferred answers. Ballot-box stuffing in the form of false interview records can easily be done, especially if respondents' names are not recorded, but also when they are. Polling agencies do abbreviated repeat interviews on a partial spot-check basis to check on whether some interviewing was actually done. This is to check against a lazy interviewer inventing interviews. It does not check adequately on a systematic biasing of responses in the recording or transfer processes. Human memory and the vagueness of conversations make this almost impossible to check. If immediately after a bona fide interview, the interviewer were to read back his summary of respondent opinions on free-response items, the average respondent would probably feel the recording somewhat inaccurate on one third of the items. Weeks later the identification of deliberate misquoting would be hopeless. (If door-to-door interviewing employed in part a structured ballot, one verification device would be to leave a copy of this with the respondent, which, if he kept it, could be used in the repeat interview spot checks.) To avoid falsification at the survey administration level, the sample verification should be done by some truly independent agency. It should also include verification of the random sampling procedures. Under the requirement of public verifiability, the names of respondents should probably be available for independent verification efforts by protest groups challenging the study. (In the New Jersey Negative Income Tax study not even a congressional committee or the General Accounting Office has been allowed to do such verification, and for good reasons.) Another approach to verification would be to have different agencies each do half of the surveying, with agreement in results being the verification. (To some extent, the opinion polling agencies keep each other honest by publishing competing results on the same topics.)

3. Telephone Interviews. In commercial opinion surveying these are a major alternative to door-to-door interviewing, and should be included in what we consider even if not in what we recommend. They have been used, for example, in simultaneous surveys of radio and TV viewing ("what program are you tuned into at this moment") to avoid the intrusiveness of door-to-door interviewing in evening hours. Costs are no doubt less, although in part because shorter interviews are used. (For half-hour or shorter interviews with structured alternatives, cost as low as $5.00 per respondent might be achieved.) Refusal rates and the accompanying biases might be fully as high as in door-to-door interviewing, the ease of hanging up compensating for the lower fear of intrusion. These biases might be expected to be more stable than for most procedures. Anonymity is lost, and distrust as to whom the interviewer really is might be greater than in face-to-face interviewing. Thus fear of retaliation is a problem. Problems of honesty and verifiability are as great as for any technique, greater than most.

4. *Mailed Questionnaires.* These are an important means, and one we are going to recommend in spite of the many weaknesses. Its main weakness is low and selective return rate. Election type voting and door-to-door interviewing probably get returns from some 50% or more of those invited. Mailed questionnaires occasionally got much better return rates than that, but figures as low as 10% also occur and 25% might be a better overall estimate. At this return rate, and for electronic scoring of structured questions, costs as low as $1.50 per respondent might be estimated. Such low costs would make possible (R.) *high frequency of measurement,* providing the "fine-grained time series" so desirable for the time-series designs, particularly for a program that is going to be introducing different innovations at different times of the year. Thus 4 to 12 waves of measurement per year would be possible. This might be combined with the goal of perceived representativeness so that once per year each person was questioned, the total address list being randomly divided into 12 sublists, one for each month. Anonymity is readily achieved if wanted, although it makes ballot-box stuffing easier, by community groups, through collecting and filling out unused ballots or by printing their own, and by the surveying agency, and makes verifiability impossible. Even if something like polling-place voting records could be achieved by having each person also return a signed postcard stating that he had sent in his anonymous survey, ballot substitution in the data analysis process and people filling out other people's ballots could easily occur.

On this latter point, consider two extremes. If the person to whom the ballot is mailed asks some neighbor to help fill it out, or even turns it over to someone to fill out, the processes of democratic representation are still probably well served. The opinion reported is a genuine community opinion. But with three fourths of the ballots mailed out lying around unused, it would be easy for an alert community organization to collect them and fill them out in accordance with the organization program. This would still represent community opinion, but in a statistical sense many fewer opinions than ballots, over-weighting the opinion of a few leaders. Probably the tendency to allow this to be done would be much less with signed ballots. But how different would this be in practice from a community organization preparing a sample questionnaire with detailed recommendations on how to respond? This latter would seem to be a perfectly proper electioneering procedure. It could play havoc with a time series, particularly if the persons interpreting the results were unaware of the campaign. It would be hoped that if a meaningful channel for community opinion were to be established, that community organizations would see its value and work to preserve its usefulness by preserving its credibility.

(S.) *Comprehensibility* is a problem in any such survey. Bureaucratic agencies and social science academics generate forms and questionnaires that are incomprehensible to the bulk of U.S. citizens. Familiarity with questionnaires and tests is a middle-class trait. Questionnaires use an arbitrary shorthand, which makes for efficient responding once understood, but is baffling when first encountered. While more readible and clear questionnaires can be achieved, this tends to make them longer and more formidable for this reason. Thus comprehensibility is always a disadvantage for questionnaires in contrast to individual interview procedures.

Questionnaires can be "structured," with fixed multiple-choice answers, or "free response," requiring written answers, and introducing the problem of (T.) *writing fluency*. It is hard for the middle-class person whose job requires daily practice at writing, to realize what an obstacle this can be for a person who may have occasion to write only once or so a month. Infrequency of use of writing also affects the size of the script, and middle-class questionnaire constructors regularly make the blanks too small for those who do not write often.

The problem of fluency of writing argues for use of structured rather than free-response questions, where possible. But there are many contents where the structured format is very awkward. As discussed in more detail in a subsequent section, inquiring as to what problems a citizen has had, and what agencies he has gone to for help, is utterly unfeasible in a structured format. On such topics, individual interviews are much to be preferred.

What mailing lists are to be used? For some purposes these could be names of present recipients of state services. But to cover those who should be recipients and are not now, it must be broader than this. For the best sampling procedures, a list of residence addresses (with or without names) would be needed; mail could then be addressed to "Occupant, Apartment 2b, 6565 South Woodlawn, Chicago 60637." (The fact that one apartment may house several unrelated families is a problem.) Sampling by blocks, instead of persons, and with cooperation from postmen, one might use a nonspecific "Postal Patron, Local," without a specific street address.

5. *Delivered Questionnaires*. In conversation between us and the Woodlawn Service Program staff there has emerged a suggested procedure halfway between the door-to-door interview and the mailed questionnaire. In this, questionnaires would be delivered to households by a special staff rather than the mailman. If residents were at home, as much explanation and help as wanted would be given. If they were away, they would be left with an explanatory letter. The questionnaires could be filled out while the deliverer waited or made other calls in the block, or they could be picked up on a later day, or mailed in. Undoubtedly this could achieve a higher return rate and greater comprehension than a mailing. It adds some of the costs and problems of intrusiveness, fear of retaliation, excess guidance, and ballot-box-stuffing opportunities of door-to-door interviewing.

6. *Agency-Distributed Questionnaires*. Another model that has been discussed with WSP is to have in each service agency office brief questionnaires in which customers are asked to evaluate the service that they have received, much as is sometimes done by restaurants and airlines. This would reach a relevant clientele for some evaluative purposes, though not those who should be getting the service. If filled out immediately and deposited, or if signed, it would maximize fear of retaliation by withdrawal of future services. If anonymous, whether deposited in the office or to be mailed later, it would be too easy

and too tempting for agency personnel to fill them out instead of actually distributing them to customers, in order to give their agency a good report.

Other forms of distribution that we have at least briefly considered include questionnaires printed in community newspapers, or distributed in stores and on street corners.

7. Other Problems. Going through these several possible ways of getting community opinion have raised many problems, but not all. As soon as people come to believe that their opinions are influencing the distribution of funds with more funds going to more needy areas, we run the risk of (U.) *exaggerated complaint,* in which people portray their situation as bad just to be sure they get at least their share of government attention. The direction of this bias might be expected to be opposite to fear of retaliation on most topics. The recognition of the usefulness of exaggerated complaint would probably be greatest in those communities with active local protest organizations, and this could produce spurious regional differences in apparent need. No easy way of controlling this bias seems available. Conditions of anonymity might make respondents more irresponsible in this. Campaigns by local organizations to encourage this type of response might be looked for. Familiarity with the survey procedures might reduce fear of retaliation and increase sophistication, producing results that made it look like things were getting worse even while they were getting better. Basically, all community opinion survey procedures must be used with caution in comparing regional needs. They will be much more interpretable as a basis for deciding which local problem area deserves most attention. (This ties in with the concept of "control topics," above.)

Another danger that has emerged in our discussions with the Woodlawn Service Program is the potential role of public problem surveys in creating (V.) *frustration due to raised expectations.* Thus if we start surveying dissatisfaction on a given topic too long before WSP is going to be able to do anything about it, we may create false expectations of immediate improvement and anger when nothing happens. This problem would be particularly bad in the control areas where no special program improvements were to be taking place. In part this is a matter of how introduction and questions are worded. One of the special goals in pretesting instruments should be to check on this. Wordings that are misleading in the expectations they generate should be avoided. On the other hand, if the asking of the questions mobilizes public demand that something be done about problems, this is an outcome intrinsic to the goal of providing a meaningful and useful voice for the community in governmental decision making.

The policy of giving respondents full access to tabulations made from their answers will undoubtedly produce some changes in the answers given at first. We will name this problem after its most likely form, (W.) *the bandwagon effect.* Judging from college classroom studies, telling people how their group as a whole has voted leads some persons to change their vote so as to agree with the majority, thus increasing the size of the majority on a second vote. From a simple-minded application of conformity principles, a larger majority should be more impressive than a smaller one, and thus one might expect repeated voting with feedback to push all majority positions up toward 100%. This implication has never been checked, as far as we know, and almost certainly is wrong as far as one can judge from practical experience. Making votes public should have this effect, even though attenuated by the 2- to 4-year delays between votes. Perhaps the one-party areas are kept so through the help of this mechanism, but for most districts such trends are nonexistent. Since the advent some 40 years ago of published public opinion polls predicting election outcomes, there has been fear of such an effect, but no clear illustrations are available, and trends in the opposite direction occur as frequently. If there are such effects, they probably diminish after the first few waves. Since our general orientation is toward relative measurement, rather than absolute, once the process has settled down, repeated surveys accompanied by prompt feedback should produce interpretable trends for the evaluation of other impacts. (By delaying feedback for a random half of the reporting units, an experiment on the effect could be built into the early stages of the introduction of a measurement program.)

When combined with a likely fear of retaliation for criticism, the bandwagon effect might be of a selective nature. Seeing from the results that others have been brave enough to complain, and with apparent impunity, might thus increase the number of respondents willing to express complaints. Complaint frequencies less than majorities should have some of this effect. No parallel process would occur for expressions of satisfaction, since these would have been under no inhibition. A related effect might result from seeing the results from neighboring regions, stimulating competitive complaining as discussed above as exaggerated complaint.

Our main concern must be those methodological problems that will cause shifts in measures that might be misinterpreted as program effects. The repeated answering of the same questions may well produce (X.) *boredom due to repetition*. This would most likely appear as a reduction in the number of respondents, and therefore, on some instruments, a reduction in the number of complaints, on others a reduction in the number of reports of satisfactory service.

RECOMMENDED PROCEDURES FOR CUSTOMER AND POTENTIAL CUSTOMER EVALUATION

Certified Satisfied Customers Accounting. Among the goals of Woodlawn Service Program (WSP) is focusing agency attention on maximizing the number of units of high quality service that they provide recipients. Whereas at present agencies tend to define their missions narrowly and in borderline cases refer applicants to other agencies if possible, WSP aspires to create a situation in which agencies compete for the opportunity to be of genuine service. WSP is also deliberately placing contracted services from private agencies in direct competition with state agencies offering the same service.

Presumably WSP will be having agencies report monthly on the services rendered customers. For comparison base purposes, similar reports should be requested for control areas. What we propose here is that recipients be given an opportunity to confirm these reports and to evaluate briefly the quality of service. Figure 16.1 is a suggested form letter for this purpose. If these forms were not returned, this would be taken as presumptive evidence that the agency account was correct. The opportunity for the recipients to reply should be enough to avoid inflated reports from the agencies.

This suggestion is our best judgment as to how to implement Clinton McKay's desire that customer satisfaction be evaluated in some brief form such as used by restaurants and airlines. It also builds upon the procedures he used in Pennsylvania. In that setting, an "ombudsman" or public helper in dealing with government gave the potential recipient an "Introduction Card" to take to the service agency with which an appointment had been made. The lower half of that card was to be mailed to the governor with an evaluation of

Mr. John Doe
6705 A. Woodlawn Avenue
Chicago, Illinois 60638

Dear Mr. Doe:

The state of Illinois is trying to make sure that agencies are delivering the services to the people that they are supposed to. For this reason the State is asking all agencies for a list of the customers they have served.

The *Woodlawn Chicago Office* of the State Dept. of Public Welfare has reported that they have provided you or your family with six hours of family budgeting advice on the dates of October 7, 9, and 10th involving delays of two hours in waiting room. We are asking you to confirm or correct this report.

                                              Sincerely yours,

                                              Leroy S. Wehrle, Director
                                              Illinois Institute for Social Policy
                                              Room 302, Armory Building,
                                              Springfield, Illinois 62706

1.   a. I received this service as reported.
     b. The report needs correcting as I have marked it above.
     c. I did not receive any such service.
2.   The service was: a. very helpful
                        b. some help
                        c. little help
                        d. no help at all
3.   a. I was treated with a lot of respect and courtesy.
     b. I was treated with some respect and courtesy.
     c. I got no respect and no courtesy.
4.   a. The State should hire more people to do this kind of work.
     b. This service is staffed all right as it is.
     c. The State should hire fewer people to do this kind of work.
5.   I have these suggestions to improve this service: _____
_____
6.   Other comments: _____
_____

Figure 16.1. Rough Draft of Form Letter for "Certified Satisfied Customers Accounting"

the quality of service eventually received. While very few of these cards were mailed in, it seems certain that the conspicuous presence of this easy opportunity to complain had its effect on the service agency staff, and that were service to have become worse, complaints would have increased. While WSP is not at present introducing the ombudsman, the office in which self-certification for financial assistance eventually takes place will also no doubt serve to direct people to the service agencies they need. Peoria is considering a centralized intake office for all types of need. In both of these settings, the "Introduction Card" could be used in the Pennsylvania pattern. We believe that the present suggestion is superior, however. It covers recipients who get to the service agency on their own. The Introduction Card may seem to ask for an evaluation right under the nose of the evaluated agency. The "Certified Satisfied Customers Accounting" letter (see Figure 16.1) is mailed at a later time and thus calls for a judgment of the overall assistance that may have taken several appointments and several weeks, while the Introduction Card is most conveniently mailed in immediately after the first appointment. Since the service agencies will be told in detail how their reports of service will be verified, this follow-up letter should more directly than the Introduction Card increase both agency honesty in reporting service rendered and their eagerness to achieve a large number of satisfied customers.

In the suggested form (as in the Introduction Card) the respondent signs his name. Fear of retaliation from the service agency criticized (e.g., through taking the recipient off financial aid, or withdrawing services) is reduced through having the complaint addressed not to the agency itself but to a quite separate branch of government. This pattern fits in with the traditional American theory of government of "checks and balances" and "separation of powers." It fits in with the modern trend in governmental evaluation policy in which the evaluation section of OEO, for example, is made as organizationally separate from the operating agency as possible (Wholey, 1970; Williams & Evans, 1969). In terms of social perception, it is good that the evaluation is mailed to a separate city as well as to a separate branch of government.

It would be simple, and perhaps desirable, to experiment with an unsigned version. In this latter case, the evaluative portion of the letter would be on a separate sheet, and only it would be mailed back, unsigned. One could easily take 2,000 reports of service and randomly assign half to the unsigned, half to the signed, and check whether or not there were more responses, and more critical responses, on the unsigned form. However, if distrust of government has gone so far that recipients of government services do not dare sign their names to complaints about those services, then that very distrust will also make them believe that (through secret markings, fingerprints, or some other way) the government can tell who the sheet came from and is trying to trap them with the appearance of anonymity. Asking for signatures may arouse less suspicion.

(Such secret markings are of course a real possibility, and have been used by psychologists and sociologists to identify questionnaires for statistical analysis, in ways that harm no one. In the case of anonymous questionnaires, the research staff might like to identify the residential area, type of service received, data, and perhaps even age, sex, marital status, etc., for purposes of purely statistical analysis that would not in fact harm the respondent and would make the analyses much more useful in guiding agency reorganization. Where such identifications are hidden or inconspicuous, they can also be used to break anonymity, and thus their use lends credence to suspicion. Probably the research management should abstain from such disguise, and on any anonymous form sent out indicate openly: "For statistical analysis, this ballot will be classified as region: *Woodlawn,* Agency: *employment office,* Date: *January year.*)

A word should be said about content. The final determination of that will of course have to be approved by the many relevant decision makers and by the results of pretesting. Space limits what can be covered, and longer forms reduce response rate. Within these limits, there has been an effort to (a) provide creditability to the Woodlawn Service Program's important concept of Units of Service Delivered, (b) to offer recipients an opportunity to evaluate the usefulness of the service (and thus to support WSP's goal of making agency activities more useful and to provide direct guidance from the customers to the state on funding priorities.

A special word needs to be said about Question 3 of the form. In the suburbs and prosperous areas of town, state agencies provide services to citizens as though they deserved them. In the poor areas, these same services are lumped with "welfare" services, and delivered as though the recipient were somehow guilty of his need for them, as an improvident person receiving undeserved charity. We have tried in Item 3 to create an opportunity to record a change in these attitudes. While we are not yet satisfied with the wording, we recommend that this goal be represented among the very few topics that a one-page form can cover.

Agencies also show disregard of their clients in the attitude that poor people have nothing to do with their time anyway, so that hours spent in waiting rooms are unimportant. Asking agencies to report on the delays experienced by their clients (as is assumed in the top part of the suggested form) should focus agency attention upon the frustration of their customers. At the same time, this aspect of the record-keeping serves the agency in communicating their need for more staff to handle promptly the demands for their services. However, this feature is not worth hanging on to if it jeopardizes the procedure.

This Certified Satisfied Customers Accounting proves a good opportunity to measure increased numbers of persons served and increased satisfaction with that service. It does not provide any voice to those who need service but are not yet getting it. Hopefully, the system would lead service agencies to seek out such persons insofar as they had time and staff to do so. (State budgeting should continue to increase services as long as the number served was increasing.) But for overall assessment of unmet needs, other procedures are needed.

Surveying of all recipients, rather than just a sample, should be possible. (Where the same person is reported as being provided the same service month after month by a given agency, verification should be asked for not oftener than once each 6 months.) These should result in sufficient responses to plot monthly figures.

Implementation Recommendations

1. Require of all agency offices regular monthly reports on customers served. To provide some retrospective extension, the initial report should go back 3 months. (This request should go to Welfare, Employment, and *all* other agencies that are *eventually* to be coordinated under WSP). In communicating this report requirement, the verification procedures would be explained in detail, to avoid tempting the agencies into inflated reports on this initial request.

2. Require the same for the First Comparison Area. The First Comparison Area is to start measurement at the same time as the experimental area. Ideally this control area should be served by different local offices of each type of service. This may be impossible to achieve for all agencies in selecting a comparison. It is desirable because some of the changes introduced by WSP in, say, the local Employment Office, will no doubt improve their treatment of customers

from all areas. In a subsequent section we are going to present the need for a delayed-measurement control area, for which the requirement of nonoverlapping offices will be essential. Comparison areas should be as similar as possible to the experimental areas.

3. Get permission from the state government to use the confirmation letter in its present form and with future changes of a "nonsensitive" nature. (Changes with policy implications should of course require new approvals.) Get advice and approval from the WSP Community Advisory Board, the Welfare Rights Organization, and the Woodlawn Organization, as to the wording and content, with the understanding that this was only one of several efforts to be made to get community feedback. The principle that those surveyed have representational participation in the decisions on the survey should be maintained.

4. Select a small sample (e.g., 100) of names supplied in 1 and 2, above, to be mailed the letter in its present form. After a 10-day delay to sample return rates these recipients will then be interviewed about their reactions to the form, comprehension of it, suggested changes, fears, reasons for not returning, and so on.

5. Settle on a final form letter. If at any future time it becomes desirable to change this form, the interpretability of the time series should be preserved by using a 6-month split sample overlap period, during which one random half of each mailing received the old form, the other the new form. It is important to start full-scale usage as soon as possible so that several months' records are available before program changes.

6. Establish analysis procedures. The suggested sample letter presupposes using machine tallying by optical scanner. This procedure avoids the drudgery of hand tallying, makes results from fixed alternative questions available promptly, and is probably more accurate. All revisions made as instructed under 1b would be examined and referred to the reporting agency, as also all 1c answers. For questions 5 and 6, all answers would be read and the usefulness of coding and counting certain answer types would be considered. This is a very expensive process, however, and probably could only be done on a sample basis using, for example, a random sample of 500 written answers taken from all write-ins received in a 6-month period.

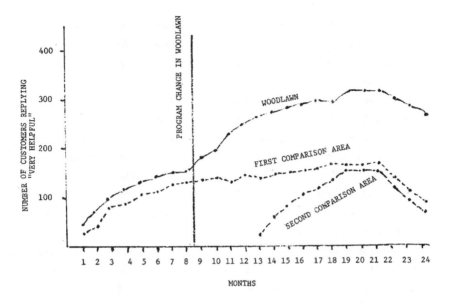

Figure 16.2. Time series comparing Woodlawn with a First Comparison Area in which Certified Satisfied Customers Accounting (CSCA) is started at the same time (in the first month) and with a Second Comparison Area in which CSCA is started one year later. During months 22, 23, and 24 the effects of a business depression are evident.

7. Establish report distribution policy. The introductory report and monthly supplements should be distributed to the service agency offices, to interested government officials, and "to the public." As has been argued above, if we are to avoid exploitative research, we must make available to the people the results of the surveys they have contributed to, and accept the political consequences of this information service. The mechanisms of such public distribution need to be specified. We recommend that copies be sent to all community newspapers, public library branches, high school and college libraries, and to the community organizations claiming to represent the people of the community. This should be done for both experimental and control areas. This distribution should provoke both challenges enough to keep the system honest and excuses and explanations from the agency that will help interpret changes.

Interpreting Results. In Figure 16.2, we have graphed a hypothesized successful outcome on one out of the dozen or so indicators that the data would provide. In the very first months Woodlawn starts out ahead, due to imperfect matching and unknown reasons. (It might also start out below the comparison area.) These inequalities can be troublesome, but must be lived with rather than adjusted away. In this hypothetical case, both curves start rising before WSP treatment is started. This effect would be very troublesome to interpret without a comparison group. It might be due to the effects of the Certified Satisfied Customers Accounting producing improved and increased service, or it might be due to a change in economic conditions. (To illustrate the latter, note the business depression in the final 3 months plotted.) We interpret the program introduced in the 8th month as successful because Woodlawn is similar to the control area prior to treatment and then rises relative to the first area, not just because it rises in an absolute sense. This relative rise continues even during the depression, shown as a smaller drop.

The design as discussed so far will test the effect of WSP changes in ways of distributing state services, once the customer feedback process has been initiated. *It does not measure* the effect of the Certified Satisfied Customers Accounting itself. Yet as Clinton McKay emphasizes, this feedback system may be the most important change agent in the whole package. Can we measure its effect?

For this purpose, we proposed designating for each experimental area a Second Comparison area. If we are able to locate in presently existing archives, such as welfare records, appropriate social indicators, we can plot a time series going back a year or so prior to introducing the Certified Satisfied Customers Accounting (CSCA), for both Experiment and First Comparison areas, and include in that graph data from the Second Comparison Area into which the CSCA is never introduced, or only much later. Let us hope that such data are available, but they may not be. If they are not, we are left with a weaker but still worthwhile design illustrated in Figure 16.2. In this hypothetical case, the CSCA feedback procedures are introduced in the Second Comparison Area 12 months later than in the first two areas. It then shows the rapid improvement that the others showed 12 months earlier, and ends up paralleling the First Comparison Area. We interpret most of the difference between the First and Second Comparison Areas at month 13 as due to the CSCA feedback process.

Whereas in our usual experimental procedure, our argument goes from no difference before treatment to difference after, there is an opposite design that goes from pretest difference to posttest equality. This may turn out to be common in reform programs. We have begun to explore the design in the Evanston elementary school desegregation study in which the experimental group segregated at the time of the pretest became like the always integrated control group at the posttest. Here in the time-series setting we have something analogous. Note that in Woodlawn versus First Comparison Group, we believe that the First Comparison Group is appropriate both because of similarity on background data and because of similarity in the shape of the time series before the experimental treatment was introduced in Woodlawn. In using the First versus Second Comparison Group comparison, we argue the interpretability on the basis of background similarity and the similarity of curves *after* the CSCA feedback system has become well established in both. On these grounds we argue that at month 13 they would have been similar had it not been for the effect of CSCA.

In the final analysis, interpretability depends upon coherence among many indicators having independent methodological problems, rather than upon single graphs such as Figure 16.2. We will not attempt to illustrate in advance this full complexity. But this may be the appropriate place to note a very important kind of record that should go along with this and other time series. This is the *Event Log*. In this log are to be kept all potential causes for a change in the indicator as they are noted day by day. Local newspapers should be regularly watched for these, and the agencies whose reputations are on the line should be encouraged to suggest them. An agency office closed for remodeling or due to a strike, changes in other local services, a local factory lay-off, general changes in unemployment, all should be noted. Not all will end up being judged plausible rival explanations of the changes in the time series, but they must be given careful consideration. Campaigns by local organizations to get recipients to return the CSCA letters, or to fill them out in specific ways, would of course be noted, as would news stories complaining about, praising, or informing about agency services, results of previous CSCA evaluations, and so forth. Such a log must also be kept for each comparison area.

STAFF MEMBER EVALUATIONS OF AGENCY PROGRAMS

Agency personnel, especially those who are in direct contact with people requesting services, are in an excellent position to be aware of the success their agency is having in meeting the needs of the community. They should be sensitive to a number of things, such as an increase or decrease in complaints from clients, changes in client attitudes, changes in the kind and availability of help they can obtain for their clients, and more. They also can delineate their own reactions to various changes—reactions that will have considerable bearing on the type of service that clients receive from them. Finally, they may have suggestions for improvements in the way agency policy is formulated and applied, and these suggestions should be taken into account. For these reasons, evaluation by agency staff members of the way their agency is functioning seems to be an important part of the evaluation of the effects of WSP—whose chief purpose is to tie agencies into a "service delivery network." It will also be useful in evaluating the actual changes in structure.

The best way of obtaining evaluation data from agency staff would seem to be through a relatively short questionnaire that could be distributed and filled out during office hours. Figure 16.3 presents a tentative version of such a form.

The preparation of this report has been supported by the Illinois Institute of Social Policy and the Russell Sage Foundation.

Staff Evaluation of Agency Policy and Programs

The Illinois Institute of Social Policy is entrusted with evaluating present state programs and developing new ones. While program evaluation can never be made fully scientific, and will always involve human judgment, it can be greatly improved. One way is to collect judgments from all those groups familiar with the details of program operation, including especially agency staff members such as yourself.

Your responses to the following questions will be used to evaluate programs, not persons. They will not be used to evaluate you, nor your superiors, nor your clients, but only programs and program changes. They will guide policy decisions, but not personnel decisions at any level. The results will be reported as anonymous statistical compilations of averages.

These analyses will compare average results before and after program changes, and between regions operating under different policies. These results will be made available to you, as well as to governmental decision makers. These statistical analyses will be made within the Illinois Institute of Social Policy, and only they will see the individual questionnaires.

Thus, while space is provided for you to sign your name, your answers will be effectively anonymous. Signing your name is optional. Your judgments will be useful even if you do not sign your name. But they will be more useful if you do sign. With the normal personnel turnover, there is the danger that some changes in average rating that actually are due to a change in the persons doing the ratings may be misinterpreted as the effect of a change in the program. This source of confusion can be avoided if the statisticians can identify which ratings at two different times are made by the same persons.

Two types of questions are asked. The first calls for your reactions to present policies in your own words. These questions are of greatest value in revising present policies and in designing new ones. The second type of question asks for numerical ratings on the present status of problems (from 1 = very bad problems, to 5 = no problem at all) and on the direction of change in the problem during the past 6 months or since the previous report (– = getting worse, 0 = no change, + = getting better). For many questions, answers of "Too Much" or "Too Little" are needed, with an intermediate "OK." Many careful people find it difficult and frustrating to convert their complex judgments and impressions into these narrow numerical categories. Please do the best you can. It may help to know that these ratings will be used comparatively, rather than absolutely. It will be the differences in average ratings from one time to the next, or in comparing ratings on different topics, that will be used. These quantitative ratings will be used to plot the ups and downs over time. Thus you will be asked to fill out this same form once every 6 months or so, and perhaps more often in periods of rapid program change.

(continued)

Figure 16.3. Proposed Questionnaire for Agency Staff

Your Name (optional) _____ Agency Type _____

Office _____ Position (optional) _____

1. Policies and programs as they affect the client's or recipient's well-being:

    a. What are the strong points or desirable policy features of the present program of your agency, as it affects the client's well-being?

    b. What are the aspects of present policy as they affect clients that need to be changed? How would you recommend changing them?

2. Policies and programs as they affect the ability of you and other staff members to do a good job and have satisfying professional careers:

    a. What are the most important favorable aspects of present policies and programs as far as your own job satisfaction is concerned?

    b. What aspects of present policies and programs, as they relate to your job satisfaction, need to be changed? How would you recommend changing them?

Your Name (optional) _____   Agency Type _____

Office _____   Position (optional) _____

On the following items, you are to fill in with a black lead pencil the space between the red dashes corresponding to your answer. If the question does not apply, fill in the dashes under that heading. Erase completely any error. If you wish to comment on a question, fill in the "comment" blank, then write your comment on the back, indicating the number of the item to which it applies.

Policy or Program Feature	too much	OK	too little	Present Status bad problem — no problem					Recent change			Does not apply	Comment
				1	2	3	4	5	−	0	+		
1. Amount of monetary aid providing recipients													
2. Ease to recipient of obtaining monetary aid													
3. Procedures designed to preserve recipient dignity and self-respect													
4. Services to clients other than money (in general)													
5. Aid in securing jobs													
6. Job training													
7. Child care services													
8. Home-making advice													
9. Aid in securing housing													
10. Efforts to prevent welfare cheating													
11. Size of agency staff, as allocated (i.e., if all budgeted positions were filled)													
12. Size of agency staff as now operating													
13. Training or experience required of staff													
14. Inservice training provided													
15. Office space													
16. Secretarial and clerical assistance													
17. Case load													
18. Time available to render service to clients													
19. Salary of agency staff													
20. Efforts to coordinate government service agencies													
21. Amount of paperwork													

~ PART V ~

ETHICS AND RIGHTS
OF SUBJECTS

———•◆•———

ost social scientists are aware of the experiment performed by Stanley Milgram in the early 1960s at Yale University, examining the conflict between obedience to authority and personal conscience. Unknowing subjects of the experiment, called "teachers," were asked to administer electric shocks of increasing intensity to "learners" for each mistake made during the experiment. The "learners" were confederates who acted as if they had been shocked, although no shocks were actually administered. Since some of the unknowing "teachers" felt a great deal of psychological stress as a result of the study, this example is often cited to exemplify the plight of the subject in social research and to foster discussion of ethical issues in social research.

Throughout the pages of this volume, Campbell "worries" about the research participant. In Chapter 8, he refers to the exploitative attitude taken by some researchers who, in trying to devise unobtrusive measures, consider with glee the "gullible suckers" who serve as subjects. Campbell suggests that the term *subject* may even encourage that type of attitude, and prefers instead the term *respondent*. He is quick to point out that the importance of the finding may justify a certain amount of deception, even in some cases where psychic damage may have occurred, such as in the Milgram study. Yet, he maintains that the researcher is ultimately responsible for protecting those who, wittingly or unwittingly, participate in the research. The test constructor should attempt to anticipate future uses of an instrument or measure to ensure it will not have a negative impact. For example, an indirect measure that appears to be a test of knowledge may actually be measuring an attitude, and the score may preclude certain individuals from getting or keeping a job. This type of test denies an individual the chance to respond self-defensively. Even when not used for decisions regarding employment, indirect tests might result in embarrassment or resentment.

In Chapter 16, Campbell discusses how program participants might fear retaliation for negative comments about a program's effectiveness. This fear is increased if comments are provided directly to the agency providing the service. The program evaluator can allay these fears by assigning outside sources to collect such comments, such as a governmental agency that will ensure confidentiality. Anonymity is another way to protect those providing the comments.

Beyond psychological implications and invasion of privacy, information provided by individuals may lead to their arrest if information on illegal activities is collected. This information can become available if data are subpoenaed, for example. Identifying information of an individual or individuals may inadvertently become public through a research report. Shared files, even when no identifying information is present, may finger certain individuals by a combination of variables in two files. This unique combination of variables may identify only a single individual. Finally, there is always the possibility that individuals involved in the research enterprise might be bribed or otherwise induced to release data or may gossip about the confidential information.

Campbell's concern extends to agencies or programs that are subject to evaluation. He recognizes that there may be resistance, because administrators feel that they, rather than their programs, are targeted. Moreover, if the evaluation has a disappointing outcome, they are fearful that they might lose their funding, their jobs, or both. Campbell recommends that social scientists refuse to conduct ad hominem research and that new innovative programs should be ready to replace those that have been demonstrated to be ineffective.

Finally, in Campbell's view, research participants are co-owners of the research. When possible, they should know to whom they are providing the information, and they should have access to the research results.

In the last two chapters, Campbell deals with both the rights of the research participant and the duties of the social scientist toward human subjects. Chapter 17 discusses several methods that can be used by the researcher to ensure confidentiality when using administrative records or combining files containing information of a private nature. The techniques are extremely conservative and can be used with the most sensitive of data. In the final chapter of this volume, Campbell and Cecil present a list of proposals for ensuring the protection of research participants. These proposals were condoned by a number of individuals familiar with topics of ethics, privacy, confidentiality, and the rights of subjects. This system of regulation, as proposed, provides safeguards for the researcher as well as protection for those who participate in the research.

————•◆•————

OVERVIEW OF CHAPTER 17

———— ·◆· ————

In Chapter 15, Campbell states that he is against the use of a unified national data bank. He believes, however, that there are a number of social indicators that should be accessible for program evaluation. With the appropriate safeguards, the researcher can ensure the privacy of those included in the databases. This chapter, which Campbell coauthored with Boruch, Schwartz, and Steinberg, offers methods by which sensitive data can be shared for meaningful evaluation while protecting the identity of those included in the database.

The authors agree with a number of recommendations for the management of archives: Do not collect unnecessary sensitive personal data. Identifying information should not be collected if not necessary. Individuals should have a copy of their own data. It should be made clear to the respondent that the data will be used for statistical summaries. The collected data should never be used to investigate individuals. Code numbers should replace identifying information and the code key protected. Formal rules should be established for staff members who have access to the data.

The following are recommendations that they feel unnecessarily restrict the use of public records. Social Security numbers are not to be used as identifiers for databases, yet the authors believe that they can safely be used as identifiers for mutually insulating file linkage (discussed later).

The recommendation to destroy all files after 5 or 10 years does not allow for longer-term follow-up. Requiring an informed consent for each statistical analysis is needless when identifiable data are not being released from files. Finally, the authors disagree with the recommendation to eliminate all individual identified files in any form, which they feel seriously hampers program evaluation.

The procedures described are the most conservative approaches available to protect respondents with the most sensitive of data. Intrafile analysis by outsiders involves a situation where all statistical analyses are to be done in a single file. Interfile linkage of confidential data involves linking files in which one or both files are confidential.

When conducting intrafile analysis by outsiders, names, Social Security numbers, and addresses should be deleted from all files used for reanalysis. Further precautions should be taken if there are a number of items on each person or if the file includes items on public lists that include names. In this later instance, only larger report categories should be released; for example, year of birth rather than the full date. If a combination of public variables can be used to identify an individual, the researcher should apply a minimum lower bound restriction so that no combination of public variables would relate to fewer than three individuals. The authors recommend giving researchers doing secondary analysis only the public variables of highest priority to their studies. When data are being released to several researchers, each with different public variables but with the same unique variables, one cannot guarantee that these researchers will not share the files among themselves. If two or more of these files were merged, the possibility exists that certain individuals can be identified with the new combination of public variables. Releasing only random samples of the data can protect identities under these circumstances, providing the total population is large and that the public and unique variables are few enough to ensure that many persons end up with identical patterns.

Another way to protect individual data is through microaggregation, that is, releasing only aggregates of smaller subsamples. For example, instead of releasing individual data on 1,200 individuals, secondary analysis can be performed on the means of 240 subsamples each comprised of 5 individuals. A single microaggregate should contain only experimentals or only controls. Aggregations can be based on any unit relevant to a study, such as city, region, or ethnicity.

If a file includes sensitive unique variables that might be incriminating, the researcher can use error inoculation of individual data. After identifiers are removed, all public variables should be error inoculated so that no record can be matched by using all the public variables. This can be done by adding random error to continuous public variables or by random score substitution when the public variables are categorical.

Statistical analysis requested by an outsider can be done by those who archive the data. If numerous analyses are requested by the same researcher, subtractive code-breaking could occur in which the data from a single individual might be identified. This can be avoided in several ways: by deleting a different individual from each cell for each reanalysis; by modifying the count by a random factor with a range of 0.5 to 1.5; or by random rounding.

Interfile linkage allows statistical analysis of data contained in two confidential files, at the same time, avoiding invasion of privacy. Using archival data is valuable for evaluation research, since the cost of retrieval is minimal, and data are available on a larger number of subjects than could be gathered through interviews. Experimental design is possible since data are available on both recipients of ameliorative programs as well as on eligible applicants who could not be served. Four procedures are discussed: microaggregation, synthetic linkage by matching, link file brokerage, and mutually insulated file linkage.

If social programs could be allocated by small units, such as census tracts or blocks, two files with relevant data can be linked providing they use the same criterion for aggregation (e.g., census tract). Only aggregated data would be released. For this method to work, the program being tested must be widely distributed in the experimental units.

Synthetic linkage by matching involves releasing data of similar individuals, but not necessarily the same individuals. If a researcher is interested in the relationship between two variables, one that is unique to one file, and the other that is unique to a second file, individuals could be matched on a number of variables shared by both files. The relationship between two variables of interest will be lost if they are independent from the variables used for the match. Even when there are rather strong relationships between the matched variables and the variables of interest, the relationship between the two variables of interest will be attenuated. The authors believe that the consequences of using this method should be studied in greater detail.

The link file brokerage method involves appointing a responsible broker to link two files with confidential data. The identifiers from the initial files are used to match the individual's data and then deleted. One must take care, however, because in certain instances, individuals might be identified based on the data remaining in the file. Also, the researchers requesting the linkage may have in their possession original files including identifiers, allowing them access to the confidential information in the other file. This can be avoided in several ways. First, the researcher can be required to destroy all identifiers once the data are transmitted to the broker. Another possibility is that the broker does the analysis. Finally, if the merged file is shared with those providing an original file, sufficient error inoculation must be applied to protect the identity of the respondents.

The authors describe an example of mutually insulated file linkage in which a local Job Corps program is to be related to Social Security Administration records on earnings subject to FICA deductions. Both files are to be kept confidential from each other. The Job Corps would first group subjects in both the experimental and control groups by some meaningful variable, in this case, socioeconomic status (SES). In some SES groupings, there would be a higher number of subjects, and these groupings will be divided into smaller groupings. Each of these groupings is randomly assigned a list code, in this case, a letter from A to Z. The data contained in each list would simply be the individual identifiers, which would be sent to the Social Security Administration (SSA). The SSA would then delete one individual at random from each list, locate the data on the remaining individuals, and provide the descriptive statistics identified by their list code. The Job Corps would then reassemble these data into a meaningful dimensional order, that is, SES rather than the A-to-Z list codes, and compute summary statistics. In this way, the SSA gets lists identified only by letters of the alphabet and no interpretable data about these individuals. The Job Corps gets only summary statistics on a group. In their report, the Job Corps must further aggregate the data so that the aggregation scheme will be undecodable by the SSA.

SEVENTEEN

PRESERVING CONFIDENTIALITY

———•◆•———

*T*here is great concern about invasion of privacy and confidentiality and about the threat to individual freedom represented by data banks. Such concerns are currently much stronger than are demands for increased objectivity in the evaluation of governmental programs. It is our belief that both concerns can be reconciled—that data archive use for program evaluation can be achieved without increasing the dangers of invasion of privacy. But we also believe that the means of such reconciliation are too little recognized and that there is a real danger of ill-considered solutions to the privacy problem that would needlessly preclude the use of archives in program evaluation. At its worst,the privacy issue becomes a rationalization for evading meaningful program evaluation.

The present analysis starts out by assuming the existence of administrative records and of archived statistical research data and then asks how both of these can be further used to generate nonindividual statistical products without

Campbell, D. T., Boruch, R. F., Schwartz, R. D., & Steinberg, J. (1977). Confidentiality-preserving modes of access to files and to interfile exchange for useful statistical analysis. *Evaluation Quarterly, 1*(2), 269-299.

increasing the risks to individuals that are already implicit in these existing files. Such a focus is tangential to many of the main concerns in the discussion of the threats of data banks. While we favor a number of the proposals for the reform of government data archiving, both present practice and these reforms are compatible with the recommendations in this chapter.

Thus, although not the focus of this chapter, we join others in a number of recommendations on the management of data archives.

1. Administrative data collectors and evaluation researchers should refrain from collecting sensitive personal data not directly relevant to the government's legitimate concerns appropriate to the transaction at hand.

2. Identifying information should not be collected at all; that is, respondents should be kept anonymous from the beginning where this is compatible with the purposes of the evaluation.

3. For the purposes here represented, there would be no loss and perhaps some gain if individuals were given a copy of their own data at the time it is filed, with the opportunity to correct it if necessary, and with the right to future access.

4. In regard to the desirability of restricting the uses of data to those that the individual anticipated and was agreeable to when providing the data, it would probably be desirable if the forms used for data collection (e.g., income tax returns) announced that the data would also be used for statistical summaries in which the individual would be unidentifiable.

5. Restrictions would be desirable to prevent any secondary use of archived date for "intelligence" or investigatory purposes, that is, for actions or descriptions targeted on the individual; all secondary uses of data would be restricted to statistical products in which individuals were unidentifiable.

6. For statistical research data files, individual identifiers should be replaced with code numbers for data processing and computer storage, and the code key kept under tight security. For administrative data files this may not always be feasible, but certainly should be required for any computer memory storage on a time-sharing basis.

7. Formal rules and guidelines should be promulgated to guarantee high standards of confidentiality and security management on the part of all data file staff.

8. For the data uses we advocate, a unified national data bank is not required. Such a data bank is feared because it multiplies the power of a corrupt employee to blackmail, or of the government to police, the individuals on whom data are recorded.

On the other hand, there are some recommended reforms of public record-keeping that would preclude the uses here advocated and that we regard as both needless and contrary to the public interest.

1. Abolition of the use of social security numbers for all but Social Security Administration files. Our recommendation is quite the opposite, namely, that social security numbers be recorded where possible. The abolition recommendation was designed to preclude merging files into larger data banks. Through the "mutually insulated file linkage" described in this chapter, some types of the file linkage can be achieved without merging, that is, in a manner that prevents either file from acquiring identifiable individual information from the other file. This procedure does require, however, that common identifiers, such as names and Social Security numbers, exist in each file. We believe that were this procedure adopted, the reasons for the suggested prohibition on Social Security numbers would be eliminated.

2. The destruction of personal data files after a specified period, say 5 or 10 years. Many social innovations call for longer-term statistical follow-ups that would be precluded by such a rule.

3. The requirement of a specific, separate permission statement and explicit informed consent for each separate statistical research use of an administrative file. We regard this recommendation as contrary to the public interest as well as needless when no individually identifiable data are being released from the file, as in procedures described below.

4. Elimination of all individually identified files in any form. Needless to say, we regard this as impossible for administrative files in their administrative use, unneeded for protection of individuals since this can adequately be done in other ways, and seriously detrimental to our capacity for program evaluation.

The requirements for safeguarding confidentiality are, of course, the responsibility of the administrators of each specific data file. The precautions and procedures necessary will vary from setting to setting. This chapter focuses on the most cautious and conservative approaches, not to recommend that they be required in all settings, but rather to emphasize that, for even the most sensitive settings, there are safe modes of access that will permit important statistical analyses. These conservative approaches do set limits to the degree of refinement possible in the statistical analyses, and, to avoid such costs, one should not use a more conservative approach than is called for by the requirements of the situation.

The major sections of this chapter discuss specific procedures under two main headings. The first is designated *intrafile analysis by outsiders*. In this category, all of the statistical analyses under consideration are to be done within a single data file. This category is exemplified by the U.S. Census Bureau's Decennial Census public use 1% and 0.1% samples that are released for social science research purposes, or by the Social Security Administration's

1% Continuous Work History Sample (CWHS). In the experience of the Office of Economic Opportunity (OEO), such uses are encountered in the release of data for reanalysis from the evaluations of Head Start, Performance Contracting, and the New Jersey Negative Income Tax Experiment (NJNITE; Kershaw, 1972, 1975; Watts & Rees, 1973; and the spring 1974 issue of the *Journal of Human Resources*). Six classes of procedures are considered for intrafile analysis by outsiders, concluding with the following recommendations.

> Deletion of known identifiers (name, social security number) is insufficient unless also accompanied by restrictions in number and refinement of data on variables that are publicly available elsewhere, or unless accompanied by error inoculation on public variables, especially by additive normal error.
>
> Microaggregated release is acceptable, albeit statistically costly.
>
> Best of all is in-file capacity as a public utility to run outsiders' statistical analyses, accompanied by randomized rounding of frequency tabulations to prevent disclosure through comparisons of sets of results.

The secondary category of utilization considered is *interfile linkage of confidential data,* where one or both files are confidential and the objective is to relate variables across files in statistical analyses. (Most conservatively, such exchanges can be done without merging files, i.e., with neither file acquiring the other's confidential data.) Examples of this occur when Social Security Administration data are used to evaluate Job Corps training programs, when the Census Current Population Survey data are related to IRS Statistics of Income data derived from income tax reports, or, conjecturally, if NJNITE interview data were to be related to withholding tax information or to FICA earnings. For such purposes, this chapter emphasizes the most conservative of several procedures: mutually insulated file linkage with random deletion of one respondent from each list. Link file brokerage, a widely discussed procedure, is considerably less conservative, but may be a useful strategy if adequate protection for confidentiality can be assured. There are also settings with confidentiality safeguards and legal protection from subpoena in which the still less conservative approach of direct file merging provides reasonable safeguards. Full merging has the advantage of preserving full statistical information on all relationships among all variables for any analysis or reanalysis. Where this approach is used, it would be very important for the merged file to have in-file capacity to run outsiders' statistical analyses (as discussed more extensively in the next section).

INTRAFILE ANALYSIS BY OUTSIDERS

Deletions of Identifiers

It is customary in releasing data for reanalysis to delete names, social security numbers, and addresses from the data on individuals. In some settings this may provide sufficient protection in that it may not increase the respondent's loss of privacy or increase the risks of breach of confidentiality. In other settings, deletion of identifiers is an insufficient safeguard. Two features seem crucial: the number of items of information on each person and the availability of those items on public lists with names attached. For example, deletion of identifiers might be sufficient for a 0.1% sample of the 1970 Census because of the extremely scattered nature of the sample and the absence of parallel lists. However, even in this case, if census tract, age, and specialty are given for a low-frequency, visibly listed profession, such as M.D., individual identification could frequently be made and the other information on the record thereby identified with a specific person, thus making it possible for a corrupt user to infringe upon the M.D.'s privacy (Hansen, 1971).

Where the research population is compact and where some of the variables are conveniently recorded with names on public or semi-public lists (here designated as *public variables*), the deletion of identifiers is less adequate. Thus, for a study conducted within a single school, even the date and place of birth are usually sufficient to reveal names. (Specific birth date in combination with birth place probably should always be treated as a personal identifier.)

In the case of the NJNITE, data tapes were released to outside users through the Data Center of the Institute for Research on Poverty of the University of Wisconsin. It was decided in this case that a thorough deletion of identifiers provided adequate protection. This deletion covered names, addresses, exact birth places and birth dates, social security numbers, and, in addition, the names of doctors, teachers, and the like. These data have been deleted not only from the released tapes, but also from the original interviews preserved in microfilm.

Crude Report Categories for, and
Restriction of, Public Variables

For public variables in the confidential file (variables that are readily available elsewhere with names attached), cruder report categories should be used in the data released, to the level needed to prevent disclosure: for example, county rather than census tract, year of birth rather than day or month, profession but not specialty within profession, and so on. For variables unique to the research project (unique variables), which therefore do not exist on other lists with names attached, this precaution is not necessary. Thus, for a multi-item attitude test or for an achievement test, individual item responses and exact total scores can be made available without jeopardizing confidentiality. (Such data probably should be made available because of their relevance to the estimation of error for use in generating alternate statistical adjustments, an issue of ever-increasing concern.)

Even with crude report categories on such public variables as geographic areas, places and years of schooling, age, profession, and so on, if there are enough such variables, combinations emerge in which only one or two persons occur and discovery of individual identity becomes possible. Thus, there should be a minimum lower bound restriction on the cell sizes of the full combination of public variables. For example, the rule might be adopted that there should be no combination of public variables yielding a frequency less than three persons (Fellegi & Phillips, 1974; Hansen, 1971; Hoffman & Miller, 1970). Recoding of variables using still cruder report categories, or complete deletion of some public variables, should be done until the chosen criterion is achieved. Before a criterion is chosen, tests of the anonymity-breaking potentials of various criteria should be tried out using actual bodies of data and publicly available lists.

These restrictions are obviously at the cost of some potential statistical analyses, particularly if some public variables have to be eliminated entirely. It might be thought that this could be avoided by releasing to each given user only some of the public variables, permitting the user to specify which public variables were of highest priority to the particular work. This strategy would suffice if there were only one user on one occasion or if users could be kept from sharing their data sets. But this seems impossible to guarantee, and such sharing would permit discovery of identity. For example, if user Alpha received public variables P_1 and P_2 plus all unique variables U_1 through U_n while user Beta received public variables P_3 and P_4 plus all unique variables U_1 through U_n, they could easily employ the shared unique variables to achieve perfect matches and thus generate a complete, merged deck with P_1, P_2, P_3, and P_4 on each person. This full set of public variables might then be sufficient to identify individuals with the help of public lists.

Random Subsample Release

The last-mentioned problem of multiple users sharing differentially deleted data sets and thereby gaining increased ability to disclose individual identities can be greatly attenuated by providing each user with a different randomly selected subset of the data. This approach is obviously most usable for files containing a large number of individuals. It provides most protection where the sample is a small portion of the total available population and when the public and unique variables are few enough in number and crude enough in categories so that many persons end up with identical patterns and individual identification is precluded.

Microaggregation

Feige and Watts (1970; Watts, 1972) have developed a technique of microaggregation for the release of census data on firms, as a substitute for the release of individual data. This approach has been recommended as a general approach to the release of confidential data. The idea of microaggregation is to create many synthetic average persons and to release the data on these rather than on individuals. Thus, instead of releasing individual data on the 1,200 participants of the NJNITE, as has been done, hypothetically one might group the data into 240 sets of five each and release average data on every variable for each set (probably with within-set variance as well as mean). Outside users could then do all of their secondary analyses on these 240 synthetic persons.

Feige, Watts, and their colleagues have done such analyses on Federal Reserve Board data banks and have been able to compare microaggregate analyses with individual data analyses. Their conclusion is clear that such microaggregation is much more useful than no release of data at all. It results in a loss of statistical efficiency, but does not necessarily bias the statistical estimates. For most conceivable grouping variables, anonymity and confidentiality are preserved at the individual level.

The actual acceptable basis for microaggregation must be thought through in detail for every specific body of data. The following preliminary suggestions hypothetically illustrate the problem for the NJNITE. For most purposes, aggregation should probably keep intact the experimental design, that is, aggregation should be done within treatments and in comparability across treatments. (There would be many more such aggregates in the 640-person control group than in one of the experimental groups that average around 80 persons, but each one of the experimental group aggregates should be identifiable as parallel to certain control aggregates, etc.) In the Feige and Watts discussion, local region is a preferred basis of aggregation. In the NJNITE, cities differ considerably in time of initiation of the experiment and in attrition rates. Therefore, city should be used as a basis for aggregation, and possibly region within city. Ethnicity would be wanted for some uses, but with an initial sampling model assigning as few as 16 cases per experimental treatment per city, comparability would be hard to maintain for any variable not blocked on initially. If complete data cases are aggregated separately from those lost through attrition, comparability is jeopardized, because the attrition in the NJNITE is differential, being greatest in the control and low-payment treatments. Possibly, attrition could be handled by reading out for each variable not only mean and variance, but also the number of persons on which data were computed, basing the mean on those cases providing data.

The variables used as a basis for aggregation must be independent of sampling variation to assure that an estimator (of slope, say, in a linear function) based on aggregated data is unbiased. Since the dependent variable is a function of that error, aggregation in the NJNITE data, for example, could not be based on number of hours worked by members of treatment and control groups. Similarly, any other outcome variable, such as attrition rate, could not be used as a basis for aggregation since its correlation with sampling variation would induce bias in estimators.

The possible bases for aggregation in the NJNITE data include experimental treatment, city, and ethnicity. For the purposes of relating any of these aggregation variables to each other or to any of the nonaggregation variables, there is essentially no loss of information or precision except from the crudeness of the categories of aggregation (e.g., using 3 categories of ethnicity rather than 30) if variances and cell n's are provided and distributional assumptions and assumptions about relations among variables are approximated. For relating the unique variables to each other, however, there is certain to be a loss of efficiency. In many cases, there will be no bias accompanying this loss of efficiency, given proper adjustments for the known parameters of aggregation. However, suppressions of both relationships and pseudo-relationships are possible in a complex body of data (multifactored in the factor-analysis sense). Consider an extreme example: If variables U_1 and U_2 each were to correlate zero with the variables of aggregation and if a large number of individuals were in each aggregate, then all aggregates would tend to have identical scores on U_1 and identical scores on U_2 and any true relationship between U_1 and U_2 would be suppressed. At the other extreme, if in fact U_1 and U_2 were totally uncorrelated, but if each correlated strongly with some of the variables of aggregation, then an artificial correlation would be generated between them. Obviously, such biases are less the smaller the number of individuals per aggregate, disappearing as this approaches one. Such biases are also less insofar as the variables of aggregation result in a high, all-purpose similarity among the individuals aggregated.

For reasons such as the above, Feige and Watts recommend flexible microaggregation, tailoring the biases used for aggregation so that the efficiency and lack of bias are optimal for the user's needs. Such flexible microaggregation requires that the archiving file have some statistical reanalysis capacity, probably very nearly as much as would be required for doing the customer's analyses internally, releasing only statistical indices (see below). If a user were to sequentially request different microaggregations of the same data, it might be possible to deduce individual data. As discussed more fully below, random deletions of individuals from each microaggregate would protect against this.

Error Inoculation of Individual Data

Boruch (1969, 1971) and others have suggested error inoculation as a means of rendering incriminating responses immune from subpoena. Like the randomized response method (Greenberg, Abernathy, & Horvitz, 1970; Greenberg, Abul-ela, Simon, & Horvitz, 1969; Warner, 1965), this was initially proposed for sensitive unique variables, such as drug use or abortion, rather than for public variables usable in decoding individual identity. The present suggested usage is different and has different requirements (e.g., damage from gossip and the threat of blackmail may result from randomly produced misinformation as well as from valid confidential information). Prior to error inoculation in the release of files for reanalysis, identifiers should of course be eliminated. Most or all public variables should be error inoculated and with enough error so that each individual record contains some imperfection on at least one of the public variables. That is, a potential code-breaker armed with a complete list of all names and public variables should not be able to make any exact matches. Under these conditions, unique variables, even those with sensitive or incriminating information, could be spared error inoculation. All users should be informed of the error inoculation and of its parameters.

Two types of error inoculation can be considered: (a) adding random error, and (b) random score substitution. For a continuous-dimension public variable, such as age, years of education, income (public for some institutions, such as corporations and banks, or government employees in some states), purchase cost of house, mean rental level of residence block, geographic location by latitude and longitude or miles from center of city, and the like, a random error of relatively small variance and a mean of zero can be added to each individual score. This increases the overall variance a predictable degree and attenuates all nonzero relationships (correlation coefficients, regression coefficients, slopes, t-ratios, F-ratios, etc.) a predictable amount for those relationships where the ordinary linear statistical model holds. The variance of the inoculated error can be kept small relative to the variance of the original data, thus minimally attenuating relationships, while effectively maintaining disguise since almost every score is changed to some degree (except for those very few who by chance draw a normal random number of exactly zero). This procedure affects the error of estimation, but not the degrees of freedom. It does tend to dampen curvilinear relationships, biasing the statistical decision in favor of linear ones. For all public variables whose statistically useful aspects can be converted into continuous form, this is the recommended procedure.

In many data sets, the procedure could be used for most public variables, leaving the remainder with such large cell size (see the discussion of crude report categories for public variables, above) that they could be left without error inoculation. Place of residence and place of birth, for example, could each be replaced by a number of related continuous variables: degree and minutes of longitude and latitude, population per square mile of census tract, percentage black of census tract, mean residential rental value of census tract, and the like. To each of these variables could be added normal random error (e.g., adding 5% or 10% to the variance). If this were done, it might then be unnecessary to add error to high-frequency categories, such as sex and race. For low-frequency variables that are visibly listed, such as some professions or specialties, a second kind of error inoculation might be necessary.

The second form of error inoculation, random score substitution, is the appropriate procedure for dichotomous variables and for category systems that cannot be converted into continuous dimensions. For example, suppose a sample of doctors contained 30% general practitioners, 25% internists, 20% surgeons, 10% gynecologists, 10% psychiatrists, and 5% other medical specialties. Two randomizations would be involved: first, for each person, a simple random number would be drawn to determine if her or his data were to be left as is or were to be substituted. For example, if a 5% error rate were the aim, all those assigned random numbers from 00 through 04 would be selected for response substitution. For each of these, a second two-digit random number would be selected to determine the substitute response, and this response would be so chosen that the original overall distribution would be maintained. Thus, if the second two-digit random number were between 00 and 29, general practitioner would be assigned; if 30-54, internist; if 55-74, surgeon; and so on. (By chance, the substitute specialty would sometimes be the same as the original.)

This method can also be used for continuous variables, but it would be much less desirable than error addition. For tolerable levels of error inoculation, most scores remain exactly the same under random score substitution, making presumptive identification from public variables possible; under the random error addition, most scores are changed to some degree. Under error substitution, the substitute response has no similarity to the correct response, while under normal random error addition the response is still similar to the original data, big errors are much less frequent than small ones, and thus much information is still retained. Even so, the general effect of the error inoculation by response substitution on summary statistics of association is calculable, although statistical power is inevitably reduced. (For error inoculation of statistical products rather than individual data, see below.)

In summary, error inoculation of individual data on public variables, while costly as far as statistical efficiency is concerned, is an acceptable safeguard that still permits many valuable reanalyses to be done.

In-File Capacity to Run
Outsiders' Statistical Analyses

It is already the practice of some archives of research data to provide for reanalysis of their data, not by releasing the raw data, but instead by performing on their data the statistical analyses requested by an outsider, who is charged for the costs involved. Project Talent, the American Council on Education, the Bureau of the Census, the STATPAK service of Statistics Canada, and other repositories provide such services. One of the obviously desirable features of maximally useful federal data archives would be that each be provided with such statistical analysis capacity. It is also in the interest of increasing our capacity to evaluate federal programs that nongovernmental archives with large relevant record sets be funded with federal evaluation research funds. Blue Cross/Blue Shield and other carriers of medical insurance, automobile and life insurance companies, and the like, all could be made accessible by funding each major record center with a statistician and a computer programmer for this purpose.

Where the requested outputs are summary statistics, such as means, standard deviations, correlation coefficients, regression weights, slopes, rates, and so forth, summarized over large populations, few if any threats to individual privacy are involved. For sample surveys, the lists of participants can and should be kept confidential, precluding most conceivable code-breaking efforts. Where the data represent a complete census of some small population and where an outsider user is able to request repeatedly separate analyses, he or she might be able to decode data on a single person by using knowledge of public variables to move that person from one cell to another in two subsequent analyses, keeping the other people intact, and thus learn that one person's data by subtraction. If this is a hazard, the precaution of deleting one or more persons at random from each cell (deleting different persons for each reanalysis) will preclude such a subtractive code-breaking.

Where the output requested involves frequency counts and where, as in complete census, knowledge of who is in the file is available, the anonymity-breaking possibilities are much greater. The problem is the same as is met with in the publication of detailed tabulations. Hansen (1971) describes as "random modification" an approach to altering exact count data prior to publication. To adjust counts within categories, one simply multiplies the count by a random factor whose range is, say, 0.5-1.5 and whose properties are known. The long-run average count will be accurate if the random number is drawn from a uniform distribution, but the variance of the published estimators will be large relative to unadulterated counts. The method differs from error inoculation in that modification is limited to published count data and is not introduced at the individual data level. Where the outside analyst has no access to individual re-cords, but does have access to tabulated statistical data, the Hansen variant ap-pears to be more desirable than error inoculation of individual data.

Members of the Statistics Canada staff have recommended "random rounding" for the preservation of privacy in the publication of tabular material and in performing customer-specified analyses. Fellegi and Phillips (1974) provide a convenient introduction to the papers that various members of this group have published. Even if small cell frequencies say, below three—are not reported, these can usually be reconstructed from marginal frequencies and from considering several tables jointly. Collapsing categories into cruder ones must be applied to all tables involving that dimension if reconstruction of small cell frequencies is to be precluded, and thus has a greater informational cost than random rounding. Ordinary rounding is biased through a preponderance of rounding down and, because of its fixed rules, also often permits reconstruction of the real frequencies.

In random rounding all cell frequencies are rounded, either up or down de-pending on the random number drawn. Were the true frequency exactly half-way between the rounded values (e.g., ending in a 5), then the chances of rounding up or down would be 50-50. In their system, as the true frequency is nearer the rounding up value, the chances of drawing a rounding up are in-creased so that an average of many roundings will give the true value. Marginals and total are rounded independently of cell roundings. Corre-sponding sums and averages are computed so as to be consistent both with the rounded frequencies and with the actual average per unit values computed on the unrounded data. Fellegi and Phillips report minimal bias or information loss once cell frequencies rise above 10 or 15 persons.

INTERFILE LINKAGE OF CONFIDENTIAL DATA

The second major category of use to be considered is that in which statistical relations are sought between the data contained in two confidential files. In accordance with this chapter's objective of providing very conservative but usable procedures, this can be achieved without increasing the number of file personnel or users who have access to confidential information about individuals. That is, if File A is being related to File B, the custodians of File A need not end up with confidential information from File B, or vice versa. Neither file need expand in the amount of confidential information it contains.

Even under these restrictions, interfile exchange is an extremely valuable tool in federal agency evaluation research. Once the major administrative archives of government, insurance companies, hospitals, and the like are organized and staffed for such research, the amount of interpretable outcome data on ameliorative programs can be increased tenfold.

For example, Fischer (1972) reports on the use of income tax data in a follow-up on the effectiveness of manpower training programs. While these data are not perfect or complete for the evaluation of such a training program, they are highly relevant. Claims on unemployment compensation and welfare payments would also be relevant. Cost is an important advantage. Using a different approach, Heller (1972) reports retrieval costs of $1 per person for a study of several thousand trainees. Even if $10 were more realistic, these costs are to be compared with costs of $100 or more per interview in individual follow-up interviews with ex-trainees. Rate of retrieval is another potential advantage. Follow-up interviews in urban manpower training programs have failed to locate as many as 50% of the population, and 30% loss rates would be common. Differential loss rates for experimental and control groups are also common, with the control groups less motivated to continue. In the NJNITE, over 3 years, 25.3% of the controls were lost, compared with a loss of only 6.5% of those in the most remunerative experimental condition. While retrieval rates overall might be no higher for withholding tax records, the differential bias in cooperation would probably be avoided, and the absence of data could be interpreted, with caution, as the absence of such earnings.

In many settings where programs are focused on special needs and where there are more eligible applicants than there are spaces for them, access to government records can enable program administrators to use experimental evaluation designs at minimal costs. With an excess of eligible applicants, there are several strategies available. An administrator can randomly select trainees from the pool of eligibles or from a pool of those at the borderline of eligibility, keeping records on those randomly rejected as a control group. Or the administrator can quantify the grounds of eligibility, or some component of it, admitting those who are most eligible according to this quantitative criterion, and keeping records on those above and below the cutoff point as categorized by their eligibility scores. Access to appropriate administrative file records for subsequent outcome studies then provides a low-cost estimate of program effects. Such results might be used to justify an expensive follow-up by individual interviews.

The requirements for achieving such linkage are more complicated than for intrafile reanalysis. But it can and has been done with adequate guards to confidentiality (e.g., Fischer, 1972; Schwartz & Orleans, 1967). Even though such use requires special restrictions and rituals, its potential value justifies an investment in making these procedures routinely available. In what follows, four procedures are discussed: (a) microaggregation, (b) synthetic linkage by matching, (c) link file brokerage, and (d) mutually insulated file linkage.

Microaggregation

While the focus of the Feige and Watts (1970) paper is on single file analyses, their paper suggests that files be linked after microaggregation by parallel use of the same aggregation criteria, for example, one based on geographical units—a "micro zip-code system" (Feige & Watts, 1970, p. 270). For administrative files, this would certainly be of great use. For example, to have average income data available on pseudo-census tracts or block statistics (subject to limitations on the minimum number of individuals within aggregates) would greatly expand our capacity for social reality testing. If social experiments in community services or urban renewal could be allocated by census tract or block, microaggregated administrative data would be available for program evaluation.

Such a system could not be used to link NJNITE data to census or income tax records, for example, since the treatment was not assigned by microregion. It would be usable only for those social experiments where the experimental units corresponded to census tracts, blocks, zip codes, or other compact aggregation bases in use by other files. Moreover, even in such cases, the treatment would have to saturate the area, being applied to most persons in the aggregation unit rather than just to a few selected ones. Such experiments will occur, and this method should be kept in mind. But for most federal agency evaluation research, useful interfile linkage will have to be achieved through individual identifiers.

Synthetic Linkage by Matching

This title will be used to designate a technique used by Budd and Radner (1969), Okner (1972, 1974), and others (Alter, 1974; Ruggles & Ruggles, 1974) to link the data in two files from which individual identifiers have been removed or that contain only similar individuals, not necessarily the same individuals. If there are a number of variables shared by both files, these can be used for a one-to-one matching of individual cases from which a composite individual file can be made combining the unique data of the two files. These extended files can then be analyzed as though all of the data came from the same person.

Let us call the shared variables $X_1, X_2, \ldots X_n$; the variables unique to the first file $Y_1, Y_2, \ldots Y_n$; and those unique to the second file $Z_1, Z_2, \ldots Z_n$. A typical analytic goal is to determine relationships between Y and Z variables. If the X and Y variables and/or the X and Z variables are entirely independent, any Y and Z relationships will be lost, inasmuch as an essentially random matching will have been achieved. Consideration of the effect of error and other unique variance in variables would seem to predict that even with strong X-Y and X-Z relationships, the Y-Z correlations will be underestimated since they will be attenuated not only with the unique variance of the Y and Z variables (as in a direct study) but also by the unique variance in the X variables used for matching. The extent of such underestimation will be a function of the exactness of the matching and of the two multiple correlations between the matching X variables as independent variables and the specific Y and Z variables as dependent variables. It is possible that the extent of such attenuation can be estimated.

Where the two files differ widely on the means of the X variables—as where, for example, a survey of unemployed youth were to be linked with census data or, as in an example mentioned by Okner (1974), where homeowners were matched with nonhomeowners, both from IRS files—the matching pro-

cess will systematically undermatch for the latent variables (as per considerations of the theory of error in variables and the experience with regression artifacts). Even with no file population mean differences to begin with (as he had
two sample surveys of the same population), Alter (1974) found that inexact
matches were necessary and that those cumulated to produce significant differences, even on the X variables used in matching (for other criticisms, see Sims,
1972, 1974). We should produce trial runs where all variables, X, Y, and Z, exist in the same file so that the Y-Z relationship produced by matching linkage
can be compared with the true values. For the present, we judge the technique
inferior to linkage procedures (such as the mutually insulated file linkage discussed below) based on individual identity and using individual identifiers, if
these are available.

Synthetic linkage by matching would not seem feasible for the specific
purpose of using administrative archives for follow-up measures in the evaluation of the effects of experimental programs.

Link File Brokerage

Manniche and Hayes (1957), Astin and Boruch (1970), and others have
proposed that a responsible broker, located perhaps in another country, provide
the linkage. Domestically, we can visualize this done in an agency like the Census Bureau, where records are immune from subpoena. Each file would provide a list of names or other individual identifiers and corresponding file-
specific code numbers, which would be turned over to the linkage broker.
Using the individual identifiers common to the two files, the broker would prepare a list or tape linking the two file-specific codes from which the names and
other individual identifiers would be removed. Subsequently, the files would
provide data sets to the broker identified only by file-specific codes. The broker
could then merge such decks from the two files and turn the merged deck over
to either of the files, with both file-specific codes now deleted.

This suggestion comes out of a well-justified policy of keeping the data of
a research project separated, insofar as possible, from the names and addresses
of the respondents during data analysis. But it also assumes that deletion of
identifiers provides adequate protection of confidentiality. As we have seen,
this is not always sufficient. In addition, the broker represents a new file that
has access to identified confidential information (unless it can be ensured that

the two lists linking public identifiers to the file-specific code information were destroyed immediately after use).

As originally proposed, link file brokerage also permits personal identifiers to be reconnected easily with the total merged data set if either of the original files still has its original data with personal identifiers. The replication of the unique variables on both the original data and on the new composite deck will usually provide a basis for exact matching, making the reinstatement of personal identifiers on the merged deck a simple process and thus giving one file access to the confidential information of the other file.

To avoid these difficulties, the link file brokerage device must be modified in one or more directions. In some settings it might be possible for each original file to destroy all records of names and other public identifiers after having transmitted the linking list to the broker. This would be hard to police, and particularly hard for one file to ensure on the part of the other file, as would be necessary in settings where a custodian of confidential data has assumed responsibility for restricting the dissemination of the data in individually identifiable form. Where the broker is isolated from opportunities and temptations to misuse data, or if ways can be developed to guarantee the broker's destruction of the intermediate lists containing identifiers, it would be desirable for the broker to do the analyses on the merged deck, operating as a public utility data archive, as described in a preceding section. (Such analyses could be done without the broker knowing the meaning of the variables being analyzed, although later publication could reveal variable names.) Under such conditions, the merged deck would never get back to the original files. If the merged deck is to be shared with an originating file, sufficient error inoculation of the unique variables could preclude the exact matching that would reinstate identifiers.

The use of a link file broker may be of some value in protecting against subpoena if the broker is located beyond the reach of subpoena or protected from subpoena by statute. But, for the goal of restricting identifiable data to the files for which permission has been given, this system has serious weaknesses unless much modified.

(The linking of research files by remembered or regenerated codes retained by the respondent so that longitudinal studies are made possible while files have no individual identifiers is a separate technique needing a review and analysis. Where one of the files is a government record, this does not seem feasible.)

Mutually Insulated File Linkage

This phrase is used to cover a group of similar devices for linking files without merging, preserving confidentiality. The essential notions involved have no doubt been hit upon independently on many occasions, particularly in statistical research with government records. Of published discussions, probably the first and certainly the most cited is by Schwartz and Orleans (1967), in a study linking public opinion survey responses to income tax returns. But it is clear from Fischer (1972) that similar processes have been in use in a number of government agencies.

It seems well to start with a concrete exposition of the full model in its most conservative version, and subsequently to discuss alternatives and abbreviations. The hypothetical problem in Figure 17.1 is to relate a local Job Corps experimental program to Social Security Administration records on earnings subject to FICA deductions. It is assumed that both files are to be kept confidential from each other. The experimental trainees and the control trainees would have been grouped by socioeconomic level, chosen as a useful dimension of analysis. Where there are a sufficient number of trainees within a given level, two or more lists would have been formed. The resulting 26 lists would then have been assigned list names from A to Z on a random basis. Each list itself would consist solely of person identifiers useful in SSA's retrieval operation, such as name and social security number. SSA would delete one person at random from each list, locate the data on all variables of interest for the remainder, compute for each variable a mean, variance, and frequency for the persons on the list for whom FICA deductions were on record, and send back these summary statistics, identified with their unique list designators. The Job Corps project evaluators would then reassemble these cell-by-cell data into their meaningful dimensional order and compute summary statistics. While the SSA file would get individual identifiers, they would get no interpretable data about these individuals. In return, they would send back no information about individuals, but only summary statistics about a group, which the evaluators would decode as a data cell in a statistical grid. The returned data would be microaggregated, but by an aggregation scheme unrevealed to and undecodable by the SSA. It should be emphasized that the researching agency receiving the microaggregated data (in this example, the Job Corps) must not in its published report provide results for any single list, but must further aggre-

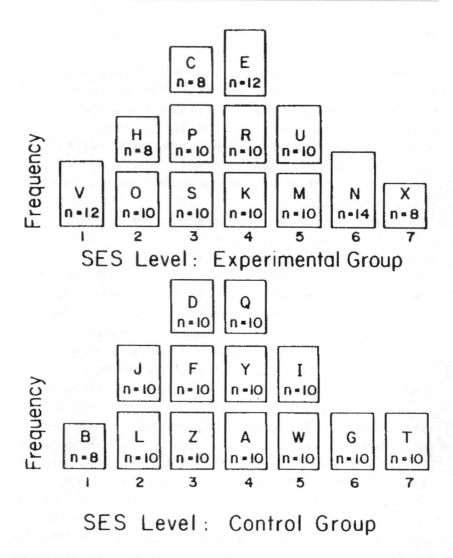

Figure 17.1. Hypothetical data from two treatment groups in a social experiment, grouped by SES level and given coded list designators A through Z.

gate the dependent-variable information received from the furnishing agency (SSA) in such a manner as to conceal the confidential characteristics of the individuals for whom the information might be sought. Otherwise, publication of the furnished information by the researching agency could provide the furnishing agency with the ability to identify the individuals in terms of the independent variables by which they are characterized.

In Figure 17.1, the vertical dimension represents frequency, but it could represent cross-classification on any other dimensional score. Note that adjacent (and even identical) scale values are assigned haphazardly nonadjacent list codes. Not only are the names of the variables disguised from the second file, but also the ordering of respondents on these variables. When the cell means and variances have been returned to the initiating file, they can be reassembled to provide publishable group means, standard deviations, t-ratios, F-ratios, covariances, correlations, regression weights, slopes, and so on. Frequency distributions, cross-tabulations, and cell means would often reveal to the second file (SSA) first file (Job Corps) information, although this might be precluded by adding random values as discussed by Hansen (1971) and above.

It probably would have been of both scientific and public policy value to have the results of the NJNITE cross-validated with SSA income data, ideally using years prior to, during, and subsequent to the 3 years of the experiment. As a hypothetical exercise, consideration of such a study will serve to develop a number of points. While not all income would be picked up in this manner, the results would still be very useful. The effects of attrition, and especially differential attrition, would be minimized, since many noncooperators in the periodic interviews would still have employers sending in reports to the SSA on earnings subject to FICA. For such a study to be done, lists would be prepared subject to the same considerations discussed under the first presentation of microaggregation above. Thus, each of the eight experimental payment plans in each of the five cities would provide 40 lists of varying size, averaging some 16 persons per list. The control subjects in each of the five cities could be randomly assigned to eight lists per city. The resulting 80 lists of names would be randomly assigned list designations and then sent to the SSA.

With these uses and procedures in mind, some more detailed problems and questions can be considered.

1. The random deletion of one individual from each list is to prevent detection of identified individual data through repeated negotiations. For example, without that precaution File A could group an individual in one list on one negotiation and delete that individual from the list on a second negotiation, keeping all of the other individuals on the list intact. The difference between

the two means would then represent this individual's score. The random deletion process prevents this possibility and would, of course, be done anew for each negotiation.

In place of random deletion, the addition of a random normal error to each set of scores for each list could be substituted. In the case of longitudinal data, this would seem to be more damaging to the analysis than the loss of one randomly selected case per list.

2. In the Schwartz and Orleans (1967) study, individual scores were provided, rather than means and variances. This was adequate safeguard in that instance, but where repeated negotiation between files has to be anticipated, it would usually permit disclosure of individual data by the device of moving a person from one list to another list on successive negotiations. A random deletion from each list would not usually protect against this.

If the general normal linear additive model is being assumed in the analysis, the cell means and variances are as useful as the individual scores, although new computational versions of standard formulas are needed. Other summary statistics, higher-order moments, indices of skewness, and so on could be added to the mean and variance data.

3. An intermediate degree of disguise can be considered, in which the originating file turns over its variables with code names for the variables (rather than, as here suggested, unique and scrambled codes for each category on each variable). This probably makes the discovery of the variable more likely and makes it definitely possible once the results are published, if the second file has kept the records of the transaction. In contrast, under mutually insulated file linkage as first presented above, the published analyses of the data by the initiating file would provide summary statistics for the whole sample, pooling the information from numerous lists, so that the second file would not be able to identify values on the variables reported in the published articles for any lists they might retain.

4. Lower limits on the number of persons in any list need to be established by practical exercises in identity breaking. Heller (1972) says only "small cells have to be withheld." Fischer (1972) suggests a three-person minimum. The random deletion of one person per cell gets very costly at this cell size. In the illustrations above, a minimum of eight has been used.

5. The requirement of minimal cell size will set limits on the number of variables or dimensions from the originating file that can be employed. One, two, or three may be common maximums. (There is no limit, however, on the number of variables from the second file.) More first-file variables can be handled by repeated negotiations. If, as for a factor analysis, one wanted to relate 20 variables from the first file with 20 from the second, one might do this in seven negotiations, each using 2 or 3 variables from File 1 and all 20 from File 2, to get the 400 cross-file correlations. The 90 intra-File 1 and the 90 intra-File 2 correlations would best be done within each file, but for the linked cases pooled from all lists. (For File 1 to do the File 2 intrafile correlations from the list aggregates it has received would potentially bias these correlations as described under microaggregation above.) The matrix of correlations would have the defect of being biased upon differing numbers of cases, but with substantial numbers this should not render a factor analysis inconsistent.

6. Because of some confusion in previous discussions of the method, it must be emphasized that the file linkage achieved is strictly limited and that file merging does not result. File 2 gets no addition at all. File 1 has access to File 2 variables for further analyses only in a micro-aggregated form. File 1 could microaggregate other File 1 variables by the lists used in a prior negotiation and could relate these means to the means on the File 2 variables received in that prior negotiation. These indirectly estimated relations would not be ascertained with the precision of those involving variables used in the initial negotiations, but rather in the form described for the relationships among unique variables ascertained from microaggregate data, as described in the first section above.

7. In the hypothetical illustration involving the NJNITE, SSA rather than IRS files were used because consideration of the latter raises several unique issues that would unduly complicate the general model. First, there are some interfile exchange settings where it is a loss of privacy and a breach of confidentiality for one file to even inform another file that a person exists. If the NJNITE were to send its lists to the IRS, this might make the IRS aware of nonfilers who should have been filing income tax returns. To avoid this, the NJNITE would need to access the IRS index files, identify the tax return document locator numbers for those who had filed returns, and negotiate only for

summary information for filers (Steinberg & Pritzker, 1969). This is probably not a realistic worry for the NJNITE, because most of its respondents were probably motivated to file tax returns in order to obtain refunds of withheld taxes. However, even if any exposed delinquent cases would likely be cases in which the IRS owed the wage earner money rather than vice versa, the best approach would still be to have the NJNITE access the IRS index files. In many studies there would be a real jeopardy, and however the researcher felt about delinquent taxpayers, she or he would realize that it was not a part of the research role to bring them to justice and would therefore arrange for screening by her or his own staff so that negotiations with the IRS would be limited to known tax filers.

8. Considering a hypothetical NJNITE-IRS exchange also raises the possibility that in some cases co-occurrence on a File 1 list might provide meaningful incriminating evidence to File 2. For example, suppose that NJNITE income supplement recipients were supposed to report this experimental income on their tax forms and that most of them had done so. The IRS's general knowledge of the experiment, plus their observation that on certain lists many persons were reporting such income, could have led them to suspect that the others on such lists should also have done so.

Such possibilities occur when the second file has partial information on a variable being used in the negotiation by the first file. Such information leads the second file to deduce a dimension of homogeneity for the list (lists must be homogeneous for the system to work). This deduction then justifies the deduction that the remaining persons on the list should also have the same value on this variable. In general, this is a very unlikely set of circumstances and would not stand in the way of most interfile exchanges. But it is an appropriate worry in this concrete case, and it should be checked. Consideration should be given to a procedure that has been used that requires embedding the File 1 population in a larger one. Random subsets would include one or more non-File 1 population members in each microaggregated list. Other lists would contain small numbers of the File 1 population and the largest portion from the larger population. This, while more expensive, creates the desired heterogeneity. In carrying out analyses using File 2 data, File 1 could discard lists primarily from the larger population. Occasionally, concerns about list homogeneity will lead one to forgo a dimension of analysis. One might decide not to use lists grouped on criminal record, or grouped on having committed a given crime, because of the danger that colisting will convey incriminating information.

For most of the wide range of federal agency evaluation research uses, such incriminating categories will not be involved. Classifying Job Corps trainees by number of months of training will produce no colisting jeopardy with either the IRS or the SSA. If family income provides jeopardy when negotiating for IRS, this variable can be sacrificed and some effects of the training still ascertained, providing that there has been a good experimental or quasi-experimental scheduling of admission.

This paper [by Campbell, Boruch, Schwartz, and Steinberg] constituted Appendix A of the 1975 final report of the NAS-NRC Committee on Federal Agency Evaluation Research: Protecting Individual Privacy in Evaluation Research. A. M. Rivlin, Chair. The efforts of Donald T. Campbell and Robert F. Boruch have been supported in part by grants from the Russell Sage Foundation, by National Science Foundation Grant GSOC-7103704, and by National Institute of Education Grant NIE-C-74-0115. The authors [Campbell, Boruch, et al.] are indebted to Professor Tore Dalenius for a careful review of an earlier draft of this manuscript. Portions of an earlier draft of the report have been used by Boruch and Campbell as a basis for pages 261-269 of H. W. Riecken, R. F. Boruch, D. T. Campbell, N. Caplan, T. K. Glennan, J. Pratt, A. Rees, and W. Williams. *Social Experimentation: A Method for Planning and Evaluating Social Intervention* (New York: Academic Press, 1974).

OVERVIEW OF CHAPTER 18

———— •◆• ————

The previous chapter suggests that social indicators provide a rich resource for the researcher involved in evaluating ameliorative programs. The chapter included several methods for protecting the privacy
of those who unknowingly participate through their inclusion in archival
records. This chapter, penned by Campbell and Cecil, provides recommendations for the National Commission for the Protection of Human
Subjects of Biomedical and Behavioral Research for protecting the privacy of individuals involved in program evaluation.

Initially, this chapter was submitted for comment to some 400 individuals familiar with the topics of ethics, privacy, confidentiality, and
rights of subjects. Seventy-five individuals returned comments, and 45
of these also completed a ballot endorsing or rejecting the specific proposals. After results were assessed and appropriate changes made, the
revised paper was again sent with ballots to the previous commentators.
The present chapter outlines the proposals that were endorsed by a majority of those responding to this second round.

The first recommendation is that all social research of this type
should conform to the federal regulations and policies developed for
these areas. All studies, not merely federally funded ones, should be subject to review. The authors recognize that this could lead to bureaucratic
overload, and they offer two options to avoid this problem. The first in-

volves conditional clearance by affidavit in which the researcher files an affidavit to be kept on file with the institutional review board. The research could proceed unless the board finds possible risks upon examination. The other option involves an expedited review in which a single member of the board can give approval to the researcher. In order for this first recommendation to be implemented, all investigators, agencies, and organizations that conduct research must have access to a review board. Review should be tied to funding, and large funding sources, such as the government or institutions, should set up review boards. All research participants should be given a written statement that informs them of their rights and provides the address and phone number of the review board to which complaints could be directed. Although the authors felt that individuals from the study participant groups should be represented on the review board, they were not able to arrive at a formal recommendation that ensures representation without also allowing the possibility that narrow political issues might interfere with the process.

The second major recommendation is that all research activities should be reviewed, but this review should not extend to nonresearch activities. The problem faced by review boards becomes the issue of defining *research*. The commission describes it very generally as a "systematic investigation" to develop knowledge. The authors caution that a change in the services offered by an agency does not imply that research is being done unless there was a concurrent effort to collect data to evaluate the changes for possible adoption by similar units. Also, data collected merely for the purpose of internal monitoring is not research.

Informed consent provides protection for the research participant and should extend to program evaluation. The consent form, after approval by the institutional review board, should be given only to individually identifiable participants. Along with the elements of the consent form recommended by the commission, it is advised that the participants be informed of anticipated uses of the data. Participants should be given any information, within reason, that might help them decide whether or not to participate. Although it may be difficult to get written consent, the onus is on the researcher to demonstrate that participants were properly informed. For this reason, researchers may wish to require signed consent forms for their own protection.

When sensitive information is collected in surveys or interviews, disclosure of this information may result in embarrassment or even the arrest of the respondent. Certain areas of research have limited protection; however, some research information can be subpoenaed. Information might also be released through audits, verifying interview data, or accidentally, through gossip. This latter threat can be avoided in one of three ways: unnecessary sensitive data should not be collected; identifying information should not be collected, if possible; or code numbers should be used instead of identifiers. Of greatest importance is that respondents be made aware of the risks involved if they choose to provide information about themselves for research or evaluation purposes.

All potential participants must be informed of the treatment and measurement processes they will experience. It is not necessary to apprise them of treatments received by other groups in the study. Envy and resentment by those not receiving desirable treatments might result in differential dropout rate and jeopardize the results of the study. When possible, control groups should eventually receive treatments that are shown to be useful. When the effects of a program are unknown, random assignment to experimental and control groups provides an equitable way of assigning treatments.

Informed consent is not required for reanalysis of research data or for statistical analysis of administrative records when no identifying information is involved. When identifiable data are released, permission must be granted by the identified individuals. One must take precautions, such as those discussed in Chapter 17, to safeguard the identity of the respondents when data are released without express permission. The use of administrative records avoids the differential attrition rate involved in experimental studies. The authors believe that the prohibition of social security numbers as individual identifiers is a needless and harmful precaution.

The final section discusses three issues that are controversial and should be given further consideration. The first involves whether social problems should be examined rather than the attributes of individuals. Studied social groups might be more cooperative if evaluators were to examine the effectiveness of the services instead of the problems of the individuals, and to include representatives of the recipient population in reviewing research instruments. A second issue concerns the rights of an entire class or category rather than the rights of individual research participants. The authors warn against recognizing broad "class" rights that would hamper most social science research, but allow that in certain instances, classes of studied individuals may experience harmful consequences. The final issue involves the rights of the respondents to the research results. Since they are coproducers of the research product, they should also be co-owners of the results.

EIGHTEEN

PROTECTION OF
RESEARCH PARTICIPANTS

———•◆•———

*T*his chapter offers a series of proposed regulations for areas of applied social research that have little risk for the research participants. Such areas include program evaluation, social experimentation, social indicators research, survey research, secondary analysis of
research data, and statistical analysis of administrative records. These areas of
research, which we will refer to collectively as "program evaluation," have
been free of publicized abuses, and relatively free of regulation common to
other areas of biomedical and behavioral research.

Although federal regulations moved away from requiring institutional review of these areas of social research (DHHS, 1981), we believe that the nature
of the data collection process in these areas results in risks to the research participants that require the measure of protection suggested by our proposed reg-

Campbell, D. T., & Cecil, J. S. (1982). A proposed system of regulation for the protection of
participants in low-risk areas of applied social research. In J. E. Sieber (Ed.), *The ethics of
social research: Fieldwork, regulation, and publication* (pp. 97-121) New York: Springer.

437

ulations. While the participants in such research clearly have rights and interests that may be violated, the nature of these risks is somewhat unique. Rarely will a risk to physical health be involved. Indeed, the participants in the experimental group often receive an apparent boon, such that the rights of the participants in the control group often may be the greater problem. The more frequent danger in program evaluation is the risk that sensitive research data will be misused. Such data may be subpoenaed by prosecutors searching for evidence of crimes, or become a source of malicious gossip or blackmail. Federally funded program evaluations frequently require audit, verification, and reanalysis. These activities may preclude a promise of complete confidentiality to the respondents and increase the risk that the information they provide will be used for purposes other than those initially intended. However, if respondents are fully informed of these risks, the quality of the research data may be diminished. From these few examples it is apparent that these areas of social research present a different set of problems from those encountered in medical and laboratory research.

A brief background on the development of this chapter is in order. In the fall of 1975, Campbell was asked to prepare a paper concerning protection of participants in program evaluations for the National Commission for the Protection of Human Subjects of Biomedical and Behavioral Research (the Commission). Cecil brought to the collaboration training in both law and program evaluation, and an interest in procedures for protecting privacy while permitting research in data archives (Boruch & Cecil, 1979, 1982; Cecil, 1978; Cecil & Griffin, 1981). A major interest in accepting the invitation to prepare the background paper was a desire to propose a regulatory scheme that permits the use of administrative records for program evaluation while protecting the privacy interests of the individuals (Boruch & Cecil, 1979; Campbell, Boruch, Schwartz, & Steinberg, 1977; Schwartz & Orleans, 1967).

In January 1976, a draft of proposed regulations was distributed to some 400 persons for comment, the names coming from various lists we obtained of committees, symposia, and conferences on the topics of ethics, privacy, confidentiality, rights of subjects, and so on, in the social sciences. Some 75 persons responded, almost all with detailed comments. Of these, 45 also expressed their preferences on the ballot that allowed specific proposals to be endorsed, rejected as "too protective," rejected as "not protective enough," or rejected for other reasons. These conscientious and thoughtful reactions were compiled and returned to the commentators in a report consisting of 73 single-spaced pages of written comments and a 23-page written summary.

In April 1977, a revised version of the paper was prepared. It eliminated six of the earlier proposed regulations that failed to achieve an endorsement by the majority (most dissents being in the "too protective" direction), though discussion of these issues was retained. Several new proposed regulations were added, especially in the area of informed consent. This second version was also circulated with ballots to previous commentators, plus a few others. Responses from some 30 persons were received. These results again were assembled, duplicated, and redistributed. These results are reported in the text that follows. All of the proposed regulations were endorsed by a majority of this group, all but one by more than 70%. Similar support was found in the first survey for those proposed regulations that were retained.

PROPOSED REGULATIONS

1. Scope of Review and Review Boards

Let us start with a concrete recommendation.

1a. Evaluation research, social indicator research, social survey research, secondary analysis of research data, and statistical analysis of data from administrative records are to conform to federal policies and regulations developed for these areas. The federal government or reviewing institution will review such research to the full extent of its authority, regardless of its sponsorship.

There is general agreement that these areas of research should be subject to some form of review, though the research involves little risk to participants and there are essentially no publicized cases of violations in these areas. However, there is less agreement on the limits of federal authority to conduct such a review (Boulay et al., 1980; de Sola Pool, 1979; Pattullo, 1980; Robertson, 1981; Swazey, 1980). We see no necessity to limit the review function only to those programs that have been funded directly by the federal government. To the greatest extent possible, we would extend this review authority to all research without regard to its sponsorship, including all university-related research, research by profit and nonprofit research corporations, and even unfunded private research. The restrictions on this review function will be determined by the constitutional and legislative limitations on federal authority to conduct such a review, and not by the nature of the research. Without attempting to determine the limits of such authority (Robertson, 1977), our effort is intended to construct a scheme for the conduct of applied social research when the regulatory power is extended to its limit. Of course, if research institutions choose to adopt a similar voluntary system of review, then the special nature of applied social research may require consideration of these suggestions.

Our proposal to require institutional review of low-risk research would permit broader review than either the past or recent regulations. The past federal regulations did not clearly specify the scope of review, and institutional review boards varied in interpreting their mandates. In the past, at least some institutional review boards felt obligated to review some of the research in these low-risk areas, even though the research was not federally funded. The Commission sought to clarify the scope of review and recommended institutional review of all "research" with "human subjects," broadly defined to include the areas of concern in this chapter with the exception of analysis of anonymous records. The proposed federal regulations followed, for the most part, the definitions proposed by the Commission, and suggest review of all research conducted by an institution receiving federal funds, to the extent that existing statutes and regulations permit. However, the final regulations extend to individual research projects (rather than institutions) that are federally supported. Furthermore, a number of exclusions are included that would deregulate survey research (unless the information may be harmful to the individual survey participant), most educational research, and most research with anonymous records. Consequently, our suggestion that research in these areas be reviewed by the research institutions would require greater regulatory authority than that suggested by the Commission or by the current federal regulations.

The problem raised by the broad scope of review we propose is the monstrous bureaucratic burden of requiring this vast area of low-risk research to go through formal institutional review processes. In response to this problem, we suggest a process of conditional clearance by affidavit. As an expeditious means of reviewing certain low-risk research in these areas, the suggested procedure should be superior to the kind of mass-produced perfunctory clearance that institutional review boards would tend to employ in those areas.

1b. Procedures for conditional clearance by affidavit and full review by institutional review boards. Before soliciting funding or initiating a research activity in the low-risk areas of evaluation research, secondary analysis of research data, or statistical analysis of data from administrative records, the principal investigator(s) shall file with the institutional review board a full research proposal and a "clearance affidavit," constituting a detailed affirmation that the rights of the participants are not jeopardized in any of the ways specified by federal policies and regulations developed for these areas. At the discretion of the review board and the request of the principal investigator, this affidavit may constitute a conditional clearance of the review process, permitting funding requests and research to proceed forthwith, unless or until the principal investigator, the institutional review board, or the funding source, requests delay for a full review by the institutional review board. The institutional review board may conduct such a full review at any time during a research proceeding under conditional affidavit clearance, and may order the cessation of research found to be in violation of the regulations.

Conditional clearance by affidavit for these low-risk areas of research might be implemented through a detailed questionnaire, signed by the principal investigator(s). These affidavits and research proposals would be kept on file by the board for the length of the research project and the subsequent period of project liability for participant injury. For these designated low-risk areas, the funding and research process could proceed if the principal investigator(s) does not choose to have a full review, and files the research proposal and clearance affidavit. The board would have the right to examine these materials in any way it chooses. Certainly a board would want to have a staff or board member examine each affidavit for combinations of features that might indicate possible risks. Since sampling is an efficient technique for quality control, perhaps a board should give full review to a random one tenth of conditional affidavit clearances. Such sample verification should discourage abuses. The board would have the right to request at any point the cessation of research activity (funding applications, data collection, data analysis, etc.) until a full review had been conducted. Such a delayed decision to hold full review or a veto of the research would be rare for these low-risk areas of research, and a principal investigator would be likely to choose a conditional clearance rather than a full review by a board.

From the investigator's point of view, conditional clearance speeds up and simplifies the review process, but prolongs the project's vulnerability to a negative review board decision. Conditional clearance may increase the likelihood that law suits will be brought against the researcher, and increase the likelihood that the board will check whether ongoing research corresponds to the proposed procedure, especially if the board receives complaints about a project.

Both the recommendations of the Commission and the recent federal regulations permit an institutional review board to offer a procedure for "expedited review" of proposals in certain low-risk areas of research. The proposed procedure for "expedited review" differs from our proposal for "conditional clearance by affidavit" in that the procedure for "expedited review" permits a single member of the review board to review and give final approval to the research. The single member of the review board must verify that the research is within a category not requiring consideration by the full review board, and that it involves no violation of ethical principles governing research with human beings. This procedure is unlike our proposal in that it would not be conditioned on subsequent verification, and the principal investigator would not be required to go through the affidavit procedure indicating why the research qualifies for the expedited procedure.

Consideration must be given to the effects of reviewing program evaluation on the functioning of review boards. One recommendation is obvious:

> 1c. Institutional review boards shall be available to review research conducted by independent investigators, profit and nonprofit research organizations, governmental agencies, and so on, as well as research conducted through universities.

The proper location of these review boards becomes a problem. It would be desirable for them to be locally available to the research participants so that complaints can easily be placed and heard. This role for review boards becomes particularly important in monitoring the conditional affidavit clearance procedure.

Presently, institutional review boards are set up in the institutions doing the research. Neither the recommendations of the Commission nor the proposed federal regulations anticipate any change in the location of the review boards. Since most research has been conducted in universities and hospitals, the research participants have had easy access to a review board. However, program evaluations may be conducted by a more distant institution. Even if the research institution has a review board, local institutions (such as public schools) whose members are frequent participants in evaluation research may wish to set up their own institutional review boards to ensure adequate access to their membership.

Local review boards seem impractical for broad public opinion surveys. City, county, and state boards are conceivable, and should be given jurisdiction if they request it (local jurisdictions that require licensing of opinion survey interviewers could insist on approval by review boards). However, it would be unreasonable to require local review boards for national surveys interviewing only a few people in any one local jurisdiction. For these, a national review board is appropriate.

Enforcement of the review requirement will be most effective when tied to funding. This suggests that each major source of funding, governmental and private, set up review boards. While some commercial and private political opinion research may avoid review, this may be the practical limit of the enforcement power. Opinion survey interviewing merges into investigative journalism, detective work, credit investigation, neighborly curiosity, and information collection activities more generally. It is in these areas that the interests of participants are in greatest jeopardy, yet we are unlikely to see such "research" activities subject to formal institution review.

1d. Where there are several appropriate institutional review boards, one review is sufficient if the review board most directly responsible for the well-being of the respondents does the review or concurs in it.

Currently, the institution receiving research funding must conduct the review. This proposal would shift the obligation to the institution most directly responsible for the research participants. Research by a university team on hospital patients would provide one example. In such a case, the hospital has the primary responsibility for the well-being of the participants and should conduct the review. If a community drug abuse treatment agency required data from high school students to be collected through the schools, the school district review board would be the one with the primary responsibility for protecting respondent rights. Proposed regulations recognize the problems posed by multiple review and suggest that joint review may be approved for institutions participating in cooperative research projects.

To adequately protect research participants' rights, it is essential for the participants to know the extent of their rights and to whom to complain if they feel their rights are in jeopardy. Fully informed research participants will be necessary to monitor the conduct of research approved under the conditional clearance procedure.

> 1e. Research participants should each be given a printed statement informing them that the research is required to conform to federal legislation and regulations and their rights under this legislation, and providing the address and telephone number of the review board to which inquiries and complaints should be directed.

In the case of a national project review board, this might include a toll-free telephone number. This recommendation is one of several that could be implemented with a statement in writing that could be left with the respondent.

Does the inclusion of the program evaluation, survey research, and the like have any special implications for the selection of review board members? A recommendation characteristic of these areas of research would be that review boards contain members of the groups from which participants are being drawn, or in the case of children, parents of such participants. Such suggestions arise out of experience with neighborhood boycotts of survey research. It is probably true that potential participants in program evaluations are more competent to judge when their own interests are threatened than are participants in medical research. A brief training program could supply the technical knowledge necessary to make an informed judgment. While we approve of having such persons on institutional review boards along with a substantial proportion of nonresearchers, we have been unable to develop a recommendation that would ensure such representation and still be feasible. A recommendation in an earlier draft for participation on review boards by representatives of organizations received the lowest approval rating by all the commentators. It is difficult to develop a method that would ensure representation of the interests of the members of the community while limiting the intrusion of narrow political issues into the review process. If such community representatives were given veto power, this would, in effect, recognize class or category rights, contrary to the recommendation in Section 7.

2. The Borderline Between Administrative Reports on Social Service Delivery and Program Evaluation

While we favor review of a broad range of research activities, we do not suggest that the review extend to nonresearch functions. The difficulty is in specifying the boundaries of research. For example, where is the borderline between a social work department delivering its regular services and a similar department testing out new procedures or giving a special evaluation to its standard method of operation? Where is the borderline between the regular instructional activities in a school and the comparative evaluation of alternative practices? Thus, parallels exist to the medical profession's problem of specifying when the doctor's exploration of alternative therapies with his patient becomes research. Neither the Commission nor the recent regulations attempt to specify the boundaries of research, beyond describing it as a "systematic investigation" to develop general knowledge.

While the borderlines for program evaluation should be recognized, these problems seem less serious than those in medical research, and it is probably wise to employ a narrow definition of program evaluation to minimize the coverage. Social service programs, employment offices, adult education programs, schools, police departments, and administrative agencies of all kinds have, in the past, had wide latitude in varying their modes of operation. It is unwise to add regulations curtailing this freedom, or adding to the bureaucratic difficulties of initiating change. Thus, it might be necessary to distinguish between variations in the services and variations in the information collection activities.

> 2a. Changes in mode of operation of a service agency that are within the legal or customary latitude for change enjoyed by the agency will not be interpreted as research within the jurisdiction of the regulations, except with regard to any novel data collection activities initiated for the purpose of evaluating the change as a program alternative capable of being adopted by other similar units.

There is an ambiguous borderline between information collected for use in an annual report of an operating agency and that collected for a program evaluation done by an in-house staff. Clearly it would be unwise to include annual reports or even special-topic operational analyses done to monitor regular operations.

> 2b. Data collection and analysis done by an institution for monitoring of its own operations (as opposed to evaluating program alternatives as policy items capable of being disseminated to other units) will not be regarded as research within the jurisdiction of the regulations.

These proposed regulations have obvious ambiguities, but rather than suggest specific refinements, it seems better to wait, allowing operating agencies to define their activities as they choose until specific problems emerge. We must remember that there are risks of exploiting others in every social institution and profession, public and private, whether doing research or not. These regulations address such problems only as they arise in a research setting.

The expressed purpose in the authorization of programs may provide guidance.

> 2c. Where funds are specifically designated for evaluation of program effectiveness, construction of social indicators, statistical analyses of administrative data, and so forth, the activities undertaken with these funds are "research" activities that should be examined by an institutional review board.

This proposed regulation does not cover the treatment (although the following one does) but merely the data collection introduced for the evaluation. Such an emphasis on the risks arising from data collection is unlike medical research, where the dangers of the treatment are usually the major concern of an institutional review board.

Consider a borderline case like Title I programs of compensatory education in public schools. In this massive national program, all districts and schools meeting specified poverty criteria are eligible to receive funds to spend on a variety of special remedial activities of their own devising or choosing, but limited to children designated as educationally deficient. While a great diversity of innovative and traditional remedial activities are involved, these are still within the range of standard operating procedures, and the program is funded as a nationwide activity, not a pilot program. However, effectiveness of a sample of Title I programs, employing new data collection activities, opinion surveys of parents, students, and school personnel, specifically administered achievement tests, and the like, would be considered research under this regulation.

There are, however, instances in which the treatment as well as the informational research procedures should be reviewed.

> 2d. Where the enabling legislation specifies a trial or experimental pilot program or demonstration project as well as an evaluation budget, and where the research contract or grant funding covers funds for treatment development and treatment delivery as well as for evaluative information collection, institutional review boards should review the treatment as well as the informational research activities of the project.

Usually the terms of the evaluation contract or research grant will provide adequate information for determining whether the treatment should also be reviewed. While the illustrations have involved governmental programs, privately supported programs also come within the scope of the recommendations.

3. Informed Consent—General

Extension of notions of informed consent from laboratory research into areas such as program evaluation and survey research may require considerable change from current practice. These changes may result in considerable opposition from some segments of the research community. The most common modification in research procedure requested by institutional review boards is in the area of informed consent (Gray & Cooke, 1980). However, informed consent is so fundamental to the protection of the interest of research participants that we recommend the endorsement of this extension.

> 3a.   Individually identifiable participants in social experimentation, survey research, and other areas of program evaluation must be informed:
>
> 3a-1.   That research is being conducted;
>
> 3a-2.   Of the procedures they will be experiencing;
>
> 3a-3.   Of the risks and benefits reasonably to be expected;
>
> 3a-4.   Of the purpose of the research;
>
> 3a-5.   Of the anticipated uses of the information;
>
> 3a-6.   Of the names, addresses, and telephone numbers of the researchers;

3a-7.   Of the names, addresses, and telephone numbers of the sponsors of the research;

3a-8.   That they are free to ask questions and may refuse to participate; and

3a-9.   That they may later withdraw from the research, and the consequences of such withdrawal (cancellation of income subsidies, etc.).

3b.   The exact wording of these statements must be approved by the institutional review board. The board may approve modifications of the elements of the informed consent agreement when:

3b-1.   The risk to a research participant is minimal; and

3b-2.   Rigid adherence to the specified elements of the informed consent agreement undermines important objectives of the research.

The elements of this informed consent agreement contain all of the elements typically required for consent in biomedical research. However, certain elements have been added to accommodate special problems that arise in the context of program evaluation.

Informed consent must be obtained only from "individually identifiable participants" in social research. This results in two important limitations. First, restriction of the informed consent requirements to "participants" in the research will not require the researcher to obtain the consent of nonparticipants who might be affected by the treatment, such as landlords in a housing allowance experiment. Second, restriction of the requirement to "individually identifiable" participants would exempt anonymous observational studies and the like that involve no jeopardy to the interests of the individual participants. In rare instances these restrictions may preclude consent by persons whose interests are directly affected by the research, such as in family research, where one family member gives information about another. In such situations, as in instances of anonymous participants and nonparticipants who may be affected by the research, the broad representation of interests on the institutional review board should ensure that the rights of such persons will be respected.

Even if consent is restricted to individually identifiable research participants, major changes in the conduct of social research will result. Social researchers will be explicitly required to obtain some kind of informed consent of the participants. Opinion surveys will be required to identify the sponsors and purposes of the survey, as well as the research firm conducting it.

In keeping with the recommendations of Section 5 below, the statements of the purpose of the research (3a-4) may stop short of telling the participants about the experimental treatments that they are not receiving. Still, even such limited information may influence the degree of cooperation by participants or modify their responses (Gardner, 1978). It is this latter possible effect that will most disturb the social research profession. However, data collected under these conditions can be almost as useful as present surveys. It is comparative differences under common contexts that are most informative. Present surveys do not provide "absolute" opinions, but rather opinions conditioned by a heterogeneous set of respondents' surmises and suspicions on the very issues that this recommendation would make explicit. Of course, the more explicit nature of this information may result in greater attention by respondents to these issues, and researchers should anticipate the resulting biases.

Recommendation 3b permits the institutional review board to modify the elements of the informed consent requirements when the risks to the research participants are minor and information regarding one or more of the elements of informed consent would undermine some important research objective. This recommendation should permit the flexibility to accommodate a wide range of social research settings. In certain extreme instances, such as assessment of the impact of Title I funding, consent of the participants in the research (e.g., consent by the parents of the school children) may not be required by the institutional review board. This would be appropriate when an institution rather than an individual is the focus of the study. In such a situation a similar informed consent can be obtained from an institution representing the interests of the participants (such as a school board or local government body).

The elements of the informed consent agreement listed in recommendation 3a anticipated the elements of consent recommended by the Commission, with the exception of our suggestion that participants be informed of anticipated uses of the information. Our commentators on earlier drafts were also suspicious of this particular element of informed consent, suggesting that such uses are difficult to anticipate. In any case, we agree with the Commission that participants should be informed of information that they may reasonably be expected to desire in deciding whether or not to participate. The recommendations of the Commission indicate that consent would not be necessary in studies of identifiable documents where the importance of the research justifies the invasion of privacy and the institutional review board protects the interest of the participants. The recent federal regulations give little guidance in this area since most program evaluation, survey research, and social experimentation are either exempt from regulations or permitted great flexibility in structuring the standard for consent. In studies where consent is required, it may be unnecessary that such consent be documented. In major experiments such as the New Jersey Negative Income Tax Experiments, participants are asked to sign a written consent form. Such formality is usually missing from survey research, even in panel studies where repeated interviews are envisioned. This recommendation anticipates that in most instances the written consent of the participant will be obtained. In situations such as telephone surveys, where it would be difficult or awkward to obtain written consent, some other means of obtaining consent will be permitted. However, researchers must bear the burden of showing that the individual was properly informed and consented to participation in the research, and therefore may wish to require a signed consent form for their own protection.

It has been suggested that separate consents be solicited for the experimental treatment and information collection components of social research (Kershaw, 1975). Such separation can improve the control and estimation of attrition bias (Riecken et al., 1974, pp. 58-59). For the most part, in program evaluation, social indicators research, and so on, and for control groups in experiments, only informational consent forms will be required.

These proposals on informed consent were not reviewed in their present form by our cooperating readers, and should be regarded with more caution than the better-tested sections of this chapter. Moreover, insofar as the content of these recommendations was covered in earlier drafts, no favorable consensus was found.

4. Rights and Interests of Respondents in Informational Surveys

A major part of social and behavioral research involves soliciting information from and about respondents by interviews and questionnaires. Respondents certainly have interests and risks with regard to the information they provide about themselves. Their interests must be recognized in determining the proper uses of any information that identifies them as the source. They also have rights to information provided by others in which they may have been identified. (It will be argued below that respondents have no rights that are jeopardized in transfers and uses of such data in which they are not identified as a source or target of the information.) The rights of participants in survey research, polling, and interviewing have received relatively little attention compared to the attention these issues have received in other areas of research. This overview will touch on these problems.

The data solicited by interview and questionnaire for program evaluation and social indicator development (or for descriptive surveys serving social science or journalistic purposes) often involves information about illegal acts. For example, information about income and income sources may indicate violation of tax or welfare laws. Disclosure of such sensitive information could result in personal embarrassment or discomfort to the respondent, and conceivably could be subpoenaed and result in the arrest of the respondent.

The procedures of survey sampling make the identity of the respondent known to the interviewer in door-to-door and telephone surveys. Procedures for checking on the honesty and accuracy of interviews through reinterviewing a portion of the respondents require recording this identity, as do research procedures involving reinterviews of the same respondents (e.g., pretests and posttests) or linking respondents to program treatments and other information sources.

Subpoena and Government Audit. In the New Jersey Negative Income Tax Experiment (Kershaw & Fair, 1976; Watts & Rees, 1977), the Mercer County prosecutor requested information about the participants as a part of a broad search for cases of welfare cheating. The power of governmental agencies to subpoena such information can jeopardize the interests of research participants. The decennial census and the interim surveys conducted by the Bureau of the Census are made exempt from such subpoena by acts of Congress. Limited statutory protection exists for certain areas of drug abuse research and criminal justice research (Boruch & Cecil, 1979). But most program evaluation research lacks such protection, and the data will be vulnerable to subpoena. In some cases researchers have gone to jail or risked going rather than release confidential information, while in other cases confidential information has been released (Carroll & Knerr, 1976).

In the Mercer County case, the evaluation project and the prosecutor reached a compromise; the project gave the prosecutor names of participants and the amounts of money they received from the project, but no information on income or anything else that respondents provided the project. We believe that this was a proper resolution of the dispute, and sets forth the policy that should be followed by statutes providing for the protection of research data. Research agencies must be accountable for their research findings and their expenditures of public funds. However, sensitive research information provided by respondents should be shielded from scrutiny by governmental officials (Nejelski & Peyser, 1975). Such protection should cover the information in all its data processing stages, rather than just in the interviewer-interviewee communication. If law enforcement agencies want this information, they should ask the respondents directly. However, such broad protection seems unlikely, and one must assume that sensitive information will be vulnerable to a subpoena by law enforcement authorities.

Required audits of federally sponsored social experiments may result in similar threats to the confidentiality of identifiable information. The General Accounting Office (GAO), pursuant to a request from a Senate committee considering preliminary analyses from the New Jersey Experiment, sought to audit and verify interviews. The project staff gave these auditors full access to the computer data from interviews with individual identifiers deleted, and the GAO produced its own parallel analyses of income guarantee effects. The staff also permitted GAO access to a sample of individually identified files to audit the accuracy of the transfer from individual files to the record systems used in the analysis, which may have been in violation of the project's promise of confidentiality. Such access was sufficient to meet the purpose of the audit without requiring GAO auditors to reinterview the respondents. A similar issue has been raised between the GAO and the Housing Allowance Experiment operated by the Department of Housing and Urban Development through the Urban Institute, Rand Corporation, and Abt and Associates (Baratz & Marvin, 1979).

Because program evaluation data are assembled as a part of a governmental decision-making process, it seems essential that audit, recount, reanalyses, and other verification processes be possible. In ordinary public opinion polls, verification by sample reinterview is a standard procedure for checking interviewer honesty and competence. This would seem to be a desirable feature for government auditing to verify sample surveys by selecting and interviewing independent samples of the same size drawn according to the same rules. But since this rarely will be feasible, it seems undesirable to preclude verification contacts with the original interviewees. It also seems undesirable to violate pledges of confidentiality to the respondents. In most cases slight changes in those pledges so as to mention the rare possibility of verification interviews to check interview honesty would suffice without reducing respondent cooperation on sensitive material. If, despite these precautions, the information is so sensitive that the threat of recontact would substantially impair participation in the research, other less intrusive means of establishing response validity should be considered (Boruch & Cecil, 1979; Committee on Evaluation Research, Social Science Research Council, 1978).

The possibilities of subpoena and of release of names to auditors for verification interact crucially with informed consent. The institutional review board should examine the specific wordings of the explanation of research purpose and pledges of confidentiality made to respondents to ascertain that relevant risks and threats to privacy are mentioned and that the investigator has not promised more protection than can be given. Recommended wording might eventually be prepared. The risks involved will depend on the type of information being requested and degree of cooperation promised by local prosecutors and police.

4a. Where the material solicited involves no obvious jeopardy to respondents, a general promise of confidentiality is acceptable. For example, "These interviews will be summarized in group statistics so that no one will learn of your individual answers. All interviews will be kept confidential. There is a remote chance that you will be contacted later to verify the fact that I actually conducted this interview and have recorded your answers accurately."

4b. Where full and honest answers to the question could jeopardize a respondent's interests in the case of a subpoena, the respondent should be so informed. For example, "These interviews are being conducted to provide statistical information in which individual answers will not be identified or identifiable. We will do everything in our power to keep your answer completely confidential. Only if so ordered by court and judge would we turn over individually identified interviews to any other group or government agency. We believe that this is very unlikely to happen, because of the assurance of cooperation we have received from _____."

4c. Where the researcher has made the data invulnerable to subpoena, as by relinquishing control over the key linking names to code numbers, this being stored beyond reach of subpoena or in some agency immune from subpoena, like the Census Bureau, or where the researcher has used other procedural or statistical techniques that ensure the anonymity of the sensitive information, the warning of possible subpoena may be omitted from the background statement to the respondent.

The devices are discussed more fully elsewhere (Boruch & Cecil, 1979; Campbell et al., 1977). While they have not been tested in the courts, they seem sufficiently sound, and the dangers of a subpoena are sufficiently remote, so that omitting mention of the possibility of a subpoena creates no real jeopardy. While in general our commentators approved of these recommended regulations, a strong minority found regulation 4b not protective enough. There was general approval of statistical and procedural devices to protect sensitive data.

Subpoena is probably a rarer threat than accidental release of individual information in the form of gossip. Blackmail, though a rare event, is also possible. Thus, respondents' rights are involved in the degree to which the data processors have access to the data in an individually identified form. We endorse the following three recommendations from the Report of the Committee on Federal Agency Evaluation Research (Rivlin et al., 1975).

4d. Sensitive information should not be collected unless it is clearly necessary to the evaluation and is to be used.

4e. Where it is feasible and does not undermine the validity of the evaluation, the anonymity of the respondent should be preserved from the beginning by not collecting identifying information at all.

4f. Identifying information, such as name and address or social security number, should be removed from the individual records at the earliest possible stage of analysis and replaced by a code number. The key linking this code number to the identifying information should be stored in a safe place and access to it severely limited. This key should be destroyed as soon as it is no longer needed.

Even with individual identifiers removed, individual data probably should not be stored on time-sharing computer systems, as this makes possible a repeated accessing of the data, using publicly available variables so as to discover the identities of some individuals.

5. Rights and Interests of Participants in Social Experiments With Regard to Treatment Variables

> 5a. All participants in an experimental program should be informed in advance of all features of the treatment and measurement process that they will be experiencing that would subject them to any obvious risk or jeopardy and that would be likely to influence their decision to participate in the program or their conduct as participants in the program. Institutional review boards should be provided with copies of the statements made to potential participants when seeking their consent.

All researchers would probably concur in this recommendation, even though there will be many settings in which living up to it will produce less valid data than if participants were not informed of certain aspects of the treatment variable, or kept in ignorance of the fact that an experiment was going on. For example, in the New Jersey Experiment, it was recognized as essential that the recipients of the income supports understand clearly that it was for 3 years only. (This has been the source of such serious criticisms about the validity of the experiment for purposes of extrapolating the impact of a permanent national program, that in later experiments small groups are getting guarantees of up to 20 years.) Were the experiment to be redone again today, the recipients should be warned that information about the payments made by the project to them would be released to government officials if requested.

There is a further degree of informed consent, however, that methodologists recommend against; that is, the informing of each group of what the other groups in the experiment are getting. In particular, methodologists caution against informing the control group of the desirable treatments the experimental groups are getting. The Social Experimentation Committee of the Social Science Research Council discussed this issue at length, and ended up approving this position, since the interests of the control group are not jeopardized and since more complete disclosure would have potentially destructive effects on the conduct of the research. For example, in the New Jersey Negative Income Tax Experiment, the control group members were not informed about the maintenance payments of up to $1,000 or $2,000 per year to the experimental group members. As it was, some 26% of the control group were lost from the experiment in spite of being paid $15 per interview four times a year, while only 7% were lost from the best-paying experimental group. Envy and resentment, coming from awareness of relative deprivation of the control group, would almost certainly have added to this differential dropout rate.

Of course, there are cases in which failing to inform an untreated control group of the availability of the treatment being offered the experimental group represents a harmful deprivation of rights. The Tuskegee syphilis experiment (Brandt, 1978; DHEW, 1973; Jones, 1981) was such a case. When begun in the 1930s, the informed consent of the participants should have been secured, but the available "cures" were so ineffective that the use of a control group restricted to traditional treatments was probably not unethical. However, once penicillin became available, the dramatic (even if only quasi-experimental) evidence of its effectiveness and its plentiful availability made it unethical to withhold it from the experimental group. While a similar situation is extremely unlikely in the realm of program evaluation, the possibility should be kept in mind.

Of course, beneficial treatments are recognized and adopted through a consensus of expert judgment and popular demand. If such a consensus is present, quasi-experimental evaluation designs not involving equally needy control groups may be employed. If the treatment is in short supply, an especially powerful quasi-experimental evaluation design not involving equally needy control groups may be employed. If the treatment is in short supply, an especially powerful quasi-experimental design is made possible by making quantitatively explicit the degree of need and assigning to treatment on this basis (Riecken et al., 1974, chap. 4).

> 5b. Where there is already expert consensus on the value and feasibility of a treatment and where there are adequate supplies of the treatment available, needy control groups should not be deprived of the treatment.

It should be noted that pilot programs, experimental programs, and demonstration programs are not within this exclusion. These testings of potential policies should be done so as to learn in the most precise way the social costs and benefits of the program, and this will usually require random assignments of participants to experimental and control conditions. If there is expert consensus on the costs, benefits, feasibility, and the like, then the program could just as well be adopted as national policy at once; if controls cannot ethically be deprived of the treatment, then usually the pilot program is not worth doing.

However, without such a consensus, the drawing of lots, random assignment, is a traditional equitable method of assigning the boon. In such circumstances, the controls are not being deprived in relation to the general population, but only in relation to the temporary experimental recipients. (This condition definitely did not hold in the syphilis study.)

6. Reanalysis of Research Data and Statistical Analysis of Administrative Records

Here is an area in which some current interpretations of research participants' rights are needlessly hampering useful science. Let us begin by proposing an exclusionary rule.

> 6a. The reanalysis of research data and the statistical analysis of administrative records jeopardize no individual rights as long as no individually identifiable data are involved. For uses of research and administrative records meeting this requirement, the informed consent of the respondents is not required.

There are horror stories about institutional review boards requiring consent by each of the original participants for the statistical reanalysis of 20-year-old intelligence test data, even though names and other identifying information have been deleted from the data. This seems a totally unnecessary requirement. The Russell Sage Foundation's guidelines for the maintenance of school records (Russell Sage Foundation, 1970) suggest parental approval of each research use of a child's record. The proposed federal regulations on research involving children (DHEW, 1978) go far in protecting the privacy rights, but do not clarify the rights of children and parents to restrict access to anonymous data. Certainly each of these guidelines should be changed to require parental permission "for each research use involving the release of individually identified records," and not for release of anonymous records for research purposes. The report of the Privacy Protection Study Commission (1977) suggested that greater access to statistical and administrative records for research purposes be permitted. Several bills have been introduced in Congress to increase research and statistical access to federal records (Alexander, 1982).

As an example of the practice recommended in 6a, data of the New Jersey Negative Income Tax Experiment were available to social scientists through the Institute for Research on Poverty, University of Wisconsin. The data have been stripped of identifying information, such as names, addresses (but not cities), social security numbers, names of the family doctor, and so forth. Data archives go to great lengths to permit data sharing without compromising the privacy of the research participants (Clubb, Austin, Geda, & Traugott, 1981).

> 6b. Individually identifiable data from either research or administrative record systems may be released to new users for statistical analysis only with the permission of the identified individual.

While this rule is consistent with the spirit of the Privacy Act of 1974, the report of the Privacy Protection Study Commission suggests that the Privacy Act be amended to permit greater access to identifiable research information without the consent of the individual participants, so long as the information is not used to make a determination about any individual (Privacy Protection Study Commission, 1977). If the Act is so amended, we would support such greater access to research information.

> 6c. Release of research or administrative data to new users for statistical analysis when done without the express permission of each respondent must be done so as to adequately safeguard individual identities.

Procedures for achieving this have been described elsewhere (Boruch & Cecil, 1979; Campbell et al., 1977). Usually this would include deletion of the participant's name, address, social security number, specific birth date (but not year), and specific birthplace (but not geographical region). Where some of the research variables are publicly available and can be associated with identifiable individuals (such as lists and descriptions of members of a school or a professional association), it may also be necessary to delete this information or use crude report categories for the variables that are in these accessible lists. Even where multiple tables of frequencies or percentages are presented, rather than individual-level data, it may be possible to deduce the identities of individuals. Restrictions on minimal cell frequency and randomized rounding may be required in such cases.

> 6d. The original custodian of research or administrative data may generate and release to others statistical products in which individuals are not identifi-

able, including statistical products not anticipated by the individuals initially providing the data.

In the future the requirements of respondent confidentiality and of meaningful program evaluation will be resolved by increasing the data-analysis capabilities of administrative record files. Through the "mutually insulated file linkage" [Chapter 17 of this volume], the records of two files can be statistically linked without exchanging any individually identified data, thus conforming to this rule. But this procedure requires that the custodial file be able to do standard statistical analyses as well as internal data retrieval for individuals. For many ameliorative programs, government records on subsequent earnings and unemployment compensation would provide accurate and inexpensive measures of effects. While these procedures have their own problems, almost certainly they would avoid the differential attrition rate found for the interviews in the New Jersey study. Accordingly, it would be in the government's interest to increase the internal data retrieval and statistical analysis capacities of private health insurance, auto insurance, educational testing agencies, hospitals, schools, and so on, so that these data can be used in program evaluation and social indicator generation in ways precluding identifying individual data.

It should be noted that privacy legislation curtailing the use of social security numbers as all-purpose individual identifiers hinders the uses just described. Greater protection of individual privacy can be achieved by prohibiting unified data banks. No abuse of privacy has resulted from the limited use of social security numbers in research. The prohibition of the use of social security numbers for research purposes is a needless and harmful precaution.

7. Future Controversial Issues

The previous sections have sketched some of the current areas of concern, and also represent to a considerable degree a consensus among the social scientists who responded to our survey. (The recommendations concerning informed consent in opinion surveys may have gone beyond this consensus.) This consensus, however, may be seen as but the current form of a growing shift in attitude about the rights of research participants as a part of an increasingly equalitarian participatory democracy. It may help to consider what the parallel set of standards 10 years hence might also contain. The following three topics are included for this purpose.

Respondents' Interests in the Topics on Which Data Are Collected. A recent trend in criticism of research on social problems, including evaluation research, goes under the name "blaming the victim" (Caplan & Nelson, 1973; Ryan, 1971). There is a recurrent option in program evaluation and social indicator research as to whether evidence of a social problem is indexed as an attribute of the individual or as an attribute of the social setting and the social institutions present. When the data are indexed as individual attributes (ability, morale, personality, employment status), this predisposes the analysis to end up "blaming the victims" of social system malfunction for their lot in life. Many times there are options in the wordings of questions that can make big differences in social causation implied even while collecting very nearly the same data. Standards could be developed requiring that articulate representatives of the program recipient population be asked to check on the research instruments in this regard. Or more specific recommendations could be developed, such as recommending the social setting attributional format wherever the option existed. Shifts of this kind might be of practical value as well. In many urban ghetto settings, opinion surveys meet with mass boycott, greatly hampering the evaluation of new alternatives in social welfare services delivery. In most such instances, the program evaluation purposes would be served just as well by substituting "Is this service effective?" questions for the "Are you sick?" questions. The conceptual shift is to turn the welfare recipient into an expert on the quality of welfare services delivered rather than a source of evidence about his or her own inadequacies. This shift, and the shift recommended below concerning participants' rights to the results, will almost certainly increase the cooperation received, and turn the informational survey into a useful vehicle for communicating neighborhood complaints. We have not developed a recommendation in this area, and the reactions of our panel of commentators to the earlier draft show that no consensus exists to support such a recommendation. In fact, proposed regulations in earlier drafts that would have permitted participation by representatives of various groups in the development of research instruments were among the least popular of all the draft proposed regulations. Most critics felt that these recommendations exceeded the appropriate degree of community participation in the research process. Note that the "blaming the victim" theme is only one illustration of such respondents' interests. The more general issue is discussed in the next section.

Class or Category, Privacy, Interests, and Rights. This chapter assumes that the rights of research participants are individual rights. Most discussions of rights of research participants join us in this. Jeopardy to the rights of a class or category to which the research participant belongs has not been considered. If "class" is interpreted broadly, recognition of class rights could preclude most social science research. We recommend that such broad class rights not be recognized in making determinations about research ethics, but we make this decision self-consciously, with some recognition of the issues we are neglecting. Following are some examples.

The American Council on Education prepared a profile from anonymous surveys of college students of the activist campus radicals who had been involved in destruction of property, disruption of speeches, and so on. No respondent was placed in jeopardy by confessing to past acts, since the data were collected anonymously through a mailed ballot. However, the interests of current and future radicals were jeopardized. For example, college admissions offices seeking to exclude such students could do so on an actuarial basis by asking applicants the profile questions about backgrounds, interests, activities, and values, and excluding those applicants who fit the profile. In such a case, the proper protection may be to increase the accountability of college admissions procedures by prohibiting the use of anything but academic competence criteria. However, regulation of research to protect the interests of such classes or categories seems to us to be unacceptable.

A statistical analysis by the Internal Revenue Service might show that medical doctors in certain specialties have twice the income of other professionals. This jeopardizes the interests of these medical doctors by increasing the frequency with which they are approached by fund-raisers, confidence men, and burglars, and by the focused zeal of Internal Revenue agents. Yet such descriptive statistics for occupational and social classes seem essential for the governance of a democracy in which governmental decisions are a major determinant of income inequities.

Respondent Rights to Data Produced. It will be increasingly argued that the participants in research, the interviewees in public opinion surveys, and so on, are coproducers of the research product, and should be co-owners of that product with a right to know the results and to use that information for their own purposes. This could lead to the rule that all respondents to an informational survey should be provided with the statistical results produced. Such a rule could be implemented by having these results published in a local newspaper or placed in the public library nearest to each respondent.

Another way of arriving at such a proposal is to recognize that where such surveys are a part of governmental decision making, the voting booth rather than the animal laboratory becomes the relevant model. Just as voters get to know and use the results of elections they have voted in, so too they should know and be able to use the results of surveys and interviews they have participated in. This equalitarian emphasis is supported by an analysis that sees researchers as a potentially self-serving elite who may exploit the cooperative efforts of the respondents by producing products that may be used to harm the interests of the respondents. Unlike much medical and physical research, the results of social research will be meaningful and useful to the respondents. Participants' access to research results as advocated in an earlier draft of this chapter was rejected by a majority of the commentators. However, we believe the trends in political conscience are such that in 10 or 20 years we will have to live with these limitations.

REFERENCES

————•—————

Adorno, T. W., Frenkel-Brunswik, E., Levinson, D. J., & Sanford, R. N. (1950). *The authoritarian personality*. New York: Harper & Row.

Ager, J. W., & Dawes, R. M. (1965). Effect of judge's attitudes on judgment. *Journal of Personality and Social Psychology, 1*(5), 533-538.

Alexander, L. (1982). Proposed legislation to improve research access to federal records. In R. F. Boruch, J. Ross, & J. S. Cecil (Eds.), *Solutions to ethical and legal problems in applied social research*. New York: Academic Press.

Allen, G. (1879). *The colour-sense: Its origin and development*. London: Trubner.

Almond, G., & Verba, S. (1963). *The civic culture: Political attitudes and democracy in five nations*. Princeton, NJ: Princeton University Press.

Alper, T., & Korchin, S. J. (1952). Memory for socially relevant material. *Journal of Abnormal and Social Psychology, 47*, 25-37.

Alter, H. E. (1974). Creation of a synthetic data set by linking records of the Canadian Survey of Consumer Finances with the Family Expenditure Survey 1970. *Annals of Economic and Social Measurement, 3*, 373-394.

American Psychological Association. (1954). Technical recommendations for psychological tests and diagnostic techniques. *Psychological Bulletin, Supplement, 51, Part 2*, 1-38.

Anastasi, A. (1958). *Differential psychology* (3rd ed.). New York: Macmillan.

Anderson, R. B. W. (1967). On the comparability of meaningful stimuli in cross-cultural research. *Sociometry, 30*(2), 124-136.

Asch, S. E. (1952). *Social psychology*. Englewood Cliffs, NJ: Prentice Hall.

Astin, A. W., & Boruch, R. G. (1970). A link file system for assuring confidentiality in longitudinal studies. *American Educational Research Journal, 1*, 615-624.

Athey, K. R., Coleman, J. E., Reitman, A. P., & Tang, J. (1960). Two experiments showing the effect of the interviewer's racial background on responses to questionnaires concerning racial issues. *Journal of Applied Psychology, 44*, 244-246.

Atkinson, J. W. (Ed.). (1958). *Motives in fantasy, action, and society.* Princeton, NJ: Von Nostrand.

Ayer, A. J. (1956). *The problem of knowledge.* New York: St. Martin's.

Ayer, A. J. (Ed.). (1959). *Logical positivism.* Glencoe, IL: Free Press.

Babbitt, H. G. (1962). An attempt to produce changes in attitudes toward the self by means of verbal conditioning. *Journal of Verbal Learning and Verbal Behavior, 1*(3), 168-172.

Bagby, J. W. (1957). A cross-cultural study of perceptual predominance in binocular rivalry. *Journal of Abnormal and Social Psychology, 54,* 331-334.

Bagozzi, R. P., Yi, Y., & Phillips, L. W. (1991). Assessing construct validity in organizational research. *Administrative Science Quarterly, 36,* 421-458.

Bain, H. M., & Hecock, D. S. (1957). *Ballot position and voter's choice: The arrangement of names on the ballot and its effect on the voter.* Detroit, MI: Wayne State University Press.

Baker, F. (1968). The changing hospital organizational system: A model for evaluation. Man in systems. *Proceedings of the 14th annual meeting of the Society for General Systems Research.*

Baker, F. (1970). General systems theory, research and medical care. In A. Sheldon, F. Baker, & C. P. McLaughlin (Eds.), *Systems and medical care* (pp. 1-26). Cambridge: MIT Press.

Baldus, D. C. (1973). Welfare as a loan: An empirical study of the recovery of public assistance payments in the United States. *Stanford Law Review, 25,* 204.

Bank, L., Dishion, Y., Skinner, M., & Patterson, G. R. (1990). Method variance in structural equation modeling: Living with "Glop." In G. R. Patterson (Ed.), *Depression and aggression in family interaction.* Hillsdale, NJ: Lawrence Erlbaum.

Baratz, S. S., & Marvin, K. E. (1979). Privacy and confidentiality as problems in the audit and reanalysis of social research for policy. In R. F. Boruch, J. Ross, & J. S. Cecil (Eds.), *Proceedings and background papers. Conference on ethical and legal problems in applied social research.* Evanston, IL: Department of Psychology, Northwestern University.

Bauer, R. M. (1966). *Social indicators.* Cambridge: MIT Press.

Baumrind, D. (1964). Some thoughts on ethics of research: After reading Milgram's "Behavioral study of obedience." *American Psychologist, 19,* 421-423.

Bechtoldt, H. P. (1959). Construct validity: A critique. *American Psychologist, 14,* 201-238.

Beck, B. (1970). Cooking the welfare stew. In R. W. Habenstein (Ed.), *Pathways to data: Field methods for studying ongoing social organization.* Chicago: Aldine.

Becker, H. (1970). *Sociological work.* Chicago: Aldine.

Becker, H. M., Geer, B., & Hughes, E. C. (1968). *Making the grade.* New York: John Wiley.

Benney, M., Riesman, D., & Star, S. (1956). Age and sex in the interview. *American Journal of Sociology, 62,* 143-152.

Bennis, W. G. (1968). The case study. *Journal of Applied Behavioral Science, 4*(2), 227-231.

Bentz, V. I. (1955). *A comparison of the Spanish and English versions of the Sears Executive Battery.* Chicago: National Personnel Department, Sears, Roebuck and Company. Mimeo.

Bergmann, G., & Spence, K. W. (1941). Operationism and theory in psychology. *Psychological Review, 48,* 1-14.

Bernstein, E. M. (1935). *Money and the economic system.* Chapel Hill: University of North Carolina Press.

Berrien, F. K. (1966). Japanese and American values. *International Journal of Psychology, 1*(2), 129-141.

Berrien, F. K. (1967). Methodological and related problems in cross-cultural research. *International Journal of Psychology, 2*(1), 33-43.

Blau, P. (1955). *The dynamics of bureaucracy.* Chicago: University of Chicago Press.

Blau, P. M. (1963). *The dynamics of bureaucracy* (Rev. ed.). Chicago: University of Chicago Press.

Block, J. (1965). *The challenge of response sets.* New York: Appleton-Century-Crofts.

Borgatta, E. F. (1955). Analysis of social interaction: Actual, role-playing, and projective. *Journal of Abnormal Social Psychology, 51,* 394-405.

Boring, E. G. (1923). Intelligence as the test tests it. *New Republic, 34,* 33-36.

Boruch, R. F. (1969). *Educational research and the confidentiality of data: A case study* (ACE Research Reports 4). Washington, DC: American Council on Education.

Boruch, R. F. (1971). Maintaining confidentiality in educational research: A systematic analysis. *American Psychologist, 26,* 413-430.

Boruch, R. F., & Cecil, J. S. (1979). *Assuring the confidentiality of social research data.* Philadelphia: University of Pennsylvania Press.

Boruch, R. F., & Cecil, J. S. (Eds.). (1982). *Solutions to ethical and legal problems in social research.* New York: Academic Press.

Boruch, R. F., & Wolins, L. (1970). A procedure for estimation of trait, method and error variance attributable to a measure. *Educational and Psychological Measurement, 30,* 547-574.

Boulay, H., Goldsgtein, R., & Zisk, B. (1980). Comment on Pool's analysis—Protecting human subjects of research: Proposed amendments to HEW policy. *Political Science, 13,* 202-203.

Box, G. E. P., & Tiao, G. C. (1965). A change in level of a non-stationary time series. *Biometrika, 52,* 181-192.

Brandt, A. M. (1978). *Racism and research: The case of the Tuskegee Syphilis Study.* Hastings Center Report, Garrison, NY.

Brenner, M. H. (1973). *Mental illness and the economy.* Cambridge, MA: Harvard University Press.

Brenner, M. H. (1975). *Aggression, justice, and the economy.* Cambridge, MA: Harvard University Press.

Bridgman, P. W. (1927). *The logic of modern physics.* New York: Macmillan.

Brigham, J. C., & Cook, S. W. (1969). The influence of attitude on the recall of controversial material: A failure to conform. *Journal of Experimental Social Psychology, 5,* 240-243.

Brookover, L., & Back, K. W. (1966). Time sampling as a field technique. *Human Organization, 25,* 64-70.

Brown, H. I. (1979). *Perception, theory and commitment: The new philosophy of science.* Chicago: University of Chicago Press.

Brown, J. F. (1947). Modification of the Rosenzweig picture frustration test to study hostile interracial attitudes. *Journal of Psychology, 24,* 247-272.

Browne, M. W. (1984). The decomposition of multitrait-multimethod matrices. *British Journal of Mathematical and Statistical Psychology, 37,* 1-21.

Brownlee, K. A. (1965). *Statistical theory and methodology in science and engineering* (2nd ed.). New York: John Wiley.

Budd, E. C., & Radner, D. B. (1969). The O. B. E. size distribution series: Methods and tentative results for 1964. *American Economic Review, 59,* 435-449.

Burtt, H. E. (Ed.). (1942). *Principles of employment psychology.* New York: Harper.

Burwen, L. S., & Campbell, D. T. (1957). The generality of attitudes toward authority and nonauthority figures. *Journal of Abnormal and Social Psychology, 54,* 24-31.

Burwen, L. S., Campbell, D. T., & Kidd, J. (1956). The use of a sentence completion test in measuring attitudes toward superiors and subordinates. *Journal of Applied Psychology, 40,* 248-250.

Campbell, D. T. (1950). The indirect assessment of social attitudes. *Psychological Bulletin, 47,* 15-38.

Campbell, D. T. (1953). *A study of leadership among submarine officers.* Columbus: Ohio State University Research Foundation.

Campbell, D. T. (1954). Operational delineation of "what is learned" via the transportation experiment. *Psychological Review, 61,* 167-174.

Campbell, D. T. (1955). The prediction of superior-subordinate relationships within bomber crews. *Final Report to the Air Research and Development Command.* Mimeograph (pp. 1-15). Chicago: University of Chicago.

Campbell, D. T. (1956). *Leadership and its effects upon the group.* (Monograph No. 83). Columbus: Ohio State University Bureau of Business Research.

Campbell, D. T. (1957). Factors relevant to the validity of experiments in social settings. *Psychological Bulletin, 54*(4), 297-312.

Campbell, D. T. (1959a). Methodological suggestions from a comparative psychology of knowledge processes. *Inquiry, 2,* 152-182.

Campbell, D. T. (1959b). Systematic error on the part of human links in communication systems. *Information and Control, 1,* 334-369.

Campbell, D. T. (1960a). Blind variation and selective retention in creative thought as in other knowledge processes. *Psychological Review, 67,* 380-400.

Campbell, D. T. (1960b). Recommendations for APA test standards regarding construct, trait, or discriminant validity. *American Psychologist, 15,* 546-553.

Campbell, D. T. (1961a). Conformity in psychology's theories of acquired behavioral dispositions. In I. A. Berg & B. M. Bass (Eds.), *Conformity and deviation.* New York: Harper.

Campbell, D. T. (1961b). The mutual methodological relevance of anthropology and psychology. In F. L. K. Hsu (Ed.), *Psychological anthropology: Approaches to culture and personality* (pp. 333-352). Homewood, IL: Dorsey.

Campbell, D. T. (1963). Social attitudes and other acquired behavioral dispositions. In S. Koch (Ed.), *Psychology: A study of science: Vol. 6. Investigations of man as socius* (pp. 94-172). New York: McGraw-Hill.

Campbell, D. T. (1964). Distinguishing differences of perception from failures of communication in cross-cultural studies. In F. S. C. Northrop & H. H. Livingston (Eds.), *Cross-cultural understanding: Epistemology in anthropology* (pp. 308-336). New York: Harper & Row.

Campbell, D. T. (1965). Variation and selective retention in socio-cultural evolution. In H. R. Barringer, G. I. Blanksten, & R. W. Mack (Eds.), *Social change in developing areas: A reinterpretation of evolutionary theory* (pp. 19-48). Cambridge, MA: Schenkman.

Campbell, D. T. (1966). Pattern matching as an essential in distal knowing. In K. R. Hammond (Ed.), *The psychology of Egon Brunswik* (pp. 81-106). New York: Holt, Rinehart & Winston.

Campbell, D. T. (1967a). Administrative experimentation, institutional records, and nonreactive measures. In J. C. Stanley (Ed.), *Improving experimental design and statistical analysis.* Chicago: Rand McNally.

Campbell, D. T. (1967b). Stereotypes and the perception of group differences. *American Psychologist, 22,* 812-829.

Campbell, D. T. (1969a). Prospective: Artifact and control. In R. Rosenthal & R. L. Rosnow (Eds.), *Artifact in behavioral research* (pp. 351-382). New York: Academic Press.

Campbell, D. T. (1969b). Reforms as experiments. *American Psychologist, 24*(4), 409-429.

Campbell, D. T. (1970). Natural selection as an epistemological model. In R. Naroll & C. R. (Eds.), *A handbook of method in cultural anthropology* (pp. 51-85). New York: Natural History Press/Doubleday.

Campbell, D. T. (1974a). Evolutionary epistemology. In P. A. Schilpp (Ed.), *The philosophy of Karl Popper* (pp. 413-463). LaSalle, IL: Open Court.

Campbell, D. T. (1974b). *Qualitative knowing in action research.* Kurt Lewin Award Address, Psychological Association, New Orleans.

Campbell, D. T. (1975). "Degrees of freedom" and the case study. *Comparative Political Studies, 8*(2), 178-193.

Campbell, D. T. (1976). Focal local indicators for social program evaluation. *Social Indicators Research, 3,* 237-256.

Campbell, D. T. (1979). Assessing the impact of planned social change. *Evaluation and Program Planning, 2,* 67-90.

Campbell, D. T. (1986). Science's social system of validity-enhancing collective belief change and the problems of the social sciences. In D. W. Fiske & R. A. Shweder (Eds.), *Metatheory in social science: Pluralisms and subjectivities* (pp. 108-135). Chicago: University of Chicago Press.

Campbell, D. T. (1988). Qualitative knowing in action research. In E. S. Overman (Ed.), *Methodology and epistemology for social science: Selected papers* (pp. 360-376). Chicago: University of Chicago Press.

Campbell, D. T. (1991). Coherentist empiricism, hermeneutics, and the commensurability of paradigms. *International Journal of Educational Research, 15,* 587-597.

Campbell, D. T. (1993). Plausible coselection of belief by referent: All the "objectivity" that is possible. *Perspectives on Science: Historical, Philosophical, Social, 1,* 85-105.

Campbell, D. T., Boruch, R. F., Schwartz, R. D., & Steinberg, J. (1977). Confidentiality-preserving modes of access to files and to interfile exchange for useful statistical analysis. *Evaluation Quarterly, 1*(2), 269-299.

Campbell, D. T., & Burwen, L. S. (1956). Trait judgments from photographs as a projective device. *Journal of Clinical Psychology, 12,* 215-221.

Campbell, D. T., & Damarin, F. L. (1961). Measuring leadership attitudes through an information test. *Journal of Social Psychology, 55,* 159-176.

Campbell, D. T., & Fiske, D. W. (1959). Convergent and discriminant validation by the multitrait-multimethod matrix. *Psychological Bulletin, 56,* 81-105.

Campbell, D. T., Kruskal, W. H., & Wallace, W. P. (1966). Seating aggregation as an index of attitude. *Sociometry, 29,* 1-15.

Campbell, D. T., & LeVine, R. A. (1961). A proposal for cooperative cross-cultural research on ethnocentrism. *Journal of Conflict Resolution, 5*(1), 82-108.

Campbell, D. T., & LeVine, R. A. (1965). Propositions about ethnocentrism from social science theories. Northwestern University, mimeograph.

Campbell, D. T., & Mack, R. W. (1965). *The steepness of interracial boundaries as a function of the locus of social interaction.* Unpublished data, plans, and manuscript fragments. Lehigh University, Bethlehem, PA.

Campbell, D. T., & McCormack, T. H. (1957). Military experience and attitudes toward authority. *American Journal of Sociology, 62,* 482-490.

Campbell, D. T., & Mehra, K. (1958). Individual differences in evaluations of group discussions as a projective measure of attitude toward leadership. *Journal of Social Psychology, 47,* 101-106.

Campbell, D. T., Miller, N., Lubetsky, J., & O'Connell, E. J. (1964). Varieties of projection in trait attribution. *Psychological Monographs, 78*(15).

Campbell, D. T., & O'Connell, E. J. (1967). Methods factors in multitrait-multimethod matrices: Multiplicative rather than additive? *Multivariate Behavioral Research, 2,* 409-426.

Campbell, D. T., & O'Connell, E. (1982). Methods as diluting trait relationships rather than adding irrelevant systematic variance. In D. Brinberg & L. Kidder (Eds.), *New directions for methodology of social and behavioral science: Forms of validity in research* (Vol. 12, pp. 93-111). San Francisco: Jossey-Bass.

Campbell, D. T., & Paller, B. T. (1989). Extending evolutionary epistemology to "justifying" scientific beliefs: A sociological rapprochement with a fallibilist perceptual foundationalism? In K. Hahlweg & C. A. Hooker (Eds.), *Issues in evolutionary epistemology* (pp. 231-257). Albany: State University of New York Press.

Campbell, D. T., & Shanan, J. (1958). Semantic idiosyncrasy as a method in the study of attitudes. *Journal of Social Psychology, 47,* 107-110.

Campbell, D. T., Siegman, C. R., & Rees, M. B. (1967). Direction-of-wording effects in the relationships between scales. *Psychological Bulletin, 68,* 293-303.

Campbell, D. T., & Stanley, J. C. (1966). *Experimental and quasi-experimental designs for research.* Chicago: Rand McNally.

Cane, V. R., & Heim, A. W. (1950). The effects of repeated testing: III. Further experiments and general conclusions. *Quarterly Journal of Experimental Psychology, 2,* 182-195.

Cannell, C. F., Oksenberg, L., & Converse, J. M. (1977). Striving for response accuracy: Experiments in new interviewing techniques. *Journal of Marketing Research, 14,* 306-315.

Cantril, H. (1944). *Gauging public opinion.* Princeton, NJ: Princeton University Press.

Cantril, H. (1965). *The pattern of human concerns.* New Brunswick, NJ: Rutgers University Press.

Caplan, N., & Nelson, S. D. (1973). On being useful: The nature and consequences of psychological research on social problems. *American Psychologist, 28,* 199-211.

Capra, P. C., & Dittes, J. E. (1962). Birth order as a selective factor among volunteer subjects. *Journal of Abnormal and Social Psychology, 64,* 302.

Carroll, J. B. (1952). Ratings on traits measured by a factored personality inventory. *Journal of Abnormal and Social Psychology, 47,* 626-632.

Carroll, J. B. (1961). The nature of the data, or how to choose a correlation coefficient. *Psychometrika, 55,* 347-372.

Carroll, J. K., & Knerr, C. R. (1976). *Law and the regulation of social science research: Confidentiality as a case study.* Presented at the Symposium on Ethical Issues in Social Science Research, Department of Sociology, University of Minnesota, April 9, 1976.

Cattell, R. B., Heist, A. B., Heist, P. A., & Stewart, R. G. (1950). The objective measurement of dynamic traits. *Educational and Psychological Measurement, 10,* 224-248.

Cattell, R. B., Maxwell, E. F., Light, B. H., & Unger, M. P. (1949). The objective measurement of attitudes. *British Journal of Psychology, 40,* 81-90.

Caws, P. (1969). The structure of discovery. *Science, 166,* 1375-1380.

Cecil, J. S. (1978). *Regulation of research record systems by the Privacy Act of 1974* (Research Report of the Department of Psychology). Evanston, IL: Northwestern University.

Cecil, J. S., & Griffin, E. (1981). Legal issues in obtaining access to data. In R. F. Boruch et al. (Eds.), *Access to research data* (Report submitted to the Panel on Data Sharing, Committee on National Statistics, National Research Council, 2101 Constitution Avenue, NW, Washington, D.C., 20418.

Chapman, L. J., & Bock, R. D. (1958). Components of variance due to acquiescence and content in the F scale measure of authoritarianism. *Psychological Bulletin, 55,* 328-333.

Chapman, L. J., & Campbell, D. T. (1957a). An attempt to predict the performance of three-man teams from attitude measures. *Journal of Social Psychology, 46,* 277-286.

Chapman, L. J., & Campbell, D. T. (1957b). Response set in the F scale. *Journal of Abnormal and Social Psychology, 54,* 129-132.

Chapman, L. J., & Campbell, D. T. (1959a). Absence of acquiescence response set in the Taylor Manifest Anxiety scale. *Journal of Consulting Psychology, 23,* 465-466.

Chapman, L. J., & Campbell, D. T. (1959b). The effect of acquiescence response-set upon relationships among F scale, ethnocentrism, and intelligence. *Sociometry, 22,* 153-161.

Chein, I. (1949). On evaluating self-surveys. *Journal of Social Issues, 5,* 56-63.

Chein, I. (1956). *Community self-surveys.* Lecture given at University of Rochester, 5 November (Mimeograph, 23pp.).

Chein, I., Cook, S. W., & Harding, J. (1948a). The field of action research. *The American Psychologist, 3,* 43-50.

Chein, I., Cook, S. W., & Harding, J. (1948b). The use of research in social therapy. *Human Relations, 1,* 497-510.

Child, A. (1965). *Interpretation: A general theory.* Berkeley: University of California Press.

Christie, R. (1954). Authoritarianism reexamined. In R. Christie & M. Jahoda (Eds.), *Studies in the scope and the method of the authoritarian personality* (pp. 123-196). Glencoe, IL: Free Press.

Christie, R., Havel, J., & Seidenberg, B. (1958). Is the F scale irreversible? *Journal of Abnormal and Social Psychology, 56,* 143-159.

Clarke, R. B., & Campbell, D. T. (1955). A demonstration of bias in estimates of Negro ability. *Journal of Abnormal and Social Psychology, 51,* 585-588.

Clignet, R. (1970). A critical evaluation of concomitant variation studies. In R. Naroll & R. Cohen (Eds.), *A handbook of method in cultural anthropology.* Garden City, NY: Natural History Press.

Clubb, J. M., Austin, E. W., Geda, C. L., & Traugott, M. W. (1981). *Sharing research data.* A report submitted to the Panel on Data Sharing, Committee on National Statistics, National Research Council, 2101 Constitution Avenue, NW, Washington, D C., 20418.

Coffin, T. E. (1941). Some conditions of suggestion and suggestibility: A study of certain attitudinal and situational factors influencing the process of suggestion. *Psychological Monographs, 4,* 1-241.

College Study in Intergroup Relations. (1948). *Study forms and technics in intergroup relations.* Supplemental Sheet 5 (Mimeograph), Wayne State University, Detroit, MI.

Commission on Community Interrelations of the American Jewish Congress. (1947-1948). *The face game.* Unpublished research on a modified version (by Chein & Schreiber) of a test originally developed by Marian Radke. (Available from author at 2583 E. 84th Street, New York, NY 10028)

Committee on Evaluation Research, Social Science Research Council. (1978). *Audits and experiments: A report prepared for the U.S. General Accounting Office, U.S.G.A.O., October.*

Cook, S. W. (1962). The systematic analysis of socially significant events: A strategy for social research. *The Journal of Social Issues, 18,* 66-84.

Cook, S. W. (1968). *Studies of attitude and attitude measurement* (Mimeograph, AFOSR Technical Report, pp. 1-130). Institute of Behavioral Science, University of Colorado.

Cook, S. W., Johnson, R. C., & Scott, W. A. (1969). Comparative validities of direct and indirect attitude measures. Unpublished manuscript. University of Colorado.

Cook, S. W., & Selltiz, C. (1964). A multiple-indicator approach to attitude measurement. *Psychological Bulletin, 62,* 36-55.

Cook, T. D., & Campbell, D. T. (1979). *Quasi-experimentation: Design and analysis for field settings.* Boston: Houghton Mifflin.

Cook, T. D., & Campbell, D. T. (1986). The causal assumptions of quasi-experimental practice. *Synthese, 68,* 141-180.

Corsini, R. J. (1956). Understanding and similarity in marriage. *Journal of Abnormal Social Psychology, 52,* 327-332.

Crespi, L. P. (1948). The interview effect on polling. *Public Opinion Quarterly, 12,* 99-111.

Cronbach, L. J. (1946). Response sets and test validity. *Educational Psychological Measurement, 6,* 475-494.

Cronbach, L. J. (1950). Further evidence on response sets and test design. *Educational Psychological Measurement, 10,* 3-31.

Cronbach, L. J. (1951). Coefficient alpha and the internal structure of tests. *Psychometrika, 16,* 297-334.

Cronbach, L. J. (1958). Proposals leading to analytic treatment of social perception scores. In R. Tagiuri & L. Petrullo (Eds.), *Person perception and interpersonal behavior* (pp. 353-379). Stanford, CA: Stanford University Press.

Cronbach, L. J. (1989). Construct validation after 30 years. In R. L. Linn (Ed.), *Intelligence: Measurement theory and public policy*. Champaign: University of Illinois Press.

Cronbach, L. J., & Meehl, P. E. (1955). Construct validity in psychological tests. *Psychological Bulletin, 52,* 281-302.

Davidson, D. (1984). *Inquiries into truth and interpretation*. Oxford: Clarendon.

Department of Health and Human Services. (1981). Final regulations amending basic HHS policy for the protection of human research subjects. *Federal Register, 46*(16), 8366-8392.

Department of Health, Education, and Welfare. (1973). *Final report of the Tuskegee Syphilis Study Ad Hoc Advisory Panel.* Washington, DC: Government Printing Office.

Department of Health, Education, and Welfare. (1978). Proposed regulations on research involving children. *Federal Register, 43*(141), 31786-31794.

Deri, S., Dinnerstein, D., Harding, J., & Pepitone, A. D. (1948). Techniques for the diagnosis and measurement of intergroup attitudes and behavior. *Psychological Bulletin, 45,* 248-271.

de Sola Pool, I. (1979). Protecting human subjects of research: An analysis of proposed amendments to HEW policy. *Political Science, 12,* 452-455.

Diab, L. M. (1965). Studies in social attitudes: III. Attitude assessment through the semantic differential technique. *Journal of Social Psychology, 67*(2), 303-314.

Dicken, C. F. (1959). Simulated patterns on the Edwards Personnel Preference Schedule. *Journal of Applied Psychology, 43,* 372-378.

Dicken, C. F. (1960). Simulated patterns of the California Psychological Inventory. *Journal of Counseling Psychology, 7,* 24-31.

Doob, L. W. (1953). Effects of initial serial position and attitude upon recall under conditions of low motivation. *Journal of Abnormal and Social Psychology, 48,* 199-205.

Doob, L. W. (1965). Psychology. In R. A. Lystad (Ed.), *The African world: A survey of social research* (pp. 373-416). New York: Praeger.

Douglas, J. D. (1967). *The social meanings of suicide.* Princeton, NJ: Princeton University Press.

Drummond, B. (1978, May 22). Statistics mislead: Black illegitimacy not rising. *Minneapolis Star,* p. 2a.

Dubin, S. S. (1940). Verbal attitude scores predicted from responses in a projective technique. *Sociometry, 3,* 24-28.

Duijker, H. C. J. (1955). Comparative research in social science with special reference to attitude research. *International Social Science Bulletin, 7,* 555-556.

Duncan, O. D., & Duncan, B. (1955). A methodological analysis of segregation indexes. *American Sociological Review, 20.*

Duncan, O. D., Cuzzort, R. P., & Duncan, B. (1961). *Statistical geography.* Glencoe, IL: Free Press.

Duncker, K. (1929). Uber induzierte Bewegung. Ein Beitrag zur Theorie optisch wahrgenommener Bewegung. *Psychologishe Forschung, 12*(6), 180-259.

Edwards, A. L. (1957). *The social desirability variable in personality assessment and research.* New York: Dryden.

Eggan, F. (1954). Social anthropology and the method of controlled comparison. *American Anthropologist, 56,* 5, Part 1.

Eisenman, R., Bernard, J. L., & Jannon, J. E. (1966). Benevolence, potency, and God: A semantic differential study of the Rorschach. *Perceptual and Motor Skills, 22*(1), 75-78.

Ekelblad, F. A. (1962). *The statistical method in business.* New York: John Wiley.

Ervin, S., & Bower, R. T. (1952). Translation problems in international surveys. *Public Opinion Quarterly, 16,* 595-604.

Ervin, S. M. (1964). Language and TAT content in bilinguals. *Journal of Abnormal Social Psychology, 68,* 500-507.

Etzioni, A., & Lehman, E. W. (1967). Some dangers in "valid" social measurement. *Annals of the American Academy of Political and Social Science, 373,* 1-15.

Evans, M. C., & Chein, I. (1948). *The movie story game: A projective test of interracial attitudes for use with Negro and white children.* Paper presented at the American Psychological Association, Boston.

Everhart, R. B. (1975). Problems of doing fieldwork in educational evaluation. *Human Organization, 32*(2), 205-215.

Eyer, J. (1976). Review of mental illness and the economy. *International Journal of Health Services, 6,* 139-148.

Feather, N. T. (1964). Acceptance and rejection of arguments in relation to attitude strength, critical ability, and intolerance of inconsistency. *Journal of Abnormal and Social Psychology, 69*(2), 127-136.

Feige, E. L., & Watts, H. W. (1970). Protection of privacy through microaggregation. In R. L. Bisco (Ed.), *Data bases, computers, and the social sciences.* New York: Wiley-Interscience.

Feigl, H. (1945). Operationism and scientific method. *Psychological Review, 52,* 250-259.

Feigl, H. (1958). The mental and the physical. In H. Feigl, M. Scriven, & G. Maxwell (Eds.), *Concepts, theories and the mind-body problem* (Minnesota Studies in the Philosophy of Science, Vol. 2). Minneapolis: University of Minnesota Press.

Fellegi, I. P., & Phillips, J. L. (1974). Statistical confidentiality: Some theory and applications to data dissemination. *Annals of Economic and Social Measurement, 3,* 399-409.

Feyerabend, P. K. (1970). Against method: Outline of an anarchistic theory of knowledge. In M. Radner & S. Winokur (Eds.), *Analyses of theories and methods of physics and psychology* (Minnesota Studies in the Philosophy of Science, Vol. 4, pp. 17-130). Minneapolis: University of Minnesota Press.

Fidler, D. S., & Kleinknecht, R. E. (1977). Randomized response versus direct questioning: Two data-collection methods for sensitive information. *Psychological Bulletin, 84,* 1045-1049.

Fischer, J. L. (1972). The uses of Internal Revenue Service data. In M. E. Borus (Ed.), *Evaluating the impact of Manpower Programs.* Lexington, MA: D. C. Heath.

Fisher, I. (1923). *The making of index numbers.* Boston: Houghton Mifflin.

Fiske, D. W. (1947). The validation of naval aviation cadet selection tests against training criteria. *Journal of Applied Psychology, 31,* 601-614.

Fiske, D. W. (1949). Consistency of the factorial structures of personality ratings from different sources. *Journal of Abnormal and Social Psychology, 44,* 329-344.

Fiske, D. W. (1971). *Measuring the concepts of personality.* Chicago: Aldine-Atherton.

Fiske, D. W. (1978). *Strategies for personality research: The observation versus interpretation of behavior* (Vol. 9). San Francisco: Jossey-Bass.

Fiske, D. W. (Ed.). (1981). *Problems with language imprecision. New directions for methodology of social and behavioral research* (Vol. 9). San Francisco: Jossey-Bass.

Fiske, D. W. (1982). Convergent-discriminant validation in measurements and research strategies. In D. Brinberg & L. Kidder (Eds.), *New directions for methodology of social and behavioral science: Forms of validity in research* (Vol. 12, pp. 72-92). San Francisco: Jossey-Bass.

Fiske, D. W. (1986). Specificity of method and knowledge in social science. In D. W. Fiske & R. A. Shweder (Eds.), *Metatheory in social science: Pluralisms and subjectivities* (pp. 61-82). Chicago: University of Chicago Press.

Fiske, D. W., & Baughman, E. E. (1953). Relationships between Rorschach scoring categories and total number of responses. *Journal of Abnormal and Social Psychology, 48,* 25-32.

Fiske, D. W., & Campbell, D. T. (1992). Citations do not solve problems. *Psychological Bulletin, 112,* 292-295.

Fiske, D. W., & Shweder, R. A. (Eds.). (1986). *Metatheory in social science: Pluralisms and subjectivities.* Chicago: University of Chicago Press.

Frank, P. (1955). Foundations of physics. In O. Neurath, R. Carnap, & C. Morris (Eds.), *International encyclopedia of unified science* (Vol. 2). Chicago: University of Chicago Press.

Frankel, B. (1986). Two extremes on the social science commitment continuum. In D. W. Fiske & R. A. Shweder (Eds.), *Metatheory in social science: Pluralisms and subjectivities* (pp. 353-361). Chicago: University of Chicago Press.

Freeman, H. E., & Sherwood, C. C. (1970). *Social policy and social research.* Englewood Cliffs, NJ: Prentice Hall.

Freeman, L. C., & Pilger, J. (1964). *Segregation: A micro-measure based upon compactness* (Residential Segregation Study, Maxwell School of Citizenship and Public Affairs). Syracuse, NY.

Freeman, L. C., & Pilger, J. (1965). *Segregation: A micro-measure based on well-mixedness.* Residential Segregation Study, Maxwell School of Citizenship and Public Affairs, Syracuse University.

French, E. G. (1955). Some characteristics of achievement motivation. *Journal of Experimental Psychology, 50,* 232-236.

Frenkel-Brunswik, E., Jones, H. E. (Directors), Rokeach, M., Jarvik, M., & Campbell, D. T. (Staff). (1946-1947). [Unpublished research on the personality correlates of antiminority attitudes among grade school children]. Financed by a grant from the American Jewish Committee.

Frenkel-Brunswik, E., Levinson, D., & Sanford, R. N. (1947). The anti-democratic personality. In T. M. Newcomb & E. L. Hartley (Eds.), *Readings in social psychology.* New York: Holt.

Frenkel-Brunswick, E., & Reichert, S. (1946-1947). *Personality and prejudice in women.* Unpublished manuscript.

Frey, P. W. (1973). Student ratings of teaching: Validity of several rating factors. *Science, 182,* 83-85.

Frijda, N., & Jahoda, G. (1966). On the scope and methods of cross cultural research. *International Journal of Psychology, 1*(2), 109-127.

Fromme, A. (1941). On use of qualitative methods of attitude research. *Journal of Social Psychology, 13,* 429-460.

Gage, N. L., Leavitt, G. S., & Stone, G. C. (1956). The intermediary key in the analysis of interpersonal perception. *Psychological Bulletin, 53,* 258-266.

Gardner, G. T. (1978). Effect of federal human subjects regulations on data obtained in environmental stress research. *Journal of Personality and Social Psychology, 36*(6), 628-634.

Garfinkel, H. (1967). "Good" organizational reasons for "bad" clinical records. In H. Garfinkel (Ed.), *Studies in ethnomethodology* (pp. 186-207). Englewood Cliffs, NJ: Prentice Hall.

Garner, W. R. (1954). Context effects and the validity of loudness scales. *Journal of Experimental Psychology, 48,* 218-224.

Garner, W. R., Hake, H. W., & Eriksen, C. W. (1956). Operationism and the concept of perception. *Psychological Review, 63,* 149-159.

Gatty, R., & Hamje, K. H. (1961). *The error-choice technique in image research.* Unpublished manuscript, Rutgers State University.

Getzels, J. W., & Walsh, J. J. (1958). The method of paired direct and projective questionnaires in the study of attitude structure and socialization. *Psychological Monographs, 72,* 1-454.

Ghiselli, E. E., & Brown, C. W. (1955). *Personnel and industrial psychology* (2nd ed.). New York: McGraw-Hill.

Gilbert, H. H. (1941). Secondary science and pupil prejudice. *Journal of Educational Research,* *35,* 294-299.

Gilbert, N., & Specht, H. (1973). The model cities program: A comparative analysis of participating cities process, product, performance, and prediction. Marshall Kaplan, Gans and Kahn, Inc. of San Francisco. Washington, D.C., Department of Housing and Urban Development, Office of Community Development, Evaluation Division. U.S. Gov. Printing Office, Washington, D.C. 20402, GPO Bookstore Stock Number 2300-00242.

Glass, G. V., Tiao, G. C., & Maguire, T. O. (1971). Analysis of data on the 1900 revision of the German divorce laws as a quasi-experiment. *Law and Society Review, 6,* 539-562.

Glass, G. V., Willson, V. L., & Gottman, J. M. (1975). *Design and analysis of times series experiments.* Boulder: Colorado Associated University Press.

Glazer, E. M. (1941). *An experiment in the development of critical thinking.* Teachers College Contributions to Education, 843. New York: Bureau of Publications, Teachers College, Columbia University.

Goffin, R. D. (1987). *The analysis of multitrait-multimethod matrices: An empirical and Monte Carlo comparison of two procedures.* Unpublished doctoral thesis, University of Western Ontario, London, Ontario, Canada.

Goffin, R. D., & Jackson, D. N. (1992). Analysis of multitrait-multirater performance appraisal data: Composite direct product method versus confirmatory factor analysis. *Multivariate Behavior Research, 27,* 363-385.

Goffman, E. (1959). *The presentation of self in everyday life.* Garden City, NY: Doubleday.

Goldman, A. I. (1985). What is justified belief? In H. Kornblith (Ed.), *Naturalizing epistemology* (pp. 91-113). Cambridge: MIT Press.

Goodman, N. (1955). *Fact, fiction, and forecast.* Cambridge, MA: Harvard University Press.

Gordon, A. C., Campbell, D. T., Appleton, H., & Conner, R. F. (1971). *Recommended accounting procedures for the evaluation of improvements in the delivery of state social services.* Russell Sage Foundation and Illinois Institute of Social Policy.

Gordon, L. V. (1967). Q-typing of Oriental and American youth: Initial and clarifying studies. *Journal of Social Psychology, 71,* 185-195.

Gordon, L. V., & Kikuchi, A. (1966). American personality tests in cross-cultural research—A caution. *Journal of Social Psychology, 69,* 179-183.

Gordon, S. (1947). *Exploration of social attitudes through humor.* Unpublished master's thesis, University of Illinois.

Gough, H. G. (1966a). An appraisal of social maturity by means of the CPI. *Journal of Abnormal Psychology, 71*(3), 189-195.

Gough, H. G. (1966b). A cross-cultural analysis of the CPI Femininity Scale. *Journal of Consulting Psychology, 30*(2), 136-141.

Gray, B., & Cooke, R. A. (1980). The impact of institutional review boards on research. *Hastings Center Report,* February 1980, 36-41.

Green, J. (1954). *The use of an information test about the Negro as an indirect technique for measuring attitudes, beliefs, and self-perceptions.* Unpublished doctoral dissertation, University of Southern California.

Green, R. T., & Stacey, B. G. (1966). A flexible projective technique applied to the measurement of the self-images of voters. *Journal of Projective Techniques and Personality Assessment, 30*(1), 12-15.

Greenberg, B. G., Abernathy, J. R., & Horvitz, D. G. (1970). A new survey technique and its application in the field of public health. *Milbank Memorial Fund, 68,* 39-55.

Greenberg, B. G., Abul-ela, A. A., Simon, W. R., & Horvitz, D. G. (1969). The unrelated question randomized response model: Theoretical framework. *Journal of the American Statistical Association, 64,* 520-539.

Greenstone, J. D., & Peterson, P. E. (1973). *Race and authority in urban politics: Community participation and the war on poverty.* New York: Russell Sage.

Greenwald, A. B., & Sakumura, J. S. (1967). Attitude and selective learning: Where are the phenomena of yesteryear? *Journal of Personality and Social Psychology, 7,* 387-397.

Grings, W. W. (1942). The verbal summator technique and abnormal mental states. *Journal of Abnormal and Social Psychology, 37,* 529-545.

Guilford, J. P. (1954). *Psychometric methods.* New York: McGraw-Hill.

Guttentag, M. (1971). Models and methods in evaluation research. *Journal for the Theory of Social Behavior, 1*(1), 75-95.

Guttentag, M. (1973). Evaluation of social intervention programs. *Annals of the New York Academy of Sciences, 17,* 144-163.

Habermas, J. (1971). *Knowledge and human interests.* Boston: Beacon.

Habermas, J. (1983). Interpretive social science vs. hermeneuticism. In N. Haan, R. N. Bellah, P. Rabinow, & W. M. Sullivan (Eds.), *Social science as moral inquiry* (pp. 251-269). New York: Columbia University Press.

Hafner, E. M., & Presswood, S. (1965). Strong inference and weak interactions. *Science, 149,* 503-510.

Halbwachs, M. (1930). *Les causes de suicide.* Paris: Felix Alcan.

Hammond, K. R. (1948). Measuring attitudes by error-choice: An indirect method. *Journal of Abnormal and Social Psychology, 43,* 38-48.

Hanfmann, E., & Getzels, J. W. (1953). Studies of the sentence-completion test. *Journal of Projective Techniques, 17,* 280-294.

Hansen, A. H. (1921). *Cycles of prosperity and depression in the United States.* University of Wisconsin Studies in Social Sciences and History.

Hansen, M. H. (1971). *Insuring confidentiality of individual records in data storage and retrieval for statistical purposes* (Federal Statistics, Vol. II. Report of the President's Commission [No. 4000-0269]). Washington, DC: Government Printing Office.

Hanson, N. R. (1958). *Patterns of discovery: An inquiry into the conceptual foundations of science.* Cambridge: Cambridge University Press.

Harding, J. (1948, March 5). Community self-surveys: A form of combating discrimination. *Congress Weekly: A Review of Jewish Interests.*

Harmon, G. (1985). Positive versus negative undermining in belief revision. In H. Kornblith (Ed.), *Naturalizing epistemology* (pp. 231-248). Cambridge: MIT Press.

Hartley, E. L. (1946). *Problems in prejudice.* New York: Kings Crown Press.

Hartley, E. L., & Schwartz, S. (1948). A pictorial doll-play approach for the study of children's intergroup attitudes. Mimeographed preliminary draft. Research Institute in American Jewish Education, American Jewish Committee. (Available from American Jewish Committee, 165 E. 65th Street, New York, NY 10022)

Havron, M. D., Nordlie, P. G., & Cofer, C. N. (1957). Measurement of attitudes by a simple word association technique. *Journal of Social Psychology, 46,* 81-89.

Heller, R. N. (1972). The uses of Social Security Administration data. In M. E. Borus (Ed.), *Evaluating the impact of Manpower Programs.* Lexington, MA: D. C. Heath.

Herskovits, M. J., Campbell, D. T., & Segall, M. H. (1969). *Materials for a cross-cultural study of perception* (2nd ed.). Indianapolis, IN: Bobbs-Merrill.

Hesse, M. (1980). *Revolutions and reconstructions in the philosophy of science.* Bloomington: Indiana University Press.

Hicks, J. M. (1967). Comparative validation of attitude measures by the multitrait-multimethod matrix. *Educational and Psychological Measurement, 27,* 985-995.

Hildum, D. C., & Brown, R. W. (1956). Verbal reinforcement and interviewer bias. *Journal of Abnormal and Social Psychology, 53,* 108-111.

Himmelfarb, S. (1966). Studies in the perception of ethnic group members: I. Accuracy, response bias, and anti-Semitism. *Journal of Personality and Social Psychology, 4*(3), 347-355.

Hochberg, H. (1959). *Intervening variables, hypothetical constructs and metaphysics.* Paper read at American Association for the Advancement of Science, Chicago.

Hodgkinson, H. (1971). Cited in human factors: Unobtrusive measures. *Behavior Today, 2,* 3.

Hoffman, L. J., & Miller, W. F. (1970). How to obtain a personal dossier from a data bank. *Datamation, 16,* 75-76.

Holmes, L. D. (1958). *Ta'u: Stability and change in a Samoan village* (Reprint No. 7). Wellington, New Zealand: Polynesian Society.

Holtzman, W. H., Mosely, E. C., Reinehr, R. C., & Abbott, E. (1963). Comparison of the group method and the standard individual version of the Holtzman inkblot test. *Journal of Clinical Psychology, 19,* 441-449.

Hoover, E. D. (1978). Index numbers: Practical applications. In W. H. Kruskal & J. M. Tanur (Eds.), *International encyclopedia of statistics* (Vol. 5, pp. 456-463). New York: Free Press/Macmillan.

Horowitz, E. L., & Horowitz, R. E. (1938). Development of social attitudes in children. *Sociometry, 1,* 301-338.

Hovland, C. I., & Sears, R. R. (1940). Minor studies of aggression: VI. Correlation of lynchings with economic indices. *Journal of Psychology, 9,* 301-310.

Hovland, C. I., & Sherif, M. (1952). Judgmental phenomena and scales of attitude measurement: Item displacement in Thurstone scales. *Journal of Abnormal and Social Psychology, 47,* 822-833.

Hsü, E. H. (1949). An experimental study of rationalization. *Journal of Abnormal and Social Psychology, 44,* 277-278.

Hyman, H. H., Cobb, W. J., Feldman, J. J., Hart, C. W., & Stember, C. H. (1954). *Interviewing in social research.* Chicago: University of Chicago Press.

Hyman, H. H., & Sheatsly, P. B. (1964). Attitudes on desegregation. *Scientific American, 211,* 16-23.

Jackson, D. N. (1970). A sequential system for personality scale development. *Current Topics in Clinical and Community Psychology, 2,* 61-96.

Jackson, D. N. (1975). Multimethod factor analysis: A reformulation. *Multivariate Behavioral Research, 10,* 259-275.

Jackson, D. N., & Carlson, K. A. (1973). Convergent and discriminant validation of the Differential Personality Inventory. *Journal of Clinical Psychology, 29,* 214-219.

Jackson, D. N., & Messick, S. (1962). Response styles on the MMPI: Comparison of clinical and normal samples. *Journal of Abnormal and Social Psychology, 65,* 285-299.

Jackson, D. N., & Messick, S. (1965, September). *Acquiescence: The nonvanishing variance component.* Paper presented at the meeting of the American Psychological Association, Chicago. (Republished: *Research Bulletin No. 18,* March 1966, University of Western Ontario, Department of Psychology)

Jacobson, E. H. (1954). Methods used for producing comparable data in the OCSR: Seven-Nation Attitude Study. *Journal of Social Issues, 10,* 40-51.

Jaffe, A. J., & Stewart, C. D. (1951). *Manpower, resources and utilizations.* New York: John Wiley.

James, J. (1951). A preliminary study of the size determinant in small group interaction. *American Sociological Review, 16,* 474-477.

Janis, I. L., & Frick, F. (1943). The relationship between attitudes toward conclusions and errors in judging logical validity of syllogisms. *Journal of Experimental Psychology, 33,* 73-77.

Jastrow, J. (1900). *Fact and fable in psychology.* Boston: Houghton Mifflin.

Jessor, R., & Hammond, K. R. (1957). Construct validity and the Taylor Anxiety Scale. *Psychological Bulletin, 54,* 161-170.

Johnson, C. G. (1949). *An experimental analysis of the origin and development of racial attitudes with special emphasis on the role of bilingualism.* Unpublished doctoral dissertation, University of Colorado.

Jones, E. E., & Aneshansel, J. (1956). The learning and utilization of contravaluant material. *Journal of Abnormal and Social Psychology, 53,* 27-33.

Jones, E. E., & Kohler, R. (1958). The effects of plausibility on the learning of controversial statements. *Journal of Abnormal and Social Psychology, 57,* 315-320.

Jones, J. (1981). *Bad blood.* New York: Free Press.

Jones, R. W. (1973). *Principles of biological regulation: An introduction to feedback systems.* New York: Academic Press.

Jöreskog, K. G. (1969). Factoring the multitest-multioccasion correlation matrix. *Research Bulletin* (pp. 59-62). Princeton, NJ: Educational Testing Service.

Jöreskog, K. G. (1970). Estimation and testing of simplex models. *The British Journal of Mathematical and Statistical Psychology, 23,* 121-145.

Jöreskog, K. G., & Sörbom, D. (1979). *Advances in factor analysis and structural equation models.* Cambridge, MA: Abt Books.

Kadish, S. (1964). On the tactics of police-prosecution oriented critics of the courts. *Cornell Law Quarterly, 49,* 436-477.

Kahn, R. L., & Cannell, C. F. (1957). *The dynamics of interviewing: Theory, technique and cases.* New York: John Wiley.

Kaplan, B. (1961a). Cross-cultural use of projective techniques. In F. L. K. Hsü (Ed.), *Psychological anthropology.* Homewood, IL: Dorsey Press.

Kaplan, B. (Ed.). (1961b). *Studying personality cross-culturally.* New York: Harper.

Katz, D. (1942). Do interviewers bias poll results? *Public Opinion Quarterly, 6,* 248-268.

Katz, M., R. (1947). A hypothesis on anti-Negro prejudice. *American Journal of Sociology, 53,* 100-104.

Kelley, T. L., & Krey, A. C. (1934). *Tests and measurements in the social sciences.* New York: Scribner.

Kelly, E. L., & Fiske, D. W. (1951). *The prediction of performance in clinical psychology.* Ann Arbor: University of Michigan Press.

Kelly, G. A. (1955). *The psychology of personal constructs.* New York: Norton.

Kenny, D. A., & Kashy, D. A. (1992). Analysis of the multitrait-multimethod matrix by confirmatory factor analysis. *Psychological Bulletin, 112,* 165-172.

Kenyatta, J. (1938). *Facing Mount Kenya.* London: Secker & Warburg.

Kershaw, D. (1975). Comments. In A. M. Rivlin & D. M. Timpane (Eds.), *Ethical and legal issues of social experimentation.* Washington, DC: Brookings Institution.

Kershaw, D. N. (1972). A negative income tax experiment. *Scientific American, 227,* 19-25.

Kershaw, D., & Fair, J. (1976). *The New Jersey income maintenance experiment: Vol. 1. Operations, surveys, and administration.* New York: Academic Press.

Kidder, L. H. (1969). *Comparisons of a direct and an indirect attitude test: Their relative susceptibility to distortion.* Unpublished master's thesis, Northwestern University.

Kidder, L. H. (1971). *Foreign visitors: A study of the changes of selves, skills, and attitudes of Westerners in India.* Northwestern University.

Kikuchi, A., & Gordon, L. V. (1966). Evaluation and cross-cultural application of a Japanese form of the Survey of Interpersonal Values. *Journal of Social Psychology, 69,* 185-195.

Kitsuse, J. K., & Cicourel, A. V. (1963). A note on the uses of official statistics. *Social Problems, 11,* 131-139.

Klineberg, O. (1940). *Social psychology.* New York: Henry Holt.

Komorita, S. S. (1963). Attitude content, intensity, and the neutral point on a Likert-type scale. *Journal of Social Psychology, 61,* 327-334.

Krasner, L. (1958). Studies of the conditioning of verbal behavior. *Psychological Bulletin, 55,* 148-170.

Krech, D., & Crutchfield, R. S. (1948). *Theory and problems of social psychology.* New York: McGraw-Hill.

Kremen, E. O. (1949). *An attempt to ameliorate hostility toward the Negro through role playing.* Unpublished master's thesis, Ohio State University.

Kuethe, J. L. (1962a). Social schemas. *Journal of Abnormal and Social Psychology, 64,* 31-38.

Kuethe, J. L. (1962b). Social schemas and the reconstruction of social object displays from memory. *Journal of Abnormal and Social Psychology, 65,* 71-74.

Kuethe, J. L. (1964). Prejudice and aggression: A study of specific social schemata. *Perceptual and Motor Skills, 18*(1), 107-115.

Kuethe, J. L., & Stricker, G. (1963). Man and woman: Social schemata of males and females. *Psychological Reports, 13,* 655-661.

Kuhn, T. S. (1962). *The structure of scientific revolutions.* Chicago: University of Chicago Press.

Kuhn, T. S. (1970). Logic of discovery or psychology of research? and reflections on my critics. In I. Lakatos & A. Musgrave (Eds.), *Criticism and the growth of knowledge* (pp. 1-23 and 231-278). Cambridge: Cambridge University Press.

Lakatos, I. (1970). Falsification and the methodology of scientific research programmes. In I. Lakatos & A. Musgrave (Eds.), *Criticism and the growth of knowledge* (pp. 91-230). Cambridge: Cambridge University Press.

Lana, R. E. (1964). Perceptions of social controversy in professors and college students. *Journal of Psychology, 57*(1), 213-218.

Lansdell, H. (1946). A study of distorted syllogistic reasoning as a means of discovering covert attitudes toward marriage. *Bulletin of Canadian Psychological Association (Abstract), 6,* 98.

Larwood, L., Zalkind, D., & Legault, J. (1975). The bank job: A field study of sexually discriminatory performance on a neutral-role task. *Journal of Applied Social Psychology, 5,* 68-74.

Laughlin, P. R., & Laughlin, R. M. (1968). Source effects in the judgment of social argot. *Journal of Social Psychology, 78,* 257-264.

Leavitt, H. J., Hax, H., & Roche, J. H. (1955). "Authoritarianism" and agreement with things authoritative. *Journal of Psychology, 40,* 215-221.

Lehrer, K. (1974). *Knowledge.* Oxford: Clarendon.

Lehrer, K. (1990). *Theory of knowledge.* Boulder, CO: Westview.

Lenski, G. E., & Leggett, J. C. (1960). Caste, class, and deference in the research interview. *American Journal of Sociology, 65,* 463-467.

Levine, M. (1974). Scientific method and the adversary model: Some preliminary thoughts. *American Psychologist, 29*(9), 661-677.

LeVine, R. A. (1965). Socialization, social structure, and intersocietal images. In H. Kelman (Ed.), *International behavior: A social psychological analysis.* New York: Holt, Rinehart, and Winston.

LeVine, R. A. (1966). Outsiders' judgments: An ethnographic approach to group differences in personality. *Southwestern Journal of Anthropology, 22*(2), 101-116.

LeVine, R. A. (1970). Research design in anthropological field work. In R. Naroll & R. Cohen (Eds.), *A handbook of method in cultural anthropology.* Garden City, NY: Natural History Press.

LeVine, R. A., & Campbell, D. T. (1965). *Ethnocentrism field manual.* The cross-cultural study of ethnocentrism, supported by a grant from the Carnegie Corporation of New York to Northwestern University. (Available from Carnegie Corporation, 437 Madison Avenue, New York, NY 10022)

Lewin, K. (1946). Action research and minority problems. *Journal of Social Issues, 2,* 34-46.

Lewin, K. (1947). Frontiers in group dynamics, Part II-B. *Human Relations, 1,* 147-153. Reprinted as Feedback problems in social diagnosis and action. In W. Buckley (Ed.), *Modern systems research for the behavioral scientist* (pp. 441-444). Chicago: Aldine, 1968.

Lijphart, A. (1971). Comparative politics and the comparative method. *American Political Science Review, 65,* 682-693.

Lindholm, H. (1983). Sectorized psychiatry: A methodological study of the effects of reorganization on patients treated at a mental hospital. *Acta Psychiatrica Scandinavica, 67,* Suppl. No. 304.

Lindzey, G. (1961). *Projective techniques and cross-cultural research.* New York: Appleton-Century-Crofts.

Lippitt, R., & Radke, M. (1946). New trends in the investigation of prejudice. *The Annals of the American Academy of Political and Social Science,* p. 244.

Lipset, S. M., Lazarsfeld, P. F., Barton, A. H., & Linz, J. (1954). The psychology of voting: An analysis of political behavior. In G. Lindzey (Ed.), *Handbook of social psychology.* Cambridge, MA: Addison-Wesley.

Loevinger, J. (1957). Objective tests as instruments of psychological theory. *Psychological Reports, 3,* 635-694.

Loevinger, J., Gleser, G. C., & DuBois, P. H. (1953). Maximizing the discriminating power of a multiple-score test. *Psychometrika, 18,* 309-317.

Long, S. B. (1980). The continuing debate over the use of ratio variables: Facts and fiction. In K. F. Schuessler (Ed.), *Sociological methodology* (pp. 37-67). San Francisco: Jossey-Bass.

Lonner, W. J. (1968). The SVIB visits German, Austrian and Swiss psychologists. *American Psychologist, 23,* 164-179.

Lorge, I. (1937). Gen-like: Halo or reality? *Psychological Bulletin, 16,* 545-546.

Lucas, D. B., & Britt, S. H. (1950). *Advertising psychology and research.* New York: McGraw-Hill.

Lucas, D. B., & Britt, S. H. (1963). *Measuring advertising effectiveness.* New York: McGraw-Hill.

MacCorquodale, K., & Meehl, P. E. (1948). On a distinction between hypothetical constructs and intervening variables. *Psychological Review, 55,* 95-107.

Magnus, H. (1883). *Uber ethnologische untersuchungen des farbensinnes.* Breslau.

Maher, B. A., Watt, N., & Campbell, D. T. (1960). Comparative validity of two projective and two structured attitude tests in a prison population. *Journal of Applied Psychology, 44,* 284-288.

Manniche, E., & Hayes, D. P. (1957). Respondent anonymity and data matching. *Public Opinion Quarterly, 21,* 384-388.

Margenau, H. (1950). *The nature of physical reality.* New York: McGraw-Hill.

Margenau, H. (1954). On interpretations and misinterpretations of operationalism. *Scientific Monitor, 79,* 209-210.

Marrow, A. J. (1969). *The practical theorist: The life and work of Kurt Lewin.* New York: Basic Books.

Marsh, H. W. (1988). Multitrait-multimethod analysis. In J. P. Keeves (Ed.), *Educational research, methodology, and measurement.* Elmsford, NY: Pergamon.

Matarazzo, J. D. (1962). *Control of interview behavior.* Paper presented at the American Psychological Association, St. Louis.

Matarazzo, J. D., Wiens, A. N., Saslow, G., Dunham, R. M., & Voas, R. B. (1964). Speech durations of astronaut and ground communicator. *Science, 143,* 148-150.

McCarthy, P. J. (1978). Index numbers: Sampling. In W. H. Kruskal & J. M. Tanur (Eds.), *International encyclopedia of statistics* (Vol. 5, pp. 463-467). New York: Free Press/Macmillan.

McNemar, Q. (1946). Opinion-attitude methodology. *Psychological Bulletin, 43,* 289-374.

Mead, M. (1953). National character. In A. L. Kroeber et al. (Eds.), *Anthropology today: An encyclopedia inventory* (p. 648). Chicago: University of Chicago Press.

Meehl, P. E. (1967). Theory-testing in psychology and physics: A methodological paradox. *Philosophy of Science, 34,* 103-115.

Meehl, P. E. (1986). What social scientists don't understand. In D. W. Fiske & R. A. Shweder (Eds.), *Metatheory in social science: Pluralisms and subjectivities* (pp. 315-338). Chicago: University of Chicago Press.

Meehl, P. E. (1990). Appraising and amending theories: The strategy of Lakatosian defense and two principles that warrant using it. *Psychological Inquiry, 1,* 108-141.

Meehl, P. E. (1992). Cliometrics and metatheory. *Psychological Reports Monograph Supplement 1, 71,* 339-467.

Melton, A. W. (1933a). Some behavior characteristics of museum visitors. *Psychological Bulletin, 30,* 720-721.

Melton, A. W. (1933b). Studies of installation at the Pennsylvania Museum of Art. *Museum News, 11,* 508.

Melton, A. W. (1935). Problems of installation in museums of art. In *Studies in museum education.* Washington, DC: American Association of Museums.

Melton, A. W. (1936). Distribution of attention in galleries in a museum of science and industry. *Museum News, 13,* 3, 5-8.

Melton, A. W., Feldman, N. G., & Mason, C. W. (1936). Experimental studies of the education of children in a museum of science. *Publications of the American Association of Museums,* New Series, No. 15.

Milgram, S. (1963). Behavioral study of obedience. *Journal of Abnormal and Social Psychology, 67,* 371-378.

Milgram, S. (1964). Group pressure and action against a person. *Journal of Abnormal and Social Psychology, 69,* 137-143.

Mills, F. C. (1927). *The behavior of prices.* New York: National Bureau of Economic Research.

Minturn, L., & Lambert, W. W. (1964). *Mothers of six cultures: Antecedents of child rearing.* New York: John Wiley.

Mintz, A. (1946). A re-examination of correlations between lynchings and economic indices. *Journal of Abnormal and Social Psychology, 41,* 154-160.

Mitchell, R. E. (1965). Survey materials collected in the developing countries: Sampling measurement, and interviewing obstacles to intra- and international comparisons. *International Social Science Journal, 17,* 677.

Mitchell, W. C. (1921). *Index numbers of wholesale prices in the U.S. and foreign countries: I. The making and using of index numbers* (Bulletin No. 284). Washington, DC: U.S. Department of Labor, Bureau of Labor Statistics.

Moore, W. E. (1953). The exploitability of the "labor force" concept. *American Sociological Review, 18,* 68-72.

Morgan, J. J. B. (1943). Distorted reasoning as an index of public opinion. *School and Society, 57,* 333-335.

Morgan, J. J. B. (1945). Attitudes of students toward the Japanese. *Journal of Social Psychology, 21,* 219-246.

Morgan, J. J. B., & Morton, J. T. (1944). The distortion of syllogistic reasoning produced by personal convictions. *Journal of Social Psychology, 20,* 39-59.

Morgan, L. H. (1871). *Systems of consanguinity and affinity in the human family.* Smithsonian Contribution to Knowledge, Vol. 17. Washington, DC: Government Printing Office.

Morgenstern, O. (1963). *On the accuracy of economic observations* (2nd ed.). Princeton, NJ: Princeton University Press.

Morrissey, W. R. (1972). Nixon anti-crime plan undermines crime statistics. *Justice Magazine, 1*(5/6), 8-11, 14.

Morton, J. T. (1942). *The distortion of syllogistic reasoning produced by personal convictions.* Unpublished doctoral dissertation, Northwestern University.

Mudgett, B. D. (1951). *Index numbers.* New York: John Wiley.

Murdock, G. P. (1949). *Social structure.* New York: Macmillan.

Murphy, G., & Likert, R. (1937). *Public opinion and the individual.* New York: Harper.

Murray, H. A., & Morgan, C. D. (1945). A clinical study of sentiments. I and II. *Genetic Psychological Monographs, 32,* 3-311.

Myrdal, G. (1944). *An American dilemma* (Vol. II). New York: Harper.

Naroll, R. (1962). *Data quality control: A new research technique.* New York: Free Press of Glencoe.

National Research Council, Committee on Federal Agency Evaluation Research of the National Academy of Sciences. (1975). *Protecting individual privacy in evaluation research.* Washington, DC: Washington, DC: Author.

Neel, R. G., & Neel, A. F. (1953). *A demonstration of the validity of a picture technique for measuring attitude.* Paper presented at the Midwest Psychology Association, Columbus, OH.

Nejelski, P., & Peyser, H. (1975). A researcher's shield statute: Guarding against the compulsory disclosure of research data. Appendix B. In A. M. Rivlin & D. M. Timpane (Eds.), *Ethical and legal issues of social experimentation.* Washington, DC: Brookings Institution.

Nelson, H., & Giannotta, F. J. (1974b). *Research methodology in alternative education settings: The MET plan.* Minneapolis, MN: Aries Corporation. (Submitted to the National Institute of Education pursuant to Contract No. OEC-0-71-4752.)

Nelson, H., & Giannotta, F. J. (1974a). [Draft]. *MET interim report on southeast alternatives ESP project. Vol. I: Project context and rationale of research.* Minneapolis, MN: Aries Corporation.

Nelson, H., Reynolds, J., French, L. R., & Giannotta, F. J. (1974). [Draft]. *MET interim report on southeast alternatives ESP project: Vol. IIA. School ethnographic studies: Tuttle, Pratt-Motley, Marchy. Vol. IIB. Southeast and Free School and Marshall University High School.* Minneapolis, MN: Aries Corporation.

Neurath, O. (1959). Protocol sentences. In A. J. Ayer (Ed.), *Logical positivism* (pp. 199-208). Glencoe, IL: Free Press.

Newcomb, T. M. (1943). *Personality and social change.* New York: Dryden.

Newcomb, T. M. (1946). The influence of attitude climate upon some determinants of information. *Journal of Abnormal and Social Psychology, 41,* 291-302.

Nisbett, R. E., & Ross, I. (1980). *Human inference: Strategies and shortcomings of social judgment.* Englewood Cliffs, NJ: Prentice Hall.

Nunnally, J., & Husek, T. R. (1958). The phony language examination: An approach to the measurement of response bias. *Educational and Psychological Measurement, 18,* 275-282.

Office of Community Development Evaluation Division, Department of Housing and Urban Development. (1973). *The model cities program: A comparative analysis of city response patterns and their relation to future urban policy.* Washington, DC: Government Printing Office

Okner, B. A. (1972). Constructing a new data base from existing microdata sets: The 1966 merge file. *Annals of Economic and Social Measurement, 1,* 325-342.

Okner, B. A. (1974). Data matching and merging: An overview. *Annals of Economic and Social Measurement, 3,* 347-352.

Orne, M. T. (1959). The nature of hypnosis: Artifact and essence. *Journal of Abnormal and Social Psychology, 58,* 277-299.

Orne, M. T. (1962). On the social psychology of the psychological experiment: With particular reference to demand characteristics and their implications. *American Psychologist, 17,* 776-783.

Orne, M. T., & Evans, F. J. (1965). Social control in the psychological experiment: Antisocial behavior and hypnosis. *Journal of Personality and Social Psychology, 1,* 189-200.

Orne, M. T., & Scheibe, K. E. (1964). The contribution of nondeprivation factors in the production of sensory deprivation effects: The psychology of the "panic button." *Journal of Abnormal and Social Psychology, 68,* 3-12.

Parrish, J. A. (1948). *The direct and indirect assessment of attitudes as influenced by propagandized radio transcriptions.* Unpublished master's thesis, Ohio State University.

Parrish, J. A., & Campbell, D. T. (1953). Measuring propaganda effects with direct and indirect attitude tests. *Journal of Abnormal and Social Psychology, 48*(1), 3-9.

Pattullo, E. L. (1980). *Who risks what in social research?* Hastings Center Report, Garrison, NY.

Paul, B. D. (1953). Interview techniques and field relationships. In A. L. Kroeber et al. (Eds.), *Anthropology today: An encyclopedia inventory* (pp. 443-444). Chicago: University of Chicago Press.

Peabody, D. (1961). Attitude content and agreement set in scales of authoritarianism, dogmatism, anti-Semitism, and economic conservatism. *Journal of Abnormal and Social Psychology, 63,* 1-11.

Pearson, K. (1892). The grammar of science (1st ed.). London: A. and C. Black.

Peterson, D. R. (1965). Scope and generality of verbally-defined personality factors. *Psychological Review, 72,* 48-59.

Pettigrew, T. F., Allport, G. W., & Barnett, E. O. (1958). Binocular resolution and perception of race in South Africa. *British Journal of Psychology, 49,* 265-278.

Phillips, H. P. (1959). Problems of translating and meaning in field work. *Human Organization, 18,* 184-192.

Platt, J. R. (1964). Strong inference. *Science, 146,* 347-353.

Poincaré, H. (1913). Mathematical creation. In H. Poincaré (Ed.), *The foundations of science.* New York: Science Press.

Polanyi, M. (1958). *Personal knowledge: Toward a post-critical philosophy.* London: Routledge & Kegan Paul.

Politz Media Studies. (1959). *A study of outside transit poster exposure.* New York: Alfred Politz.

Popper, K. R. (1935). *Logik der Forschung.* Vienna: Springer-Verlag.

Popper, K. R. (1959). *The logic of scientific discovery.* New York: Basic Books.

Popper, K. R. (1963). *Conjectures and refutations: The growth of scientific knowledge.* New York: Basic Books.

Popper, K. R. (1972). *Objective knowledge: An evolutionary approach.* Oxford: Clarendon.

Privacy Protection Study Commission (PPSC). (1977). *Personal privacy in an information society.* Washington, DC: Government Printing Office.

Proshansky, H. (1943). A projective method for the study of attitudes. *Journal of Abnormal and Social Psychology, 38,* 393-395.

Quine, W. V. (1951). Two dogmas of empiricism. *Philosophical Review, 60,* 20-43.

Quine, W. V. (1953). *From a logical point of view.* Cambridge, MA: Harvard University Press.

Quine, W. V. (1960). *Word and object.* New York: John Wiley.

Quine, W. V. (1969a). Epistemology naturalized. In W. V. Quine (Ed.), *Ontological relativity and other essays* (pp. 69-90). New York: Columbia University Press.

Quine, W. V. (1969b). *Ontological relativity and other essays.* New York: Columbia University Press.

Radke, M., & Trager, H. G. (1950). Children's perceptions of the social roles of Negroes and whites. *Journal of Psychology, 29,* 3-33.

Radke, M., Trager, H. G., & Davis, H. (1949). Social perceptions and attitudes of children. *Genetic Psychological Monographs, 40,* 327-447.

Radke, M., Sutherland, J., & Rosenberg, P. (1950). Racial attitudes of children. *Sociometry, 13,* 154-171.

Rankin, R. E. (1951). *The galvanic skin response as a physiological measure of social attitudes.* Unpublished master's thesis, Ohio State University.

Rankin, R. E., & Campbell, D. T. (1959). Galvanic skin response to Negro and white experimenters. *Journal of Abnormal and Social Psychology, 51,* 30-33.

Raser, J. R. (1969). *Simulation and society.* Boston: Allyn & Bacon.

Rechtschaffen, A., & Mednick, S. A. (1955). The autokinetic word technique. *Journal of Abnormal and Social Psychology, 51,* 346.

Reichardt, C. S., & Coleman, S. C. (1995). The criteria for convergent and discriminant validity in a multitrait-multimethod matrix. *Multivariate Behavioral Researech, 30,* 513-538.

Remmers, H. H. (1934). Generalized attitude scales—Studies in social psychological measurements. Purdue University Studies in Higher Education. *Studies in Attitudes—A contribution to Social Psychological Research Methods,* No. 26, pp. 7-17.

Remmers, H. H. (1954). *Introduction to opinion and attitude measurement.* New York: Harper.

Remmers, H. H., & Silance, E. B. (1934). Generalized attitude scales. *Journal of Social Psychology, 5,* 298-312.

Reynolds, D., & Toch, H. H. (1965). Perceptual correlates of prejudice: Stereoscopic constancy using biracial stereograms. *Journal of Social Psychology, 66*(1), 127-133.

Reynolds, R. T. (1949). Racial attitudes revealed by a projective technique. *Journal of Consulting Psychology, 13,* 396-399.

Riddleberger, A. B., & Motz, A. B. (1957). Prejudice and perception. *American Journal of Sociology, 62,* 498-503.

Ridgeway, V. (1956). Dysfunctional consequences of performance measures. *Administrative Science Quarterly, 1*(2), 240-247.

Riecken, H. W., Boruch, R. F., Campbell, D. T., Caplan, N., Glennan, T. K., Pratt, J., Rees, A., & Williams, W. (1974). *Social experimentation: A method for planning and evaluating social intervention.* New York: Academic Press.

Riesman, D. (1956). Orbits of tolerance, interviewers and elites. *Public Opinion Quarterly, 20,* 49-73.

Riesman, D., & Ehrlich, J. (1961). Age and authority in the interview. *Public Opinion Quarterly, 25,* 39-56.

Robertson, J. A. (1977). The scientists' right to research. *University of Southern California Law Review, 51,* 1203-1279.

Robertson, J. A. (1981). The judicial conference experiment: Social experiments and prior ethical review. *I. R. B.: A Review of Human Subjects Research, 3,* 1-3.

Robinson, D., & Rohde, S. (1946). Two experiments with an anti-Semitism poll. *Journal of Abnormal and Social Psychology, 41,* 136-144.

Robinson, E. S. (1928). The behavior of the museum visitor. *Publications of the American Association of Museums,* New Series, No. 5.

Roethlisberger, F. J., & Dickson, W. J. (1939). *Management and the worker.* Cambridge, MA: Harvard University Press.

Rokeach, M. (1952). Attitude as a determinant of distortions in recall. *Journal of Abnormal and Social Psychology, 47,* 482-488.

Rokeach, M. (1956). Political and religious dogmatism: An alternative to authoritarian personality. *Psychological Monographs, 70,* 18, Whole No. 425.

Rokeach, M. (1960). *The open and closed mind.* New York: Basic Books.

Rorer, L. G. (1965). The great response-style myth (Soc. Meas.). *Psychological Bulletin, 63,* 129-156.

Rorer, L. G., & Goldberg, L. R. (1965). Acquiescence in the MMPI? *Educational and Psychological Measurement, 25,* 801-817.

Rose, A. (1948). *Studies in reduction of prejudice.* Chicago: American Council on Race Relations.

Rosenberg, M. J. (1965). When dissonance fails: On eliminating evaluation apprehension from attitude measurement. *Journal of Personality and Social Psychology, 1,* 28-42.

Rosenberg, M. J. (1969). The conditions and consequences of evaluation apprehension. In R. Rosenthal & R. Rosnow (Eds.), *Artifact in social research.* New York: Academic Press.

Rosenthal, R. (1966). *Experimenter effects in behavioral research.* New York: Appleton-Century-Crofts.

Rosenthal, R. (1976). *Experimenter effects in behavioral research* (Enlarged ed.). New York: Irvington.

Rosenthal, R., & Rosnow, R. L. (1975). *The volunteer subjects.* New York: Wiley-Interscience.

Ross, H. L. (1963). The inaccessible respondent: A note on privacy in city and country. *Public Opinion Quarterly, 27,* 269-275.

Ross, H. L. (1973). Law, science, and accidents: The British Road Safety Act of 1967. *Journal of Legal Studies, 2,* 1-78.

Ross, H. L., Campbell, D. T., & Glass, G. V. (1970). Determining the social effects of a legal reform: The British "breathalyser" crackdown of 1967. *American Behavioral Scientist, 13,* 493-509.

Ross, L., & Lepper, M. R. (1980). The perseverance of beliefs: Empirical and normative considerations. In R. A. Shweder (Ed.), *New directions for methodology of social and behavioral science: Fallible judgment in behavioral research* (Vol. 4). San Francisco: Jossey-Bass.

Rotter, J. B., & Willerman, B. (1947). The incomplete sentences tests as a method of studying personality. *Journal of Consulting Psychology, 11,* 43-48.

Royal Anthropological Institute of Great Britain and Ireland, A Committee of. (1874). *Notes and queries on anthropology.* London: Routledge & Kegan Paul (1st ed., 1874; 6th ed., 1951).

Ruggles, N., & Ruggles, R. (1974). A strategy for merging and matching microdata sets. *Annals of Economic and Social Measurement, 3,* 353-371.

Ruist, E. (1978). Index numbers: Theoretical aspects. In W. H. Kruskal & J. M. Tanur (Eds.), *International encyclopedia of statistics* (Vol. 5, pp. 451-456). New York: Free Press/Macmillan.

Russell Sage Foundation. (1970). *Guidelines for the collection, maintenance and dissemination of pupil records.* New York: Author.

Ryan, T. A. (1960). Significance tests for multiple comparisons of proportions, variances, and other statistics. *Psychological Bulletin, 57,* 318-328.

Ryan, W. (1971). *Blaming the victim.* New York: Pantheon.

Saadi, M., & Farnsworth, P. R. (1934). The degrees of acceptance of dogmatic statements and preferences. *Journal of Abnormal and Social Psychology, 29,* 143-150.

Sanford, F. H. (1950). The use of a projective device in attitude surveying. *Public Opinion Quarterly, 14,* 697-709.

Sanford, F. H., & Rosenstock, I. M. (1952). Project techniques on the doorstep. *Journal of Abnormal and Social Psychology, 47,* 3-16.

Schachter, S. (1954). Interpretative and methodological problems of replicated research. *Journal of Social Issues, 10,* 52-60.

Schanck, R. L., & Goodman, C. (1939). Reactions to propaganda on both sides of a controversial issue. *Public Opinion Quarterly, 3,* 107-112.

Scheffé, H. (1953). A method for judging all contrasts in analysis of variance. *Biometrika, 40,* 87-104.

Schulberg, H. C., & Baker, F. (1968). Program evaluation models and the implementation of research findings. *American Journal of Public Health, 58,* 1248-1255. Reprinted in Schulberg, Sheldon, & Baker, 1969, pp. 562-572.

Schulberg, E. H., Sheldon, A., & Baker, F. (1969). Introduction. In *Program evaluation in the health fields* (pp. 3-28). New York: Behavioral Publications.

Schuman, H., & Converse, J. M. (1971). The effect of black and white interviewers on black responses in 1968. *Public Opinion Quarterly, 35,* 44-68.

Schwartz, R. D. (1961). Field experimentation in sociolegal research. *Journal of Legal Education, 13,* 401-410.

Schwartz, R. D., & Orleans, S. (1967). On legal sanctions. *University of Chicago Law Review, 34,* 274-300.

Sechrest, L. (1998). Don Campbell and measurement in the social sciences. *American Journal of Evaluation, 19,* 403-406.

Seeman, M. (1947). Moral judgments: A study in racial frames of references. *American Sociological Review, 12,* 404-411.

Segall, M. H., Campbell, D. T., & Herskovits, M. J. (1966). *The influence of culture on visual perception.* Indianapolis, IN: Bobbs-Merrill.

Seidman, D., & Couzens, M. (1972, September). *Crime statistics and the great American anticrime crusade: Police misreporting of crime and political pressures.* Paper presented at the meeting of the American Political Science Association, Washington, D.C.

Selltiz, C. (1956). The use of survey methods in a citizens' campaign against discrimination. *Human Organization, 14,* 19-25.

Selltiz, C., & Cook, S. W. (1948). Can research in social science be both socially useful and scientifically meaningful? *American Sociological Review, 13,* 454-459.

Selltiz, C., Jahoda, M., Deutsch, M., & Cook, S. W. (1959). *Research methods in social relations. Published for the Society for the Psychological Study of Social Issues* (Rev. ed.). New York: Holt, Rinehart & Winston.

Selvin, H. C., & Stuart, A. (1966). Data-dredging procedures in survey analysis. *American Statistician, 20,* 20-23.

Shadish, W. R., & Fuller, S. (1994). *Social psychology of science.* New York: Guilford.

Sheldon, E. H., & Moore, W. E. (Eds.). (1968). *Indicators of social change: Concepts and measurements.* New York: Russell Sage.

Shelley, H. P., & Davis, R. E. (1957). Relationship of attitude to logical problem-solving. *Psychological Reports, 3,* 525-530.

Sherif, M. (1935). A study of some social factors in perception. *Archives of Psychology,* New York, No. 187.

Sherif, M., & Hovland, C. I. (1953). Judgmental phenomena and scales of attitude measurement: Placement of items with individual choice of number of categories. *Journal of Abnormal and Social Psychology, 48,* 135-141.

Sherriffs, A. C. (1948). The "intuition questionnaire": A new projective test. *Journal of Abnormal and Social Psychology, 48,* 326-337.

Shimony, A. (1970). Scientific influence. In R. Colodny (Ed.), *Pittsburgh studies in the philosophy of science* (Vol. 4, pp. 79-172). Pittsburgh, PA: University of Pittsburgh Press.

Shweder, R. A., & D'Andrade, R. G. (1980). The systematic distortion hypothesis. In R. A. Shweder (Ed.), *New directions for methodology of social and behavioral science: Fallible judgment in behavioral research* (Vol. 4). San Francisco: Jossey-Bass.

Silverman, L. H. (1959). A Q-sort study of the validity of evaluations made from projective techniques. *Psychological Monographs, 73*(7, Whole No. 477).

Sims, C. A. (1972). "Comments" to Okner's 1966 merge file. *Annals of Economic and Social Measurement, 1,* 343-345.

Sims, C. A. (1974). Comment: January 17, 1974. *Annals of Economic and Social Measurement, 3,* 395-397.

Sletto, R. F. (1937). *A construction of personality scales by the criterion of internal consistency.* Hanover, NH: Sociological Press.

Slobin, D. I., Ervin-Tripp, S. M., Gumperz, J. J., Brukman, J., Kernan, K., Mitchell, C., & Stross, B. (1967). *A field manual for cross-cultural study of the acquisition of communicative competence.* University of California, Berkeley. Multilith, second draft.

Smith, G. H. (1947). Beliefs in statements labeled fact and rumor. *Journal of Abnormal and Social Psychology, 42,* 80-90.

Smith, L. D. (1986). *Behaviorism and logical positivism: A reassessment of the alliance.* Stanford, CA: Stanford University Press.

Solomon, R. W. (1949). An extension of control group design. *Psychological Bulletin, 46,* 137-150.

Sommer, R. (1954). On the Brown adaptation of the Rosenzweig P-F assessing social attitudes. *Journal of Abnormal and Social Psychology, 49,* 125-128.

Stanley, J. C. (1961). Analysis of unreplicated three-way classifications, with applications to rater bias and trait independence. *Psychometrika, 26,* 205-220.

Steinberg, J., & Pritzker, L. (1969). Some experiences with the reflections on data linkage in the United States. *Bulletin of the International Statistical Institutes. 42,* 786-805.

Stephan, F. F., & McCarthy, P. J. (1958). *Sampling opinions.* New York: John Wiley.

Stern, E., & D'Epinay, R. L. (1948). Some polling experiences in Switzerland. *Public Opinion Quarterly, 11,* 553-557.

Stewart, V. M. (1973). Tests of the "carpentered world" hypothesis by race and environment in America and Zambia. *International Journal of Psychology, 8*(2), 83-94.

Strang, R. (1930). Relation of social intelligence to certain other factors. *School & Sociology, 32,* 268-272.

Stricker, G. (1963). The use of the semantic differential to predict voting behavior. *Journal of Social Psychology, 59*(1), 159-167.

Suchman, E. (1967). *Evaluation research.* New York: Russell Sage.

Sudman, S., & Bradburn, N. M. (1974). *Response effects in surveys: A review and synthesis.* Chicago: Aldine.

Sullivan, P. L., & Adelson, J. (1954). Ethnocentrism and misanthropy *Journal of Abnormal and Social Psychology, 49,* 246-250.

Suppe, F. (1977). *The structure of scientific theories* (2nd ed.). Urbana: University of Illinois Press.

Swazey, J. P. (1980). *Professional protectionism rides again.* Hastings Center Report, Garrison, NY.

Sweet, L. (1929). *The measurement of personal attitudes in younger boys.* New York: Association Press.

Symonds, P. M. (1931). *Diagnosing personality and conduct.* New York: Appleton-Century.

Taft, R. (1954). Selective recall and memory distortion of favorable and unfavorable material. *Journal of Abnormal and Social Psychology, 49,* 23-28.

Taylor, J. A. (1953). A personality scale of manifest anxiety. *Journal of Abnormal and Social Psychology, 48,* 285-290.

Taylor, J. A. (1956). Drive theory and manifest anxiety. *Psychological Bulletin, 53,* 303-320.

Thistlethwaite, D. (1950). Attitude and structure as factors in the distortion of reasoning. *Journal of Abnormal and Social Psychology, 45,* 442-458.

Thorndike, E. L. (1920). A constant error in psychological ratings. *Journal of Applied Psychology, 4,* 25-29.

Thorndike, R. L. (1936). Factor analysis of social and abstract intelligence. *Journal of Educational Psychology, 27,* 231-233.

Thorndike, R. L. (1949). *Personnel selection*. New York: John Wiley.

Thouless, R. H. (1959). Effect of prejudice on reasoning. *British Journal of Psychology, 50*, 289-293.

Thurstone, L. L. (1937). *The reliability and validity of tests*. Ann Arbor, MI: Edwards.

Tolman, E. C., & Krechevsky, I. (1933). Means-end-readiness and hypothesis. *Psychological Review, 40*, 60-70.

Toulmin, S. E. (1961). *Foresight and understanding: An inquiry into the aims of science*. Bloomington: Indiana University Press.

Toulmin, S. E. (1972). *Human understanding: The evolution of collective understanding* (Vol. 1). Princeton, NJ: Princeton University Press.

Travers, R. M. W. (1941). A study in judging the opinions of groups. *Archives of Psychology* (New York), No. 266.

Tryon, R. C. (1942). Individual differences. In F. A. Moss (Ed.), *Comparative psychology* (2nd ed., pp. 330-365). New York: Prentice Hall.

Turner, C. F., & Krauss, E. (1978). Fallible indicators of the subjective state of the nation. *American Psychologist, 33*, 456-470.

Twigg, R. (1972). Downgrading of crimes verified in Baltimore. *Justice Magazine, 1*(5/6).

Underwood, B. J. (1957). *Psychological research*. New York: Appleton-Century-Crofts.

Vaughan, G. M., & Thompson, R. H. T. (1961). New Zealand children's attitudes toward Maoris. *Journal of Abnormal and Social Psychology, 62*, 701-704.

Vernon, P. E. (1957). *Educational ability and psychological factors. Address given to the Joint Education-Psychology Colloquium*. Chicago: University of Illinois.

Vernon, P. E. (1958). *Educational testing and test-form factors* (Res. Bull. RB-58-3.). Princeton, NJ: Educational Testing Service.

Vidich, A. J., & Bensman, J. (1954). The validity of field data. *Human Organization, 13*(1), 20-27.

Vincent, C. E. (1964). Socioeconomic status and familial variables in mail questionnaire responses. *American Journal of Sociology, 69*, 647-653.

Wallen, R. (1943). Individuals' estimates of group opinion. *Journal of Abnormal and Social Psychology, 17*, 269-274.

Waly, P., & Cook, S. W. (1965). Effect of attitude on judgments of plausibility. *Journal of Personality and Social Psychology, 2*, 745-749.

Waly, P., & Cook, S. W. (1966). Attitude as a determinant of learning and memory: A failure to confirm. *Journal of Personality and Social Psychology, 4*, 280-288.

Warner, S. L. (1965). Randomized response: A survey technique for eliminating evasive answer bias. *Journal of the American Statistical Association, 60*, 63-69.

Watson, G. B. (1925). *The measurement of fair-mindedness*. Teachers College Contribution to Education No. 176. New York: Teachers College, Columbia University.

Watson, J. B. (1963). A micro-evolution study in New Guinea. *Journal of the Polynesian Society, 72*, 188-192.

Watts, H. W. (1972). Microdata: Lessons from the SEO and the Graduated Work Incentive Experiment. *Economics and Social Measurement, 1*, 183-192.

Watts, H. W., & Rees, A. (Eds.). (1973). *Final report of the New Jersey Graduated Work Incentive Experiment: Vol. I. An overview of the labor supply results of central labor-supply results. Vol. II. Studies relating to the validity and generalizability of the results. Vol. III. Response with respect to expenditure, health, and social behavior technical notes*. Madison: University of Wisconsin Institute for Research on Poverty. (Unpublished paper)

Watts, H. W., & Rees, A. (Eds.). (1977). *The New Jersey income maintenance experiment: Vol. 3. Expenditures, health and social behavior and the quality of the evidence*. New York: Academic Press.

Webb, E. J., Campbell, D. T., Schwartz, R. D., & Sechrest, L. B. (1966). *Unobtrusive measures: Nonreactive research in the social sciences.* Chicago: Rand McNally.

Webb, E. J., Campbell, D. T., Schwartz, R. D., Sechrest, L. B., & Grove, J. B. (1981). *Nonreactive measures in the social sciences.* Boston: Houghton Mifflin.

Weiss, R. S., & Rein, M. (1970). The evaluation of broad-aim programs: Experimental design, its difficulties, and an alternative. *Administrative Science Quarterly, 15,* 97-109.

Werts, C. E., Linn, R. L., & Jöreskog, K. G. (1977). A simplex model for analyzing academic growth. *Educational and Psychological Measurement, 37,* 745-756.

Weschler, I. R. (1950). A follow-up study on the measurement of attitudes toward labor and management by means of the error-choice method. *Journal of Social Psychology, 32,* 63-69.

Weschler, I. R. (1951). Problems in the use of indirect methods of attitude measurement. *Public Opinion Quarterly, 15,* 133-138.

Westfall, R. L., Boyd, H. W., & Campbell, D. T. (1957). The use of structured techniques in motivation research. *Journal of Marketing, 22,* 134-139.

Wherry, R. J., & Gaylord, R. H. (1944). Factor pattern of test items as a function of the correlation coefficient: Content, difficulty and constant error factors. *Psychometrika, 9,* 237-244.

Whisler, T. L., & Harper, S. F. (1962). *Performance appraisal: Research and practice.* New York: Holt, Rinehart & Winston.

Whiting, B. B., Child, I. L., Lambert, W. W., & Whiting, J. W. M. (1963). *Six cultures: Studies of child rearing.* New York: John Wiley.

Whiting, J. W. M., & Child, I. L. (1953). *Child training and personality: A cross-cultural study.* New Haven, CT: Yale University Press.

Whiting, J. W. M., Child, I. L., Lambert, W. W., Fischer, A. M., Nydegger, C., Nydegger, W., Maretzki, H., Maretzki, T., Minturn, L., Romney, K., & Romney, R. (1966). *Field guide for the study of socialization.* New York: John Wiley. Multilith edition 1954.

Wholey, J. (1970). *Federal evaluation policy: Analyzing the effects of public programs.* Washington, DC: Urban Institute.

Wiggins, J. S. (1973). *Personality and prediction: Principles of personality assessment.* Reading, MA: Addison-Wesley.

Wilder, C. S. (1972). *Physician visits, volume, and interval since last visit, U.S., 1969.* National Center for Health Statistics, July (Series 10, No. 75; DHEW Pub. No. [HSM]72-1064).

Wilks, S. S. (1962). *Mathematical statistics.* New York: John Wiley.

Williams, J. E. (1964). Connotations of color names among Negroes and Caucasians. *Perceptual and Motor Skills, 18,* 721-731.

Williams, R. (1950). Probability sampling in the field: A case history *Public Opinion Quarterly, 14,* 316-330.

Williams, R. M. J. (1947). *The reduction of intergroup tensions.* New York: Social Science Research Council Bulletin No. 57.

Williams, W., & Evans, J. W. (1969). The politics of evaluation: The case of Headstart. *Annals of the American Academy of Political and Social Science, 385.*

Windle, C. (1954). Test-retest effect on personality questionnaires. *Educational and Psychological Measurement, 14,* 617-633.

Wittgenstein, L. (1953). *Philosophical investigations.* Oxford: Oxford University Press; New York: Macmillan.

Wolcott, H. F. (1973). *The man in the principal's office: An ethnography.* New York: Holt, Rinehart & Winston.

Wolf, R. L. (1974). *The application of select legal concepts to educational evaluation.* Unpublished doctoral dissertation, University of Illinois, Urbana-Champaign.

Wolff, H. A., Smith, C. E., & Murray, H. A. (1934). The psychology of humor: 1. A study of race disparagement jokes. *Journal of Abnormal and Social Psychology, 28,* 341-365.

Wothke, W. (1984). *The estimation of trait and method components in multitrait-multimethod measurement.* Unpublished doctoral dissertation, University of Chicago.

Wrightsman, L. S. (1965). Characteristics of positively scored and negatively scored items from attitude scales. *Psychological Reports, 17,* 898.

Yates, A. T. (1980). *Distinguishing trait from method variance in fitting the invariant common-factor model to observed intercorrelations among personality rating scales.* Unpublished manuscript.

Yule, G. U., & Kendall, M. G. (1950). *An introduction to the theory of statistics* (14th ed.). New York: Hafner.

Zeisel, H. (1957). *Say it with figures* (4th ed.). New York: Harper.

Zeligs, R. (1937). Racial attitudes of children. *Sociological and Social Research, 21,* 361-371.

Zillig, M. (1928). Einstellung und Aussage. *Zeitschrift fur Psychologie, 106,* 58-106.

Zimring, F. E. (1975). Firearms and federal law: The Gun Control Act of 1968. *The Journal of Legal Studies, 4,* 133-198.

Author Index

Subject Index

————— •◆• —————

ABOUT THE AUTHORS

———•◆•———

Donald T. Campbell spent the major part of his academic career at Northwestern University. Before retiring, he was Professor at Lehigh University. He held teaching positions at Syracuse University, University of Chicago, and Ohio State University. During his career, he also lectured at Oxford, Harvard, and Yale University. He served as president of the American Psychological Association and was a member of the National Academy of Sciences; he received numerous honorary degrees and awards. He wrote more than 234 articles in the areas of social psychology, sociology, anthropology, education, and philosophy, covering a broad scope of topics from social science methodology to philosophy of science. He received his AB and PhD from the University of California at Berkeley.

M. Jean Russo is research scientist at the Center for Social Research at Lehigh University. She holds academic degrees from Moravian College (BA) and Lehigh University (MA, PhD). She was a student of Donald T. Campbell's while pursuing her master's degree in Social Relations and her doctoral degree in Applied Social Research. She has applied her research expertise in a number of diverse areas, including studies of severe childhood discipline, technology transfer, the sources and allocation of R&D funds in industry, as well as in program evaluation.